Studies in Ezra Pound
Chronicles and polemic

Also by Donald Davie from Carcanet

POETRY
Collected Poems 1970-1983
Selected Poems
To Scorch or Freeze
Collected Poems

CRITICISM
Under Briggflatts: a history of
poetry in Great Britain 1960-1985

Slavic Excursions: essays on
Polish and Russian literature

AUTOBIOGRAPHY
These the Companions

STUDIES IN EZRA POUND

DONALD DAVIE

CARCANET

First published in Great Britain in 1991 by
Carcanet Press Limited
208-212 Corn Exchange Buildings
Manchester M4 3BQ

British Library Cataloguing in Publication Data

Studies in Ezra Pound.
    1. Poetry in English. American writers. Pound, Ezra, 1885–1972
    I. Davie, Donald. *1922-*
    811.52

    ISBN 0-85635-880-0

The publisher acknowledges financial assistance
from the Arts Council of Great Britain

Typeset in 10pt Bembo by Bryan Williamson, Darwen
Printed and bound in England by SRP Ltd, Exeter

Contents

Foreword

This volume documents what some will call an obsession, which I prefer to think of as a preoccupation. (Obsessions are irrational; preoccupations aren't.) My preoccupation with Ezra Pound among the poets of this century began so long ago that there is now no way to explain it. Those who would call it an infatuation have grounds for thinking so, and their case is not weakened by observing that I have as often been exasperated by Pound as exalted and delighted by him. A love affair comprehends exasperation along with exaltation. And so 'infatuation' describes the condition better than either 'obsession' or 'preoccupation'. What the infatuation has let me in for, apart from such well-advertised and horrendous matters as Fascism and anti-Semitism, is for instance a persistent and gradually more exasperated puzzle about historiography: how it is possible, and what status we can give to it among the intellectual exertions of mankind, whether or not it is allied with poetry, as it was by Pound. This wouldn't have mattered to me at all urgently if history, and historical biography, hadn't for years been my favourite reading, far more than for instance novels. And so my worryings about it, with certain Poundian texts as pretexts or provocations, may be of interest to those for whom Pound's inventions in imagery and cadence are – more's the pity! – neither here nor there. In other words, a concern with Ezra Pound's writings cannot be, and never has been, a matter of literary history narrowly considered. Accordingly, whenever in subsequent pages I seem to be trapped amidst in-fighting among Pound's devotees, it should be understood that more is at issue than certain persons' academic or more generally intellectual standing. In-fighting in this peculiarly fraught arena is necessarily out-fighting: whatever decisions we may arrive at about Pound reverberate far beyond the world where academic ranks or literary reputations are established or, for that matter, are in question.

In 1964 *Ezra Pound. Poet as Sculptor* was a book I was commissioned to write by the New York branch of Oxford University Press, who approached me, I am delighted to remember, in the person of Reuben Brower and in the unlikely milieu of Warsaw, where in 1960 an international conference on poetics – not a thing that happened every week or every year in Stalinist Poland – brought Brower and me together, along with John Hollander and Francis Berry among others. What was commissioned was a book about Pound for the common reader; the special 'spin' that I gave to it with the sub-title, 'Poet as Sculptor', was my own idea, and not one that my publishers took to at all readily. I was myself quite unprepared for finding, in subsequent years, that what had originated as merely a bright idea – an analogy between the arts of sculpture and poetry – would come to dominate and direct my thinking about not just Pound's poetry but *all* poetry, including my own. For more than twenty years after that I strove to keep abreast of publications about Pound, in the not groundless belief that every innovation in thinking about how poetry and society interacted would show up, and be brought to the test, with peculiar severity in relation to Pound's poetry, so challenging as that poetry was, and so contestable. The pieces that I here bring together and reprint mark the several stages in this odyssey: an odyssey that comes to term and fulfilment not in homing in on what Odysseus/Pound truly was, but on what his life-long witness tells us about the place that poetry has, or should have, among the intellectual exertions of mankind. (As with historiography, so with poetry; increasingly, in my sense of the matter, the one has seemed to stand or fall with the other.)

These pieces I have headed, for my convenience and the convenience of my reader, under the alternative headings of 'chronicle' and 'polemic'. But this is a rough-and-ready distinction: there is no way to chronicle Pound's career without being polemical about it and about him; and equally, though there is no lack of polemics about Pound which play fast and loose with chronology, that playing fast and loose disqualifies them. Dates, *dates*, are of the essence; and it will be found that I date quite exactly the break-down of the imaginative exploit of the *Cantos*: between the completion of the late sequence called *Rock-Drill*, and the inauguration of the next, called *Thrones*. Because most readers of the poem will have understandably lost patience before they ever get to this point, my arguments about it will look like pedantry. However, to be patient for as long as patience is rewarded may be thought, in the reader of poetry, a virtue. And when patience is at last exhausted, the exhaustion may be thought forgivable to just the extent that it was for so long postponed. Every one agrees that the exploit represented by Pound's *Cantos* somehow *fails*. So far from thinking as many do that the failure was predetermined from the first, because wrongly conceived, I offer a reading of the poem which suggests on the contrary that the crucial failure came late; and came because of a misunderstanding about historiography.

DONALD DAVIE
Exeter, 1990

Chronicle

Ezra Pound: Poet as Sculptor

Ezra Pound was sixty-nine years old, and he had been a patient for nine years in St Elizabeth's Mental Hospital in Washington, D.C., when in 1955 he published a volume under the title, *The Classic Anthology Defined by Confucius*. This was the culmination of nearly half a century's dedication by Pound to the art of verse translation: 305 poems translated from a notoriously difficult language, and from that language at an archaic stage. Moreover, the poetic strategies and conventions were as much in dispute among scholars as were the social matrix they were meant to serve, and the reasons for their preservation were hardly less a mystery than the reasons and the validity of the arrangement in which they survived. And yet these poems represented, according to Confucius himself, the core of the Confucian ethics for which Pound had been campaigning, in pamphlet and polemic, in prose translation and in his own poems, for some three decades. Thus these translations sum up more of Pound, in more compact and accessible form, than any other single volume; and there is perhaps no better place for the reader to strike into the bewilderingly various and dauntingly voluminous corpus of Pound's writings.

The volume is elaborately and elegantly, but also confusingly, arranged. The list of contents gives no page numbers but instead places the poems under four heads: Part I Folk Songs; Part II Elegantiae, or Smaller Odes; Part III The Greater Odes; and Part IV Odes of the Temple and Altar. Each of the four sections is further subdivided, Part I into no less than fifteen categories, each with a title which, so far from illuminating the reader, seems on the contrary to insist on how remote from him is the world from which these poems come and to which they refer. And truly their world is remote, not just in time and space but also in spirit.[1] Accordingly

1 For an invaluable explanation of how the arrangement of the Anthology makes good sense in the tradition of Confucian thought in China, see L.S. Dembo, *The Confucian Odes of Ezra Pound* (Berkeley and London, 1963), pp.11-13.

this is not a volume to be read solidly through from first page to last. The section which promises most, if only because it is articulated less elaborately than the others, comprising as it does only three categories, is Part III, The Greater Odes. With this the reader might start, reading to begin with only rapidly and skimmingly.

The Greater Odes start with poem number 235. The version runs to forty-nine lines of verse, arranged in seven strophes, varying between six and nine lines in length with irregular rhyme. The poem is prefixed by a brief headnote in bold type and, in the same type, an irregular quatrain as epigraph. It has to do, apparently, with the triumph of one dynasty over another through the virtue of a hero called King Wen; it counsels the new regime, or the heirs of that dispensation, to be clement toward the dispossessed and to learn humility from the overweening by which those others fell. We pick up too, a chain of words that bind the poem together in references to light: 'bright', 'glitteringly', 'sun's fountainhead', 'sun's turn', 'of light a fountainhead', 'radiant', 'gleaming', 'white', and

> Wen, like a field of grain beneath the sun
> when all the white wheat moves in unison,
> coherent, splendid in severity,
> Sought out the norm and scope of Heaven's Decree.

'Splendid', we may realize, and (in the poem's last line) 'candour', are words that by association with the imagery of light regain some of the pristine metaphorical sharpness that in common literary usage they have normally lost; but there are other words and expressions that at first sight strike as literary in a different sense, words that have not been in the spoken language of English for a long time: 'supernal', 'gat new decree', 'brought under fealty', 'clad in their antient splendid broideries'. In the last case archaic spelling underlines the archaism of vocabulary. Pound is a translator, it seems, who puts an archaic text into archaic English, for whom the archaic and exotic character of what he is translating is something not to be overcome in translation, but on the contrary reproduced there. If he wants to familiarize and make accessible, he will not do so without making his reader aware of the gulf which reader and poet together are trying to span.

Poem 236 following, forty lines long in eight strophes of various length, continues to talk of King Wen and his victory over his adversaries, though it celebrates also some women of his line and his heir who completed his conquests. A cursory reading notes this as a more forbidding poem, with more Chinese names in it, the sparse rhyming more strained, extremely crabbed in expression at certain points (for instance in 'blood-might to harm'), and in diction more obtrusively archaic ('from inwit to his act', 'laudable in his stance') and odd in other ways too, as in the line 'layed out so towering Yin'.

Poem 237 is of about the same length, in nine strophes; but the measure has shortened, with four or fewer stresses to the line, more singable and accordingly rhyming much more frequently and insistently. The poem speaks of 'Old Duke T'an Fu', apparently a subordinate officer of King Wen, whose achievement was in reconstruction and civilized settlement.[1] The diction here for the first time permits modern colloquialisms like 'after you' and 'at any rate', but the archaic flavour is preserved resourcefully and pleasingly ('a proctor of prentices'), and one notes the striking word 'chthonian', its strikingness neither colloquial on the one hand nor archaic on the other. Rather plainly, as the diction thus swings over a wider arc of the English language, so presumably does the feeling of the poem range over more various experience. The question will be whether the poem can harmonize these potentially disparate elements; cursory reading suggests that it does, reports it as attractive and exhilarating and worth returning to.

Poems 238 and 239 go together, partly because they are shorter; more importantly because they both, the second more notably, break with the narrative impulse into a more nakedly didactic style, gnomic or aphoristic; and most importantly because they have a common imagery of growing timber. The archaism here cannot easily be located in details of diction but is rather in the unabashed didacticism of the gnomic style; a word that, like 'chthonian', draws attention to itself is 'tensile' from 238.

Number 240 is unattractive. Pound gives in the margin an alternative version of the third of its five stanzas, differing so widely from the first version that we are bewildered; there is a footnote to the poem which calls for a knowledge of Chinese ancient history such as we didn't know we needed; and the rhythms lurch disjointedly. The headnote is a piece of jaunty slang 'Three generations to make a gent'; and the jauntiness rings stridently, as if trying to force on the poem a modern parallel which does not fit the poem and which, if it did, could only vulgarize it. The long poem 241 is more interesting. It is once again narrative in structure arranged in eight strophes varying between eleven lines and fifteen. It begins with a strophe of two-stress lines tightly rhyming in couplets – a fresh metre and apt to the subject matter, which seems to demand the effect of chanted chronicle. This strict and primitive form is thus firmly asserted only so that later strophes may depart from it; but

1 In fact, the old Duke was Wen's grandfather.

through much of the poem, and perhaps through all of it, the departures take the form of variations on a norm that is never lost sight of altogether. Though the rhyme, for instance, can quickly become sparse, it at the same time becomes more intricate, a matter of internal chimings and partial echoes. The diction is insistently archaic, in expressions like 'Kingstead', 'the Welkin', 'suzerain', 'fiefs', 'carrochs', 'arbalasts'. On the other hand there are colloquial or conversational expressions like 'take...in his stride' and 'a decor without great noise'. The phrase 'in jactancy' joins 'tensile' and 'chthonian': all seem to belong in the same idiosyncratic jargon. The poem ends on an exquisite cadence.

A novel feature in this poem is a wholly opaque expression put between quotation marks as if to acknowledge its opacity – 'the "string tribes".' There is an identical effect in each of the two poems following (242 and 243), and, since each of these is shorter – a ceremonial chant rather lyrical than narrative – this nugget of unexplained foreign matter in the poem is in both cases more diconcerting. Number 244, the last of the 'Decade of King Wen', praises Wen through eight stanzas of three or four lines apiece, with a refrain to each stanza on the pattern 'Wen! avatar, how!' – where the 'how', we must take it, is the Redskin ceremonial greeting familiar from Western movies. Such are the risks, and perhaps the liberties, that this translator will take!

The reader has now scanned in a deliberately unfocused way ten poems, and has found himself no doubt intrigued, arrested, and offended by turns. In any case he has the right to begin to be restive, to ask for some more solid connection than any he has yet found between the conventions of this poetry and those familiar to him from other poems in English. This he finds with poem 246. The preceding poem 245 recounts a creation myth in which, by a transition that will not seem grotesque to anthropologists, the imagery of a supernatural Nativity is crossed with imagery of the planting, nourishing, and harvesting of grain. Pound helpfully points up both elements by, in the one case, a marginal note about the lamb and the burning babe, and, in the second case, headnote references to 'John Barleycorn', in British folk-usage a sort of demigod of the cornfield and the whisky-still. Since the Chinese wines are made from grain, this prepares us for poem 246, headed 'Festal':

> Tough grow the rushes, oh!
> No passing kine break down
> their clumpy wads, and blades so glossy growin'.

Our brothers will be here at call
assembled as to rule
wherefore lay down the mat, the mat
and bring the old man his stool.

2

Put a soft straw mat on a bamboo mat
let lackeys bring in the stools,
toast against toast, wine against wine
observant of all the rules,
Then rinse the cups and bring catsups
with pickles, roast and grill,
trype and mince-meat and while drums beat
let singers show their skill.

3

The trusty bows are tough, my lads,
each arrow-point true to weight
and every shot hits plumb the spot
as our archer lines stand straight.
They shoot again and four points go in
as if they were planting trees,
For a tough wood bow and the archers row
attest the gentilities.

4

An heir to his line is lord of this wine
and the wine rich on the tongue.
But by the great peck-measure, pray in your leisure
that when you're no longer young
Your back retain strength to susteyne
and aid you kin and clan.
Luck to your age! and, by this presage,
joy in a long life-span.

Rather plainly, this poem is in itself less ambitious, and to that extent less interesting, than many that have preceded it. But it has the merits of being familiar – familiar in its type, in the conventions it uses, in the social occasions it is designed to register and celebrate. Indeed, Pound so deftly plucks, in phrase after phrase, cadence after cadence, the strings of the English folk-verse tradition, that there can be no question of hunting out and identifying all the echoes that give the piece its resonance. The very first line, for instance, echoes a folk-composition reworked memorably by Burns. Of the many traditional poems in English that this version depends upon our half-remembering, what may come to mind first is the famous 'Back and side go bare, go bare':

> I can not eate, but lytle meate
>   my stomacke is not good;
> But sure I thinke, that I can drynke
>   with him that weares a hood.
> Thoughe I go bare, take ye no care,
>   I am nothinge a cold:
> I stuff my skyn so full within
>   of ioly good Ale and olde
>   Backe and syde go bare, go bare,
>   booth foote and hand go colde;
>   But Bellye god send the good ale inoughe,
>   whether it be new or olde.
>
> I love no rost, but a nut browne toste,
>   and a crab layde in the fyre;
> A lytle bread shall do me stead
>   much breade I not desyre:
> No froste nor snow, no winde, I trowe,
>   can hurte mee if I wolde;
> I am so wrapt, and throwly lapt
>   of ioly good ale and old
>   Backe and syde go bare, &c.
>
> And Tyb my wyfe, that as her lyfe
>   loveth well good ale to seeke,
> Full ofte drynkes shee, tyll ye may see
>   the teares run downe her cheekes:
> The dooth she trowle, to mee the bowle
>   even as a mault worme shuld,
> And, sayth sweethart, I tooke my part
>   of this ioly good ale and olde
>   Backe and syde go bare, &c.
>
> Now let them drynke, tyll they nod and winke,
>   even as good felowes shoulde doe;
> They shall not mysse, to have the blisse
>   good ale doth bringe men to;
> And all poore soules that have scowred boules
>   or have them lustely trolde,

> God save the lyves of them and theyr wyves
> whether they be yonge or olde.
> Backe and syde go bare, go bare,
>   booth foote and hande go colde:
> But Bellye god sende thee good ale inoughe,
>   whether it be new or olde.

The point of our making this comparison, and of the poet's inviting it, is not just that we may see what tradition the poem is in, and what conventions it observes; but also that we may see where it diverges from that tradition. For, in proportion as the traditional norm is established firmly, to just that extent do the departures from it stand out as intentional and significant.

The first way in which the sixteenth-century poem is instructive, when set beside Pound's, is that it shows how in traditional songs of this kind the rhythms are less regular than later, more streamlined, examples might lead us to suppose. Just because the swinging rhythm is so strong and insistent, it can accommodate and ride over the roughness of extra syllables crammed and jostling in some of the lines. In 'Back and side go bare', though it is in the metre of the fourteener (which Pound admired when it was used by Arthur Golding, the Elizabethan translator of Ovid), there are several examples of extra syllables thus hurried and stumbled over; Pound contrives the same rough-hewn effect in his line about 'the great peck-measure' where the weight of the rhythm emphasized by the heavy rhymes it is slung between ('measure' / 'leisure') can easily and profitably carry a clutter of additional light syllables. At such a point the accomplished professional displays his accomplishment, as well as his taste, by contriving an unsophisticated effect.

Not all of Pound's metrical variations, however, are of this kind. In the third stanza the reader's expectations, which have been roused so confidently by the insistent simple rhythms, are dashed all the more painfully by the second line. Every reader's ear demands 'each arrow-point weighs true', and on each new reading there is a shock when we stumble instead into 'each arrow-point true to weight'. And yet it would be a very naïve reader who supposed that Pound did not find 'weighs true' for himself. Why did he reject it? Not, I think, for any 'primitive' effect, but rather so as to jar the reader into attending to what is said. For, if the traditional metre is established so insistently only to be rudely disrupted at crucial points, so the traditional sentiments are invoked only to throw into relief the places where the Chinese sentiments go beyond the tradition. These are the places where the feeling is exotic, no longer to be paralleled from Old English but, on the contrary, strange and stubbornly

Chinese. And since the object of translation, presumably, is to bring over into English modes of feeling not already extant, these points where the poem refuses to be acclimatized into the extant traditions are the most important of all, the nub of the whole enterprise. To look again at the sixteenth-century poem is to see very clearly where in the Chinese this stubborn novelty is. In a sense it is pervasive throughout, but it comes to a head in 'attest the gentilities'; what is novel and non-Western and therefore especially valuable about this drinking-chorus is that in it drinking, and the rural sports which go with drinking, are seen in a peculiarly strict and insistent way as decorous, even ceremonial. 'Assembled as to rule', 'observant of all the rules' – these are the lines, seeming unimportant at first, which are taken up in 'attest the gentilities', and are then seen to be the backbone of the poem. As the word 'decorous' will have suggested to students of Elizabethan poetry, it is in Elizabethan poems that the English tradition comes nearest to expressing this Chinese perception or range of perceptions, and so it is appropriate that, down to details like his spelling of 'susteyne', Pound should challenge comparison with sixteenth-century poets.[1]

Thus we conceive the possibility that there is more to Pound's archaism than meets the eye. In some cases at least the principle is not just to match archaic Chinese with archaic English; we seem required or invited to distinguish just what degree of archaism is being practised, precisely what period out of the long past of English poetry is being alluded to – and this so as to suggest that in just that period English approximated most nearly to such and such a Chinese perception, or cluster of perceptions. If we return to The Greater Odes, we find something similar only four poems further on from 'Festal':

> Duke Liu, the frank,
> unhoused, unhapped,
> from bound to bourne
> put all barned corn in sacks
> and ration bags
> for glorious use, stretched bow
> showed shield, lance, dagger-axe
> and squared to the open road.

1 See especially Ben Jonson; in many of Jonson's epistles the ceremonious character of unforced social encounter is brought out in almost Oriental fashion. Pound acknowledges the affinity, but very obliquely, when he gives as epigraph to Ode 57 the phrase 'Sidney's sister' from Jonson's 'To Penshurst'.

To my ear there is an echo in this, too loud to be accidental, from Robert Browning's 'Marching Along', the first of three 'Cavalier Tunes' from Browning's *Dramatic Lyrics* of 1842:

> Kentish Sir Byng stood for his King.
> Bidding the crop-headed Parliament swing:
> And, pressing a troop unable to stoop
> And see the rogues flourish and honest folk droop,
> Marched them along, fifty-score strong,
> Great-hearted gentlemen, singing this song.
>
> God for King Charles!...

This appears to be a different case from 'Back and side go bare, go bare'. That seemed to provide an illuminating commentary on the translation 'Festal'; but there was no reason to suppose that Pound had it specifically in mind, only that he had in mind poems of roughly that period and specifically that type. One may believe, on the other hand, that Pound had 'Kentish Sir Byng', if not in mind, at least echoing in his ear. What strengthens this supposition is Ode 36, which is headed '(King Charles)'; here the reference directly to Browning's 'Cavalier Tunes' cannot be doubted, though it may have more to do with the second of them:

> King Charles, and who'll do him right now?[1]

If the parallel was thus close and conscious, it is instructive to see how Browning's ringing internal rhymes – 'Byng' and 'King', 'troop' and 'stoop', 'along' and 'strong' – dissolve into the intricately delightful chimings of 'bound' and 'bourne' with 'barned' and 'corn', of 'unhoused' with 'bound', of 'bow' with 'showed'. As was seen with some of the other Odes, Pound is often rhyming most richly and elaborately when he seems to be rhyming hardly at all. To put it more exactly, by such verse as this we are made to realize that terminal rhyme is only one arbitrarily codified aspect of the multifarious orchestration by sound that should be going on all the time. And Pound appears to have trained his ear in these matters, above all through the translations he made in his youth from the intricately musical poems of medieval Provence. In any case, if we catch a submerged allusion to Browning's poem in Ode 250, we are invited to understand its hero Duke Liu by regarding him as at least in part

---

1 L.S. Dembo, however, in *The Confucian Odes of Ezra Pound*, pp.65-6, very justly and acutely defines the verse-form of Ode 36 as 'Skeltonics'.

analogous to the faithful Royalists of the English Civil War in the seventeenth century.

Having got as far as this with the *Classic Anthology*, we can begin to profit from the brief introduction to the volume, by Achilles Fang. Fang there remarks of Pound's translations:

> the choice of the ballad meter is a happy one, as it not only makes the translation readable but accurately brings out the original rhythm of the Odes. For the Odes are essentially ballads; they were all sung, and some of them were probably dance-songs as well.

Well! 'Festal' and the poem about Duke Liu are undoubtedly in ballad metres; they observe, though with variations, that metrical convention as well as other non-metrical conventions familiar from what we normally think of as ballads. On the other hand, this was not true of any of the poems we scanned more rapidly; several of these, in their stately ceremoniousness if in nothing else, seemed nearer to what is normally understood by 'ode'. In fact, if these poems are ballads, how can they be odes also? For in normal parlance these two kinds of poems are poles apart. Mr Fang declares:

> the term 'odes' applied to the 305 poems in this volume is to be understood in its etymological sense of songs meant to be sung.

And it is quite true that if we stretch our minds into ancient times, far behind any English precedents, we can just envisage, and find scholarly reasons for envisaging, a form of poetry written for singing or chanting, in which the ceremonious solemnity of what later became the ode is married indistinguishably to the artless vigour and grace of the folk poem sung to commemorate rural life and accompany rural sports. What Achilles Fang is saying, it appears, is that, because the ancient Chinese poems in the anthology are poems of this sort, the translator is under the necessity of creating, in order to be faithful to his originals, a form of poem for which no precedent exists in English. If so, this explains much of the difficulty we have with these translations; at least it should make us reluctant to jump to conclusions about them. Pound, as has been seen, can find English precedents for certain passages, certain turns of thought and feeling, and in these cases he will invoke the English precedents or analogues so as to ease the way for the English-speaking reader. But the Chinese poems as wholes, the kind of poem all of them exemplify, the body of conventions governing them as wholes, have no English precedents.

One was compelled to realize, moreover, in the case of 'Festal', which seemed to rest on an English precedent in the wassail or festive ballad, that in the end the Chinese poem in Pound's translation strained away from that English kind of poem. And what went outside the English ballad-convention was 'attest the gentilities', a sort of formal and ceremonious civility which goes rather with what we conceive of as 'ode'. Thus what seemed the exception in fact proves a rule.

It is from this same emphasis on 'gentilities' that we can understand Achilles Fang's insistence on how, in Confucius's teaching, the singing of the Odes is intricately bound up with observance of 'the rites'. At the end of the Introduction, Achilles Fang glosses the word *li*, which is sometimes translated as 'rites', by saying that in other contexts the English equivalent may be 'tact' and in still others 'character'. More generally,

> The word *li*, essentially a code of behavior, is generally rendered as 'rites' when that behavior is directed toward the supernatural or the manes, and as 'etiquette' when it concerns man's relation with his fellow men.

Plainly, the creation of a kind of poem that is neither wholly 'ode' as understood in the English tradition, nor wholly 'ballad' as so understood, that partakes of both kinds in a way for which there is no English precedent – this represents not only a fusion of the artless and spontaneous with the ceremonious and fixed, but equally a fusion of piety toward the superhuman with common courtesy among humans. We are being asked to perceive how a proper attitude toward God might be no more than just good manners toward Him, and conversely how no manners can be truly 'good' that do not introduce into human intercourse a sort of humility toward the more than human.

With these perceptions, or rather the possibility of these perceptions, held in mind, a reader is well equipped to embark upon the *Classic Anthology* as a whole. And a reader who understands by this argument how a question of poetic genre, and of the marrying of genres, is necessarily a question of entertaining certain ranges of perceptions rather than others, and of combining some perceptions with others in unprecedented ways – such a reader has the central clue to Pound's works as a whole, to the entire labyrinth. He will realize, for example – what has baffled and continues to baffle many readers – why Pound's thoughts about style and styles of poetry cannot help but spill out beyond poetry into politics, ethics, economics. For on this showing certain kinds of human behaviour, for instance certain kinds of economic behaviour, conform to or comport with certain kinds of poetry, whereas others cannot do so. And thus the poet who takes with real seriousness matters of his own vocation, such as genre and style, must by that very token pass judgment on human affairs in general.

I

The Early Collections · 'The Seafarer' · *The Spirit of Romance* ·
Canto I · *Ripostes* · Imagism

Ezra Pound set out in life by preparing himself for a career in literary
scholarship. He spent his childhood in a suburb of Philadelphia and
enrolled in the University of Pennsylvania in 1901, when he was
not quite sixteen. In 1903 he transferred to Hamilton College in
Clinton, New York, but returned to the University of Pennsylvania
in 1905. 'Belangal Alba' or 'Alba Belingalis', a translation from
Provençal which was to survive into *Personae* in 1909, first appeared
in the *Hamilton Literary Magazine* for May 1905. Returning to
Philadelphia as a graduate student now specializing in the Romance
languages, Pound by 1906 was a Graduate Fellow in that field, work-
ing under Felix E. Schelling, to whom in later years he addressed
some of his most interesting letters. When he used his fellowship
to visit Europe, he seems to have taken the advice of another Philadel-
phia scholar, Dr Hugo Rennert, who is introduced respectfully into
Pound's book of essays *The Spirit of Romance* (1910) and also into
Canto 20.

There is nothing in this pattern to disturb the picture of an enter-
prising young scholar preparing himself for an academic career in
his chosen field; and when in 1907 Pound accepted the offer of a
teaching post at Wabash College in Crawfordsville, Indiana, it must
have seemed that he was embarked upon an arrangement which has
become more familiar in later generations than his, a way of life by
which, for some years, the young poet combines without too much
trouble the writing of poems with the teaching of literature and the
pursuit of research.

The story has often been told of how provincial Mrs Grundyism
in Indiana deprived Pound of his teaching post; as Charles Norman
acutely implies,[1] his dismissal from Wabash College probably rank-
led with Pound less bitterly than the failure of the University of
Pennsylvania to stand by him by offering an alternative position.

1 Charles Norman, *Ezra Pound* (New York, 1960), p.24.

At all events, when Pound in the winter of 1908-9 lectured at the Regent Street Polytechnic in London on 'Developments of Literature in Southern Europe', and again in 1909-10 on 'Mediaeval Literature', his was not the impudent initiative of an amusing charlatan; he was thoroughly qualified to offer instruction in these fields, and *The Spirit of Romance*, which gives the substance of these lecture courses, is a piece of intelligent popularizing which suggests that his audiences got value for their money. One of Pound's hearers was Dorothy Shakespear, whose mother Mrs Olivia Shakespear was a friend of Yeats and of other writers; Ezra Pound and Dorothy Shakespear were married in 1914.

By that time, however, Pound at 29 had already published, apart from *The Spirit of Romance* and a translation, *The Sonnets and Ballate of Guido Cavalcanti* (1912), six books of original poems: *A Lume Spento*, published in Venice in June 1908; *A Quinzaine for This Yule*, published in London in December of that year; *Personae* and *Exultations*, both published in London in 1909; *Canzoni* (1911); and *Ripostes* (1912). *Ripostes* marks a new departure, but the other volumes were enough to make Pound's name in London. Of *Personae*, *The Bookman* said, 'No new book of poems for years past has had such a freshness of inspiration, such a strongly individual note'; and in *The English Review* a British poet of comparable seriousness, Edward Thomas, declared admiringly, 'He cannot be usefully compared with any living writers, though he has read Yeats'. Pound was to declare that indeed Yeats (the Yeats of *The Wind Among the Reeds*, not the greater poet who was to emerge later) was the magnet which drew him to London in the first place. But if Yeats was the only *living* poet whose voice sounded in Pound's early volumes (for instance in 'La Fraisne' from *Personae*, with its direct reference to 'The Madness of King Goll' from *The Wind Among the Reeds*), the voices of dead poets echoed there as they always must in the first volumes of young poets, and in this case more loudly than usual. Swinburne speaks in 'Anima Sola' from *A Lume Spento* and in 'Ballad for Gloom' from *Personae*, as well as in a poem from *A Lume Spento* which is patently and admiringly addressed to him, 'Salve Pontifex'; and his 'Madonna Mia' has something to do with a poem from *Exultations*, 'Sestina for Isolt'. William Morris speaks in the ballads 'Oltre la Torre: Rolando' and 'Ballad Rosalind', both from *A Lume Spento*, and in 'The House of Splendour' from *Canzoni*. There is Rossetti (though there is Browning also) in 'Fair Helena, by Rackham' from *Exultations*; and Rossetti's love sonnets contribute something to 'Camaraderie' from *Personae*.[1] Pound, by

---

1 See N. Christoph de Nagy, *The Poetry of Ezra Pound: The Pre-Imagist Stage* (Bern, 1960).

refusing to reprint these early poems in later, more definitive, collections, seems to concede that in them these influences were not properly assimilated.

These styles and models were not fashionable in Edwardian London. For British poets of that period the styles of Swinburne, of Rossetti, of Morris were available for serious use only as they had been muted and modified by the writers of the 'nineties; and for these mutings and modifications, except as they are practised in a special way by Yeats, Pound seems from the first to have had little sympathy. 'Piccadilly' from *Personae* is the only poem approaching the 'impressionism', as it was called, that inspired John Davidson and Arthur Symons, under the influence of Baudelaire, to write poems about the metropolis; and 'In Tempore Senectutis' from *A Lume Spento* advertises by its subtitle, 'An Anti-Stave for Dowson', that it is tilting polemically against another of the characteristic styles of the 'nineties. In 'The Flame' from *Canzoni*, an early poem which Pound has consented to retain in later collections, there is an alluson to Arthur Symons's *Days and Nights*, 'the first representative collection of impressionistic verse in England' (de Nagy, p.41), which seems to single this out as treading in a wrong path, as against the path trodden by Yeats, who is present in allusions to *Countess Cathleen*.

Pound's reaching back over a poetic generation to echo directly some Victorian poets must have seemed a symptom of provincialism, something possible to an American, but not to a British poet. And Pound himself was thoroughly aware of this possibility and of himself as indelibly American. Though it is British voices which sound, he knows that they sound differently in his American ear, and that just for that reason they may be fruitful for him as they could not be for his British contemporaries. He hints at this in a touchingly boyish essay of 1909, 'What I Feel About Walt Whitman', which was first published only in 1955:

> It seems to me I should like to drive Whitman into the old world. I sledge, he drill – and to scourge America with all the old beauty. (For Beauty *is* an accusation) and with a thousand thongs from Homer to Yeats, from Theocritus to Marcel Schwob. This desire is because I am young and impatient, were I old and wise I should content myself in seeing and saying that these things will come. But now, since I am by no means sure it would be true prophecy, I am fain set my own hand to the labour.
>
> It is a great thing, reading a man to know, not 'His Tricks are not as yet my Tricks, but I can easily make them mine'

but 'His message is my message. We will see that men hear it'.[1]

It was not until another four years had passed that Pound trusted himself to employ Whitman's 'tricks' and to print Whitmanesque poems. But he knew already that he must be nearer to Whitman than he could ever be to those British poets whom, just by reason of that saving distance between them, he could afford for the moment to imitate. Later he was to look for support to some of his countrymen who had been expatriates as he was himself – to James McNeill Whistler and Henry James.

It is surprising, and it is to the credit of the British reviewers of 1909, that in the author of *Personae* they recognized this American-ness, and relished it. But it is true that they had before them poems more powerful than any so far mentioned. These were the poems written under the influence of yet another British Victorian, Robert Browning: in *Exultations*, 'Piere Vidal Old' and 'Sestina: Altaforte'; and in *Personae*, 'Cino', 'Na Audiart', and 'Marvoil'. There is no denying the influence on these poems of Browning's experiments with the dramatic monologue. Pound has acknowledged his debt generously, and in *Personae*, quite apart from the amusingly affec-tionate homage to Browning in 'Mesmerism', there is, for instance, the Browningesque writing of 'Famam Librosque Cano' and of the important poem 'In Durance' with its specific allusion to Browning's 'Pictor Ignotus'. Moreover, Browning was to exert a powerful influ-ence for many years yet – up to and into the first of the Cantos. But Browning could be a more fruitful influence than William Morris, for instance, chiefly because his influence was always combined with some other. The poems just cited can draw fruitfully on Browning's previous experience in the dramatic monologue only because they are modifying that poetic form into something that Browning hardly dreamed of. On the one hand, under pressure from Pound's study of medieval Provence, the dramatic monologue becomes in his hands something much closer to translation or at least paraphrase; on the other hand, because of Yeats's ideas of the 'mask', Pound's Provençal personae are less *dramatis* personae than they are embodied aspects of his own situation and his own personality (though this is truer of some of these poems than of others).

The most impressive is 'Sestina: Altaforte'. Though this can be read, as undoubtedly and properly it most often is read, as a success-ful and stirring dramatic lyric or dramatic monologue (not that these,

1 Herbert Bergman, 'Ezra Pound and Walt Whitman', in *American Literature*, 27 (March 1955), 56-61.

in Browning's use of the terms, are the same thing), Pound's poem has, in fact, another dimension of interest available only to the erudite: it is only the instructed reader who can appreciate how close the poem is to a translation of Bertran de Born's 'Praise of War', and how the sestina is a form invented not by Bertran but by Arnaut Daniel, and how Pound switches the conventional *envoi*, the address to a named auditor (Papiols), from the end of the poem to the beginning (de Nagy, p.125). These aspects of the poem are not merely formalistic, part of the scaffolding that can be torn down once the building is erected; it was probably these considerations which, by giving the poet other things to aim at than Browning had aimed at, permitted him to draw on Browning's precedent without being overwhelmed by it. (Similarly, though in a less complicated way, Villon's French counterbalances translations of him by Rossetti and Swinburne, in 'Villonaud for This Yule' and 'A Villonaud: Ballad of the Gibbet', two near-translations in *Personae*.) What gives pre-eminence to 'Sestina: Altaforte' over a poem no less affecting and memorable, such as 'Piere Vidal Old', or over a straight translation from Bertran de Born, the 'Planh for the Young English King', is what Edward Thomas noticed: a verse-movement that breaks away from Tennysonian mellifluousness so as to replace it by something positive. The opening of 'Sestina: Altaforte' is very arresting indeed, with a quality of assured 'attack'. But the metrical effect, if one may isolate it, is more remarkable because it is harder to parallel. The verse-lines are true units, rhythmically and in meaning; and yet each of them is broken near the centre much more forcibly than by a caesura in traditional accentual-syllabic metres. The break in 'I have no life / save when the swords clash' depends upon a rising beat before the break, crammed against the emphatically falling rhythm of the trochee 'save when'. But this is not true of other lines where the break apart is just as pronounced. In any case, this breaking of the line near mid-point (which Pound at this stage cannot maintain through a whole poem) was to be the hallmark of his writing in verse. It can be found elsewhere in *Personae*; strategically placed, and to plangent rather than forcible effect, the dismembered line appears in 'Praise of Ysolt', for example, and to scornful effect in 'Au Salon'.

The rhythms which thus reappear in modern English were common enough before English metres were settled at the end of the sixteenth century as accentual-syllabic in principle. From this point of view, Pound's translation of the Old English poem, 'The Seafarer', does not come as a surprise; from every other point of view it is very surprising indeed, coming as it did in *Ripostes* (1912) from the poet who had seemed wedded to the Romance languages of Southern Europe.

The Anglo-Saxon poem, however, appealed to Pound for other than metrical reasons. A few years later, after Pound had begun translating and adapting from Chinese, he was to find much in common between the Anglo-Saxon poet and the Chinese poet whom he most admired, Li Po (AD 701-762). Later still, in his prose tract *The ABC of Reading* (1934), he related:

> I once got a man to start translating the *Seafarer* into Chinese. It came out almost directly into Chinese verse, with two solid ideograms in each half-line. Apart from the *Seafarer* I know no other European poems of the period that you can hang up with the 'Exile's Letter' of Li Po, displaying the West on a par with the Orient.

Pound's interest in metre, in the Anglo-Saxon verse-line with its heave in the middle between two alliteratively combined rhythms, is what makes him speak of the half-line rather than the line. Yet his comment shows that for him 'The Seafarer' and the Chinese poem have more than this in common, and more than is involved in their being roughly of the same date. For 'Exile's Letter' is, of all the poems which Pound was to translate, that one which presents Li Po as legendary anecdote preserves him through tradition: a drunkard, an idler, disreputable, undependable, without self-respect. The author of 'Exile's Letter' is recognizably the man of whose poems Po Chu-i complained that 'not one in ten contains any moral reflection or deeper meaning'; of whom Wang An-shih declared that 'his intellectual outlook was low and sordid'.[1] But we can thus recognize this poet in his poem only because he speaks in it very directly, reveals himself with such unhesitant nakedness. And this he has in common with the poet of 'The Seafarer' as Pound gives him through translation: in 'The Seafarer' too we are struck by the directness of the address, the completeness of the self-exposure.

Pound's version of the Old English poem is very inaccurate. And yet not all his howlers are on a par. For instance:

> Disease or oldness or sword-hate
> Beats out the breath from doom-gripped body.

1 Po Chu-i, writing about AD 816; Wang An-shih (1021-86). I take these quotations from Arthur Waley's paper to the China Society at the School of Oriental Studies, London, delivered on 21 November 1918. Mr Waley endorses these strictures. See Waley, *The Poet Li Po, AD 701-762* (London, 1919).

And for this, every earl whatever, for those speaking after –
Laud of the living, boasteth some last word,
That he will work ere he pass onward,
Frame on the fair earth 'gainst foes his malice,
Daring ado,...
So that all men shall honour him after
And his laud beyond them remain 'mid the English,...

These verses, in which the mid-line heave or thump comes with ultimately monotonous impact, correspond to those in which the Anglo-Saxon poet exhorts men to combat the malice of devils so that their good fame may live for ever with angels. Pound, wittingly or not, uses in 'remain 'mid the English' the Augustinian pun on 'Angles' and 'angels' so as to shut out the Christian reference. This can hardly be on a par with his misunderstandings elsewhere: of *stearn* (a seabird) for the stern of a ship; of *byrig* ('towns') for berries, of *thurh* ('through', 'in') for *thruh* ('tomb').[1] In the original the genuflections toward Christianity are so conspicuous that they could not escape the hastiest reading; and Pound consistently eliminates them. Many a scholar has also wished them away, since perfunctory genuflections is all that they seem to be, and their presence has led many readers to rate 'The Seafarer' below its companion piece, 'The Wanderer', which one suspects that Pound has never read. Pound had to eliminate these references if he was to give us a poet who would expose himself with the same unconcern for received opinion as Li Po exhibits in 'Exile's Letter'.

Pound does not merely eliminate the Christian values, he replaces them by something positive, not just pagan but barbaric. Kenneth Sisam says that he 'makes malice the source of everlasting renown among the English'. So he does. And he might well be impenitent about it, for one may detect in Kenneth Sisam's protest (perhaps unfairly) the same note of outraged respectability as in Wang An-shih's objection to Li Po, that his outlook was 'low and sordid'. *Épater le bourgeois* has never been beneath Pound's dignity, and there is a comically anachronistic zest about his references in 'The Seafarer' to the 'burghers' who are 'wealthy and wine-flushed'. As Li Po shocked the respectable Chinese of his day by his wine-bibbing and interest in concubines, so Pound makes the Anglo-Saxon poet shock the mores of his society by putting a high value on 'malice'.

1 See Kenneth Sisam's letter to the *Times Literary Supplement* for 25 June 1954. I am greatly indebted to Mr Sisam's letter throughout this discussion.

Épater le bourgeois in the Anglo-Saxon kingdoms of the Dark Ages! Obviously this is to romanticize. In Pound the youthful author of *The Spirit of Romance* it could hardly be anything else. And yet some pages in that first of Pound's prose works ought to shield him from any facile gibes at his anachronisms. There is, for instance, an essay on Villon:

> thief, murderer, pandar, bully to a whore, he is honoured for a few score pages of unimaginative sincerity; he sings of things as they are. He dares to show himself.

But Pound goes on to protect Villon against the romanticizing of taverns and harlots which had made the old French poet a favourite in the generations of Swinburne and R.L. Stevenson. For Pound's romanticizing has to do, not with *romanticism*, but with *romance* in the strict sense in which one speaks of 'Romance languages'. And thus his romanticizing of a medieval writer like Villon is not anachronistic at all; on the contrary, it is scholarly and historical, faithful to the romance sensibility and tradition which as a fact of chronology lay behind such a writer:

> Villon's verse is real, because he lived it; as Bertran de Born, as Arnaut Marvoil, as that mad poseur Vidal, he lived it. For these men life is in the press. No brew of books, no distillation of sources will match the tang of them.

Romantic is what Villon is, in a stricter, more disconcerting way than romanticists of the nineteenth century realized.

As Pound here compares Villon with three Provençal poets (each of whom had had a fine poem to himself in *Personae*), so elsewhere in *The Spirit of Romance* he compares him with a poet of Spain:

> His poems are gaunt as the *Poema del Cid* is gaunt; they treat of actualities, they are untainted with fancy; in the *Cid* death is death, war is war. In Villon filth is filth, crime is crime; neither crime nor filth is gilded. They are not considered as strange delights and forbidden luxuries, accessible only to adventurous spirits.

And what Pound has to say of the *Poema del Cid* strikes the by now familiar note, very excitedly:

> it is the unquenchable spirit of that very glorious bandit, Ruy Diaz, which gives life to the verse and the apparently crude rhythm.

Ruy Diaz, *el Cid* (who is to appear in Canto 3), takes his place beside Li Po and the poet of Pound's 'Seafarer' and, more sombrely, François Villon, as an engaging, because uncompromising, ruffian – 'that very glorious bandit'. This is a refreshingly unsophisticated way of responding to poetry.

But it raises questions that reach rather far if we look ahead a few years and find Pound using his 'Seafarer' measure for translating Homer.[1] For Homer, every one knows, is an epic poet; and Pound's translation from Homer's *Odyssey* inaugurates that poem, *The Cantos*, which he himself has offered as a modern epic. The *Poema del Cid*, moreover, so far as it is a *geste*, is epic no less. And yet, not only was the style of 'The Seafarer' evolved for a poem not epic at all but elegiac, but also the element Pound most values in the *Cid* as in 'The Seafarer' and the poems of Li Po, the robust fullness of self-exposure in narrator or protagonist, is a fundamentally non-epic quality. This appears very clearly in Chapter IV of *The Spirit of Romance* where Pound strenuously maintains the superiority of the *Poema del Cid* to that other epical *geste*, the *Chanson de Roland*. As might be predicted, what Pound objects to in the French *épopée* is precisely a cherished characteristic of epic writing – its impersonality:

> The personality of the author is said to be 'suppressed', although it might be more exact to say that it has been worn away by continuous oral transmission.

And, of the death of Roland, Pound observes:

> Perfect chivalric pose, perfect piety! The hero goes out of this chançon of gesture, and one feels that perhaps he and the rest of his characters are not wooden figures, that they are simply 'latin'. Heroic, his hands joined, in death he forgets not etiquette. He is the perfect hero of pre-realist literature.
>   But...one is grateful for the refreshment of the Spanish *Poema*, and for the bandit Ruy Diaz.

Moreover, the antipathy that Pound expresses thus temperately toward one of the received masterpieces of European epic is in line with his indifference to Spenser and Tasso, his lukewarmness about

1 *The Letters of Ezra Pound, 1907-1941*, ed. D.D. Paige (London, 1951), p.137: 'I don't know that one can read any trans. of the *Odyssey*. Perhaps you could read book XI. I have tried an adaptation in the 'Seafarer' metre, or something like it, but I don't expect anyone to recognize the source very quickly' (to Iris Barry, 1916).

All subsequent references to this volume will describe it as *Letters*.

Camoens,[1] and is as nothing beside his violent dislike of Virgil[2] and of Milton.[3] Unless the *Divine Comedy* is to be called an epic, Pound has pronounced an anathema upon the whole epic tradition since Homer, with the solitary eccentric exception of the *Poema del Cid*. In the only modern poet who has essayed epic in the English-speaking world, this is noteworthy.

It is proper to anticipate the Cantos this early in an account of Pound's career. For, though his readers in 1912 could not know of his epic ambitions, Pound had been setting his course toward that objective for several years. In a recent interview he has declared, 'I began the Cantos about 1904, I suppose. I had various schemes, starting in 1904 or 1905'.[4] Certainly his friend William Carlos Williams knew that he was working on an epic as early as 1908.[5] And Pound says, 'In the first sketches, a draft of the present first *Canto* was the third.' In that Canto Homer is invoked through translation to preside over the epic pretensions of the poem thus inaugurated. But it is the Homer of the *Odyssey*. The Homer who is the father of the European epic is the poet of the *Iliad*; and in the *Iliad* Pound has consistently shown comparatively little interest.[6] Yet ever since ancient times it has been realized that the *Odyssey* is hardly epic at all:

> in the *Odyssey* one might liken Homer to a setting sun; the intensity has gone, but there remains the greatness. Here the tone of those great lays of Ilium is no longer maintained – the passages on one level of sublimity with no sinking anywhere, the same stream of passion poured upon passion, the readiness of turn, the closeness to life, the throng of images all drawn from the truth: as when Ocean retires into himself, and is left lonely around his proper bounds, only the ebbings of his greatness are left to our view, and a wandering among the shallows of the fabulous and the incredible. While I say this, I have not

1 *The Spirit of Romance* (London and New York, 1910), ch. X.
2 E.g. *Letters*, p.138 (1916): 'Virgil is a second-rater, a Tennysonianized verrsion of Homer.'
3 E.g. 'Notes on Elizabethan Classicists', in *The Egoist*, IV, 120-22, 135-6, 154-6, 168; V, 8-9 (Sept. 1917 to Jan. 1918); reprinted in *Pavannes and Divisions* (New York, 1918) and in *Make It New* (London, 1934; New Haven, 1935).
4 *The Paris Review*, 28 (Summer-Fall, 1962), p.23.
5 *Selected Essays of William Carlos Williams* (New York, 1954), p.105.
6 Though see 'Translators of Greek' in *The Egoist*, V, 95-7, 106-8, 120-21, 130-31; VI, 6-9, 24-6 (Aug. 1918 to April 1919), reprinted in *Make It New* (1934).

forgotten the storms in the *Odyssey*, nor the story of the Cyclops, nor certain other passages; I am describing an old age, but the old age of Homer. Still in all these, as they follow one another, fable prevails over action.[1]

One need not follow the ancient critic in thinking the *Odyssey* inferior to the *Iliad*. But one must agree with him in thinking them profoundly different, with a difference that puts the *Odyssey* apart from the epic as traditionally conceived. The *Odyssey* is nearer to the novel than it is to the epic; as Longinus goes on to imply:

> You may recognize how the decline of passion in great writers and poets passes away into character-drawing: the sketches of the life in the household of Ulysses much resemble a comedy of character.

Indeed Pound would concur, for in his later prose polemics he would repeatedly cite the *Odyssey* as a model for the novelist.[2] What he seems not to have realized is that the nearer the *Odyssey* is to a novel, the further it is from an epic – or at any rate, that this might be argued.

It is something more than a quibble. We may well feel that a novel can speak to our modern condition as no epic can, and that one reason why the *Odyssey* may speak to us as the *Iliad* nowadays cannot is that its protagonist can be re-created by James Joyce in the figure of Leopold Bloom, and by Joyce's friend Pound as something between Li Po and the author of 'The Seafarer': 'Born un po' misero, don't want to go to war, little runt who finally has to do all the hard work, gets all Don Juan's chances with the ladies and can't really enjoy 'em'.[3] But when Pound defines epic as 'a poem including history',[4] we have the right to ask *how* Pound's epic will do this: in what spirit will history be included? And we may legitimately think that a poem which begins in the style and measure of 'The Seafarer' will 'include history' in a spirit not epical but elegiac.

The use of the 'Seafarer' metre in Canto I has been explained in another way, as a matter of chronological propriety. For this most ancient of Greek poems (Pound believes the *nekuia* episode which he translates in Canto I to be more archaic than the rest of the *Odyssey* – Letters, p.363), it was appropriate – so the argument runs – to use

---

1 Longinus, *On the Sublime*, tr. A.O. Prickard (Oxford, 1916), sect.IX.
2 Cf. *Guide to Kulchur* (London, 1938), p.146 in the New Directions (New York) reprint.
3 *Letters*, p.362 (to W.H.D. Rouse, 1935). All the letters to Rouse on his translation of the *Odyssey* are relevant.
4 'Date Line' in *Make It New*.

the most ancient of poetic styles extant in English. This argument seems too schematic to be convincing, especially if it is extended, as in logic it has to be, to explain why Pound took Homer's Greek through the medium of a translation into Renaissance Latin.[1] Similarly, the usual way of explaining Pound's choice of the *Odyssey* as his standard of poetic reference, rather than the *Iliad*, is to insist, as Pound invites us to do, on Odysseus as 'the voyager', like Hanno the Carthaginian and other navigators who are to appear in the *Cantos*, as the man who knows his world experimentally in coastlines followed and landfalls aimed at, not as configurations on a map. But this is to make of Pound's Odysseus the Odysseus of Tennyson, not the Odysseus of Homer (or of Du Bellay). For Homer's Odysseus is voyaging *home*. Thus, in the strictest sense of nostalgia,[2] Homer's Odysseus is a nostalgic hero. And nostalgia, once again, comports with elegy better than with epic. Certainly one may read quite a long way into the *Cantos* in the spirit of 'Lordly men are to earth o'er given' from 'The Seafarer'.

Apart from 'The Seafarer', *Ripostes*, the collection of 1912, is insubstantial, as if Pound had scraped his bottom drawer to find enough for a volume. For instance 'Salve Pontifex', the elaborate tribute to Swinburne, is salvaged from *A Lume Spento*. In some ways, indeed, *Ripostes* represents, not a marking time since *Personae*, but a losing of ground there gained. This is particularly true of metre: 'Portrait d'une Femme' is an interesting, even a distinguished poem (on a subject to be more characteristic of Eliot's work than of Pound's) which fails to realize its full potential because it is in blank verse; Pound had appealed and attracted attention because he was singing to other tunes than those of the iambic pentameter, yet it is those old tunes sounding here again. 'Silet', with its opening echo of a famous sonnet by Keats; 'In Exitus Cuiusdam' and 'Phasellus Ille', which admirably incorporate the modern world of letters; the appealingly vulnerable love-poems, 'The Needle' and 'A Virginal' – though in different ways each of these is distinguished and memorable, in none of them is the voice that speaks a new and unmistakable voice, the voice of 'Sestina: Altaforte'. For in all of these the measure, though it is varied more in some than in others, is still the iambic pentameter.

There are, however, two pieces of which this is not true: 'Apparuit'

1 The Latin source, together with Pound's translation, is in 'Translators of Greek', reprinted in *Make It New*.
2 See D.W. Harding, 'A Note on Nostalgia', in *Determinations*, ed. F.R. Leavis (London, 1934).

and 'The Return'. And they are very important because in them Pound experiments metrically not with the line but with the strophe. 'Apparuit' is in Sapphic stanzas and seems to be a reworking of 'The House of Splendour' from *Canzoni*. Pound draws from Sapphics a melody altogether more haunting and enervated than the urgent rapidity of earlier English Sapphics like Isaac Watts's 'Day of Judgment' or Cowper's 'Stanzas Written in a Period of Insanity'. It is this melody, once discovered, by which Pound attains a sort of unearthliness that he seems to have tried for also in 'The House of Splendour'. He was balked on that occasion by the incongruous materiality of heraldic or pageant-like imagery he seems to have taken over from Morris; all trace of Morris's influence has been purged from 'Apparuit', and whatever happens in the poem (we cannot give a name to it) is clearly happening in a dimension beyond time and space. The same is true of 'The Return', where the Sapphic stanza has a sort of phantasmal presence in or behind the first four lines, but only as a sort of musical theme which is at once thereafter developed and elaborated not quite beyond recognition but certainly beyond analysis:

> See, they return; ah, see the tentative
>   Movements, and the slow feet,
>   The trouble in the pace and the uncertain
> Wavering!
>
> See, they return, one, and by one,
> With fear, as half-awakened;
> As if the snow should hesitate
> And murmur in the wind,
>   and half turn back;
> These were the 'Wing'd-with-Awe,'
>   Inviolable.
>
> Gods of the wingèd shoe!
> With them the silver hounds,
>   sniffing the trace of air!
>
> Haie! Haie!
>   These were the swift to harry;
> These the keen-scented;
> These were the souls of blood.
>
> Slow on the leash,
>   pallid the leash-men!

The decay of classical studies? The etiolation of Hellenism as an intellectual and artistic stimulus? The virtual extinction of any sense of retributive justice in the frame of things, such as the ancients figured by the avenging furies? Even the etiolation of the Sapphic stanza, considered as the classic vehicle for expression of sexual passion? These ideas or some of them (and certainly others) are part of the 'complicated sort of significance' Pound was to claim for the poem; one might think that the poem has the sort of meaning that music normally has, but Pound found analogies for it in another art, in sculpture.[1]

It is surprising that a poet who had scored his most brilliant successes with Browningesque poems, dense with the tangible presences of men recorded in history and occupying a very particular time and space, should have wanted to write a poem like this – let alone, that he should have brought it off. But, in fact, he had tried for this effect many times without success. Among the earlier poems, 'Threnos' is like 'The Return' in its tone, though nowhere near it in accomplishment. 'In Durance' is a discursive poem arguing for a Platonic understanding of poetry, on the authority of Coleridge's essay 'On the Principles of Genial Criticism'. There is Platonism also in 'Paracelsus in Excelsis' and in the fine 'Blandula, tenulla, vagula'. And a poem from *Canzoni*, 'The Flame', is quite explicit:

> There *is* the subtler music, the clear light
> Where time burns back about th'eternal embers.
> We are not shut from all the thousand heavens:
> Lo, there are many gods whom we have seen,
> Folk of unearthly fashion, places splendid,
> Bulwarks of beryl and of chrysophrase.
>
> Sapphire Benacus, in thy mists and thee
> Nature herself's turned metaphysical,
> Who can look on that blue and not believe?

In fact, throughout the earlier collections, Pound is to be heard more often asking for a Platonic poetry of the metaphysical, transcending place and time, than for a poetry dense with the particulars of history. Over Pound's career as a whole the wish to transcend history is more

1 *Gaudier-Brzeska* (London, 1916), p.98: 'poems like "The Return", which is an objective reality and has a complicated sort of significance, like Mr Epstein's "Sun God" or Mr Brzeska's "Boy with a Coney".' Such poems, Pound says, 'are Imagisme, and insofar as they are Imagisme, they fall in with the new pictures and the new sculpture'. ('The Return' appeared originally in *The English Review* in June 1912.)

powerful than the wish to act in history, but the Cantos seem governed by the conviction that the poet has to earn the right to such transcendence, that history can be transcended only after it has been understood.

The last pages of *Ripostes* are taken up by 'The Complete Poetical Works of T.E. Hulme' (five poems), and Pound's introductory note to these, oddly evasive as it is, gives the first uncertain notice of his involvement with the programmatic movement, imagism. The history of imagism has been told several times, first by Glenn Hughes thirty years ago[1] and most recently and entertainingly by Charles Norman in his biography of Pound. With the movement thus chronicled, which began with T.E. Hulme and F.S. Flint in 1908/9 and persisted into the 'twenties under the able sponsorship of Amy Lowell, Pound's association was, though spectacular, brief and tangential. Pound's poetic path intersected at one stage with those of Flint, of James Gould Fletcher, Richard Aldington, and H.D. (Hilda Doolittle, an old acquaintance of Pound's from his college days with William Carlos Williams), but he was set on a different course and in a short time was distinguishing his 'imagisme' from the 'Amygisme' of the others. Whereas Flint, for instance, had taken his bearings from the ideas of T.E. Hulme, Pound had been set on his course by conversations with Yeats and Ford Madox Ford. It is Ford (or Hueffer, as he then called himself) who is more important than Hulme in this connection, for whereas Hulme's *Speculations* have been given deservedly close and respectful attention by students of twentieth-century poetry, Ford's contributions to that theory have been overlooked – naturally enough, since he made them in conversation, or else by implication in his own poems, now little read, or else (most significantly of all) in his brief but brilliant tenure of the editorial chair of *The English Review*. Ford's half-serious claim to be the father of imagism,[2] though it does not at all supplant the claim of Hulme, is certainly just insofar as it refers to the poems that Pound wrote in his imagist phase and, indeed, later. Pound has been at pains to acknowledge this. Ford, far more a novelist than he was a poet, insisted that the modern poet was in competition not only with great poets of the past but also with great novelists, with Turgenev, Flaubert, Stendhal, James. This conviction, the necessity

1 Glenn Hughes, *Imagism and the Imagists* (Stanford, 1931).
2 Ford Madox Ford, 'A Jubilee', in *Outlook* (London, 10 July 1915), reviewing *Some Imagist Poets* (1915). See also Ford's preface to *Imagist Anthology* (New York and London, 1930).

for this emulation of the realistic novel, had a permanent effect on Pound's poetry. It lies behind, for instance, Pound's admiration for the poetry of Crabbe[1] and also, I suspect, behind Eliot's declaration, in relation to the poems of Samuel Johnson, that 'poetry must be at least as well written as good prose'.[2]

1 See 'The Rev. G. Crabbe, LL.B.', in *Future*, I: 4 (February 1917), reprinted in *Literary Essays of Ezra Pound*, ed. T.S. Eliot (London, 1954).
2 T.S. Eliot, Introduction to *'London' and 'The Vanity of Human Wishes'*, ed. McAdam and Nichol Smith (London, 1930). See *Guide to Kulchur*, ch. 28.

II

Cathay · Arnaut Daniel · The Noh

Ode 167 from the *Classic Anthology* is a doing over of a translation, under the title 'Song of the Bowmen of Shu', that stands first in Pound's collection of 1915, *Cathay*. A comparison of the later version with the earlier one is startling and instructive. The poem in *Cathay* is called 'Song'. But in fact it nowhere recalls any of the forms of English verse for singing – not either of the forms of English ode, nor any of the many forms of English ballad, nor the 'air', nor the hymn. Ode 167, on the other hand, *is* cast very conspicuously in the form of a ballad, in this case of a modern ballad like 'The Quartermaster's Stores', such as British or American troops even today can make up for themselves to express, just as the Chinese poem does, the tribulations of campaigning.

Two consequences follow. First, Ode 167 is necessarily far more colloquial than 'Song'. What in 1915 was 'Here we are because we have the Ken-nin for our foemen' becomes in 1955 'We are here because of these huns'. The second consequence is more dismaying: because Ode 167 is an English poem for singing, it is incomplete without a musical setting; it is deliberately and conscientiously left incomplete, in order that the musician, when he comes to set the poem, shall have something to do. On the other hand the earlier version, 'Song of the Bowmen of Shu', aspires to be, and is, complete in itself, with a verbal music of its own wholly composed by the poet-translator so as to leave no margin for a musician to work with. Thus 'Song of the Bowmen of Shu' will inevitably and rightly please many more readers than Ode 167. For we have to go back to the seventeenth century to find English readers to whom it comes naturally to think of a poem as incomplete until it is set to music. We expect our poems to bring their music along with them, as the *Cathay* poems do but the *Classic Anthology* poems do not. Thus the seventeen translations offered as *Cathay* have for long been among the most popular of Pound's works; and there are good reasons for thinking they will continue to be liked much more than the more ambitious, but less appealing, translations of the Odes.

Cathay was published in April 1915 in London. It represents Pound's
first venture into understanding Chinese culture, and it is tempting
to say that it came about by accident. But this would be an injustice
to Mrs Ernest Fenollosa[1] who, since the death of her husband in
1908, had been looking out for a writer who would make the most
of what Fenollosa had left behind him: fragmentary translations from
Chinese and Japanese, with notes on these and the draft of a momen-
tous essay on the superficially recondite subject of the Chinese writ-
ten character as a medium for poetry. It was no accident, but the
sure and independent taste of Mrs Fenollosa, that made her choice
light upon Pound on the strength of a group of his poems in the
Chicago magazine *Poetry* for April 1913. Pound, when in 1916 he
had worked over Fenollosa's translations of the Japanese 'Noh' plays,
introduced them by declaring that 'the life of Ernest Fenollosa was
the romance par excellence of modern scholarship'.[2] Not only is this
true of Fenollosa, Salem-born and Harvard-educated, who became
Commissioner of Arts for the Imperial Japanese government; it is
also revealing about Pound. Some of Pound's incautious defenders
may have confused scholarship, and especially literary scholarship,
with dry-as-dust pedantry; Pound himself, in his fiercest polemics
against pedantry and the inertia of institutionalized learning, has
always honoured true scholarship and has been excited by the
romance as well as the dignity of the life of learning. Every one of
his translations is in intention a scholarly translation; and if it is true
that his scholarship has not kept pace with his zeal and enthusiasm,
this is because he has not observed a rule that the scholar must groan
under even as he is governed by it – the rule of specialization. Pound
has been interested in too many things, in particular in too many
languages, for his learning to be adequate in all of them. But he has
conspicuously refused to take the position that his expertise as a poet
absolves him, in translating, from the scruples and responsibilities
of the scholar. By a mournful paradox the scholars would have
treated him less harshly if, with the arrogance of a Bohemian, he
had thought that his talents permitted him to bypass the necessity
for a scholar's accuracy.

1 Fenollosa's second wife, born Mary McNeil of Mobile, Alabama, had
lived in Tokyo with her first husband and lived there again with Fenollosa
from 1897 to 1900. Japan is the setting of novels she later wrote under the
name Sidney McCall. See Van Wyck Brooks, *Fenollosa and His Circle* (New
York, 1962).
2 '*Noh*', *or Accomplishment, A Study of the Classical Stage of Japan* (London,
1916; New York, 1917); and *Certain Noble Plays of Japan*, from the manu-
scripts of Ernest Fenollosa, chosen and finished by Ezra Pound, with an
introduction by William Butler Yeats (Dublin: Cuala Press, 16 September
1916).

Thus, when Mrs Fenollosa suggested to Pound that he 'finish' Ernest Fenollosa's translations, she had found a man with a scholar's conscience as well as a poet's talent. Perhaps she had been shrewd enough to discover this and check on it for herself. For, although he had in the meantime made his name in London as an original poet and a man of letters, Pound had also published a scholarly translation deriving immediately from his academic training in Romance philology, his first versions of *The Sonnets and Ballate of Guido Cavalcanti* (London and Boston, 1912). All the same, Pound of course was quite inadequately equipped to apply his scholarship to Oriental texts; and *Cathay* includes one memorable howler: 'The River Song' is a conglomeration of two distinct poems by Li Po, the title of the second being versified and submerged in the four lines beginning 'And I have moped in the Emperor's garden'.

The melody of the translations in *Cathay*, wholly a poet's melody leaving no room for collaboration with a musician, is less a matter of metre than of syntax. What is most immediately striking about these poems is the frequency with which a line of verse comprises one full sentence:

South-Folk in Cold Country

The Dai horse neighs against the bleak wind of Etsu,
The birds of Etsu have no love for En, in the north,
Emotion is born out of habit.
Yesterday we went out of the Wild-Goose gate,
Today from the Dragon-Pen.
Surprised. Desert turmoil. Sea sun.
Flying snow bewilders the barbarian heaven.
Lice swarm like ants over our accoutrements.
Mind and spirit drive on the feathery banners.
Hard fight gets no reward.
Loyalty is hard to explain.
Who will be sorry for General Rishogu,
    the swift moving,
Whose white head is lost for this province?

The first three sentences, each with a line to itself, are separated only by commas, whereas later sentences, again one to a line, are closed off by full stops; this is important, for it takes us with a rush into a poem which then seems to get slower. But this is to plot the movement only generally, over the whole poem. Where the expectation of the complete sentence has been built up so strongly, the three pieces of stabbing telegraphese in the sixth line have the effect of speeding it up almost uncontrollably; but the slow pace is then reasserted. In the last three lines the break into a limp and liquid elegiac cadence is chiefly a matter of one question about General Rishogu being plangently trailed across three lines (or two and a half), whereas the measure which the poem has established is of one sentence to a line. More important, however, is the way in which we are persuaded to see or hear such a line as 'Loyalty is hard to explain' as of equal fullness, occupying as much of time as 'Flying snow bewilders the barbarian heaven' (which has the beauty of Racine), or, in a significantly dissonant tone, 'Lice swarm like ants over our accoutrements'. The poem establishes a convention by which the gauge of a poetic line is not the number of syllables or of stressed syllables or of metrical feet, but the fulfilment of the simple grammatical unit, the sentence; and, the convention thus established, we conspire in giving to naïvely abstract sentences like 'Hard fight gets no reward' and 'Loyalty is hard to explain' as much weight as to the longer sentences which make vivid images about lice on armour, and flying snow in the skies. This seems to be a wholly original and brilliant way of embodying abstractions in English poetry.

It is not clear whether, at the time of making the *Cathay* translations, Pound had already studied Fenollosa's essay on the Chinese written character, which he was to edit later. It is reasonable to suppose that he had read it through at least. Although other and more questionable parts of Fenollosa's argument have attracted more attention, one finds in this little treatise just what might have led Pound to this way of writing, an impassioned plea by Fenollosa for the sentence, in its naked anatomy of subject/ verb / object, as the natural unit of poetic perception, in Chinese but also (so Fenollosa suggests) in other languages.[1] And, in fact, other languages than Chinese could bring the same lesson home to the English-speaking reader. Bishop Lowth and Christopher Smart in the eighteenth century had recognized in Hebrew poetry what Gerard Manley Hopkins in the nineteenth was to call 'the Figure of Grammar', the way in which the structural units of, for instance, the Psalms of David are not metrical but syntactical. And occasionally, as in 'Song of the Bowmen of Shu', when Pound establishes the norm of not one but two sentences to the line, his lines for the moment echo the antiphonal structure of the Psalms or the Song of Solomon, where the grammar of the second half of the verse parallels the grammer of the first half:

1 See Donald Davie, *Articulate Energy: An Enquiry into the Syntax of English Verse* (London, 1955), ch.4.

We have no rest, three battles a month.
By heaven, his horses are tired.
The generals are on them, the soldiers are by them.
The horses are well trained, the generals have ivory
      arrows and quivers ornamented with fish-skin.
The enemy is swift, we must be careful.

The same principle operates: though the ear necessarily registers 'the generals have ivory arrows and quivers ornamented with fish-skin' as longer than 'the soldiers are by them', yet the ear takes pleasure in being persuaded by the mind that since these units are grammatically equal (being both complete sentences), the sentence about ivory arrows and fish-skin quivers takes up no more time than 'the soldiers are by them', or 'we must be careful'. All sorts of changes can be rung; for instance, in 'The River Merchant's Wife: A Letter', in which the norm is one sentence to a line but there are also many sentences strung over two lines, there is an exceptional poignancy about the one short line which comprehends two complete sentences:

They hurt me. I grow older.

Vers libre on these or similar principles has been written in French by Claudel and St-John Perse and in English by Eliot in his translation of Perse's *Anabase*.

This is not to say that the discovery or re-discovery of this principle absolves the poet from listening to what his verse sounds like; as if the reader's ear were always ready to be persuaded by his mind into taking as metrically equal two cadences of very unequal length. On the contrary, the ear permits itself to be thus persuaded only in specially favourable circumstances. And Pound goes to great pains to arrange the circumstances. Years later he was to say (Canto 81), 'To break the pentameter, that was the first heave'. And *Cathay* shows the pentameter already 'broken'.

It is important to understand what is involved. From Edmund Spenser onwards in English verse the finest art was employed in running over the verse line so as to build up larger units of movement such as the strophe, the Miltonic verse paragraph, or, in Shakespearean and other theatrical poetry, the sustained dramatic speech. This too is more an effect of syntax than of anything else: the grammatical unit, the sentence, is draped over the metrical unit, the line, so as to play off the pauses of different weight demanded by the grammar against the pauses demanded at line-endings (and sometimes within the line) by metre. This is not to 'break' the pentameter (or more generally the verse-line of whatever length), but rather to submerge it, by incorporating the line into the building of larger and more intricate rhythmical units. Even the masters of the heroic couplet, Samuel Johnson no less than Pope or Dryden, frequently incorporated their couplets into verse-paragraphs conceived as rhythmical and rhetorical wholes; and even when they do not do this, their unit rhythmically is in any case the couplet, the pair of lines, rather than the line. It was only when the line was considered as the unit of composition, as it was by Pound in *Cathay*, that there emerged the possibility of 'breaking' the line, of disrupting it from within, by throwing weight upon smaller units within the line. 'South-Folk in Cold Country' is an exceptionally simple case, but even there the ear registers in the second line the phrase 'in the north', as a rhythmical unit: isolated between commas, it is breaking free from the line of which it is a member, in a way which would be impossible for any comparable phrase in poetry that rode over line-endings as Pound's does not. Only when the line was isolated as a rhythmical unit did it become possible for the line to be rhythmically disrupted or dismembered from within. The phrase 'the swift moving', left hanging between the penultimate and the last lines of 'South-Folk in Cold Country' is not heard by the ear as itself an extra line, but rather as the rhythmical member of some vanished line, torn free and standing free on its own account. And in a piece as elaborately composed as 'Song of the Bowmen of Shu', there are lines such as:

> Sorrowful minds, sorrow is strong, we are hungry and thirsty.

or:

> Horses, his horses even, are tired. They were strong.

where the line breaks up into its rhythmical members, three in the first case and four in the second, between grammatical pauses which assert themselves as rhythmical pauses – which assert themselves thus more disruptively than would be possible in verse composed paragraph by paragraph, or strophe by strophe.

This procedure was not unprecedented, to be sure. Quite apart from the model of Hebrew poetry, which enforces similar effects in, for instance, Smart's *Rejoice in the Lamb*, the pentameter had thus been analyzed into its component rhythmical members by Thomas Campion[1] and in practice by other English poets of the seventeenth century who wrote for musical setting. Before many years were out,

---

1 See M.M. Kastendieck, *England's Musical Poet: Thomas Campion* (New York, 1938).

Pound would esteem very highly musicians and composers who at
that period thus collaborated, such men as Henry Lawes and
Edmund Waller; and he would see that, in their ways of writing,
these seventeenth-century artists were the legitimate heirs of those
Provençal poets to whom he had admiringly devoted himself ever
since his student days.

In the translations he made from the Provençal at this time, Pound
nevertheless overlooked this English precedent. William McNaughton
has declared, for example, comparing Campion's poem 'Since She,
ev'n She' with Arnaut Daniel's 'L'aura amara':

> Campion's music fits the Daniel poem perfectly, with the
> repetition of Campion's last two lines as indicated by the score:

> > Since she, ev'n she, for whom I liv'd,
> > Sweet she by Fate from me is torne
> > Why am not I of sence depriv'd,
> > Forgetting I was ever borne?
> > Why should I languish, hating light?
> > Better to sleepe an endlesse night.[1]

Campion's lines are very ready to dismember themselves, as the
music may prompt:

> > Since she
> > ev'n she
> > for whom I liv'd ...

> > > > and so on.

But Pound, when he worked at translations from the Provençal (he
meant to publish them as a book, 'Arnaut Daniel', dedicated to
William Pierce Shepard, his old teacher at Hamilton), was looking
for the musicality of poetry in such comparatively freakish or primi-
tive features as onomatopoeia and intricately regular full rhyme.
Thus of 'L'aura amara' he says: 'we have the chatter of birds in
autumn, the onomatopoeia obviously depends upon the *"-utz, -etz,
-ences* and *-ortz"* of the rhyme scheme.' And Pound's version of the
seventeen short lines of each of Daniel's strophes is painstakingly
in keeping with this conception of the poem, matching off each

1 William McNaughton, 'Ezra Pound's Meters and Rhythms', *PMLA*,
LXXVIII (March 1963), 136-46.

Provençal sound against an English sound in the precisely corres-
ponding place. The result is not happy. It is difficult to believe that
the poet who wrote *Cathay* was at much the same time writing the
'Five Canzoni of Arnaut Daniel' that appear in his volume of 1920,
Umbra.[1] What first strikes the reader is the extraordinarily indiscrimi-
nate diction of these versions: in order to get onomatopoeic and
rhyming words, Pound has to let his diction veer crazily from col-
loquial slang to bizarre archaisms like 'raik' and 'wriblis'; the syntax
is often crabbed, and word-order obscurely inverted, for the same
reason. But more important, in view of the principles behind the
distinctive melodies of *Cathay*, is the way in which the verse-line is
no longer the unit; syntax is jerked and heaved around line-endings
by violently disconcerting enjambements: 'What folly hath infected
/ Thee?' or 'Disburse / Can she, and wake / Such firm delights, that
I / Am hers, froth, lees, / Bigod! from toe to ear-ring'. The last
example recalls Browning at his worst.

The work that Pound did on Fenollosa's manuscripts about Chinese
literature introduced him to what was to be an abiding interest of
his life, and one of the causes he was to serve most zealously – the
Chinese, more particularly the Confucian, system of ethics. The far
more voluminous material which Fenollosa left bearing on Japanese
poetry served Pound's purposes less well. If we look back down the
perspective of Pound's career as a whole at the work he did, follow-
ing Fenollosa, on the Japanese Noh plays, we see that this bore fruit
in the later writings, not of Pound himself, but of an older poet
who was his close associate when he was working on this material,
W.B. Yeats. It was Yeats who, in 'At the Hawk's Well', 'The Dream-
ing of the Bones', and others of his *Plays for Dancers*, adapted into
the English and the Irish theatres the dramatic form that the Noh
plays represent, finding in these Japanese works the alternative he
had long been looking for to the naturalistic theatre of Ibsen and
Shaw. Pound, on the other hand, seems seldom to have been
attracted toward writing for the theatre – a feature of his tempera-
ment that helps to explain, for instance, the small place Shakespeare
has in his scheme of things, and the striking way in which Pound
hardly ever, whatever style he is writing in, recalls Shakespearean
ways of writing.

1 There are other translations from Daniel in an essay on him to be found
in Pound's *Instigations* (New York, 1920), and these are gathered together
with the five from *Umbra* in *The Translations of Ezra Pound*, ed. Hugh
Kenner (London, 1953).

His versions of the Noh plays[1] are not for this reason to be over-looked or given scant attention. On the contrary, these translations show better than anything else the catholicity of Pound's taste and how capable he was of responding to ways and structures of feeling that were remote from his own. It is true that at the time Pound did not see his own course clearly enough to realize that the Noh plays represented for him a blind alley. Noting that 'the plays have... a very severe construction of their own, a sort of musical construc-tion', and that where their language seems vague and pale it is because the unity of emotion the Noh seeks is to be completed in dance, he then finds in them also, more questionably, 'what we may call Unity of Image':

> At least the better plays are all built into the intensification of a single Image: the red maple leaves and the snow flurry in Nishikigi, the pines in Takasago, the blue-grey waves and wave pattern in Suma Genji, the mantle of feathers in the play of that name, Hagoromo.

Pound in a footnote tries to make a connection on this basis with the poetic programme of 'imagisme', which at this early stage he was campaigning for and substantiating in his own poems. But the connection is a strained one, as is another he makes in a later footnote between a Provençal poem and a Japanese dance-lyric or *Saibara* quoted by Fenollosa. More convincing, in its frank avowal of tem-peramental impatience and hostility which has had to be overcome, is one of several passages in which Pound alludes explicitly to Yeats:

> I dare say the play, Suma Genji, will seem undramatic to some people the first time they read it. The suspense is the suspense of waiting for a supernatural manifestation – which comes. Some will be annoyed at a form of psychology which is, in the West, relegated to spiritualistic seances. There is, however, no doubt that such psychology exists. All through the winter of 1914-15 I watched Mr Yeats correlating folk-lore (which Lady Gregory had collected in Irish cottages) and data of the occult writers, with the habits of charlatans of Bond Street. If the Japanese authors had not combined the psychology of such matters with what is to me a very fine sort of poetry, I would not bother about it.

1 In *'Noh' or Accomplishment*, Pound incorporated plays previously published in *Certain Noble Plays of Japan* and in *Poetry* (Chicago), *Drama, The Quarterly Note-Book*, and *The Quarterly Review*.

And in the next paragraph he talks of how the Noh requires a sympathy that is not 'easily acquired', that requires 'conscious effort' in order to 'get over the feeling of hostility'. He concludes, 'I have found it well worth the trial'. It does not occur to Pound that some readers' sympathies will go out to the swimming colours and fluctuating outlines of the Noh more readily than to the hard distinctness of the poems in *Cathay*. Since Pound, however, has sometimes given the impression of one who will always give instruction but never take it, it is worth emphasizing this case in which rather plainly Pound allowed himself to be persuaded by Yeats.

Sometimes he was over-persuaded, as in the first play, 'Sotoba Komachi', in which he gives to a Japanese woman prose that has too clearly felt the impress of Synge-song or Kiltartanese, the version of Irish folk-speech that Yeats, or his collaborators J.M. Synge and Lady Gregory, devised for Dublin's Abbey Theatre: 'And I had a high head, maybe, that time'. On the other hand, Pound's prose is in many pieces extremely moving. Many of the translations are wholly in prose; so that, when Pound speaks of 'a very fine sort of poetry' in these plays, he must be taken to mean the poetry that is peculiar and proper to drama, a poetry of action and confrontation to which language (whether prose or verse) is only an adjunct and ultimately, when drama becomes dance as it does here, expendable altogether. As Yeats reveals his realization of this in the imitations he made of the Noh, so Pound shows it in these translations; and doubtless the two poets must be thought of as working toward this together, with Fenollosa's manuscripts to help them. Certainly 'Tsunemasa', for instance, which is entirely in prose except for a last couplet, is full of a wonderful poetry throughout, as Pound points out in a brief foreword where he compares the Japanese poet with Dante:

Spirit   A flute's voice has moved the clouds of Shushinrei. And the phoenix came out from the cloud; they descend with their playing. Pitiful, marvellous music! I have come down to the world. I have resumed my own playing. And I was happy here. All that is soon over.

Priest   Now I can see him again, the figure I saw here; can it be Tsunemasa?

Spirit   It's a sorry face that I make here. Put down the lights if you see me.

Chorus   The sorrow of the heart is a spreading around of quick fires.

The flames are turned to thick rain. He slew by the sword
and was slain. The red wave of blood rose in fire, and now
he burns with that flame. He bade us put out the lights; he
flew as a summer moth.

'It's a sorry face that I make here' marks the momentary reappearance
of the 'Oirish' cadence. But the passage as a whole manifests what
was to be seen in *Cathay* also, the stabbing pathos which comes with
using, as Fenollosa had enjoined in his essay on the Chinese written
character, that rapid and compact grammatical form, the simple
sentence.[1]

In the verse, too, Pound sometimes seems still in *Cathay*:

> How sad a ruin is this:
> Komachi was in her day a bright flower;
> She had the blue brows of Katsura;
> She used no powder at all;
> She walked in beautiful raiment in palaces.
> Many attended her verse in our speech
> And in the speech of the foreign court.

But more typically the verse wanders into quite other areas; this is
especially true of the most haunting and beautiful of the plays, such
as 'Kinuta' or 'Nishikigi':

> At last they forget, they forget.
> The wands are no longer offered,
> The custom is faded away.
> The narrow cloth of Kefu
> Will not meet over the breast.
> 'Tis the story of Hosonuno,
> This is the tale:
> These bodies, having no weft,
> Even now are not come together.
> Truly a shameful story,
> A tale to bring shame on the gods.
> Names of love,
> Now for a little spell,
> For a faint charm only,
> For a charm as slight as the binding together

1 Fenollosa's essay in Pound's redaction first appeared in *The Little Review*,
VI (Sept., Oct., Nov., Dec. 1919). It was reprinted in *Instigations*, and,
along with translations from Confucius, in Washington, D.C., in 1951.

> Of pine-flakes in Iwashiro,
> And for saying a wish over them about sunset,
> We return, and return to our lodging.
> The evening sun leaves a shadow.

It is hard to believe that there is in the Japanese an equivalent to the submerged pun by which this speech floats onward – 'Now for a little spell' – where the spell is registered first as a spell of time but then, as the references to 'a charm' accumulate, transformed into the spell of a necromancer. Moreover, the sentence in which this phrase occurs is only by courtesy to be called a sentence at all: grammatical analysis cannot reveal its structure – and no wonder, for a firm and orderly structure would be out of place when the progression is, as it is here, oblique and dreamlike, through the irrational associations of pun. Pound was to use puns in his own poetry, but stridently, to draw attention to themselves, not as here. And, though he sometimes writes visionary poems, one can see in the perspective of his career as a whole that this poetry of the swimming contour, and the states of mind that produce such poetry and respond to it, are alien to his temperament. Within a year or so after making these Noh translations, he was to redefine his own 'imagisme' more stringently, so as to set it over against the 'symboliste' poetry which seeks out the indefinite. It is the more remarkable that, when challenged by works such as the Noh which called for symboliste treatment, Pound could write in the symboliste way very tenderly and evocatively indeed. In any case one feature of this poetry appealed to him very strongly – its tact, its good manners:

> Our own art is so much an art of emphasis, and even of over-emphasis, that it is difficult to consider the possibilities of an absolutely unemphasized art, an art where the author trusts so implicitly that his auditor will know what things are profound and important.

Others had worked at the Noh before Pound,[1] and new information was to impugn Fenollosa's scholarship. Arthur Waley's versions[2] were to make the Fenollosa-Pound versions out of date as scholarship, though not as English poetry. Meanwhile Pound had

1 See e.g. Marie Stopes, *Plays of Old Japan. The No* (London, 1912).
2 Arthur Waley, in an Introduction (1960) to a new edition (London, 1962) of his *One Hundred and Seventy Chinese Poems*, declares interestingly that 'in translating the lyric parts of Japanese Nō plays...I was as regards diction a good deal influenced by Hopkins'. When Pound made his versions he had not read Gerard Manley Hopkins.

served Mrs Fenollosa well, very deftly and beguilingly interweaving commentary of his own, the admirably vigorous reflections of Fenollosa himself, and the plays. But as early as 1918, Pound declared:

> I don't think Yeats' *Silentia Lunae* hangs together. At least, I don't think it in the same street with his Memoirs as writing. And I find *Noh* unsatisfactory. I daresay it's all that could be done with the material. I don't believe anyone else will come along to do a better book on Noh, save for encyclopaedizing the subject. And I admit there are beautiful bits in it. But it's all too damn soft. Like Pater, Fiona Macleod and James Matthew Barrie, not good enough.
>
> I think I am justified in having spent the time I did on it, but not much more than that. (*Letters*, p.197.)

There is no evidence that he changed his mind later.

III

Gaudier-Brzeska · Vorticism · *Lustra*

Pound's most explicit attempt to distinguish his poetry, which he calls 'imagiste', from symboliste poetry is to be found in what is unfortunately the most incoherent though also one of the most important of his prose works, his memoir of the French sculptor Gaudier-Brzeska, who was killed in the trenches in 1915 at the age of twenty-three. Pound had been associated with Gaudier-Brzeska, and with the painters Percy Wyndham Lewis and Edward Wadsworth, in a movement that christened itself 'vorticism' and ran its own polemical magazine, the once notorious *Blast*. The vorticist movement is interesting as a deliberate attempt to embrace all the arts under one rubric and to help an artist in any one medium by inviting him to find analogies with what his colleagues were doing in the others. Because of this manifesto-programme element, Pound in the memoir more than once invokes approvingly Pater's dictum, 'All the arts aspire to the condition of music'. But, in fact, the vorticist group did not include any musicians, and so the analogy with music, so important to symbolisme, is little explored by Pound; because Gaudier-Brzeska was a sculptor, it is the analogy between poetry and sculpture with which Pound is principally concerned. So he defines his own 'imagiste' poetry as 'a sort of poetry where painting or sculpture seems as it were "just coming over into speech".'[1] Since sculpture, or at least one aspect of sculpture, can be expressed in terms of a relationship between plane surfaces, Pound speaks in these terms of images in a poem:

> The pine-tree in nist upon the far hill looks like a fragment of Japanese armour.

> The beauty of this pine-tree in the mist is not caused by its resemblance to the plates of the armour.

1 *Gaudier-Brzeska* (London, 1916), p.95.

The armour, if it be beautiful at all, is not beautiful *because* of its resemblance to the pine in the mist.

In either case the beauty, in so far as it is beauty of form, is the result of 'planes in relation'.

The tree and the armour are beautiful because their diverse planes overlie in a certain manner. (pp.146-7)

This way of talking about poetry is not so useless as it seems: no other vocabulary can render the method and the effect of Pound's late cantos, which significantly are entitled *Rock-Drill* after a sculpture by Epstein. Similarly, more than juggling with words is involved when Pound defines the poetic image in specifically vorticist terms:

The image is not an idea. It is a radiant node or cluster; it is what I can, and must perforce, call a VORTEX, from which, and through which, and into which, ideas are constantly rushing. In decency one can only call it a VORTEX. And from this necessity came the name 'vorticism'. *Nomina sunt consequentia rerum*, and never was that statement of Aquinas more true than in the case of the vorticist movement. (p.106)

Nomina sunt consequentia rerum – 'names are the consequences of things'. But in symboliste poetry the logic works all the other way – things are the consequences of names; for we find in such a case as Eliot's 'penny world', from 'A Cooking Egg', that we cannot find a referent for this collocation, nothing of which 'penny world' is the name. Rather we agree (as, surprisingly, we find we can) that in the universe created by the poem, the two words thus forced into conjunction call up a thing, a 'penny world', to which they refer, which they name. Words, then, *can* create things – and do so continually in symboliste poetry. But Pound, as his appeal to Aquinas shows, is in this matter (as in surprisingly many others when one comes to look) content to be a traditionalist. For 'penny' and 'world' are not, in Pound's understanding nor, surely, in ours, images; and Eliot's cramming of them together does not, therefore, create images whose 'diverse planes overlie in a certain manner'. It is words that are put together, not images; and while it seems to be true that the right words put together at the right moment in the right way can create by fiat a thing of which they are thenceforward the name, this is a capacity of language which Pound is content to leave to symbolisme – symbolisme which has, so far as he is concerned, 'degraded the symbol to the status of a word'.

Particularly revealing of Pound's constant tendency to see the objective world as indeed objectively there is his comment, again in *Gaudier-Brzeska*, on a famous poem of his own, the two-line poem like a Japanese *hokku* called 'In a Station of the Metro':

> The apparition of these faces in the crowd;
> Petals, on a wet, black bough.

Pound comments: 'I dare say it is meaningless unless one has drifted into a certain vein of thought. In a poem of this sort one is trying to record the precise instant when a thing outward and objective transforms itself, or darts into a thing inward and subjective'.[1] Here once again one sees the traffic being run all the other way from the symbolistes. For to Pound it is the outward that transforms itself into the inward, whereas to the devotee of the objective correlative it is always the inward (the poet's state of mind or state of feeling) that seeks in the outward world something to correspond to itself. Pound's poem answers to what he gives as his intention in writing it. The syntactical dislocation between the two lines permits two comparisons at once: the first, a simple register of the outward, by which the white faces against the gloom of the underground station are like white petals against a black bough; the second, a register of the inward state evoked as a response in the perceiver's mind, by which not the faces but the apparition of them stands out against the gloom of the observer's mind as petals stand out against the bough. It is surely untrue, therefore, that the poem 'is meaningless unless one has drifted into a certain vein of thought'. Its compactness is not superficial, but real and masterly.

Part of the trouble with *Gaudier-Brzeska* is that Pound is fighting on too many fronts at once. His quarrel with symbolisme, for instance, is blurred because Pound, insisting on how his poetry, unlike symboliste poetry, hews close to the contours of the perceivable world, is forced to insist that on the other hand the art he is promoting is not simply representational. Some progress is made, however sluggishly and lop-sidedly, and it is surely no longer necessary to insist:

> We have again arrived at an age when men can consider a statue as a statue. The hard stone is not the live coney. Its beauty cannot be the same beauty. (p.127)

---

1 *Gaudier-Brzeska*, p.103. See, on this poem and more generally on Pound's debt to *hokku* or *haiku* (alternative names for one verse-form), Earl Miner, 'Pound, *Haiku*, and the Image', *The Hudson Review*, IX (Winter, 1956-57), 570-84.

And yet one cannot be sure: it is still easy to find critics for whom an imagiste poem such as 'In a Station of the Metro' is a simple register of sense appearances, all outwardness, never darting 'into a thing inward and subjective'. In these circumstances one can only baldly assert that no retreat to representationalism is involved when Pound borrows from Whistler for his *profession de foi*:

> 'Nature contains the elements.' It is to be noted that one is not forbidden any element, any key because it is geological rather than vegetable, or because it belongs to the realm of magnetic currents or to the binding of steel girders and not to the flopping of grass or the contours of the parochial churchyard.
>
> The artist is born to pick and choose, and *group with science*, these elements, that the result may be beautiful...
> (p.153; italics as in the original)

On the other hand, the emphasis must certainly fall upon the worthiness of the external world to be imitated – and imitated not in the recondite sense by which Aristotle called music the most mimetic of the arts, but in the straightforward sense that recalls what Yeats, in an untypical moment, claimed for Bishop Berkeley: 'Berkeley has brought back to us the world that only exists because it shines and sounds.' It is this shining and sounding world for the recovery of which, in all its glory, Pound is finally grateful to Gaudier-Brzeska and Epstein, to Wyndham Lewis and the other vorticists:

> These new men have made me see form, have made me more conscious of the appearance of the sky where it juts down between houses, of the bright pattern of sunlight which the bath water throws up on the ceiling, of the great 'V's' of light that dart through the chinks over the curtain rings, all these are new chords, new keys of design. (pp.155/6)

It is this shining and sounding world, this system of keys, not to an unapparent world of essence and Idea, but to design, which is carried over on to page after page of Pound's *Cantos*, as it could not be carried onto the page of Eliot, which arranges only objective correlatives, nor to the page of Yeats, the poet for whom the realm of the senses was so often only 'this pragmatical, preposterous pig of a world'. Silk purses have been made out of that sow's ear.

In *Lustra*, the collection belonging to the same period as the Gaudier memoir,[1] the poem that most clearly illustrates the memoir is 'The Game of Chess', an exciting and attractive bravura piece. But a profounder treatment, though a more oblique one, is 'A Song of the Degrees', a poem which looks forward over twenty years to the Usura cantos 45 and 51, which similarly explore the morality implicit in the painter's use of hue.

Pound's development since *Ripostes* had been so rapid, and he had advanced on so many fronts, that *Lustra*, though a very distinguished collection, is also very heterogeneous. It contains, for instance, all but one of the twelve poems published in *Poetry*, II, in April 1913 under the title 'Contemporania', and within this group there are elements so different as markedly Whitmanesque pieces ('Salutation', 'Salutation the Second', 'Commission', 'A Pact') and 'In a Station of the Metro' which one would have sworn came later, out of vorticist theory and the reading of Fenollosa. 'Further Instructions', 'Dum Capitolium Scandet', and 'Coda' are other Whitmanesque poems in *Lustra*[2] that consort oddly with the terse obliquities of Chinese pieces such as 'After Ch'u Yuan', 'Liu Ch'e', and 'Fan-Piece, for Her Imperial Lord'.[3]

'Ancora', 'Surgit Fama', 'April', 'Gentildonna', and 'Les Millwin' are other poems which were in print as early as 1913, and some of these are important and beautiful. By contrast the poems from *Lustra* which appeared first in magazines of the next year, 1914, are mostly slight and often unsatisfactory: the four epigrams headed 'Ladies',[4] for instance, seem to have no point beyond the assertion of a very precarious urbanity, flawed and precarious because it is always toppling over into calculated insolence or a mere wish to shock. Some of these are idle squibs or lampoons which may once have had some topical or polemical point but now are only irritating – for instance, 'The New Cake of Soap' or 'L'Art, 1910', both from the first issue of *Blast*. Some, however, have interest of another, technical kind in the perspective of Pound's efforts to 'break the pentameter'. A case in point is the second of the pieces called 'Amitiés' which ends on a carefully calculated and interesting free-verse cadence. Another

1 *Lustra*, trade edition, London, 1916; private edition, London, 1916; trade edition, New York, 1917; private edition, New York, 1917. Each of these editions differs slightly from all the others.
2 See C.B. Willard, 'Ezra Pound's Debt to Walt Whitman', in *Studies in Philology*, LIV (Oct. 1957), 573-81.
3 See Achilles Fang, 'Fenollosa and Pound', in *Harvard Journal of Asiatic Studies*, 20 (1957), 213-38. The Chinese poems in *Lustra* are derived not from Fenollosa but from Giles's *History of Chinese Literature* (1901) or else his *Chinese Poetry in English Verse* (1884).
4 First printed in *Poetry*, IV: 5 (1914).

such five-finger-exercise is '"Ione, Dead the Long Year".' And as early as 1917 Pound was warning a reviewer against supposing that because *Cathay* preceded *Lustra* the poems in the latter showed him applying to his original work lessons learned from his Chinese translations (*Letters*, p.154); so much of *Lustra* had appeared in magazines two or three years earlier that this could not be the case.

In particular Pound observes, 'I think you will find all the verbal constructions of *Cathay* already tried in "Provincia Deserta".' 'Provincia Deserta' is one of the most masterly poems to be found not just in *Lustra* but in the whole body of Pound's work; and its 'verbal constructions' and rhythmical arrangements are, if not identical with those of *Cathay*, without doubt very closely related and even more elaborate:

> At Calais
>   is a pleached arbour;
> Old pensioners and old protected women
> Have the right there –
>   it is charity.
> I have crept over old rafters,
>   peering down
> Over the Dronne,
>   over a stream full of lilies.
> Eastward the road lies,
>   Aubeterre is eastward,
> With a garrulous old man at the inn.
> I know the roads in that place:
> Mareuil to the north-east,
>   La Tour,
> There are three keeps near Mareuil,
> And an old woman,
>   glad to hear Arnaut,
> Glad to lend one dry clothing.

If 'Old pensioners and old protected women' were allowed to set an iambic tone for the rest, there might emerge something like this, in regular though varied blank verse:

> Old pensioners and old protected women
> Have the right there, out of charity.
> I have crept along old rafters, peering down
> Over the Dronne, a stream there full of lilies.
> Eastward lies the road to Aubeterre,
> Where a garrulous old man is at the inn.

> I know the roads in that place; know Mareuil
> To the north-east, La Tour, the three keeps near,
> And an old woman glad to hear Arnaut...

But everything is lost by such a rearrangement. The information about 'charity' is now delivered with a blank poker-face, whereas in Pound's poem it is spoken of haltingly and the speaker is as if wide-eyed. In the next lines the sense conveyed, the image presented, is completely changed, for the pentameter makes the creeping and the peering happen together, whereas in Pound's poem the man is seen first to creep, and then to peer. Moreover, in Pound's arrangement the reading eye as it moves over the page *discovers* that the Dronne is a stream full of lilies, just as the speaker may have known beforehand that the Dronne was what he was going to see, but not that it had lilies in it; we do not discover it for ourselves as the speaker did. In Pound's poem the speaker sees the road wind eastwards, and then reflects that Aubeterre is where it leads to; or else he reflects first on where the road is, then on where it is going. In the blank verse Aubeterre and the road are parts of a single act, in such a way that the road is swallowed up in 'Aubeterre' and has no physical presence of its own. Pound's poem enacts the process of remembering about Mareuil, naming 'La Tour' but then eddying back as the speaker reminds himself that there are three keeps in the vicinity (perhaps two more besides 'La Tour'); in the blank verse the speaker does not remind himself of anything. And so on: Pound's lineation points up the distinctness of each image or action as it occurs, and thus insists on the sequence they occur in, whereas blank verse, by speeding up the sequence, blurs them together. As William Carlos Williams was writing at just this time:

> The virtue of strength lies not in the grossness of the fiber but in the fiber itself. Thus a poem is tough by no quality it borrows from a logical recital of events nor from the events themselves but solely from the attenuated power which draws perhaps many broken things into a dance by giving them thus a full being.[1]

The pentameter's interwoven strands of sisal rope are replaced by one wiry and flexible steel cable.

---

1 Prologue to 'Kora in Hell', in *Selected Essays of William Carlos Williams* (New York, 1954), p.14.

The impression *Lustra* gives, of a bewildering but by no means aimless eclecticism, is crowned by the inclusion in the volume, among so many innovations, of an ambitious piece in one of the manners Pound had made his own almost from the start, the manner of Browning. This is the poem 'Near Perigord', which had appeared first in *Poetry* for December 1915. It deals, like 'Sestina: Altaforte', with the figure of Bertran de Born, and like 'Sestina: Altaforte' its way of dealing with the subject is Browning's way. However, this is another Browning from the poet of dramatic monologues and dramatic lyrics. The one who presides over 'Near Perigord' is the Browning of *The Ring and the Book*. Pound's poem, like *The Ring and the Book*, dramatizes the processes of historical research, forcing the reader to confront the conflicting testimonies and mutually exclusive hypotheses which are all that often enough the scrupulous historian has to show after all his labours among sparse and contradictory and dubiously authentic documents. Was Bertran, when he praised the Lady Maent, expressing his love for her? Or was this a fiction designed to permit his jongleur to spy into the strongholds of Bertran's neighbours and rivals, and to set them by the ears so as to improve Bertran's precariously exposed position among them? 'Is it a love poem? Did he sing of war?' Which? The poem, by trying and failing to answer this question, dramatizes the difficulty of ever knowing anything with certainty; thus it asserts how in history, as in natural history, the investigator is faced, sooner than we like to realize, with something irreducible and inscrutable – historical reality, like physical reality, resists us and can only to a limited extent be either manipulated or 'seen through'.

Looking back at this poem out of the *Cantos*, one sees how near this is to one central and governing concern of that later writing, in which the life and person of Sigismundo Malatesta, for instance, is to set just the same riddle as Bertran de Born sets in 'Near Perigord', and the attempt to solve the riddle will proceed in the same way.

Though the investigation must break off inconclusively, the poem demands to be concluded, resolved. The resolution is in the last line, 'A broken bundle of mirrors....' Grammatically this refers to the lady herself, Maent; but, concluding as it does a poem that has restlessly moved from one hypothesis to the next, it has the effect of summing up, not just Maent, but the whole situation involving Bertran and her and others. Thus, 'a broken bundle of mirrors' is what the whole of recorded history is. It should also describe, and in a sense it *does* describe, the nature of a poem which, like 'Near Perigord' and later the *Cantos*, stays close to historical record. And yet the very line that acknowledges this, because it is felt to be a satisfying resolution, denies what it states. One bundle differs from the next; and there is a poet's way of tying up the bundle of mirrors (for instance, Dante's way in lines on Bertran that Pound's poem incorporates) that somehow clarifies and harmonizes. 'Near Perigord' acknowledges this and trusts the poet's harmonizing vision; it is doubtful whether that acknowledgement and that trust govern the writing of the *Cantos*.

IV

Gourmont

In the earliest of his comments on translating Greek drama, Pound considers the 'Agamemnon' of Browning:

> His weakness in this work is where it essentially lay in all of his expression, it rests in the term 'ideas'. – 'Thought' as Browning understood it – 'ideas' as the term is current, are poor two-dimensional stuff, a scant, scratch covering, 'Damn ideas, anyhow'. An idea is only an imperfect inducement from fact.[1]

This is just the criticism of Victorian poetry in general that W.B. Yeats had been voicing ever since the 1890s.[2] But Pound almost certainly took it not from Yeats but from *Le Problème du style* by the French poet, novelist, and critic, Rémy de Gourmont: 'Une idée n'est qu'une sensation défraîchie, une image effacée'. (An idea is no more than a sensation that has faded, an image erased.) It was similarly from Gourmont that T.S. Eliot took his famous debating point about 'the dissociation of sensibility'.[3] And Frank Kermode is doubtless right to see behind the theory, in Gourmont and Eliot alike, 'the historical effort of Symbolism... to identify a period happily ignorant of the war between Image and discourse....'[4] Pound is by no means free of the historical nostalgia this involves. Yet, when he says that an idea is 'only an imperfect induction from fact', this is not the same as calling it 'une image effacée'. And in the maddening hotchpotch that Pound presented in 1918 as an essay on Gourmont,[5] though he concedes that 'in the symbolistes Gourmont had his begin-

1 'Translators of Greek', *The Egoist*, V and VI (Aug. 1918 to April 1919); reprinted in *Make It New* (London, 1934; New Haven, 1935), p.147.
2 W.B. Yeats, *Ideas of Good and Evil* (London, 1900).
3 See F.W. Bateson, in *Essays in Criticism* (Oxford), I: 3 (July 1951).
4 Frank Kermode, *Romantic Image* (London, 1957), p.150.
5 'Rémy de Gourmont: A Distinction Followed by Notes', *The Little Review*, V (Feb.-March 1919), [1]-19; reprinted in *Make It New*, p.309.

ning', he speaks also of 'funny symboliste trappings, "sin", satanism, rosy cross, heavy lilies', and declares that the symboliste phase of the nineteenth century no less than earlier phases 'had mislaid the light of the eighteenth century'.

This is the point at which current explanations of Pound go astray; he is not (as T.S. Eliot perhaps is) a 'post-symboliste' writer, except in the narrowest chronological sense; what he deserves on the contrary is the lame though honorific title 'realist'. This contention must rest in the first place upon the poems Pound has written; secondly on the theories of poetry he has peddled, particularly those which he called 'imagism' and 'vorticism'; and only in the third place on his choice of writers to applaud, through translation or otherwise. Among these last, however, Gourmont is a particularly important case, because if 'the historical effort of Symbolism' did enlist Pound's energies (as is claimed), then it must have been through Gourmont that the meaning and motive of that effort were communicated to him.

Gourmont, however, though as editor of the *Mercure de France* he provided a platform for symboliste ideas among others, was at no time really close to the centre of symboliste theory and practice, in Mallarmé's apartment in the rue de Rome. Even during the years from 1886 to 1895 when he wrote polemically as a self-avowed symboliste, the symboliste venture seems to have been for him more a matter of personal and professional friendships (with J.K. Huysmans, for instance) than it was a cause to which he was dedicated. And, indeed, his deliberately uncommitted stance, which often made his writings contradict themselves, unfitted him for the role of spokesman. Of his works that Pound cites most often, one, *Le Latin mystique* of 1892, a scholarly popularization of some Latin poetry of the mediaeval Church, is undoubtedly conceived in part as symboliste propaganda:

> Plus d'un trait de figure caractéristique des poètes latins du christianisme se retrouve en la présente poésie française, – et deux sont frappants: la quête d'un idéal différent des postulats officiels de la nation résumés en une vocifération vers un paganisme scientifique et confortable...; et, pour ce qui est des normes prosodiques, un grand dédain.[1]

1 Rémy de Gourmont, *Le Latin mystique, les poètes de l'antiphonaire et la symbolique au Moyen Age*, 2nd edn. (Paris, 1892), Introduction.
(More than one feature characteristic of the Latin poets of Christianity is to be found again in current French poetry, and two are striking: the search for an ideal different from the authorized postulates of the nation summarized in clamour for a comfortable, scientific paganism...; and, for what has to do with the norms of versification, a great disdain.)

Undoubtedly, however Pound regarded the first of these features of French symboliste poetry, the second, the matter of rhythm, interested him greatly. In the selections from French poets that Pound contributed, with commentary, to *The Little Review* for February 1918 (IV, 10), Gourmont is represented by his 'Litanies de la rose', which Pound commends particularly for its intoxicating unmetrical rhythms. The intoxication is there certainly, as is the dismemberment of the poetic line in ways sometimes reminiscent of Scripture, for instance of the Song of Songs. But Gourmont, like Claudel and St.-John Perse later, has extended the line so far that it is a line no longer and can afford no model for Pound's efforts 'to break the pentameter'. Moreover, the substance of Gourmont's poem is far from novel, and it recalls in its excited eroticism some poems of that other intoxicating metrist, Swinburne, more than it recalls Mallarmé or Laforgue. Other features of Gourmont's symbolisme would be comfortably familiar to any reader of Dowson or other poets of the English 'nineties; for instance, an attitudinizing languor which is naïvely paraded in *Le Latin mystique*:

> Seule, que l'on soit croyant ou non, seule la littérature mystique convient à notre immense fatigue, et pour nous qui ne prévoyons qu'un au delà de misères de plus en plus surement, de plus en plus rapidement réalisé, nous voulons nous borner à la connaissance de nous-mêmes et des obscurs rêves, divins ou sataniques, qui se donnent rendezvous en nos âmes de jadis. (Introduction)[1]

And the 'rêve... satanique' is indulged as early as the second chapter, in an excited meditation on the tortures peculiarly reserved for female martyrs. In all this there is more of what Pound very sensibly called 'funny symboliste trappings' than there is of symbolisme as a serious poetic programme.

One may suspect in fact that by 1918 Gourmont keeps his place beside Rimbaud and others, in Pound's reading of French poetry, chiefly out of the old loyalty that five years earlier had led Pound to invoke Gourmont's metrical practice when providing a skeletal analysis of the Bengali measures of Rabindranath Tagore's

---

1 Nothing else, whether we are believers or not, nothing else but mystical literature agrees with our immense fatigue, and so far as we are concerned, we who look forward only to a hereafter of miseries more and more certainly, more and more rapidly realized, we want to limit ourselves to the knowledge of ourselves and of the obscure dreams, divine or diabolical, that come together in our souls from past times.

Gitanjali.[1] Moreover, in 1918, Pound had probably not read *Le Latin mystique* at all recently or closely, for he declares of Gourmont that 'influenced presumably by the mediaeval sequaires, and particularly by Goddeschalk's quoted in *Le Latin mystique*, he recreated the "litanies".' In fact, as the word would lead us to suppose, Gourmont's litanies owe much more to the mediaeval litanies (also discussed in *Le Latin mystique*) than they do to the *sequaires*. And Pound seems to remember the *sequaire* of Goddeschalk (which is always the case he cites from this book by Gourmont) for a reason which has nothing to do with form and rhythm – for what Goddeschalk says to Christ about Mary Magdalen, '*Amas ut pulchram facias*'.[2]

Gourmont built up a solid reputation in France on critical and philosophical essays published after 1900, in particular on *Le Problème du style* (1902).[3] This is one of Gourmont's writings that plainly influenced the early criticism of T.S. Eliot. Its importance for Pound is much less obvious and can easily be overestimated. Indeed, since it is a sustained sarcastic polemic against a textbook by Albalat written on the assumption that one may learn literary style by imitating the classic 'stylists', much of Gourmont's book seems at odds with the position that Pound was later to take up in *How To Read*,[4] a work that could as well be entitled 'How To Write', in which Pound seems near to proceeding on precisely Albalat's assumption. In fact, Pound could square his position with Gourmont's only by driving hard a distinction Gourmont makes between imitation of foreign writers (which may be fruitful) and the imitation of writers in one's own tongue. Another of Gourmont's emphases that must have been antipathetic to Pound is on impersonality. The impersonality that Gourmont argues for is of the peculiar kind that T.S. Eliot eagerly elaborated in his influential essay on 'Tradition and the Individual Talent'.[5] Both Gourmont and Eliot argue for an absolute discontinuity between the affective experience of the writer at all times when he is not writing, and the allegedly quite distinct sort of emotional experience that conditions his composition. Pound on the other hand admired Li Po and Villon just because the man who is

1 *The Fortnightly Review* XCIII (N.S.), 1913, p.555: 'This metre is... not quantitive as the Greek or Sanscrit measures, but the length of the syllables is considered, and the musical time of the bars is even. The measures are more interesting than any now being used in Europe, except those of certain of the most advanced French writers, as, for instance, the arrangements of sound in Rémy de Gourmont's "Fleurs de Jadis" or his "Litanies de la Rose".'
2 Gourmont, op. cit., 2nd ed., p.115: 'Tu l'aimes afin qu'elle soit belle, – "Amas ut pulchram facias", – ô noble cervelle si avancée en idéalisme!'
3 See Karl-David Uitti, *La Passion littéraire de Rémy de Gourmont* (Paris, 1962).
4 *How To Read* (London, 1931; Boston, 1932).
5 'Tradition and the Individual Talent', *The Sacred Wood* (London, 1920).

personally present in the writing is recognizably the same who lived the dishevelled and turbulent life known from record, anecdote, and legend.

But what does most to bring Eliot to mind rather than Pound, in relation to *Le Problème du style*, is the tone and manner of Gourmont's procedure. In his dealings with the unfortunate Albalat, in his dealings with ideas, and in his dealings with the reader, the play of Gourmont's intelligence is very free indeed. *Le Problème du style* is a brilliant book, in every sense of 'brilliant' including those that shade off into 'superficial' and even 'journalistic'. It is continually arresting, it is not always judicious. F.W. Bateson remarks sourly, 'Gourmont was never afraid to follow a bright idea to a nonsensical conclusion'. And Gourmont himself admitted as much:

> . . . il y a des nuances infinies; mais il faut toujours pousser une théorie a l'extrème, si l'on ne veut pas être tout à fait incompris.[1]

Pound has certainly driven to nonsensical conclusions himself, but unwittingly, seldom with this air of calculated insolence. It is this in Gourmont that accounted for the rather sudden extinction of his reputation soon after his death in 1915. After his death, as for some years before, Gourmont came under heavy attack on this score in the *Nouvelle Revue Française* at the hands of Gide, whom Gourmont had assisted and admired for many years beginning in 1891. Already in 1910 Gide, accusing Gourmont of 'facilité intellectuelle', declared:

> la pensée n'est point chez [Gourmont] le résultat d'une contention, d'un effort; comme d'autres à la paresse il s'abandonne à la pensée et c'est comme en se jouant qu'il écrit.[2]

As regards *Le Problème du style* at any rate, Gide's objection, though harsh, is no more than just. Indeed, Gourmont seems to have admitted its justice, regretting his own facility; and so in *Le Problème du style* he goes out of his way to give credit to honest inarticulate clumsiness in writing. Even so, his own facility may have been more damaging than he realized.

---

1 *Le Problème du style*, 13th edn. (Paris, 1924), p.68 (. . . there are infinite shadings; but one always has to push a theory to its extreme, if one does not wish to be altogether misunderstood).
2 Quoted by Uitti, op. cit., p.47 (with Gourmont thought is not at all the result of a struggle, an effort; as others give themselves up to indolence, he gives himself up to thinking and he writes as if he were making sport).

Pound certainly recognized this quality in Gourmont but he seems to have misinterpreted it in a way not uncommon among British and American Francophiles, who mistake this tone for the tone of Voltaire. Pound, in an obituary notice of Gourmont, explicitly made the connection:

> Voltaire called in a certain glitter to assist him. De Gourmont's ultimate significance may not be less than Voltaire's. He walked gently through the field of his mind.[1]

And Pound's 'glitter' seems to mean that he is, if anything, readier to see meretricious brilliance in Voltaire. Elsewhere in the obituary Pound compares Gourmont with Anatole France, Henri de Regnier, Francis Jammes, and Laurent Tailhade, and decides

> from Rémy de Gourmont alone there proceeded a personal living force. 'Force' is almost a misnomer; let us call it a personal light.

That note was struck again in the essay *Make It New* ('the light of the eighteenth century'); it suggests that Pound saw Gourmont as a lineal successor of the French Enlightenment. And, sure enough, at the period when Pound was most concerned with Gourmont he was also reading admiringly some of the *philosophes*, and Voltaire especially.[2] But in any case Pound's attachment to the French eighteenth century went deep and has remained strong. A product of it at this time was his translation of some of the dialogues of Fontanelle,[3] but it did not end with his youth. On the contrary perhaps the profoundest insight into Pound's later Confucianism was Yeats's brilliant *aperçu* about how Pound's Confucius 'should have worn an Eighteenth Century wig and preached in St. Paul's'.[4] For indeed, it could not be otherwise. When Pound discovered that the central insights of Confucian metaphysics were carried in images from the behaviour of light, like those that were central also to Dante and Cavalcanti, he could not fail to take seriously the metaphor in the very words 'age of enlightenment' or 'age des lumières'. It was this too which led him back into the historical experience of the American, for the America of the Founding Fathers,

1 *The Fortnightly Review*, XCVIII (N.S.), 1915, p.588.
2 See the poem, 'Impressions of François-Marie Arouet (de Voltaire)', originally in *To-Day*, I: 5 (1917), also 'Genesis or The First Book in the Bible', and *Letters*, pp.140, 150, 193-4.
3 Originally in *The Egoist* III and IV (May 1916-June 1917).
4 *The Letters of W.B. Yeats*, ed. Allan Wade (New York, 1955), p.774.

Jefferson and John Adams, was (or so he was to say) specifically an Enlightenment product, a transplanting to American soil of the noblest values of that French eighteenth century which had also, as a matter of historical record, first introduced Europe to the experience of Confucian and pre-Confucian China.[1] Pound's understanding of all European and American history is jeopardized, and his political miscalculations about the history of his own times are explained, as soon as we question whether the light that shone in the Englightenment on Voltaire and Jefferson was the same light that beamed on ancient China out of *The Unwobbling Pivot*, or on the Middle Ages out of Cavalcanti's 'Donna mi prega' and Dante's *Paradiso*.

By the time he wrote *Le Problème du style*, Gourmont could have claimed kinship with figures cf the Enlightenment in at least one important respect; no more than Voltaire or Fontenelle did he regard scientific discovery and theory as a world either closed to the man of letters or beneath his consideration. Gourmont seems to have entertained the delusory, and no doubt pointless, hope of making literary criticism into a science, and some of his allusions to scientific advances are tendentious coat-trailing, like T.S. Eliot's notoriously inexact analogy, in 'Tradition and the Individual Talent', between the artistic sensibility in the act of creation and a bar of platinum acting as catalyst in a chemical solution. But Gourmont's interest in science went deeper than this, and *Le Problème du style*, no less than his *Physique de l'amour* of 1904, is an attempt to apply at least partially the theories of some biologists of his time, particularly the Lamarckian scholar De Vries (Uitti, p.77). As Fenollosa writing of literature was guided by the scientific procedures of the biologist Agassiz, so Gourmont appealed not just to the classic French case of Buffon but also to the pioneering entomologist J.H. Fabre, and admired Taine as an earlier writer who had tried to apply scientific discipline to the writing of literary history. Out of Gourmont Fabre came to stand beside Agassiz and (later) Frobenius in Pound's gallery of admirable practitioners of scientific method, and it is certain that Gourmont won Pound's admiration at least in part for the same reason as Fenollosa.

---

1 Cf. 'Fenollosa on the Noh', *The Translations of Ezra Pound* (London, 1953), p.269: 'Bishop Percy, who afterwards revived our knowledge of the mediaeval ballad, published early in the 1760's the first appreciative English account of Chinese poetry; and Bishop Hood wrote an essay on the Chinese theatre, seriously comparing it with the Greek. A few years later Voltaire published his first Chinese tragedy, modified from a Jesuit translation; and an independent English version held the London stage till 1824'. And cf. *Guide to Kulchur* (1938), p.205, on 'P. Lacharme ex soc. Jesu', who between 1733 and 1752 translated the Confucian odes into Latin.

It is this that makes Gourmont's campaigning for 'the image' into something different from what symbolist or post-symbolist writers claimed for 'the symbol'. One cardinal case of 'the image', for Gourmont as for Pound, is the carefully exact image the biologist constructs of the organisms he studies – an image created by nothing more recondite than scrupulously close and disciplined observation of the object as his senses apprehend it. It is not clear whether this is ever in T.S. Eliot's mind when he uses the word 'image'; it is difficult to see how it can be, for 'image', as Eliot used the word, seems to comprise also what he has called 'the objective correlative'.[1] And according to Eliot, the artist, in constructing his objective correlative out of phenomena offered to his senses, is not at all interested in these phenomena for themselves, in their objectivity, but only to the extent that they may *stand in for* the subjective phenomena (such as states of mind or of feeling) which can thus be objectified through them. The theory of the objective correlative seems much nearer to symboliste theory than Gourmont's or Pound's ideas of the image and, accordingly, much further from scientific method – so far indeed as to be quite incompatible with the assumptions on which a Fabre or an Agassiz proceeded. In fact, of course, the principle on which scientific empiricism proceeds, Locke's famous formulation *Nihil in intellectu quod non prius in sensu*, was called into question as soon as Coleridge (to cite only the principal English authority) pointed out that the processes of human perception are much less simple than Locke had supposed. Eliot's theories, like those of such symbolistes as Mallarmé and Valéry, have the merit of acknowledging the discoveries made by romanticism about the complexities of perception. Gourmont and Pound appear, by comparison, naïve, as nineteenth-century scientists seem naïve beside a twentieth-century physicist. Nevertheless, to get the record straight, it seems that they should be regarded not as post-symboliste theorists but rather as harking back to pre-symboliste and even pre-romantic convictions. In Pound's case, for instance, the element of sharp and exact observation that enters into his notion of the image relates him more closely to Ruskin than to any of the symbolistes or to a thinker in the symboliste tradition such as Eliot.

Accordingly, it comes as no surprise that the work by Gourmont

---

1 T.S. Eliot, 'Hamlet and His Problems', *The Sacred Wood*. When Graham Hough, on p.16 of his *Image and Experience* (London, 1960), calls the theory of the objective correlative 'one of the most celebrated offshoots of the Imagist idea', he is wrong unless he is using 'imagism' in a sense too inconclusive to be either serviceable or historically exact.

that Pound chose to translate, the *Physique de l'amour*,[1] is that in which Gourmont draws most directly and continually on the entomological observations of Fabre and others; nor that Gourmont in this work, as Pound translates him, should be heard echoing Ernest Fenollosa's strictures on 'the old logic': 'Far from wishing to impart human logic to nature, one attempts here to introduce a little natural logic into the old classic logic'.

The translation is a careless performance. Occasionally Pound seems to achieve the charming Latinate elegance of an eighteenth-century naturalist like Gilbert White, as when he writes, 'The salacity of certain birds is well known, and one does not see that the absence of an exterior penis diminishes their ardour, or attenuates the pleasure which they find in these succinct contacts'. But alas! this is a delusion: the word 'succinct' is an irresponsible Gallicism, for the French may speak of *un repas succinct* to mean 'a meagre meal', and all that Gourmont means by the word is 'brief' or 'meagre'. Gourmont writes in his fourth chapter:

> Chez les insectes, la femelle est presque toujours l'individu supérieur. Ce n'est pas ce petit animal merveilleux, roi divergent et minuscule de la nature, qui donnerait le spectacle de cette douve, la bilhargie, dont la femelle, médiocre lame, vit, telle une épée au fourreau, dans le ventre creusé du mâle![2]

Here, by omitting to translate *cette douve*, Pound depends upon our recognizing in 'the bilharzia' (though the word is not to be found in the Shorter Oxford English Dictionary) not an insect at all but a parasite-worm; otherwise we shall make the second half of Gourmont's sentence contradict the first half. And in Chapter 7 a similar heedlessness translates *en clôture* as 'into cloisters'.

All the same, *The Natural Philosophy of Love* is an amusing and instructive book. It has its sinister side, as when Gourmont's Lamarckian persuasion ('Instinct is merely a mode of intelligence') does not stop him arguing from a survival of the fittest to justify the enslavement of the black and brown races by the white. Darwinian arguments were used to the same end by jingo imperialists among Gourmont's

1 *Physique de l'amour, Essai sur l'instinct sexuel* (Paris, 1904). Pound's translation, entitled *The Natural Philosophy of Love*, first appeared in New York in 1922.
2 Among insects the female is nearly always the superior individual. This is not that marvellous little creature, deviant and infinitesimal king of nature, which we should find if we inspected that worm, the bilharzia, of which the female lives, a mere blade, like a sword in its scabbard, in the hollowed belly of the male.

British contemporaries, to the disgust of the Sussex squire Wilfrid Scawen Blunt, whom Pound admired. And when Gourmont goes on to prove from the behaviour of bees that to neuter a part of a population is not unnatural, this casts forward a longer and even blacker shadow to the images of castration which were to run through Pound's mind at the height of his anti-Semitism. But there is an entertaining and admirably pointed wit to Gourmont's remark on polygamy among sticklebacks:

> When the stickleback world becomes reasonable, that is to say absurd, their philosophers will demand 'Why should the father alone be charged with the education of his offspring?' Up to the present one knows nothing except that he educates them with joy and affection. Among sticklebacks and among men there is no answer to such a question save the answer given by facts. One might as well ask why humanity is not hermaphrodite like the snails, who strictly divide the pleasures and burdens of love, for all snails commit the male act, and all lay. Why has the female ovaries, and the male testicles; and this flower pistils, and that one stamens? One ends in baby-talk. The wish to correct nature is unnecessary. It is hard enough to understand her, even a little, as she is.

This too is a passage that would appeal to one who had read in manuscript Fenollosa's *Essay on the Chinese Written Character*, where there are passages informed by the same, perhaps naïve but certainly energetic, respect for natural processes.

V

Homage to Sextus Propertius · Imaginary Letters · Hugh Selwyn Mauberley

By 1916, the work on or toward the *Cantos*, which had been in progress intermittently for ten years or more, had advanced to the stage where Pound was prepared to publish. *Three Cantos* appeared in the magazine *Poetry* in 1917.[1] These versions of Cantos I, II, and III were, as Yvor Winters was to remark, 'awkward Browningesque affairs which bear little resemblance to the later *Cantos* or to their own later forms'.[2] Nevertheless, they are worth taking note of, for this false start on the *Cantos* helps to get into focus the new start Pound made as soon as these were abandoned. For instance, it was of the new start (the first thirty Cantos) that Mr Winters wrote in 1937:

> In the best *Cantos*, at least, Mr Pound is successful, whether in fragments or on the whole, but he presents merely a psychological progression or flux, the convention being sometimes that of wandering reverie, sometimes that of wandering conversation. The range of such a convention is narrowly limited, not only as regards formulable content, but as regards feeling.[3]

And Mr Winters may be right. But wandering reverie or wandering conversation is far more conspicuously the convention of the three cantos of the false start than of the received text – to such an extent, indeed, that Pound's reason for abandoning his first start appears to have been precisely what Mr Winters goes on to observe:

> The feelings attendant upon reverie and amiable conversation tend to great similarity notwithstanding the subject matter, and they simply are not the most vigorous or important feelings of which the human being is capable.

1 *Poetry*, X (June, July, and August 1917).
2 Yvor Winters, *The Anatomy of Nonsense* (Norfolk, Conn., 1943); reprinted in *In Defense of Reason* (Denver, 1947), p.495.
3 *Primitivism and Decadence* (1937), in *In Defense of Reason*, p.145.

If the convention of the *Cantos* is such as Mr Winters says, at least this is unintentional on Pound's part; the abortive three cantos reveal that he had seen the damaging limitations of this convention, and when he started again was trying to avoid it.

The poems Pound wrote between 1917 and 1920 have been the subject of so many claims and counterclaims, so much vilification and approbation, that to get at the poems one has to fight through a cloud of witnesses. Certainly this is true of *Homage to Sextus Propertius* which, punctiliously dated by the poet as of 1917, was not printed until 1919 (in *New Age*, XXV). No poem by Pound has caused more offence. The protests began when a part of the sequence in *Poetry*, XIII, 6 (March 1919), provoked Professor William Gardner Hale into attacking Pound for mistranslation. The attack, which was reproduced in part in the Chicago *Tribune*, was particularly awkward since Hale was a friend of Harriet Monroe, the editor of *Poetry* (*Letters*, p.310); and it broke up the association between Pound and Miss Monroe that had made *Poetry* the principal organ by which 'the new poetry' (of Pound, but also of others whom he campaigned for generously) had got into print.

And yet Pound's defence against Hale's charges was impregnable: there could be no mistranslation, since, as Pound wrote in 1919, 'there was never any question of translation' (*Letters*, p.211). Later, he elaborated this:

> No, I have not done a translation of Propertius. That fool in Chicago took the *Homage* for a translation, despite the mention of Wordsworth and the parodied line from Yeats (As if, had one wanted to pretend to more Latin than one knew, it wdn't have been perfectly easy to correct one's divergencies from a Bohn crib. Price 5 shillings.) (*Letters*, p.245.)

The parody of Yeats is in Section IV:

> Sadness hung over the house, and the desolated female attendants
> Were desolated because she had told them her dreams.[1]

And Wordsworth is named in Section XII.

This should have been conclusive. That it was not so – that Robert Graves should to this day bring the charge of mistranslation, and

---

[1] Cf. Yeats: 'I have spread my dreams under your feet; / Tread softly because you tread on my dreams'. (*The Wind Among the Reeds*, 1899.)

Robert Conquest expatiate upon it in a truly scandalous article as late as 1963[1] – this is partly Pound's fault, but more the fault of his apologists and admirers. T.S. Eliot in 1928, Hugh Kenner in 1951, John Espey in 1955, J.P. Sullivan in 1960[2] – every one of them is determined to eat his cake and have it, to assert that *Homage to Sextus Propertius* is not a translation and yet that somehow it is. As soon as Espey, for example, observes that Pound's poem 'requires, for its fullest savour, some knowledge of the text on which it is based', he opens the door to regarding the poem as translation; and Robert Conquest has the right to complain. And Espey is surely wrong, as are Eliot and Kenner and Sullivan also; so far from a knowledge of Propertius's Latin being a help to the understanding of Pound's poem, it is a perhaps insurmountable hindrance, as Conquest's essay proves. Pound's poem is *in no sense* a translation – not in the sense, for instance, in which Pope's 'Imitations of Horace' are translations of Horace, or Johnson's 'Vanity of Human Wishes' is a translation of Juvenal. Indeed, it appears that training as a Latinist tends to debar the reader from appreciating Pound's poem, and so one may commiserate with Robert Conquest on his deprivation. But of course he in turn is wrong to claim that 'even "homages" should have some connection with the spirit of the original'. A 'homage' means whatever Pound wants it to mean, since it is an *ad hoc* term he has invented. And again Conquest is wrong to say that Pound's poem 'relies entirely on the kudos, and on the properties, of the original'. How can this be true in the case of a reader who has not enough Latin to know the original? And whereas in 1919 perhaps two out of every three readers would be in this position, nowadays nine out of every ten will be thus fortunately insulated, debarred from making the comparison that spoils the poem for Conquest.

T.S. Eliot was in 1928 so far from agreeing that he declared, astonishingly, 'If the uninstructed reader is not a classical scholar, he will make nothing of it'. The readers the poem has found in the years since 1928 – years when 'classical scholars' have become ever thinner on the ground – seem to disprove Eliot; but since Robert Conquest will maintain that these readers have been bullied by academically institutionalized literary criticism, it is worthwhile spelling out how a reader with no Latin (though with a sense of how much the Latin civilization has contributed to the English) may come at Pound's poem.

1 *The London Magazine*, III: 1 (April 1963), 33-49.
2 T.S. Eliot, Introduction to *Ezra Pound: Selected Poems* (London, 1928); Hugh Kenner, *The Poetry of Ezra Pound* (London, 1951); J.J. Espey, *Ezra Pound*'s Mauberley (London, 1955); J.P. Sullivan, 'Pound's *Homage to Propertius*: The Structure of a Mask', in *Essays in Criticism* (Oxford), X: 3 (1960).

Two earlier poems by Pound, and one piece of prose, should prepare such a reader. One poem is 'Prayer for His Lady's Life' from *Canzoni*, 1911, which is glossed 'From Propertius, Elegiae, Lib. III, 26'. It is an early attempt at what becomes the second part of Section IX of *Homage to Sextus Propertius*, and the very title given to the earlier version ('His Lady') indicates how in 1911 the best Pound could do was to convert Propertius into Villon's 'Où sont les neiges d'antan?' as seen through the spectacles of Rossetti and Swinburne. As the uninstructed reader compares 'Ye might let one remain above with us' (1911) with 'There are enough women in hell' (1917), he will not care whether he is getting any nearer to Augustan Rome; he will know that he is moving from the nineteenth century into the twentieth.

The other poem that will help is 'Au Salon':

> I suppose there are a few dozen verities
> That no shift of mood can shake from us:
>
> One place where we'd rather have tea
> (Thus far hath modernity brought us)
> 'Tea' (Damn you!)
> > > Have tea, damn the Caesars,
> Talk of the latest success, give wing to some scandal,
> Garble a name we detest, and for prejudice?

Here the poet has the wish to speak in the accents of the present century, but not the capacity to do so. The most successful of his early poems had been those where we overhear him speaking to himself, privately; 'Au Salon' is one where he tries for a public voice, one which we shall hear, not overhear. The only public voice that he can command, however, is the voice of Whitman; his dissatisfaction with that voice is presumably what prompts unsuccessful but praiseworthy attempts to find another voice, as hear, where the 'Damn you!' in its frustrated stridency betrays at once the desperation of the wish and the impossibility of fulfilling it. The epigrams of *Lustra*, their style painstakingly evolved out of Chinese and Japanese models, out of Latin models such as Martial, and out of the French model of Laforgue, represent another attempt to find a public voice, and a significant but still partial and precarious advance in that direction. Only with the style of *Homage to Sextus Propertius* does Pound find the public voice he has been looking and listening for.

This distinction between the public voice and the private, between (in the terms of John Stuart Mill) the poem that we hear and the poem that we overhear, was overlooked by Pound when he adumbrated his notion of the *persona*:

In the 'search for oneself', in the search for 'sincere self-expression', one gropes... for some seeming verity. One says 'I am' this, that or the other, and with the words scarcely uttered one ceases to be that thing.... I began this search for the real in a book called *Personae*, casting off, as it were complete masks of the self in each poem. I continued in a long series of translations, which were but more elaborate masks.[1]

The word 'mask' suggests here a direct influence from the conversation of Yeats; and commentators have eagerly fastened upon this theory precisely because it seems to provide common ground between Eliot, Yeats, and Pound. But the naturally histrionic talent of the Anglo-Irishman, Yeats, needs to speak through the masks of assumed characters in a different way from Pound and Eliot, and for different reasons. In the case of the American expatriates the need arises, one suspects, only when they want to use a public voice; it arises in fact from the awkwardness of the relation between the poet and the public in Britain and America, the inability of the British and the American publics, then as now, to determine what status to give to the poet and to poetic utterance. Certainly Pound sells the pass on his own translations when he calls them 'but more elaborate masks'. If *Cathay*, if 'The Seafarer', if 'Planh for the Young English King' were indeed nothing but masks for Pound, we should not value them so highly as we do. Their virtue as translations is precisely that they are so much more than masks for the translator. Sextus Propertius on the other hand is truly nothing but a mask; and this is why *Homage to Sextus Propertius* is not and cannot be in any sense a translation. When T.S. Eliot says that the *Homage* 'is also a criticism of Propertius', and when Pound himself says that it 'has scholastic value' (*Letters*, p.245), they are surely wrong, because, for this to be true, Pound's poem would need to be far more of a translation than it is.

'Au Salon', though it is spoken in what aspires to be a public voice, is in fact an excited plea for the poet's right to be private, to eschew civic responsibilities in what he writes. And this is not paradoxical. When the poet announces his determination to speak about matters of the bedroom or the salon rather than the market place (and this is the substance of *Homage to Sextus Propertius*, as of 'Au Salon'), it is in the market place that the announcement must be made; the poet announces at the top of his voice the right to speak *sotto voce*, he denies in a voice of thunder that he is in duty bound to speak thus always. Similarly Pound the publicist in prose

---

1 *Gaudier-Brzeska: A Memoir*, p.98; quoted by J.P. Sullivan, loc. cit.

is never so shrill and vehement as when he complains that his function as a publicist is a distraction from his main concerns, a distraction forced upon him by the heedlessness and stupidity of the public:

> Time was when the poet lay in a green field with his head against a tree and played his diversion on a ha'penny whistle, and Caesar's predecessors conquered the earth, and the predecessors of golden Crassus embezzled, and fashions had their say, and let him alone. . . .

> Metastasio, and he should know if any one, assures us that this age endures – even though the modern poet is expected to holloa his verses down a speaking tube to the editors of cheap magazines – S.S. McClure, or some one of that sort – even though hordes of authors meet in dreariness and drink healths to the 'Copyright Bill'; even though these things be, the age of gold pertains. Imperceivably, if you like, but pertains.[1]

Metastasio figures in just this connection in one of the abortive cantos published in 1917:

> 'Non è fuggi.'
> > 'It is not gone.' Metastasio
> is right, we have that world about us.

And the ambitious work of that year, the *Homage to Sextus Propertius*, has no other theme than this, says nothing more devious or abstruse than had been said in the unconsidered prose of 1912. Nothing, indeed, is more striking and astonishing than the discrepancy between the straightforward obviousness of what *Homage to Sextus Propertius* has to say, and the intricacy of what commentators have to say about it. True, once Pound's poem is set beside the poems of Propertius from which it is quarried, there emerge all the baffling layers of irony which so delight some of the commentators; and it is just for this reason perhaps that they insist on bringing the Latin poet into consideration. But this is to regard the *Homage* as a translation. The *Homage*, considered apart from its Latin sources, says something so simple that the question arises whether the poem is not too long for what it has to say. It is the easiest of Pound's poems, and it has been treated as one of the hardest.

To be sure, what could safely and inoffensively be said in 1912

---

1 'Prolegomena', from *The Poetry Review* (edited by Harold Monro), 1912. Reprinted in 'A Retrospect' (*Pavannes and Divisions*, New York, 1918; and *Literary Essays of Ezra Pound*, ed. T.S. Eliot, London, 1954, p.8).

had become, by 1917, something very offensive indeed. For an expatriate American to tell London, after the Flanders trenches had endured three years of hideous futility, that the poet had the right and sometimes the duty to turn his back on all affairs of state and national destiny, in order to celebrate his love affairs with witty cynicism – this was a very perilous enterprise. And it was doubtless this (though also, one may suppose, common decency of feeling) that caused Pound not to print the sequence until after the war was over. On the other hand, it was precisely because the thing to be said was much harder to say in 1917 than in 1912 that the poet at the later date found it worth saying – and in plangent and mordant verse, not journalist's prose. Because Pound had taken care to date the poem, he carried conviction when he declared of it in 1931:

> ...it presents certain emotions as vital to me in 1917, faced with the infinite and ineffable imbecility of the British Empire, as they were to Propertius some centuries earlier, when faced with the infinite and ineffable imbecility of the Roman Empire. These emotions are defined largely, but not entirely, in Propertius' own terms. If the reader does not find relation to life defined in the poem, he may conclude that I have been unsuccessful in my endeavour.   (*Letters*, p.310.)

The *Homage* is in the fullest sense an occasional poem. And it is only when we remember the occasion that we see it as written against imperialism and against war.

Yeats in 1936, introducing *The Oxford Book of Modern Verse*, said of Pound:

> Even where the style is sustained throughout one gets an impression, especially when he is writing in vers libre, that he has not got all the wine into the bowl, that he is a brilliant improvisator translating at sight from an unknown Greek masterpiece.

Of no poem is this more true than of *Homage to Sextus Propertius*, yet it is just as true of poems where no question of translation arises, of many of the *Lustra* epigrams for example. And Yeats's example (which explains why he makes the unknown masterpiece Greek) is a wholly original poem, 'The Return'.

Robert Conquest's way of making Yeats's point is to say (having noted that 'the howlers are not mere accident: Pound could not have really thought that "votas" meant "votes"'):

Such mistakes lend colour to the notion of his just writing down how the thing appeared to him at first sight, without dictionary, and without taking much trouble either, and then simply not bothering.

Just so. And why not? There may be some rules about how to translate: but there are no rules about how to make poems, and if Pound chose to make his poem in this way, what follows? Conquest concludes with boyish petulance, 'He is just seeing how much he can get away with'. Yeats, who had found in Pound 'at moments more style, more deliberate nobility and the means to convey it than in any contemporary poet known to me', limits himself to noting the effect, though it is clear that he was at a loss to see why the effect was worth attaining – as much at a loss as the less modest Conquest is. Yet it is not hard to see what point there might be. Why should a poet contrive the effect of translating carelessly when in fact he is doing something else? To begin with, Yeats's *desiderata* can be stood on their head: a poet might contrive this effect because he wants *not* to seem to have 'got all the wine into the bowl', because 'deliberate nobility' is the last thing he is after. If he is sure that there is more to his subject (more perhaps to any subject) than he got out of it, or ever could get out of it, if he believes that all the wine never *can* be got into the bowl or into any bowl, then, like Michelangelo leaving some portion of stone unworked in his sculptures, the poet will deliberately seek an effect of improvisation, of haste and rough edges. For only in this way can he be true to his sense of the inexhaustibility of the human and non-human nature he is working with, a sense which makes him feel not noble but humble. And the same reason will make him use rhythms which seem, or are, uncontrollable, not to be measured – free verse measures which diverge from any measurable course or pattern – in order to compass the unforeseen which inexhaustible nature necessarily and continually provides.

The *Homage*, then, is written in 'translatorese'. In particular Pound makes the most of the grotesque and risible discrepancy between the vocabularies of poetry and of prose, a discrepancy which is known to any one who has made a rough working translation from a foreign poem into English prose:

> Me happy, night, night full of brightness;
> Oh couch made happy by my long delectations;
> How many words talked out with abundant candles;
> Struggles when the lights were taken away;
> Now with bared breasts she wrestled against me,

Tunic spread in delay;
And she then opening my eyelids fallen in sleep,
Her lips upon them; and it was her mouth saying:
    Sluggard!

'Me happy' is an expression that has no home in English except in
the schoolchild's painful transliteration in the classroom; similarly
the whole of the second line recalls nothing but the stilted, partly
comic and partly touching expressions that arrange themselves
across the page of an exercise-book when foreign words are looked
up one by one and their dictionary equivalents are written down.
'Delectations' in particular is a word that exists in a dictionary, and
nowhere else. It is typical of the Latinate polysyllables that trumpet
mournfully and uncertainly on every page of the *Homage*. It is usual
to say that the function of these is ironical, and that Pound learned
the trick of them from Laforgue. There is little doubt that Laforgue's
poems, still more perhaps the Laforguian English poems of the
young T.S. Eliot, have contributed to the diction of the *Homage*.
Yet, on this showing, the irony of the *Homage* is disconcertingly
pervasive and undirected: the speaker is being ironical about civic
and imperial affairs, certainly, and about the poetry that celebrates
these affairs; but he is ironical no less about his young lady, about
himself, even about his art. The irony begins to define something
only when the pompously polysyllabic words are seen as the pro-
ducts of 'translatorese', not of Jules Laforgue. It is true that Pound
was later to claim that Propertius and Laforgue were two of a kind,
and to define the kind as 'logopoeic'.[1] But this is unconvincing, and
irrelevant to the *Homage*. In the *Homage* as a poem in English, the
irony carried in the polysyllabic words is directed at the reader; the
diction puts the reader in the position of one who has transliterated
into his own pompous and civic English a poem that deserves to be
read precisely because it derides and denies all pompous and civic
pretensions.

Thus, *Homage to Sextus Propertius* is in verse, and yet its diction
is that of verse translated into prose:

The twisted rhombs ceased their clamour of accompaniment;
The scorched laurel lay in the fire-dust;
The moon still declined to descend out of heaven,

But the black ominous owl hoot was audible.

1 'How To Read', *New York Herald Tribune Books*, V, Nos. 17, 18, and 19
(13, 20, and 27 Jan. 1929). In *Literary Essays of Ezra Pound*, pp.25, 33.

In 'declined to', and the absurdly stilted passive construction 'was audible', the discrepancy between prose language and verse language, which is brought out by translatorese, is exploited to ends that are no longer grotesque or awkwardly touching so much as comical.

But what happens to rhythm in verse like this where the diction persuades us that what we are reading is a clumsy translation of verse into prose? Something very similar to what happened in *Cathay*. Of the four lines just quoted, no one line is to the ear equal to any of the others; yet, as when reading *Cathay*, the ear allows itself to be persuaded by the mind into regarding the lines as metrically equal because they are equal syntactically. Moreover, in this poem, which is not a translation yet creates the illusion that it is, just as in the poems of *Cathay* that truly *are* translations, the ear is the readier to be persuaded in this way since we are persuaded to think that each line, thus heavily end-stopped, corresponds to a line of the real or fictitious original. The same is true of the first four lines of the passage beginning, 'Me happy, night...'; these lines are unequal to the ear, yet the ear permits itself to regard them as equal because they are syntactically equal (being all syntactically imperfect in just the same way).

Where all these lines differ, however, from the characteristic lines of *Cathay* is that in none of them is there any sign of the verse-line being dismembered into smaller rhythmical components. True, there is

> Me happy, night, night full of brightness,

where the commas indicate pauses that make the line musically delightful, but that is their sole purpose: to be easy on the ear. We should be grateful. Nevertheless, this way of pausing is different from the pauses that dismember the lines of *Cathay* and of 'Provincia Deserta' – different, and less serious, for those pauses enacted or sharpened or invigorated perceptions, as these do not. The difference becomes very clear when the lines begin to surge across their end-stoppings:

> Now with bared breasts she wrestled against me,
>> Tunic spread in delay;
> And she then opening my eyelids fallen in sleep,
>> Her lips upon them; and it was her mouth saying:
>> Sluggard!

There is no longer any wish 'to break the pentameter'. The pentameter, indeed, was broken for good and all long before; here the iambic rhythm makes not even a phantasmal appearance. But there is no longer any wish to break the verse-line, of whatever meter, into its rhythmical members; the intention is no longer to dismember the verse-line, but rather, in the traditional way, to submerge it by enjambement into the larger rhythmical unit of the strophe. And thus, in a very special and esoteric way, the rhythms of the *Homage* show Pound, even so early, making his peace with Milton.

To be sure, there are many more lines that are end-stopped than there are lines that are 'run over'. Pound husbands his resources so that only at long and calculated intervals does he permit composition by strophe to supervene upon the composition by verse-line that is still his staple procedure. One place where this happens is in Section V, where it permits the masterly and audacious pun on 'volume':

> If she goes in a gleam of Cos, in a slither of dyed stuff,
> There is a volume in the matter;...

The start of Section VI is another place where it happens, and the most beautiful example of all comes when Pound rehandles the passage he had translated in 1911 – in the second part of Section IX, where the strophe comes to rest on the rocking rhythms of two lines that untypically *are* dismembered in the manner of *Cathay*:

> Beauty is not eternal, no man has perennial fortune,
> Slow foot, or swift foot, death delays but for a season.

Here indeed, as Charles Norman says, 'Pound's rhythms stride with giant steps, and there are great gulps of air instead of mere caesurae in the clash of syllables'.[1]

Yet by and large, if 'Provincia Deserta' represents one development from the vers libre of *Cathay*, the *Homage to Sextus Propertius* represents another, radically different. Both kinds of writing appear in the *Cantos*.

In 1918 Percy Wyndham Lewis went into the army, and Pound continued a series of 'imaginary letters' that Lewis had been contributing to *The Little Review*. Though Pound's imaginary letters have been twice reprinted (in Paris in 1930, and in London in 1960), they are among the least known of his works, and yet they cast light on one of the best known and most often discussed, on *Hugh Selwyn Mauberley*.

1 *Ezra Pound* (New York, 1960), p.209.

The•supposed author of the imaginary letters is one Walter Viller-
ant, a man more interesting than likeable. He writes to 'Mrs Bland
Burn', whom he addresses as 'My dear Lydia'. In the first letter he
refuses to marry:

> I am, with qualifications, Malthusian. I should consent to breed
> under pressure, if I were convinced in any way of the reason-
> ableness of reproducing the species. But my nerves and the
> nerves of any woman I could live with three months, would
> produce only a victim – beautiful perhaps, but a victim; expir-
> ing of aromatic pain from the jasmine, lacking in impulse, a
> mere bundle of discriminations.

This is very like a type of personality that appears in *Hugh Selwyn
Mauberley*:

> Drifted... drifted precipitate,
> Asking time to be rid of...
> Of his bewilderment; to designate
> His new found orchid....
>
> To be certain... certain...
> (Amid ærial flowers)... time for arrangements –
> Drifted on
> To the final estrangement;

Hugh Selwyn Mauberley exists as two intricately linked poem-
sequences, one of thirteen poems dated 1919, and a further sequence
of five poems dated 1920. In the piece just quoted, the second in the
1920 sequence, there is a phrase ('He had moved amid her phantas-
magoria') which Kenner has noted as an allusion to *The Ambassadors*
of Henry James.[1] But then Walter Villerant, who borrows from
'The Author of "Beltraffio"' in this very letter, is in an unsubtle
way a very Jamesian person, at least as 'Jamesian' is commonly
understood; before the first letter we are wondering, for instance,
if he is not an American expatriate – a haughty passage on Coney
Island and the racial melting-pot seems to suggest as much.

His first allegiance is, in any case, in a very self-congratulating
way, to 'art':

---

1 Cf. Lambert Strether in *The Ambassadors*: 'Of course I moved among
miracles. It was all phantasmagoric....'

It may be fitting that men should enjoy equal 'civic and political rights', these things are a matter of man's exterior acts, of exterior contacts. (Machiavelli believed in democracy: it lay beyond his experience.) The arts have nothing to do with this. They are man's life within himself. The king's writ does not run there. The voice of the majority is powerless to make me enjoy, or disenjoy, the lines of Catullus. I dispense with a vote without inconvenience; Villon I would not dispense with.

And this attitude is echoed elsewhere in the 1920 sequence:

> The glow of porcelain
> Brought no reforming sense
> To his perception
> Of the social inconsequence.
>
> Thus, if her colour
> Came against his gaze,
> Tempered as if
> It were through a perfect glaze
>
> He made no immediate application
> Of this to relation of the state
> To the individual, the month was more temperate
> Because this beauty had been.

This, however, does not catch the supercilious tone of Villerant; nearer to it are some quatrains from the 1919 sequence:

> Even the Christian beauty
> Defects – after Samothrace;
> We see τὸ καλὸυ
> Decreed in the market place.
>
> Faun's flesh is not to us,
> Nor the saint's vision.
> We have the press for wafer;
> Franchise for circumcision.

And yet there is energy in this, and anger behind it, which are foreign to Walter Villerant. Villerant, parading his detachment, fails to convince us of it; the speaker of the 1919 poem convinces us of his detachment, and earns our respect for it, precisely because anger is contained in it, controlled by it. The speaker of the 1920 poem

('The glow of porcelain...') has detachment of another kind again, diagnostic and therefore dispassionate, superior to Villerant's because it is in no way self-regarding; but he does not sustain this throughout his poem, which degenerates into precisely Villerant's dandified diction and cadence:

> A Minoan undulation,
> Seen, we admit, amid ambrosial circumstances...

From most points of view, in a poetry like this which manoeuvres in the fluctuating and elusive medium of 'tone', these differences in the tone of voice are precisely what matter, far more than the identiy of what is said. On the other hand, the identity is striking and must be significant.

In his second letter Villerant takes on the lineaments of Ford Madox Ford rather than Henry James, particularly in a passage where Dante is compared with French realists of the novel. And Ford is also thought to be in the background of *Hugh Selwyn Mauberley*; in particular Ford's situation in the first year after the Armistice seems to have suggested the tenth poem in the 1919 sequence, three quatrains about 'the stylist' finding refuge in a country cottage.[1] There is a good deal in this letter about Swinburne, who fails to satisfy Villerant as he had not failed to satisfy the author of *Personae*; but the author of 'Yeux Glauques', sixth in the 1919 sequence,[2] sees Swinburne and his Victorian contemporaries with something of Villerant's coolness. Something more striking emerges when Villerant refuses to be interested in the Russian writers with the solitary and significant exception of Turgenev – it was James's exception, and Ford's, and George Moore's, as well as Pound's. Villerant declares:

> I mistrust this liking for Russians; having passed years in one barbarous country I cannot be expected to take interest in another. All that is worth anything is the product of metropoles. Swill out these nationalist movements. Ireland is a suburb of Liverpool.

And Villerant's 'barbarous country' seems to be the United States,

---

1 The piece owes much to two poems by Gautier, 'Fumée' and 'La Mansarde'.
2 With 'Yeux Glauques' cf. Gautier's 'Caerulei Oculi'. *Glauque* is a word to which Pound draws attention in 'A Study of French Poets' (*Little Review*, 1918); for another unusual word, *maquero*, see Ford quoted in Douglas Goldring, *The Last Pre-Raphaelite* (London, 1948), p.216.

as does the 'half savage country' of the first poem in *Hugh Selwyn Mauberley*:

> Wrong from the start –
>
> No, hardly, but seeing he had been born
> In a half savage country, out of date;

The sneer at Ireland as a suburb of Liverpool also gets into *Hugh Selwyn Mauberley*, but thickly disguised. Through his association with Yeats presumably, but still more through his correspondence with the enlightened patron John Quinn in New York, Pound had come in touch with the Irish nationalists in London, and specifically with the intransigent revolutionary Maud Gonne, object of Yeats's hopeless passion until she married John MacBride, one of the leaders and martyrs of the Dublin rising in 1916. In January 1918 (*Letters*, pp.189-90) Pound wrote to John Quinn reporting the result of an intervention he had made at the Home Office on Maud Gonne's behalf, and plainly feeling little sympathy with her. In November of that year he wrote to Quinn again, no longer concealing his annoyance and coupling Maud Gonne's fanaticism with Yeats's about psychic phenomena:

> The other point M.G. omits from her case is that she went to Ireland without permit and in disguise, in the first place, during war time.
> 'Conservatrice des traditions Milésiennes', as de Gourmont calls them. There are people who have no sense of the value of 'civilization' or public order.
> She is still full of admiration for Lenin. (I, on the other hand, have talked with Russians.) The sum of it being that I am glad she is out of gaol, and I hope no one will be ass enough to let her get to Ireland.   (*Letters*, p.201.)

The tag from Gourmont turns up in the eleventh poem of the 1919 sequence:

> 'Conservatrix of Milésien'
> Habits of mind and feeling,
> Possibly. But in Ealing
> With the most bank-clerkly of Englishmen?
>
> No, 'Milesian' is an exaggeration.
> No instinct has survived in her

Older than those her grandmother
Told her would fit her station.

And this closes the circuit back into the *Imaginary Letters*, for with
the fourth of these we seem to be launched on an epistolary novel:
Mrs Bland Burn has left her husband, and Villerant rebukes her for
it on the grounds that her new mate will take her into an unsavoury
milieu, which he calls 'suburbia'. Temporarily he recalls Henry
James (or perhaps George Moore) when he justifies this snobbery.
The suburb that Lydia has gone to (by way of 'Bohemia', we under-
stand) is Pinner; in the poem it is Ealing. The whole of this imaginary
letter, dealing with woman's unsatisfactory function in society,
seems a necessary gloss on the eight lines of the poem.

Meanwhile it has been established beyond much doubt that Viller-
ant is American. In the third letter he has confessed to 'anglophilia'
and says, in words that recall one of Pound's letters to W.C. Williams
about America, that he 'was born in a more nervous and arid climate'.
Much of this letter is impatient about how pietism and mysticism
seem to have supplanted in France, now that Gourmont is dead, the
better intellectual tradition Gourmont had represented. Pound's dis-
like of neo-Catholicism in France appears in his correspondence but
not in *Hugh Selwyn Mauberley*, unless it has to do with the anti-
Christian sentiments of the third poem in the sequence.

The *Imaginary Letters* tail off disappointingly in a section called
'Mr Villerant's Morning Outburst', four letters addressed to three
other ladies than Lydia. The first of these is about the unsatisfactor-
iness of having recourse to prostitutes. (We may remember from
Hugh Selwyn Mauberley that 'Dowson found harlots cheaper than
hotels'.) The second letter is of little interest; the third, however,
not only rejects Christianity, but rejects it in favour of Confucianism,
and Villerant even gives his version of one of the Analects – a version
in startling contrast to what Pound was to make of it thirty years
later, in contrast also to what he had made of it by 1924, when it
was incorporated very beautifully in Canto 13.

It may not be clear why the *Imaginary Letters* are worth bothering
about in relation to *Hugh Selwyn Mauberley*. But that poem has been
the subject of much debate, and the disputes about it can all be
reduced to the question how far at this time Pound was capable of
creating and sustaining a persona, a fictitious mask to speak through.
We have already found reasons for thinking that Pound's remarks
about 'personae' and 'masks' are so many red herrings since his talent
was not histrionic, like Yeats's, but rather took him toward speaking

confessionally *in propria persona*. So long as Pound's criticism was unsophisticated, in *The Spirit of Romance* for instance, he responded most eagerly to precisely what a theory of the 'persona' tends to exclude – that is to say, robust self-exposure on the part of the poet speaking. The *Imaginary Letters* support this view of Pound, for it is impossible to read them without at first suspecting, and later feeling sure, that Pound disliked Villerant much less than we are likely to; that Pound mistook his undergraduate superciliousness for a rather grand aristocratic disdain. Though Pound wrote in the summer of 1917 to Wyndham Lewis about Villerant's 'effete and over civilised organism',[1] so much of what Villerant says is what Pound had said or was to say elsewhere, and so much more of what he says recalls men whom Pound admired, that the distance between Villerant and his creator narrows, until in the end they are identical. The identification is complete when we find Villerant in his last letter exalting Gautier above Baudelaire and discussing how hard it is to translate Gautier into English – this at the very time when the author of *Hugh Selwyn Mauberley* was throughout that poem translating Gautier, as J.J. Espey has shown.[2]

If the mask of Walter Villerant slipped so betrayingly from Pound's face, can we believe that at the same time he was capable of wearing another mask, that of H.S. Mauberley, without once betraying himself, but on the contrary keeping a constant distance between that surrogate person's character and his own? This is what many admiring commentators on *Hugh Selwyn Mauberley* ask us to believe. And they have some reason on their side. In the first place we have seen already from examples how much more sure of himself Pound was in verse than in prose, how the tight though unmetrical quatrains made sharp and distinguished in the poem what from the pen of Walter Villerant had been preenings and inanities. In the second place (a closely related point), though Pound had perhaps little talent for histrionics, he had abundant talent, as all translators have, for mimicry, for pastiche. Like the born translator he was, Pound can add cubits to his stature as soon as he begins to match himself with the master he is trying to emulate. It was a recognition of this in himself that made him stress so often the usefulness of technical apprenticeships. Pound was generous to others and serious about his vocation, as Walter Villerant could not have been; but there is evidence that otherwise, in conversation and in society, Pound in 1918 created just such an impression as Villerant creates,

1 Donald Gallup, *A Bibliography of Ezra Pound* (London, 1963; New York, 1964), p.73.
2 J.J. Espey, *Ezra Pound's* Mauberley.

no more likeable, no less mannered and self-regarding. It was emulating Gautier that purified and raised to a new power attitudes that in life were callow and unresolved; for, in learning the measure of Gautier's cadence and the dynamic shape of Gautier's stanzas, Pound by that very token became, for as long as he was writing the poem, as intelligent as Gautier and as civilized.[1] This at any rate is what a comparison with the *Imaginary Letters* suggests. And, therefore, it suggests further that the appearance of intricate planning behind the interlinked sequences of *Hugh Selwyn Mauberley* is an illusion, an *ex post facto* rationalization; that the work was in fact written 'by ear', by improvising and feeling forward from one poem to the next, not according to any pre-ordained scheme.

If so, it follows that most of the disputes about *Hugh Selwyn Mauberley* have been misconceived, for they have turned on the question of what Pound intended; and on this showing all that Pound intended was to do in English what Gautier had done in French.[2] On the one hand are those who find that H.S. Mauberley is a transparent fiction, who identify the poet at all points with his persona, and so read the two sequences as a clear-sighted and painfully honest judgment by Pound on the limitations of his own talent, and so on the reasons why he could never surpass the limited, though fine, achievement of this very poem. It is hard to square this reading with the fact that the author of *Hugh Selwyn Mauberley* had long before embarked on the *Cantos*, and was still working on them; and accordingly other readers have maintained that the persona, Mauberley, is at nearly all points distinct from the poet who created him – as distinct (so some have dared to suggest) as Lambert Strether was from Henry James. Pound has not unnaturally given his approval

---

1 See Pound in 'Harold Munro', *The Criterion*, XI (October 1931 – July 1932), p.590: 'at a particular time in a particular room, two authors, neither engaged in picking the other's pocket, decided that the dilutation of *vers libre*... had gone too far and that some countercurrent must be set going. Parallel situation years ago in China. Remedy prescribed *'Emaux et Camées'* (or the Bay State Hymn Book). Rhyme and regular strophes.'

'Results: Poems in Mr. Eliot's second volume, not contained in his first..., also H.S. Mauberley'. (We may doubt if, despite Pound's suggestion, the Bay State Hymn Book would have served him as well as Gautier's *Emaux et Camées*.)

2 Gautier is the over-riding influence; there are others, e.g. Bion in the fourth poem of the sequence. And for the piece which is in most respects the high point of the whole work, the Envoi to the 1919 sequence, the model was Edmund Waller. Despite George Dekker's objections (*Sailing After Knowledge*, London, 1963, p.157), I still believe with T.E. Connolly (*Accent*, Winter, 1956) that the 'her' of this Envoi is England. (Canto 80 for me supports this reading of the second stanza.)

to this second reading,[1] but this may be only another rationalization after the fact.

The point at issue comes out most clearly in relation to the poem that closes the second sequence, and so closes the whole work. It is called 'Medallion'. In order to sustain the case that Mauberley and Pound are distinct (in other words, that H.S. Mauberley is truly a created fiction), one has to believe that this poem is offered as Mauberley's work, not Pound's; that the exactness this poem achieves is in Pound's opinion bought at too great a cost, in view of the metallic inertness with which the imagery endows the subject. Yet at the end of the *Imaginary Letters*, Walter Villerant briefly discusses Joyce:

> The metal finish alarms people. They will no more endure Joyce's hardness than they will Pound's sterilized surgery. The decayed-lily verbiage which the Wilde school scattered over the decadence is much more to the popular taste.

Are we to believe that Villerant admires Joyce for the wrong reasons, or perhaps for the right reasons but without the necessary qualifications? We must believe this if we are to take 'Medallion', with its conspicuously 'metal finish', as Mauberley's poem rather than Pound's. In any case it looks more than ever as if Walter Villerant and Hugh Selwyn Mauberley are the same person. If so, then Pound's relation to the one fiction, Villerant, illuminates his relation to the other, Mauberley. Those who argue that Pound never loses control of the persona, Mauberley, require us to see the latter as an inadequate person whose inadequacies Pound is indicating. But as we have seen, Villerant, so largely assembled of components from men whom Pound admired (James, Ford, Gourmont), appears to differ from Pound not as a limited person whom Pound will surpass but, much of the time, as an ideally civilized person whom Pound aspires to emulate. Pound surpasses Villerant in only one particular, in the barbaric virtue of energy. And this seems true of Pound's relation to Mauberley also.

In other words, just as we are cheated of our expectations when the *Imaginary Letters* seem to be leading into an epistolary novel, so in *Hugh Selwyn Mauberley* we look in vain for the developing 'plot' that commentators of all persuasions (including the present writer)

1 See Pound, as quoted by Thomas E. Connolly in *Accent* (Winter, 1956), speaking of commentators on *Hugh Selwyn Mauberley*: 'The worst muddle they make is in failing to see that Mauberley buries E.P. in the first poem; gets rid of all his troublesome energies'.

have thought they found.[1] Such 'plots' can indeed be found – all too many of them. The trouble is that any one of them requires that we give Pound the benefit of every doubt, on the score of elusive shifts of tone, a raised eyebrow here, a half-smile somewhere else, a momentary puckering of the brow. 'Tone' will not do so much, so certainly, as the most admiring commentators ask us to believe. Therefore, the two sequences are much more loosely jointed than they seem to be. Hardly anything is lost, and much is gained, if the poems are read one at a time, as so many poems by Pound, and if the Mauberley persona is dismissed as a distracting nuisance. *Hugh Selwyn Mauberley* thus falls to pieces, though the pieces are brilliant, intelligent always, and sometimes moving (for Gautier repeatedly enabled Pound to surpass himself). As for the theory of the persona, which served Yeats so well, it seems only to have confused Pound and led him to confuse his readers.

1 For a more generous as well as more detailed examination of *Hugh Selwyn Mauberley*, see Donald Davie, 'Ezra Pound's Hugh Selwyn Mauberley', in *The Modern Age* (*Pelican Guide to English Literature*, London, 1961), pp.315-29.

VI

Cavalcanti

It was in relation to Ernest Fenollosa that Pound wrote of 'the romance of modern scholarship'. But what he meant by that, and how vividly he responded to it, appear most plainly in a footnote to his volume of essays *Make It New*,[1] at a point where he is discussing the attribution to Guido Cavalcanti of certain disputed poems and fragments. The essay, 'Cavalcanti', is dated '1910/1931', and the footnote reads:

> 1934. Whole question of authenticity of the other canzoni thrown wide open again by examination of manuscript I.ix.18 in Communale di Siena. For further details, see my *Guido Cavalcanti: Rime*, Genoa, anno x.

The Cavalcanti: Rime to which Pound refers[2] represents his most determined bid for academic respect. The bid appears to have failed with the Romance philologists. But Pound's dealings with Cavalcanti manifest at least the scholarly virtue of pertinacity and another, rarer one, the ability to change an opinion and confess as much. From the first translation of 1912[3] through to his edition of *Tre Canzoni* in 1949,[4] Pound has worried away at the poems of Cavalcanti more doggedly than at any other body of literature, even the Confucian scriptures. And to review Pound's dealings with this author, in chronological sequence over the years, is to follow with exceptional intimacy the poet's gradually growing awareness of what verse translation entails, or what it may entail in the case of

1 *Make It New* (London, 1934; New Haven, 1935). Most of the essay on Cavalcanti from this volume had appeared in various issues of *The Dial* through 1928 and 1929.
2 *Guido Cavalcanti: Rime*, texts, with notes, (Genoa, 1931).
3 *The Sonnets and Ballate of Guido Cavalcanti*, with translation and introduction (London and Boston, 1912).
4 *Tre Canzoni di Guido Cavalcanti*, con i fac-simili dei manoscritti senesi e la vita del poeta di Celso Cittadini (Siena, 1949).

an author so recondite as Cavalcanti. Unfortunately, the biblio-
graphy is so far from clear that it is impossible to date exactly all of
the versions from Cavalcanti that Pound has made. The *Translations
of Ezra Pound* (London, 1953), a book not at all so inclusive as its
title suggests, gives no indication of when any given translation
was made, nor of where a later version has been substituted for an
earlier one. And Anne Paolucci,[1] though she usefully shows how
even in 1912, despite Pound's declaration of indebtedness at that
time to D.G. Rossetti's versions, his intentions were very different
from Rossetti's, on the other hand weakens her case by resting it
on such poems as Sonnets VII and XVI, to which Pound returned
after 1912, discarding the earlier translations which she asks us to
admire.

Of the thirty-five sonnets by Cavalcanti, Sonnets VII, XIII, XIV,
XVI, and XVII are given in *The Translations of Ezra Pound* in versions
different from those that appear in the *Sonnets and Ballate* of 1912.
The changes were not always for the better; and Miss Paolucci's
case for the first version of XVI, for instance, reflects adversely on
the later version. But Sonnet VII is one case where the issue is hardly
in doubt. In 1912 (and again in *Umbra*, 1920, where several of the
versions were reprinted), this ran:

> Who is she coming, drawing all men's gaze,
> Who makes the air one trembling clarity
> Till none can speak but each sighs piteously
> Where she leads Love adown her trodden ways?
>
> Ah God! The thing she's like when her glance strays,
> Let Amor tell. 'Tis no fit speech for me.
> Mistress she seems of such great modesty
> That every other woman were called 'Wrath'.
>
> No one could ever tell the charm she hath
> For all the noble powers bend toward her
> She being beauty's godhead manifest.
>
> Our daring ne'er before held such high quest;
> But ye! There is not in you so much grace
> That we can understand her rightfully.

Miss Paolucci cites the fifth line in particular as an example of how

1 A. Paolucci, 'Ezra Pound and D.G. Rossetti as Translators of Guido
Cavalcanti', in *Romantic Review*, LI (1960), 256-67.

much more closely Pound translates than Rossetti, and Pound, as
will be seen, takes exception to other lines as rendered by Rossetti.
Yet it is hard to have any patience with such slack poeticisms as
'adown', eking out metrical regularity with a redundant prefix, or,
to light upon something more important, the commercialized vul-
garity of 'charm' ('the charm she hath') for 'la sua piacenza'.

In *Make It New* Pound supplies a later translation which has rightly
supplanted the earlier one:

> Who is she that comes, makyng turn every man's eye
> And makyng the air to tremble with a bright clearenesse
> That leadeth with her Love, in such nearness
> No man may proffer of speech more than a sigh?
>
> Ah God, what she is like when her owne eye turneth, is
> Fit for Amor to speak, for I cannot at all;
> Such is her modesty, I would call
> Every woman else but an useless uneasiness.
>
> No one could ever tell all of her pleasauntness
> In that every high noble vertu leaneth to herward,
> So Beauty sheweth her forth as her Godhede;
>
> Never before so high was our mind led,
> Nor have we so much of heal as will afford
> That our mind may take her immediate in its embrace.

I shall take it for granted that this version is more to modern taste.
And yet it is not easy, if the two versions are compared, to explain
what makes the later version the better one.

In the first place, if one proceeds like Miss Paolucci to look above
all for closeness, line by line and phrase by phrase, the early version
comes out better. For this is the Italian poem:

> Chi è questa che vien, ch'ogni uom la mira,
> Che fa dí clarità l'aer tremare,
> E mena seco Amor, sí che parlare
> Null' uom ne puote, ma ciascun sospira?
>
> Ahi, Dio, che sembra quando gli occhi gira?
> Dicalo Amor, ch'io nol saprei contare:
> Cotanto d'umiltà donna mi pare,
> Che ciascun' altra in vêr di lei chiam' ira.

Non si potria contar la sua piacenza,
Ch' a lei s'inchina ogni gentil virtute,
E la beltate per sua Dea la mostra.

Non fu sì alta già la mente nostra,
E non si è posta in noi tanta salute,
Che propriamente n'abbiam conoscenza.

Here much has been gained by reading in the penultimate line 'in noi' instead of, as in 1912, 'in voi'; this gets rid of the awkward but in 1912 inescapable switch from 'ye' and 'you' to 'we' in the last line. There remains, however, 'ira' at the end of the eighth line, which plainly underwrites the 'Wrath' of the first version whereas it affords remarkably little grounds for the delightful 'useless uneasiness' of the revision.

We might go further and point out that there is no justification in the original for the strenuous enjambement of the later version, 'is / Fit for Amor to speake'. But this would be captious. For this is not felt as an enjambement; on the contrary the syllable of 'is' is felt to be necessary to the rhythmical completeness of the line it occurs in. And this surely brings out what is the really potent difference between the first version and the second: it is the difference of rhythm. In his essay in *Make It New* Pound remarks, 'Another prevalent error is that of dealing with Italian hendecasyllables as if they were English "iambic pentameter".' It was an error into which he had fallen himself in his versions of 1912; and, although in his Introduction to those versions he had declared, gallantly and vulnerably, 'I believe in an ultimate and absolute rhythm as I believe in an absolute symbol or metaphor', his use in his translations of an iambic pentameter line quite nullifies this assertion and makes nonsense of his further claim that 'the rhythm set in a line of poetry connotes its symphony, which, had we a little more skill, we could score for orchestra'. The tunes played in the translations of 1912 prompt no reader into dreaming up novel 'symphonies', since Shakespearean and Miltonic and other symphonies come to his mind as soon as the traditional measure is sounded. In *Make It New* Pound further observes, following an unnamed authority, 'that Dante's hendecasyllables were composed of combinations of rhythm units of various shapes and sizes and that these pieces were put together in lines so as to make, roughly, eleven syllables in all. I say "roughly" because of the liberties allowed in elision'. Although Pound goes on to claim that he had discovered this for himself 'in Indiana', his versions of 1912 do not suggest as much. It is only in the later versions that one gets the effect of 'rhythm units of various shapes and sizes'. In the

very first line, for instance, of 'Chi è questa che vien', there is a
much sharper break apart on 'she that comes, makyng' in the second
version, than on 'she coming, drawing' in the first; and, because in
the second version the iambic beat has been so much disconcerted,
the ear demands another break between 'turn' and 'every man's eye'.
Where in the early version the pentameter line breaks, if at all, only
weakly on the caesura, in the later version it divides itself markedly
into three distinct units of rhythm. In fact, this is that dismember-
ment of the line from within that was noted as the distinctive rhyth-
mical pleasure of poems in *Cathay*. Even in the Fenollosa notes on
the Noh, Pound had encountered a similar notion of the poetic line
as constituted, not out of so many equal feet, but out of two unequal
rhythmical units in the proportions 7 to 5 or 5 to 7; and Pound had
drawn attention to this in an intrigued but baffled footnote about
Arnaut Daniel. Out of his own practice in *Cathay* and 'The Seafarer',
out of the meters of the Noh, and now out of the hendecasyllables
of Dante and Cavalcanti, the same recognition was pressed upon
him: there were rhythms to be found by reconstituting the line,
rather than stanza or paragraph, as the poetic unit, and then by
dismembering the line into musical units larger than the metrical
feet of traditional prosody. 'To break the pentameter, that was the
first heave'. Because for purposes of polemic Pound chose at times
to play the iconoclast, it is easy to see his abandonment of the trad-
itional pentameter as something deliberate and programmatic; his
translations of Cavalcanti from 1912 onwards suggest on the con-
trary that he broke with the pentameter reluctantly, grudgingly,
and, as it were, of necessity. By the time of the essay in *Make It
New* he had discovered belatedly some seventeenth-century English
precedents for this manner of proceeding, and he acknowledges them
in his dedication to the centrepiece of the Cavalcanti essay, a trans-
lation of the canzone 'Donna mi prega': 'To Thomas Campion his
ghost, and to the ghost of Henry Lawes, as prayer for the revival
of music'.

Another way in which the later version of this sonnet differs
notably from the first version is in its use of archaic diction. To the
translations of 1912 Pound prefixed two lines of verse:

> I have owned service to the deathless dead.
> Grudge not the gold I bear in livery.

And part of what this means is, I think, a plea by the translator to
be allowed to use a lofty and ornate language – that surely is part
of 'the gold' which he bears 'in livery'. Insofar as the loftiness and
ornateness is achieved by use of archaisms like 'adown', most readers,

rightly or wrongly, will refuse to accept Pound's plea, will not feel that the grounds on which he enters this plea are sufficient. (And one may wonder, incidentally, whether the plea was accepted by those to whom the volume was dedicated, 'my friends, Violet and Ford Maddox (sic) Hueffer', for, according to Pound's later testimony, Hueffer's advice to him in these years was always that he should compete with the novelists by making his language as prosaic and hard as, for instance, Stendhal's.) Apart from this, Pound's remarks on diction in the Introduction of 1912 are limited to specific crucial words in the Italian – *gentile, mente, spiriti, valore, virtute* – and to the English words by which Pound has rendered these. But larger issues, of diction only in the first place, are opened up when Pound objects to Rossetti's version of one of the lines from Sonnet VII:

Ch'a lei s'inchina ogni gentil virtute.

Rossetti's version – 'To whom are subject all things virtuous' – will not do because, says Pound, 'the *inchina* implies not the homage of an object but the direction of a force'; in other words, the 'she' of the poem 'acts as a magnet for every "gentil virtute", that is, the noble spiritual powers, the invigorating forces of life and beauty bend towards her....' In both of Pound's versions this meaning of *s'inchina* is duly reproduced: in 1912, 'all the noble powers bend toward her'; twenty-five years later, 'every high noble vertu leaneth to herward'. But it is in the later version that the point is rammed home, that the difference between Rossetti's version and Pound's is made irreconcilable. This is a function of the much denser and more conspicuous archaism of the revised version; in other words, the much heavier archaism of the second version is not for the sake of loftiness and ornateness but, on the contrary, it serves to cleave more closely to the sense as Pound perceives it. In the final version the archaism of the language is not, after all, at odds with the prosaicism Hueffer had recommended; it is the archaism 'to herward' that permits a precision, a hard definiteness of meaning.

A great deal is involved here, and in 1912 Pound saw much of what was involved, though he had not yet found a verse style to deal with it in his translations. For instance, if the lady in Sonnet VII acts as a magnet, this is not peculiar to her, for elsewhere in the Introduction of 1912 Pound says of Cavalcanti's world:

Virtù is the potency, the efficient property of a substance or person. Thus modern science shows us radium with a noble virtue of energy. Each thing or person was held to send forth magnetisms of certain effect; ...

It thus appears that, behind the problem of how to English one line by Cavalcanti, there lie considerations involving the physics and the metaphysics of the thirteenth century and of the twentieth. As he continued to work on Cavalcanti, Pound came to think that the greatness of Cavalcanti lay in the way the Italian poet could imply, by his vocabulary in a love poem, abstruse and indeed highly technical problems of speculation. And these scattered observations of 1912 about magnetism and potency and energy are elaborated and systematized in the pages of *Make It New* so as to produce some of Pound's most important formulations – important not only as they bear on Cavalcanti and the ultimately insoluble problem of how to translate him, but also because Pound seems to have composed his own metaphysics chiefly out of these mediaeval documents.

In the first section of the *Make It New* essay on Cavalcanti – a section which is an essay in itself, entitled 'Mediaevalism' – Pound explains what he finds uniquely valuable in Cavalcanti by defining what is lost to Italian poetry as it moves from Cavalcanti to Petrarch, or as it moves (so an old-fashioned scholar might say) from the Middle Ages into the Renaissance. Between Cavalcanti and Petrarch, Pound says,

> We appear to have lost the radiant world where one thought cuts through another with clean edge, a world of moving energies *'mezzo oscuro rade'*, *'risplende in se perpetuale effecto'*, magnetisms that take form, that are seen, or that border the visible, the matter of Dante's paradiso, the glass under water, the form that seems a form seen in a mirror, these realities perceptible to the sense, interacting, *'a lui si tiri'*. . . .

Pound contrasts this way of thinking and feeling, which a few pages later he will attempt to illustrate from a treatise on light by a mediaeval Bishop of Lincoln,[1] to what he sees as the modern scientist's image of the same world:

> For the modern scientist energy has no borders, it is a shapeless 'mass' of force; even his capacity to differentiate it to a degree never dreamed by the ancients has not led him to think of its shape or even its loci. The rose that his magnet makes in the iron filings, does not lead him to think of the force in botanic terms, or wish to visualize that force as floral and extant (*ex stare*).

1 Robert Grosseteste, *De Luce et de Incohatione Formarum*, in Etienne Gilson, *Philosophie du Moyen Age* (Paris, 1925), and *Make It New*, pp.356-62.

A mediaeval 'natural philosopher' would find this modern world full of enchantments, not only the light in the electric bulb, but the thought of the current hidden in air and in wire would give him a mind full of forms, 'Fuor di color' or having their hyper-colours. The mediaeval philosopher would probably have been unable to think the electric world, and *not* think of it as a world of forms. . . .

This may seem a long way from the matter of archaism in poetic diction. But this is not so. Not just the diction of Pound's revised translations, but their rhythms also, hinge upon this notion that 'something was lost' between Cavalcanti and Petrarch. The loss was not only in Italian poetry but also, we must say, to the mind of Western Europe, for it is a commonplace of literary history that Petrarch exerted much influence on English poetry over a period that can be defined quite exactly. (That this influence came from only a few aspects of Petrarch, not from the whole of him, is for present purposes irrelevant.) The literary histories name, as the originators of this Petrarchan vogue in England, two poets of the court of Henry VIII, Sir Thomas Wyatt and Henry Howard, Earl of Surrey; and Surrey (Wyatt admittedly is a more complicated and interesting case) also figures in the histories as the poet who established the iambic pentameter as the norm of English versification. Thus, to translate Cavalcanti into iambic pentameters, as Pound did for the most part in 1912, is to translate him into a meter devised for precisely the poet, Petrarch, from whom Pound is anxious to distinguish him. Moreover, it is again a commonplace of literary history that between Chaucer and Surrey English poets were using, though often with little success, a poetic line that rhythmically rocks apart in the middle as in the alliterative verse of Middle English. Accordingly, not just diction but rhythm also becomes archaic, simply through the endeavour after strict accuracy, as soon as Pound tries to 'reach back to pre-Elizabethan English'. Those are his own words for what he had in mind when he decided to try again at 'Chi è questa che vien'. As with some of the Odes from the *Classic Anthology*, so with Pound's Cavalcanti versions, it is not enough to observe that the diction is archaic; one is meant to ask also, 'How archaic? Archaic of what period? What English precedents or analogues is this archaism meant to bring to mind?' In the present case, it might be said that the 1912 version of 'Chi è questa che vien' prompts us to find the English precedent or analogue in the Earl of Surrey; whereas the later version makes us envisage rather some non-existent, perhaps anonymous, English lyricist of a hundred years earlier than that.

When Pound, in *Make It New*, publishes the Italian text of Caval-
canti's masterpiece, the canzone 'Donna mi prega', he presents to
the reader's eye that rhythmical dismemberment of Cavalcanti's line
that he hopes will in any case sound in the reader's ear. He does this
by spacing out the line in print, making it float or step across, as
well as down, the printed page:

> Donna mi priegha
> perch'i volglio dire
> D'un accidente
> che sovente
> é fero

And he claims, 'The melodic structure is properly indicated – and
for the first time – by my disposition of the Italian text. . . .' This is
an elaboration of the expedient that was announced as soon as the
phrase 'the swift moving' was printed so as to hang ambiguously
between the last two lines of 'South Folk in Cold Country' from
Cathay. Pound in the *Cantos* had already begun to explore more
audaciously the resources modern typography provides for thus con-
trolling very imperiously the tempo, the stops and starts, that the
reader is to observe in his reading. Other poets, notably Pound's
life-long associate William Carlos Williams, were to seize upon this
range of expedients; and whole poems by Williams and others are
stepped across the page in tripartite arrangements such as Pound's
typographer gives to Cavalcanti's second line. Already, when Pound
was working at Cavalcanti in the 'twenties, E.E. Cummings was
making play with other devices not just of typesetting machines but
of the typewriter also – devices such as upper-case and lower-case,
single and double quotation marks, and punctuation stops. These
devices, especially in the case of Cummings, have been crassly mis-
understood by many critics and reviewers, who have frequently
condemned them as 'merely typographical'. But why 'merely'? Of
course it is true that the ear will allow itself to be persuaded by the
eye only up to a point; and when a poet tries by typography to
persuade the ear of a rhythm that to the ear is nonexistent, then it
must be allowed that his arrangement is 'merely typographical', and
for this he may be blamed. But not only may the reader's ear be
assisted, simply by the look of the verse on the printed page, to hear
a rhythm it might otherwise have missed; but at times the look on
the page may actually *create* a rhythm that could not be conveyed
to the reader's ear by any other means. As Charles Olson remarks:

> It is the advantage of the typewriter that, due to its rigidity
> and its space precisions, it can, for a poet, indicate exactly the

breath, the pauses, the suspensions even of syllables, the jux-
tapositions even of parts of phrases, which he intends. For the
first time the poet has the stave and bar a musician has had.
For the first time he can, without the convention of rime and
meter, record the listening he has done to his own speech and
by that one act indicate how he would want any reader, silently
or otherise, to voice his work.

It is time we picked the fruits of the experiments of Cummings,
Pound, Williams, each of whom has, after his way, already
used the machine as a scoring to his composing, as a script to
its vocalization.[1]

And Mr Olson is usefully specific:

> If a contemporary poet leaves a space as long as the phrase
> before it, he means that space to be held, by the breath, an
> equal length of time. If he suspends a word or a syllable at the
> end of a line... he means that time to pass that it takes the eye
> – that hair of time suspended – to pick up the next line. If he
> wishes a pause so light it hardly separates the words, yet does
> not want a comma – which is an interruption of the meaning
> rather than the sounding of the line – follow him when he uses
> a symbol the typewriter has ready to hand:

> What does not change/is the will to change.

Observe him, when he takes advantage of the machine's mul-
tiple margins, to juxtapose:

Sd he:

> to dream takes no effort
>   to think is easy
>   to act is more difficult...

The examples, from Charles Olson's own poems, illustrate Pound's
use, in his later work, of the conventions of the typewriter. Such
devices are mannerisms or 'gimmicks' only when we cannot see, in
the poet's use of them, 'the listening he has done to his own speech'.
In Pound's case he was led to them, not just by the availability of a
typewriting machine, but by seeking to translate a poet of mediaeval
Italy so scrupulously as to bring over even what that poet's speech
sounded like in that poet's ear.

1 Charles Olson, 'Projective Verse', *Poetry New York*, 3 (1950); republished
as a pamphlet (New York, 1959) and as a 'Statement on Poetics' in D.M.
Allen, ed., *The New American Poetry: 1945-1960* (New York, 1960).

Thus the breaking down of Cavalcanti's line into its constitutive members is indicated by Pound in the typographical arrangement he gives to it. But one notices that Cavalcanti himself had taken steps to this end by rhyming:

> D'un accidente
>> che sovente...

And it is obvious that this is another way to 'break the pentameter': the poet makes the rhyme-word within the line mark off one rhythmical member from another. This seems to be what Pound means when he speaks, with annoying slanginess, of how Cavalcanti uses internal rhyme to 'stop the line from going heavy'. Pound was thus to use typography and rhyme together to translate the lyric choruses of Sophocles' *Trachiniae*, and it is characteristic of many of his versions in the other late translation, the Classic Odes, that he makes terminal rhyme sparse only so as to enrich internal rhyme. According to William McNaughton, there is precedent for this in the original Chinese poems 'many of which are in lines of four syllables, rhymed on the third or penultimate syllable'.[1]

The work on 'Donna mi prega', however, shows Pound attempting to reconstitute a longer poetic unit than the line while still holding on to the rhythmical dismemberment of the line from within. He speaks not of members within the line but of 'lobes' within the strophe.

> Each strophe is articulated by 14 terminal and 12 inner rhyme sounds, which means that 52 out of every 154 syllables are bound into the pattern. The strophe reverses the proportions of the sonnet, as the short lobes precede the longer.

It is worth dwelling on this curious word 'lobe', so unexpected in this sort of context. What one is likely to feel first is that a lobe *hangs*, like the lobe of an ear; as the Shorter Oxford English Dictionary defines it, 'the lower soft pendulous part of the external ear'. And this seems a curiously inert, inactive way to describe how one part of a poem may depend upon, or depend from, a preceding part. And when we look elsewhere in the dictionary definition ('A roundish projecting part, usually one of two or more separated by a fissure. . . . A rounded projection or part of a leaf or other organ'), it will appear that Pound's use of the term has everything to do, and

1 W. McNaughton, 'Ezra Pound's Meters and Rhythms', *PMLA*, LXXVIII (March 1963), 136-46.

quite exactly, with what the poem looks like on the page; but nothing at all to do with what it sounds like, actually or in imagination, in the reader's ear. Yet, in fact, Pound is at this point very concerned indeed with what the poem sounds like, since he is talking of how it was written for musical setting and how the exigencies of music determine its form:

> The strophes of canzoni are perforce symmetrical as the musical composition is only one-fifth or one-sixth the length of the verbal composition and has to be repeated.

Thus, unless we are to believe that Pound is at this point unbelievably confused between the senses of sight and of sound, we are forced to find some meaning in terms of sound for an expression like 'hanging suspended'. And we can do this: we can speak meaningfully of how a sound 'hung in the air'. In fact, when we spoke of how 'the swift-moving' hangs between the last two lines of a poem from *Cathay*, we meant that the sound it makes hangs between the sounds that they make. And thus what we have to conceive of, as the effect of Cavalcanti's canzone, is an effect by which, just as units of a few syllables float free of the line of verse and the sound of them hangs in the air, so units of three or four lines of verse at a time float or hang free of the strophe which, taken together, they constitute.

It cannot be said that the translation Pound offers in *Make It New* does in the event create this effect. When he says in his commentary that 'The melodic structure is properly indicated... by my disposition of the Italian text', he seems to mean that his own translation, on the other hand, is devoted to bringing out other features of the poem than this. For he warns us:

> I have not given an English 'equivalent' for the *Donna mi Prega*; at the utmost I have provided the reader, unfamiliar with old Italian, an instrument that may assist him in gauging *some* of the qualities of the original.

The italics are Pound's.

The most cursory look at the translation reveals one quality of the original that is being emphasized: it is a feature of Cavalcanti's vocabulary to which Pound gives much space in his commentary. There he argues that the Italian poet was using with philosophical strictness terms from the physics and metaphysics of his time. And it is this emphasis that produces in Pound's English the string of words 'affect', '*virtu*', 'force', 'essence', 'mode', 'placation', 'locus', 'sensate', 'modus', 'quality', 'postulate', 'intention', 'property' 'emanation'. When Pound speaks of 'the atrocities of my translation', we may take him to mean, among other things, these rebarbative locutions, especially at points where they are crammed one upon another. He will hammer this point home even if it means emphasizing this feature of the diction out of all proportion with other features of the poem. This is why he can confess to 'atrocities', and yet go on to declare them 'intentional'.

One of these words deserves to detain us if only because it rouses an echo – the word 'locus':

> In memory's locus taketh he his state
> Formed there in manner as a mist of light
> Upon a dusk that is come from Mars and stays

The word is used again, though not at quite the same point, in another translation Pound made of this poem, which stands as the first part of Canto 36. But we have encountered it already in Pound's introduction to the *Make It New* translation:

> For the modern scientist energy has no borders, it is a shapeless 'mass' of force; even his capacity to differentiate it to a degree never dreamed by the ancients has not led him to think of its shape or even its loci. The rose that his magnet makes in the iron filings, does not lead him to think of the force in botanic terms, or wish to visualize that force as floral and extant.

Among the energies that animate the created world is that one which Cavalcanti calls Amor or Love, which he can talk of therefore in the technical vocabulary usual in his day for defining other sorts of energy, physical or metaphysical. Such at least is Pound's contention. Another such animating energy (if indeed all of them are not different modes of one) is the psychic energy that creates poems, of which accordingly Pound may talk as something 'floral', borrowing the botanical term 'lobe'.

This explains why this poem which is so concerned with energy is so unenergetic. For this is surely the case. In either of Pound's versions the last thing we would ascribe to Cavalcanti's poem is impetus, momentum. The same thing is true of his 'Who is she that comes, makyng turn every man's eye', just as it is true also of *Cathay*. And, indeed, how could it be otherwise? The metrical sign of kinetic energy, of impetus, is inevitably the enjambement, which swings or whirls the reader on a torrent of feeling out of one line and into the next. Yet Pound the translator, as we have seen, had to eschew enjambement, for in no other way could that breaking of the pentameter which his originals forced upon him, the rhythmical dismemberment of the verse-line from within, be brought about. For the members of the line to achieve some rhythmical independence of the line, it was essential that the rhythmical impetus through the line as a whole be slackened; for the 'lobes' to achieve status independent of the strophe, it was essential that the momentum through the strophe be slackened. And so the poetry of *Cathay* and of the later Cavalcanti versions is a static poetry; its constituent parts seem to be almost as much components of an arrangement in space, as phases of a process through time. In *Cathay*, for instance, one might have expected that the reinstatement of the sentence as a poetic unit would have brought with it the impetus of active transitive verbs – indeed, Fenollosa, in his essay on the Chinese written character, assumed that this would be the case. But in the event, precisely because a line ends when a sentence ends, in 'South-Folk in Cold Country' the active verbs have none of the activating force they would have had if the sentence had been strung across the line by enjambement. Accordingly, of the lines in this poem it seems more accurate to say that they are placed one beneath another, than to say that one comes after another.

Several commentators have been struck by the paradox that a dynamic character such as Pound should have produced such undynamic poetry as in these translations. And it has been taken to show that the goal of his poetic endeavours was no different from that of the so-called Aesthetic Movement of the previous generation: the deliberate prolongation of what Walter Pater calls the 'intervals of time' in which aesthetic perception occurs, the isolation of these not for analysis of them (as by Mallarmé sometimes), but simply for their artificial prolongation in a tranced stillness. Pound would claim, it seems, that the stillness is achieved for the purposes of analysis – analysis, that is, of the sort that poetry practises, notably by rhythm – but that the analysis was conducted, in the Italian poems as in the Chinese poems, from a standpoint and according to categories which to the modern reader are strange, though he is impoverished for lack of them.

However this may be, it is true that poetry of this kind, whether practised by Pound himself or by others such as William Carlos Williams and Charles Olson and Robert Creeley, is a poetry that characteristically moves forward only hesitantly, gropingly, and slowly; which often seems to float across the page as much as it moves down it; in which, if the perceptions are cast in the form of sentences, the sentence is bracketed off and, as it were, folded in on itself so as to seem equal with a disjointed phrase; a poetry (we might almost say) of the noun rather than the verb.

VII

A Draft of XXX Cantos · The Malatesta Cantos · Canto 17 · Canto 20

Pound left London and England at the end of 1920, when he was thirty-four; from 1921 to 1924 he was domiciled in Paris, though travelling frequently, especially to Italy; and in 1925 he set up house in what was to be the most permanent of his homes, Rapallo, on the Ligurian coast.

He was still in London when in 1920 he got a rude shock from the oldest of his friends, William Carlos Williams. In this year the radical disagreements between them, which can be heard muttering and grumbling on several pages of the *Letters* from 1908 onwards, came to a head when Williams published a piece he had composed in 1918, the Prologue to his *Kora in Hell: Improvisations*. Here Williams defends some stay-at-home American poets, such as himself, against the successful expatriates Eliot and Pound. He scores some entertaining hits:

> I do not overlook De Gourmont's plea for a meeting of the nations, but I do believe that when they meet Paris will be more than slightly abashed to find parodies of the middle ages, Dante and Langue d'Oc foisted upon it as the best in United States poetry.[1]

As a debating point this is unanswerable, and when Pound tried to answer it in a letter he came off very lamely. But of course a debating point is all it is. More interesting are some of the positive points that Williams makes about his own ideas of what poetry should be:

> The true value is that peculiarity which gives an object a character by itself. The associational or sentimental value is the false. Its imposition is due to lack of imagination, to an easy lateral sliding. . . .
> . . . The imagination goes from one thing to another. Given

---

1 Quoted in *Letters*, footnote to p.225.

many things of nearly totally divergent natures but possessing one-thousandth part of a quality in common, provided that be new, distinguished, these things belong to an imaginative category and not in a gross natural array. To me this is the gist of the whole matter....

... the thing that stands eternally in the way of really good writing is always one: the virtual impossibility of lifting to the imagination those things which lie under the direct scrutiny of the senses, close to the nose. It is this difficulty that sets a value upon all works of art and makes them a necessity.[1]

To all of this, with its emphasis on 'the direct scrutiny of the senses', Pound would give a hearty assent, schooled as he had been (by Fenollosa and Gourmont alike) into admiring the controlled observations of empirical science as akin to poetic apprehensions. The heroism of the scientist was to be celebrated in a naïvely generous way in the figure of Pierre Curie, in Cantos 23 and 27, which Pound was shortly to write. Williams was a practising physician and to that extent a scientist himself; and he can see, as the men of letters Pound and Gourmont do not, how natural science can lend its prestige to an itemizing, inert apprehension of particulars that is thoroughly anti-poetic:

The senses witnessing what is immediately before them in detail see a finality which they cling to in despair, not knowing which way to turn. Thus the so-called natural or scientific array becomes fixed, the walking devil of modern life. (Williams, pp.11–12.)

What Williams rightly insists on is an imaginative 'category' of inter-related items, not an inert 'array' of items as items; it is a distinction that Pound, at least in theory, overlooked. But for Williams too the items that offer themselves for apprehension by the poet as 'images' are the same as those the scientist isolates for observation. Although the items are thereafter inter-related by the poet's imagination, they retain first and last their character as items, sharply distinct. Williams, like Pound and indeed T.E. Hulme, sets great store by this distinctness; it is part of the hard-edgedness which imagism demanded of poetic images.

When Williams more than a dozen years later jotted down his impressions of the first thirty of Pound's *Cantos*, it was this quality that he singled out for praise:

1 'Prologue to "Kora in Hell",' in *Selected Essays of William Carlos Williams* (New York, 1954), p.11.

It stands out from almost all other verse by a faceted quality that is not muzzy, painty, wet. It is a dry, clean use of words.[1]

One of Pound's words for this was 'cut'. It is the word he uses for a quality of perception to be found in Cavalcanti's world and since lost, but he uses it in other contexts also, and it can be related to a context that Pound overlooks – to the world of the cinema where an Eisenstein 'cuts' from one shot to the next. It was the principle of 'cut' that necessitated a fresh start after the three cantos, later abandoned, which appeared in *Quia Pauper Amavi*; there were to be no more transitions from image to image by 'an easy lateral sliding', but gaps were to be left between images as the poet, like a film director, cut from one to the next. In Canto 4, for instance, Pound cuts rapidly from mediaeval Provence to mythopoeic Greece and back again, as he shuttles the reader from the troubadour biographies of Guillem de Cabestanh and Piere Vidal to the myths of Procne and of Actaeon respectively. More than one commentary is available,[2] and several commentators have followed Hugh Kenner in seeing here what is to be a common procedure in many of the cantos, a procedure that they call 'cultural overlayering'. (For instance, in the next two or three cantos mediaeval Provence seems frequently to correspond to Homeric Greece, Renaissance Italy to late Greece and republican Rome, contemporary Europe to Rome's decline.) But the important point was made by Williams:

> Only superficially do the Cantos fuse the various temporal phases of the material Pound has chosen, into a synthesis. (p.110.)

One culture may 'overlayer' another; but the layers remain, and are meant to remain, distinct. What is intended is a sort of lamination, by no means a compounding or fusing of distinct historical phases into an undifferentiated amalgam. This is what Pater had asked for, confusedly, as early as 1868 in his essay 'Aesthetic Poetry'. And it is what Williams means by insisting that Pound's object is analysis, not synthesis.

This has to be true because, as Williams rightly insists, it goes down into the structure of the verse-line. The breaking of the pentameter made possible, indeed it enforced, the breaking down of

---

1 'Excerpts from a Critical Sketch. A Draft of XXX Cantos by Ezra Pound' (*The Symposium*, 1931), in *Selected Essays of William Carlos Williams*, p.111.
2 See, for instance, Warren Ramsey, 'Pound, Laforgue, and Dramatic Structure', in *Comparative Literature*, III (Winter 1951), 47-56.

experience into related but distinct items. On the other hand, any submergence of the line by enjambement into larger units inevitably produced that blurring of edges that Pound and all the imagists, no less than Williams, would castigate as 'muzzy'; this is why these poets had to denigrate Milton, the master of the blank-verse paragraph. After the fresh start on the *Cantos*, the verse-line there often dismembers itself into two members or sometimes three or four, cranking apart as the Anglo-Saxon line did, or the line of mediaeval English alliterative verse, or the hendecasyllables of Cavalcanti, or the Japanese verse-line of the Noh plays. Sometimes typography makes this clear, as in Canto 2, a story sumptuously retold from the *Metamorphoses* of Ovid:

> Olive grey in the near,
>   far, smoke grey of the rock-slide,
> Salmon-pink wings of the fish-hawk
>   cast grey shadows in water,
> The tower like a one-eyed great goose
>   cranes up out of the olive-grove.

More often the dismemberment of the line (its integrity despite dismemberment is often, as here, a matter of grammar) is too complex to be indicated by typography, resourceful as Pound is in juggling with variations of type. But the principle is always the same: this is verse in which enjambement is impossible; what has been reinstated as the poetic unit is the verse-line – continually dismembered, but never disintegrated.

How close Williams and Pound were in their purposes, despite their much publicized disagreements, appears if Williams's prose masterpiece of 1925, *In The American Grain*, is compared with Cantos 8 to 11, published in *The Criterion* in 1923 under the title *Malatesta Cantos*. On these cantos too the spade work of exegesis has been carried out very thoroughly.[1] They present, by way of much reproduction of original documents, a telescoped and jumbled account of the *condottiere*, Sigismundo Malatesta, Lord of Rimini; and Pound's method is precisely that of Williams when in his book the latter deals with Cotton Mather or Franklin or John Paul Jones. 'Where possible,' Williams writes,[2] 'I copied and used the original writings. . . . I did this with malice aforethought to prove the truth of my book, since the originals fitted into it without effort on my

1 See John Drummond, 'The Italian Background to the Cantos', in *Ezra Pound: A Collection of Essays for Ezra Pound on His Sixty-fifth Birthday*, ed. Peter Russell (London, 1950).
2 *Selected Letters of William Carlos Williams*, ed. J.C. Thirlwall (New York, 1957) p.187.

part, perfectly, leaving not a seam'. And thus Williams can add exultantly, of his chapter given to John Paul Jones, 'no word is my own', meaning that the whole section is a scissors-and-paste fabrication out of Jones's own dispatches. 'Leaving not a seam' is no part of Pound's intention; on the contrary, he leaves the original documents to stand out as foreign bodies embedded in his poem. But his motive, surely, is that of Williams: 'to prove the truth of my book'. Pound's inclusions of such foreign bodies, his refusal to mask his quotations by translating them out of their original language – these features of the *Cantos* are sometimes taken as proof of incurable dilettantism in the author; but they may just as well prove the direct opposite: his determination to hew to the contours of his subject, to 'prove the truth' of his book. Pound in the *Cantos* and Williams in *In the American Grain* are writing as historians. But in history too (so they would maintain) many of the rules of scientific method apply; in particular, the specimens to be examined must not be tampered with before being offered for inspection. And in this way Williams, critical as he is on other counts, can blithely accept what sticks in the gullets of so many, the undeniable fact that Pound's poem, in these cantos and in many others, includes much that must be called prose.

We are no wiser when we have read the Malatesta cantos about what was involved for Malatesta at any point in his incessant campaigning. Indeed, 'reading' is an unsatisfactory word for what the eye does as it resentfully labours over and among these blocks of dusty historical debris. We get lost in ever murkier chaos, an ever more tangled web of alliances, counteralliances, betrayals, changing of sides, sieges and the raising of sieges, marches and countermarches; it is impossible to remember whose side Malatesta is on at any time or why. But this is precisely what we were promised by the lines that introduce the sequence:

> These fragments you have shelved (shored).
> 'Slut!' 'Bitch!' Truth and Calliope
> Slanging each other sous les lauriers:

The fragments that Pound has shored against his ruins[1] turn out to

---

1 Cf. T.S. Eliot, *The Waste Land* (London, 1922). George Dekker, in *Sailing After Knowledge* (London, 1963) perceives a pun in Pound's 'shelved', which makes this allusion to *The Waste Land* a hostile one: 'Eliot's poetic method in *The Waste Land*, far from making the useful part of the past more available, rather "shelves" it again. Pound, on the other hand, will "unshelve" the useful part of the past, as he does in the Malatesta Cantos'. Dekker's case rests on his brilliant reading of the preceding Canto 7 (op. cit., pp.14-28).

be snarled imprecations, a hubbub of charge and countercharge, the truth inextricably tangled, all wasteful, all remote. All Malatesta's military exploits were wasted, pointless, a hand-to-mouth snatching at eleventh-hour expedients. Yet out of this ignoble manoeuvring we hear Malatesta writing to Florence for a painter, meeting the philosopher Gemistus Pletho, getting stone from Verona for the building he projected in Rimini, receiving illiterate letters from his builder about the plans of his architect, Alberti. The only thing that justifies Malatesta's warfare and his shabby diplomacy is the work of art that was coming out of it, the Tempio.

For it is important to remember another of the meanings Pound, especially in his *Gaudier-Brzeska* and *Hugh Selwyn Mauberley*, had given to 'cut'. 'Cut' for him involves an admiration for cut stone, and for related arts like intaglio and the making of medals, as the image of a moral and cultural positive. In particular, he has been very interested in bas-relief; no more than Adrian Stokes could Pound agree with writers on aesthetics who see carving in low relief as a bastard form between sculpture and painting.

Adrian Stokes, who met Pound many times in 1927, 1928, and 1929, both in Rapallo and in Venice, has written several books that make an illuminating, perhaps indispensable commentary on the *Cantos*. The most important of these is *The Stones of Rimini* (1934). Here Stokes makes a great deal of the derivation of marble from limestone, which is of all stones the one that has most affinity with the element of water. He maintains that great carvers of marble, such as Agostino di Duccio, the sculptor of Sigismundo's Tempio,[1] express their material through the medium of figures they carve from it; and that in doing so they try (unconsciously) to do justice to the stone's watery origin. This fantasy, he argues, would be particularly common and potent in Venice, built upon water, its power and prosperity based on naval supremacy and sea-going trade. Hence, he is particularly interested in the Istrian marble used by the Venetian builders and carvers:

> Istrian marble blackens in the shade, is snow or salt-white where exposed to the sun. . . .
> . . . For this Istrian stone seems compact of salt's bright yet shaggy crystals. Air eats into it, the brightness remains. Amid the sea Venice is built from the essence of the sea. . . .
> Again, if in fantasy the stones of Venice appear as the wave's petrifaction, then Venetian glass, compost of Venetian sand

1 According to John Pope-Hennessy, *Italian Renaissance Sculpture* (London, 1958), p.328, much of this carving is now attributed to Matteo de Pasti.

and water, expresses the taut curvature of the cold undersea, the slow, oppressed yet brittle curves of dimly translucent water.

If we would understand a visual art, we ourselves must cherish some fantasy of the material that stimulated the artist, and ourselves feel some emotional reason why his imagination chose... to employ one material rather than another. Poets alone are trustworthy interpreters. They alone possess the insight with which to re-create subjectively the unconscious fantasies that are general.[1]

Those last sentences seem to be Stokes's oblique acknowledgment that he draws authority here from the early cantos, which, as we know, he had read with excitement some seven years before, and from one of these in particular, Canto 17, which Yeats was later to choose for inclusion in his *Oxford Book of Modern Verse*.

In Canto 17 there appears, to begin with, the very epithet for stone which Stokes was to use, 'salt-white'. Elsewhere in the Canto Pound compresses into a single perception the whole process of the composition of marble from the incrustation of sunken timber by algae, through shell-encrusted cliff and cave, to the hewn stone of the palazzo with its feet in water. Thus 'Marble trunks out of stillness' are balks of timber encrusted by limestone deposits, but they are no less ('On past the palazzi') the hewn columns of some Venetian portico, which is 'the rock sea-worn' as well as the wood stone-encrusted. The light is said to be 'not of the sun', and this for all sorts of reasons: because it is light as reflected off water in the open air or inside a cave or inside a Venetian portico, because it is light refracted through water when we imagine ourselves submerged along with the just-forming limestone.

When, a few lines later, a man comes by boat talking of 'stone trees' and 'the forest of marble', he may be taken as one who brings to a Venice not yet revetted in stone the news of marble to be quarried, together with his excited sense of an affinity between city and quarry, a fittingness about bringing the stone of the one to dress the other; or he may be conceived as one who returns to another part of Italy with excited news of the city of stone on water that the Venetians are making. He speaks of the beaks of gondolas rising and falling, and of the glass-blowers from Murano in terms that look forward to Stokes's argument about the marine fantasies inspiring them. The transition from this, in two lines of verse, to 'Dye-pots in the torch-light', may be glossed from another book by Adrian Stokes:

1 Adrian Stokes, *The Stones of Rimini* (London, 1934), pp.19-20.

> There is no doubt that the Venetian painters were directly inspired in their use of oil paint by the achievements of the glass makers at Murano.[1]

This stone Venice is seen in the poem as a product of Mediterranean sensibility (related, for instance, to the Greek culture, similarly maritime, similarly marble-loving) and not, as Ruskin thought, related northward to Gothic. The place spoken of is identified as Venice only at the end of the Canto, and then only obliquely (by way of two names, Borso and Carmagnola). And this is right, for the pleached arbour of stone, besides being Venice and besides being the quarries from which Venice was built, is the good place, a sort of heaven of cut and squared masonry, which the broken but indomitable hero earns by his resolution and courage.

The *Cantos* force us to dismiss from our minds most of the familiar connotations of 'marmoreal' or 'stony'. Where 'marble' appears, or 'stone', it is a sign of resurgence and renewed hope. The most striking example is in Canto 16, where the first glimmer of convalescence after the passage through infernal regions, which occupied Cantos 14 and 15 also, is a hand clutching marble. After the marble comes the new inflow, the embryonic, the new potential; and twelve lines later in Canto 16 a new amplitude and tranquillity: 'The grey stone posts,/and the stair of gray stone....'

It is this casing in hewn and chiselled stone that, in the *Cantos*, justifies Sigismundo Malatesta. It may seem that all is to be forgiven Sigismundo – and there is much to forgive – just because he was good to artists, because he chose them well and set them to work on a worthwhile project. And it is true, as Williams noticed, that at times in these early cantos there is a disconcertingly great weight attached to enlightened patronage of the arts in a quite general sense, such as Pound had argued for in his *Patria Mia*.[2] But Malatesta is established as a type of individual for whom the modern sense of 'patron' is inadequate, just as it is inadequate for the 'onlie begetter' celebrated in Shakespeare's sonnets. Adrian Stokes exclaims, of the Tempio, 'It is a tight fit, this holding of one man's emblem'; and he elaborates on this:

> Sigismundo's Tempio expresses Sigismundo. There he is, projected directly into stone, not as a succession or a story, but as something immediate. It is an effect impossible to other generations. All the fifteenth century genius for emblem, for

1 Adrian Stokes, *Colour and Form* (London, 1937), p.111.
2 (Chicago, 1950), but written forty years earlier.

outwardness, centred in Sigismundo.... Each characteristic passed easily into a form of art, non-musical, tense.[1]

Clearly, if this is a sort of patronage quite different from what may be found and hoped for in the twentieth century, it is different also from, for instance, the mediaeval patronage of Abbot Suger of St Denis, 'onlie begetter' of French Gothic:

> The great man of the Renaissance asserted his personality centripetally, so to speak: he swallowed up the world that surrounded him until his whole environment had been absorbed by his own self. Suger asserted his personality centrifugally: he projected his ego into the world that surrounded him until his whole self had been absorbed by his environment.[2]

Malatesta was the sort of patron who 'swallowed up the world that surrounded him until his whole environment had been absorbed by his own self'. That is the achievement which Pound celebrates. And, if we understand why, we go near to the nerve of all the early cantos, for of all spiritual manifestations, the one that Pound at this stage showed himself surest about, and most excited by, was that which in the Renaissance went by the name of *virtù*:

> That hath the light of the doer, as it were
> a form cleaving to it.

The virtù which is the light of a personality cleaving to act or artifact, moulding and forming it, is all the more impressively *there*, all the more certainly a proof that the spiritual resources of the person can modify and indelibly mark the physical, when we perceive it as in the Rimini Tempio transmitted through intermediaries as well as through a medium – the *virtù* not of doer or artificer, but of the patron who caused things to be done, caused artifacts to be made. For the Tempio, according to Adrian Stokes, expresses not Alberti's personality nor Agostino di Duccio's, but Sigismundo's. This was the emphasis Pound was to give to Sigismundo in *Guide to Kulchur*: 'There is no other single man's effort equally registered'.

The man of Pound's own time who might come nearest to registering his effort with equal authority, Pound would come to think, was Mussolini. Thus this powerful strain of feeling in the poet had its sinister side, as Williams perceived:

1 Adrian Stokes, *The Quattro Cento* (London, 1932), p.188.
2 Erwin Panofsky, *Meaning in the Visual Arts* (Garden City, N.Y., 1955), p.137.

It is still a Lenin, striking through the mass, whipping it about, that engages his attention. That is the force Pound believes in. (op. cit., p.111.)

When Pound opens Canto 30 with the haunting mediaeval pastiche of his 'complaint of Artemis', reversing Chaucer's 'Complaint unto Pity' into an argument for a proper ruthlessness (because 'Pity spareth so many an evil thing'), although we may realize that the point is well taken, we have to feel with the benefit of hindsight that this was a woefully inappropriate time for taking it. It was characteristic of the whole of Pound's generation to sway toward totalitarian politics in the late 'twenties and early 'thirties: Eliot in 'Coriolan', D.H. Lawrence in his letters, Wyndham Lewis in *The Art of Being Ruled*, Yeats in his marching songs for O'Duffy's blue-shirts – all similarly failed to read the signs of the times. Pound was the only one of them to persist in his misreading and to be brought to book for it.

When Adrian Stokes wrote of the Tempio as Sigismundo's emblem, he was making another distinction besides that between the Renaissance patron and other kinds of patron. He insists that Sigismundo is 'projected directly into stone, not as a succession or a story', and that 'each characteristic passed easily into a form of art, non-musical, tense'. When he writes 'not as a succession... non-musical', he is deploring the confusion of non-successive arts like sculpture and architecture with the 'successive' arts of music, a confusion that he lays at the door of Brunelleschi. Pound had made the same protest, but from the side of, and on behalf of, music:

> The early students of harmony were so accustomed to think of music as something with a strong lateral or horizontal motion that they never imagined any one, ANY ONE, could be stupid enough to think of it as static; it never entered their heads that people would make music like steam ascending from a morass.[1]

But what of literature, of poetry? Is not poetry necessarily a 'successive' art like music, carving its structures out of lapsing time? Certainly the symbolists thought so, with their 'De la musique avant toute chose'. But Pound as early as *Gaudier-Brzeska* was opposed to symbolism on these grounds as on others, and was speculating about

1 Pound, *Patria Mia and The Treatise on Harmony* (London, 1962), p.80.

poetry by analogy with the spatial art of sculpture rather than the temporal art of music. Moreover, in his typographical laying out of 'Donna mi prega', a layout which seems to have been the model for many pages of the *Cantos*, Pound had contrived at least the illusion of a poetry that is ranged across as well as down in the space of the printed page.

In 1927 he was still imagining his poetry in these sculptural and spatial terms. This appears from a letter written in that year to his father, a document which is invaluable in any case as it is the nearest we come to an exegesis by the poet of one of his own cantos, specifically, of Canto 20.

This canto opens with interlarded scraps of verse from the Provençal of Bernart de Ventadour and the Latin of Catullus and Propertius. It moves into a pleasantly relaxed and affectionate reminiscence of Pound's visit, on the advice of his teacher Hugo Rennert, to the scholar of Provençal, Emile Lévy, with a problem of vocabulary from Arnaut Daniel. There ensues a passage of natural description, whether of Provence or of Lévy's Freiburg is not clear. Pound's exegesis for his father begins with the first line of a fourth section, 'He was playing there at the palla'. Pound writes that this section represents 'Nicolo d'Este in sort of delirium after execution of Parisina and Ugo' (that is, of Nicolo's wife and his own natural son, who had been her lover). And Pound's note goes on:

> The whole reminiscence jumbled or 'candied' in Nicolo's delirium. Take that as a sort of bounding surface from which one gives the main subject of the Canto, the lotophagoi: lotus eaters, or respectable dope smokers; and general paradiso. You have had a hell in Canti XIV, XV; purgatorio in XVI etc. (*Letters*, p.285.)

Nicolo's delirium plays with or plays over a great deal more than this. It includes, as Pound notes, memories of a passage of the *Iliad* when the old men of Troy talk of returning Helen to the Greeks and so ending the war; and this is confounded with another beautiful woman on another wall – Elvira, in Lope's play *Las Almenas de Toro*, which is described in *The Spirit of Romance*. Another episode that weaves in and out of Nicolo d'Este's disordered mind is the death of Roland; and it is in *The Spirit of Romance* that Pound objects to the treatment of this in *The Song of Roland* as stiff and frigid. Pound's extremely shrill and wooden retelling of it is open to Williams's objection:

> His words affect modernity with too much violence (at times) – a straining after slang effects, engendered by their effort to

> escape from that which is their instinctive quality – a taking
> character from classic similes and modes. (op. cit., p.107.)

And this makes something unintentionally warped and coarsely tex-
tured out of the 'bounding surface' that the delirium was meant to
provide. However, if Pound had spoken of this as 'a background',
there would have been no difficulty in approving at least the inten-
tion: against the tumultuous violence of love and war in Nicolo's
delirium the serenity of what follows was to stand out seductively.
By speaking instead of 'a bounding surface' (one imagines something
like a rough-hewn concave shell, half-enclosing sculpted masses in
its shadow), Pound shows that he is conceiving of his poetic space
in three dimensions, in sculptural terms rather than painterly.

As for the subsequent treatment of the lotus-eaters, this has been
much admired, for instance by Hugh Kenner. Yet one can only be
astonished at the impression the passage gives, which Pound's letter
to his father confirms, that the lotus-eaters are offered naïvely to be
admired by the reader as having attained one stage toward an all-
important illumination. In cantos written twenty-five years after
this, Pound was to insist that 'Le Paradis n'est pas artificiel'; but at
this stage the Paradiso certainly is very close to the 'paradis artificiel'
of the drug-takers. A paradiso thus infected with nineteenth-century
diabolism and self-admiring 'decadence' is surely damned by the
Dantesque parallel which Pound too presumptuously invites.

VIII

Cantos 30-36 · Guide to Kulchur

Cantos 31 to 34, first published in magazines in the years 1931-33, are the first instalment of what have come to be called the American History cantos. Cantos 31 and 32 and the first half of 33 have been put together out of snippets from letters exchanged between John Adams and Thomas Jefferson. According to William Vasse, these pages are devoted to 'outlining some of the main points of the early American economic, political, legal and ideological struggles'.[1] But the only struggle we find documented in the verse (and even this we find with difficulty) is the ideological difference between Jefferson's respect for doctrinaire theorists like Tom Paine and Condorcet and even Franklin, and Adams's distrust of them. Thus ten lines of Canto 31 are made up from a very respectful letter from Jefferson to Paine, whom Adams on the contrary (though this is not in the canto) described as 'a disastrous meteor'.[2] Elsewhere in the canto Adams is quoted describing Condorcet, Franklin, and others as grossly ignorant; and in still other lines Adams mocks Franklin for his notions of 'the exalted dignity of human nature'. Yet in Canto 33, when Adams renews his attacks on what he calls 'ideology' (borrowing the word from Napoleon), the point is blurred because Pound omits from the beginning of his quotation the words 'establishing a free republican government'. It is kindest, therefore, to suppose that Pound intended by these cantos to do no more than tease the reader into looking up his sources.

This is not true, however, of Canto 34, which is similarly a catena of quotations from a selected edition of the diaries of John Quincy Adams, son of John Adams.[3] Though in this canto too there are teasingly cryptic references, and though I think Vasse takes the will

1 W. Vasse, 'American History and the Cantos', *The Pound Newsletter*, 5 (Jan. 1955).
2 *The Works of John Adams*, ed. Charles Francis Adams, 10 vols. (Boston, 1850-57), II, 507.
3 *The Diary of John Quincy Adams, 1794-1845*, ed. Allan Nevins (New York, 1928).

for the deed in finding that some citations from John Quincy Adams's term as president contrast him with his father as more the observer and less the actor, yet the canto by itself, without recourse to the *Diary* it is hewn from, establishes John Quincy Adams as a rounded and sympathetic character. This is effected by strictly poetic means; the rhythms, while necessarily still prosaic, are repeatedly tauter than in the preceding cantos. Moreover, the alleged decline in standards of taste and enlightenment from the heyday of John Adams to that of his son is wittily and convincingly depicted. And there are lines at the end of the canto which can sustain comparison with Eliot's 'Coriolan', to which they indeed appear to be related:

> The firemen's torchlight procession,
> Firemen's torchlight procession,
> Science as a principle of political action
>
> Firemen's torchlight procession!

The exclamation mark does an amusing amount of work. The *Diary* records that Adams was accorded this peculiar honour three times running – in Buffalo, in Rochester, in Utica. 'Science as a principle of political action' refers, however, to a visit to Cincinnati that succeeded the visit to these towns of New York State. Thus the *Diary* confirms what the lineation of the verse suggests: the second repetition of 'Firemen's torchlight procession' represents a delayed reaction to the absurdity of a piece of *ad hoc* ceremonial which at first was accepted bemusedly. And it stands, with its exclamation mark, as a self-sufficient comment upon a society where the ceremonies are pompous and on a gross scale, yet uninformed by precedent or by any symbolic aptness of invention; the Diary confirms that the public life of America in 1843, as Adams saw it, was indeed the tasteless and raucous America that Dickens was to hold up to exasperated mockery in *American Notes* and *Martin Chuzzlewit*.

This is the America also of Canto 37, which is quarried from the autobiography of yet another President of the United States, Martin Van Buren. Unfortunately, the vulgarity of Van Buren, the extent to which he was himself a product of tasteless demagoguery, is concealed in Pound's canto and is revealed only when we inspect in the autobiography the language of Van Buren himself which, with its fulsome capital letters on 'the People' and 'the Party', is an eloquent witness to that tyranny of the majority that John Adams had foreseen ('a country where popularity had more omnipotence than the British parliament assumed'[1]), that Fenimore Cooper

1 Adams, *Works*, X, p.53.

fought against and suffered by throughout his life, that Dickens rightly mocked and castigated. Pound declared, in *The ABC of Reading*, 'A people that grows accustomed to sloppy writing is a people in process of losing grip on its empire and on itself'.[1] And yet he finds a hero of sorts in a man whose own language is sloppy and blowsy in the extreme. It is here one has the right to say that Pound's new-found 'conspiracy' theory of fiscal history was distorting and over-riding his own earlier insights. For Van Buren earns his place in the *Cantos* and is accorded the title of 'fisci liberator' because he was the champion of Jacksonian democracy in its war with the Banks. It is true that in Canto 34 John Quincy Adams was allowed to record 'L'ami de tout le monde, Martin Van Buren'. But it is worth returning this judgment to its context:

> Finished reading Holland's Life of Martin Van Buren, a partisan electioneering work, written with much of that fraudulent democracy by the profession of which Thomas Jefferson rose to power in this country, and of which he set the first successful example. Van Buren's personal character bears, however, a stronger resemblance to that of Mr. Madison than to Jefferson's. These are both remarkable for their extreme caution in avoiding and averting personal collisions. Van Buren, like the Sosie of Molière's *Amphitryon*, is 'l'ami de tout le monde'. This is perhaps the great secret of his success in public life. . . .[2]

This reveals, if it reveals nothing else, the animosity of the Adamses to many of their famous contemporaries, something that Pound's treatment of American history conceals. Of course the principle may be wrong; perhaps we should judge Martin Van Buren as much by his recorded actions as by his utterances. But Pound had seemed to maintain that integrity in action and integrity in language necessarily go together. And a reading in Van Buren's autobiography confirms, by the language Van Buren employs, John Quincy Adams's estimate of him as a crafty, fulsome, and slippery demagogue.

Between the John Quincy Adams canto and the Van Buren canto stand Cantos 35 and 36. Canto 35 contains the first display of Pound's anti-Semitism. There is no point in denying that this is what it is. And yet we must observe that, without the appalling hindsight we have from subsequent history and subsequent cantos, Canto 35, though it would in any case give offence to many Jews, is seen to make an arguable and interesting point about Jewish social life:

1 (London and New Haven, 1934), p.86.
2 *The Diary of John Quincy Adams*, p.465 (Apr. 13, 1836).

>   this is Mitteleuropa
>   and Tsievitz
>   has explained to me the warmth of affections,
>   the intramural, the almost intravaginal warmth of
>   hebrew affections, in the family, and nearly everything else. . . .
>   pointing out that Mr. Lewinesholme has suffered by
>   deprivation
>   of same and exposure to American snobbery . . . 'I am a
>   product,'
>   said the young lady, 'of Mitteleuropa,'
>   but she seemed to have been able to mobilize
>   and the fine thing was that the family did not
>   wire about papa's death for fear of disturbing the concert
>   which might seem to contradict the general indefinite wobble.
>   It must be rather like some internal organ,
>   some communal life of the pancreas . . . sensitivity
>   without direction . . . this is . . .

If Pound had never gone further than this into anti-Semitism, one could argue that this has as much to do with his ideas about music as expressed in *Antheil and The Treatise on Harmony*, and that, most of the executants being Jewish, there is a witty and legitimate connection between their music and the rest of their emotional life. What is in any case equally disturbing in this canto is the increased abstractness of Pound's thought: this permits him, as elsewhere to write off with a confident generalization whole tracts of recorded history, so here to dispose with absurd jauntiness of a large tract of the earth's surface – 'So this is (may we take it) Mitteleuropa'.

Canto 35 ends with an extended reference to Mantua, and this is carried on in the next canto in a reference to the Mantuan Sordello, who survives into the *Cantos* out of the Browningesque first draft of the first three, where he had played the lead. But most of Canto 36 is taken up, surprisingly enough, with a new translation of 'Donna mi prega', a translation even more opaque than the already all but impenetrable version given in *Make It New*. The best explanation of this is George Dekker's,[1] who argues that the point is precisely the opacity. In literature and history, as in the sciences, there are phemonena surviving that for certain reasons (in this case, the erosion through time of the intellectual context of Cavalcanti's poem) are simply and blankly unaccountable, inscrutable. In such cases the most faithful translation is the one making least sense, and this corresponds to what Pound has always required of historians – that

1 *Sailing After Knowledge* (London, 1963), pp.126-8.

they leave blanks in their writings for 'what they don't know'.[1] Thus
Cavalcanti's poem is lodged in the centre of the Cantos, a hard
nugget of foreign matter, to enforce humility.

Pound's *Guide to Kulchur*[2] is an incomparable book – not incompar-
ably good, just incomparable. In what other work could one find
the author conceding after thirty pages: 'I cd. by opening volumes
I haven't seen for 25 or more years find data that run counter to
what I am saying or what I shall say in the next ten pages'? No
doubt many authors have admitted this to themselves on their thir-
tieth page, and yet gone on to write three hundred and forty pages
more. But who has done this who has made the admission not to
himself but his readers? None, surely, whose purpose is, as Pound's
is, pedagogical; for no pedagogue can afford such an admission.
Pound can afford it, and that is his unique qualification, as he realizes:

> It is my intention in this booklet to COMMIT myself on as
> many points as possible, that means that I shall make a number
> of statements which very few men can AFFORD to make, for
> the simple reason that such taking sides might jeopard their
> incomes (directly) or their prestige or 'position' in one or other
> of the professional 'worlds'. Given my freedom, I may be a
> fool to use it, but I wd. be a cad not to.

Some may think that Pound, having used the poet's freedom to
the pedagogue's ends, has misled as many readers as, for instance,
Robert Graves, who in some of his prose has made the same use of
his poet's freedom; but Pound saw that the freedom involved respon-
sibility. This appears from the passage just quoted from the Preface,
but the best evidence is the damaging admission we started with,
to which there is no parallel in Graves. And halfway through the
book, at the start of Section VIII, Pound reminds himself again of
what he is doing, and how risky it is:

> Ridiculous title, stunt piece. Challenge? Guide,
> ought to mean help other fellow to get there.

1 Canto 13: And Kung said "Wang ruled with moderation,
             "In his day the State was well kept,
          "And even I can remember
          "A day when the historians left blanks in their writings,
          "I mean for things they didn't know, . . ."
2 (London, 1938); *Culture* is the title of the American printing in the same
year.

What is involved is a genuine educational experiment. The experiment may fail, but it was undertaken in all seriousness, not irresponsibly. And the same is true of the earlier pilot experiments, *How To Read* and *The ABC of Reading*. After all, Pound commenced life as a pedagogue, and in 1938 he was still the man who had written *The Spirit of Romance*.

The method he experiments with is determined by certain self-imposed ordinances. Not all of these are clear at first, but one of them is:

> In the main, I am to write this new Vade Mecum without opening other volumes, I am to put down so far as possible only what has resisted the erosion of time, and forgetfulness.

'In the main' is a saving clause. And with that qualification the rule might seem to have been followed as much in the *Cantos* as in the pedagogical treatise. In the poem, however, there is far more 'opening other volumes' – more's the pity, perhaps, for it means that in the poem, when we come on inaccuracies (as we do, repeatedly), they are far more damaging than they are in *Guide to Kulchur*, where we have been forewarned of them. At any rate, the reason for relying on memory is the same in the prose as in the poetry; the knowledge that has 'resisted the erosion of time, and forgetfulness' is a different sort of knowledge from the sort that has to be refreshed, the knowledge of 'where to look it up'. And there are plausible reasons for thinking that knowledge of the first sort is superior to the second sort, so superior that perhaps the second is not properly to be called knowledge at at all. We have not read many pages of *Guide to Kulchur* before we find that the distinction between the two kinds of knowledge not only determines Pound's way of writing, it is also, quite centrally, what he is talking about.

The knowledge we have of the Ionian philosophers is necessarily, he suggests, knowledge of the second sort; if we want to recall what Heraclitus said besides 'everything flows', or what he meant by that gnomic, because too conclusive, proposition, we always have to 'look it up'. This knowledge we have of Heraclitus is obviously different from knowledge we have which, once acquired, is a permanent possession. Pound's example of the second sort of knowledge is connoisseurship, in painting and in literature; the sort of 'feel', or rule of thumb, derived from experience, by which in the first place the connoisseur makes his attributions. Pound identifies this sort of knowledge as that which the Confucian tradition deals with and deals in, whereas the Greek tradition (even in Plato, even in Aristotle) deals only in knowledge of the other, academic sort. Pound's attempt to demonstrate this by excerpts from the Analects is unconvincing. Yet the failure of this example does not invalidate the distinction as such between the two kinds of knowledge; in fact, the distinction is endorsed always by common sense, and, as Pound realizes, it has been made many times before. Keats was making it when he distinguished between knowledge that is 'felt on the pulses' and other kinds of knowledge. And Pound is surely in a very strong position when he implies that the distinction, since it exists, ought to be the first distinction made in pedagogical theory and that all pedagogical practice should be conducted in the light of it.

In fact, even as Pound wrote *Guide to Kulchur*, an attempt was being made to apply just these insights to the teaching of literature – an attempt sustained mostly in the University of Cambridge and associated with the name of F.R. Leavis and the magazine that he founded, *Scrutiny*. This Cambridge experiment is not irrelevant to a discussion of Pound, since Leavis, in his *How To Teach Reading, A Primer for Ezra Pound*, was the only academic figure to take anything by Pound (in this case, *How To Read*) seriously enough to retort to it; and in his *New Bearings in English Poetry* Leavis at a later date drew admiring attention to *Hugh Selwyn Mauberley* at the same time as he condemned the *Cantos* and nearly everything else by Pound except *Homage to Sextus Propertius*. In fact, Leavis condemns *How To Read* and the *Cantos* by Poundian principles, since he seems to believe in the last resort that there can be no knowledge of literature 'on the pulses' except of literature in one's native language. It is reasonable for any self-respecting pedagogue to decide that the only knowledge that is worth imparting is knowledge that shall be a permanent acquisition, not mere book-learning; and yet inevitably, with Pound as more conspicuously with Leavis, this position produces a canon of approved authors and an index of proscribed books. Among their opponents, a slack irresponsibility, taste at the whim of fashion and idiosyncrasy, masquerades as open-mindedness. Yet open-mindedness *is* the cornerstone of the edifice of learning; and Pound's anathemas, like Leavis's, close the minds of their disciples. The dispute is a bitter one, and interminable, because both parties are in the right. Every man's mind is closed eventually, when time and energy run out on him before he has acquainted himself with more than a tiny fraction of what is worth knowing; and it is Pound's sense of the sands running out for his pupils, and of the unmanageable copiousness of what may be known, that justifies Pound, like Leavis, in trying to close the student's mind to what seems sterile or inessential. Moreover, in Pound this concern takes the very practical form of demanding better co-ordination internationally inside the world of learning.

Pound does not in any case proscribe whole bodies of knowledge. On the contrary, unlike Leavis but like many pedagogues of the 'thirties, Pound urges the student of literature and philosophy into, for instance, economic theory and economic history. He differs from the majority, who made this recommendation under Marxist auspices, by considering particularly important the history of fiscal policy. It soon appears that his lukewarmness about Plato and Aristotle (he stops far short of proscription of these authors) has to do with their being Athenians, citizens of a state where fiscal and economic practice was determined by the needs of maritime commerce. Like Pater in *Plato and Platonism*, Pound's sympathies are instead with Sparta, a totalitarian state with a less mercantile economy, and with Rome. And as Pound boldly associates the figure of 30 per cent interest with Athens, and of 6 per cent with Rome, as he credits St Ambrose with transmitting the best of imperial Rome into the mediaeval Church, as he reprints Gaudier's 'Vortex' as a 'history of sculpture', we perceive that Pound is not the sort of educator who proscribes whole subjects as useless; he is, on the contrary, the more buoyant but perhaps more dangerous kind who will save the time that he and his students so desperately need, by using mnemonics, on the understanding that in most subjects of discourse the essential truths can be stated on the back of a postcard or at most on a few sheets of notepaper. His 'gists and piths', as he calls them, are the mnemonics, the essential truths. The mnemonic for St Ambrose, for instance, from this time forward in Pound's writing, is 'captans annonam' or 'hoggers of harvest'; there is no intimation that we need to know more of St Ambrose than this single phrase in order to esteem him as highly as Pound does. Quite consistently, when he rightly comes to consider how a culture can be maintained by social custom and habit for some time after creative minds have ceased to fructify it, he gives as proof and example an observation and an anecdote from the conversation of an acquaintance, Urquell, a Russian White Guard émigré. It is easy to laugh this out of court, indignantly; but it must be agreed that if the only 'real' knowledge is that which stays in the memory permanently, then perhaps a mnemonic is all that stands between St Ambrose and oblivion, and all that he deserves in the unmanageable plenitude of so much else that is worth knowing.

In Part II of *Guide to Kulchur* (five chapters), the disorder is not just apparent but real. Yet the observant reader will perceive that Pound is here making a new estimate of his own career to date. Already on an earlier page he had written (Chapter 4):

My generation found criticism of the arts cluttered with work of men who persistently defined the works of one art in terms of another.

For a decade or so we tried to get the arts sorted out.

And to any reader who remembers the memoir of Gaudier, and Pound's definition of his own poetry as 'painting or sculpture just coming over into speech', this will seem disingenuous to say the least. For Pound himself had been one of those men who, in the climate of opinion inaugurated by Pater, 'persistently defined the works of one art in terms of another'. The Pound of 1938 is disowning the Pound of 1916, and to set the record straight he needs to make this explicit. He does so when in Part II he relates his own activities between 1916 and 1921 to contemporaneous French movements connected with the names of Picabia, Marcel Duchamp, and Erik Satie; that is to say, his and Wyndham Lewis's work for *Blast* (no less, in a rather special way, Joyce's in *Ulysses*) are now considered as wholly, though necessarily, destructive or at least disruptive – the vorticist movement corresponds to Dadaism across the Channel in being deliberately anarchical, a summing up or clinical clearing out and breaking down of categories and conventions inherited from the nineteenth century. It can be justified only retrospectively when it produced by reaction Cocteau's *Rappel à l'ordre*. Cocteau is declared to be a poet of genius, the presiding genius of the 'twenties, and yet his work too is only preparatory. It prepares for 'the new synthesis, the totalitarian'. 'Totalitarianism' as used by Pound refers to more than politics, but it is a term of politics in the first place, and *Guide to Kulchur* is an overtly Fascist book.[1] Pound even compliments Wyndham Lewis on having discovered Hitler before he, Pound, discovered Mussolini. Though one dislikes admitting it, nothing has happened since to invalidate this logical and chronological connection between modernism in the arts and Fascism in politics; Thomas Mann discerned it also. There is further corroboration in Chapter 20, where the Vou club in totalitarian Japan, with which Pound corresponds through Katue Kitasono, is said to have been founded by admirers of Satie.

In some places Pound's Fascism is just a straightforward enthusiasm for all things Italian, no more sophisticated (despite his years of residence in Rapallo) than the enthusiasm of any British or American middle-aged couple after a holiday in Sestri Levante. In Chapter 16 he is unashamedly the tourist, telling his readers to take walking tours in France but in Italy to take the bus, and (pretentiously knowledgeable) declaring gravely that 'Le Voyage Gastronomique is a

1 As had been, for instance, Pound's *Jefferson And/Or Mussolini* (London, 1935).

French pai-deuma'. On the other hand, Chapter 21, on the excellence of the textbooks in Italian schools, gives food for thought. And elsewhere the totalitarianism is much more serious. For instance, what Pound envisages as totalitarianism in art ('the new synthesis') becomes clearer with an interesting passage in Chapter 19, where he speaks of Bartók's Fifth Quartet, as played at Rapallo in 1937 by the New Hungarian Four, as 'the record of a personal struggle', as 'too interesting', as having 'the defects inherent in a record of struggle', which are 'the defects or disadvantages of my Cantos'. Set against the Bartók is a work by Boccherini, played on the same occasion by the same musicians, in which 'no trace of effort remained', any more than it remains in the disconcerting limpidity of the Analects or in the simplicity of 'the jokes in Boccaccio'. Totalitarian art will be simple and transparent; the obscurity and oddity of modernist art like the *Cantos* will nowhere be treated with such contumely as in the totalitarian states – and Pound almost brings himself to admit this. However, such totalitarian art is not just round the corner; for the necessary preparatory labour of clarification, co-ordination, and research is all to be done – as Pound vividly illustrates in respect to the very composers he is talking about, Boccherini and Vivaldi.[1] The difference between Boccherini and Bartók is not, in any ordinary sense of 'totalitarian', the difference between totalitarian and non-totalitarian art. As Pound acutely and instructively says, it is the difference between an art that has a culture behind it and an art (Bartók's, Pound's, perhaps even Beethoven's) that is produced out of a solitary artist's struggle *against* the cultural conditions he is born to. The two kinds of art correspond to the two kinds of knowledge. As Pound says:

> Knowledge is NOT culture. The domain of culture begins when one HAS 'forgotten-what-book'.

The knowledge that one possesses securely is not safeguarded consciously, nor even is it so acquired; it is like a trained reflex, not maintained nor extended by any act of will. Commonsense knows that this is so, but it is difficult and perilous for educators to acknowledge it.

Pound is repeatedly aware of the perils to education, and to

1 Pound, himself the composer of an opera, *The Testament of François Villon*, was not only a pioneer in the appreciation of Vivaldi, but gave to the locating of Vivaldi's manuscripts (and their interpretation) the benefit of his experience years before in locating manuscripts of troubadour songs for the edition he did with Walter Morse Rummel. (See *Hesternae Rosae* by Walter Morse Rummel, London, 1911.) Pound the musician and musicologist deserves a book to himself.

scholarship. Academic freedom, like the freedom of the press, is worthless unless freedom brings responsibility. Even open-mindedness is worthless except in the service of curiosity. Pound knows that he himself is a man with bees in his bonnet. In Chapter 28 he calls himself 'a credit-crank'. And in Chapter 31 he says, 'I am not satisfied with my own journalism. I suspect it of being coloured by my convictions'. Yet, he says, 'even this mania, this one-trackness occasionally ploughs up more truth than mere lack of direction', because 'some kind of line to hang one's facts on is better than no line at all'. Thus:

> The indifferent or 'cold' historian may leave a more accurate account of what happens, but he will never understand WHY it happens.
>
> I have seen the nitchevo journalists missing the mainspring, almost always missing the mainsprings.
>
> A complete laissez-faire, a conviction of universal vanity, a disgust with the metier itself, a belief in their own impotence, an attribution of similar lack of motivation, of constructivity, of volition to all other men, leaves them on the outside.

The dilemma is familiar to every literary scholar, and there are none who are not, wittingly or unwittingly, caught upon the horns of it, as Pound is. Unless an investigation is made with an open mind it cannot be scholarly, but will ignore whatever does not fall in with the investigator's preconceptions. And yet there is open-mindedness that is indistinguishable from indifference; and indifference, under the specious masks of impartiality and detachment, may be scholarly indeed, but it is also sterile and sterilizing. Even curiosity is worth very little if it is omnivorous, if it makes every item of information equal to every other. Nevertheless, Pound is superior to, for instance, F.R. Leavis, who at this period is making similar points with similar courage, because Pound holds on to curiosity as the irreplaceable saving grace. Scholarship is damned, and its pretensions to open-mindedness are seen to be hollow, if it can be shown to be incurious. And Pound, who has pointed out how incurious the musicologists are (for instance, about Vivaldi), can easily make the same charge stick upon the scholars of literature. 'Philology', in the inclusive German sense which was taken over from the Germans in Europe generally and in the United States, was the discipline of literary scholarship into which Pound was initiated at the University of Pennsylvania in 1907, just as the young graduate is initiated into it today in Pennsylvania or in Cambridge, England. Pound blames it, as others have done, for fostering and depending upon an impartiality which is really indifference, which recognizes no hierarchy of significance by which some items of information are more important than others. The peculiar strength of Pound's case is that he also shows how incurious it is. The Germans who initiated this scholarly method are the least to be blamed for it; and Anglo-American sneers at 'Teutonic scholarship' are particularly out of place since, as Pound shows, not only is German scholarship better co-ordinated than any other (for instance in the Institute that Frobenius founded at Frankfurt), but also, in each field Pound turns to for examples of how incurious the literary scholars are, such solitary pioneers as can be found turn out to be Germans, like Klabund in the field of ancient Chinese poetry. When Pound compares Klabund's versions with the eighteenth-century Latin versions of Lacharme (a Frenchman, but reprinted in the present century by Germans), he is inspired by the Latin to a rough English version which is the first intimation of his translation of the *Classic Anthology* twenty years later. And this, like the admirable versions of African folk-poems in the preceding two chapters of *Guide to Kulchur*, is not only an example of the effortless limpidity to be expected of totalitarian art; it stands also as evidence of how incurious literary scholarship is, which will allow such poems to lie hidden in unknown languages or in the archives of anthropologists.

Nobody can suppose that *Guide to Kulchur* was written according to a plan worked out beforehand. Chapter by chapter, even paragraph by paragraph, Pound is improvising, and no one can be deceived for more than a moment by Pound's pretence that the abruptness of his transitions is really a matter of pregnant juxtapositions, contrived according to the so-called 'ideogrammic method' as recommended by Fenollosa. On the contrary, the appeal of *Guide to Kulchur*, and its uniqueness, are in its being so desperate and so harried, and in Pound's vulnerability which, in consequence, he exposes consciously as well as unconsciously. For Pound surprises himself as well as surprising his readers. Ever more discouraged as the book drags toward its close, Pound is compelled for a second time to review his own half-century of effort, and to see his achievement as partial, limited, in part misdirected, and at best eccentric. Most unexpectedly (since the most strident of Pound's diatribes have throughout been reserved for England), it is a British writer, Hardy, who provokes Pound to this second and more painful self-assessment. In a letter of 1937 he had written of Hardy's *Collected Poems*, 'Now *there is* the harvest of having written 20 novels first' (*Letters*, p.386). And this is the note struck in *Guide to Kulchur* also (Chapter 52):

20 novels form as good a gradus ad Parnassum as does metrical exercise, I dare say they form a better if the gods have granted light by that route. Hardy is Gautier's successor as Swinburne could not be.

In consequence,

> a craft that occupies itself solely with imitating Gerard Hopkins or in any other metrical experiment is a craft misdirected. We engage in technical exercise faute de mieux, a necessary defensive activity.

Here Pound is not quite unsaying what he had said many times in earlier years, for he saves himself (with a spurt of renewed pugnacity) by observing, 'Out of these sentences you may omit neither the "solely" nor the "necessary" without destroying their meaning'. But the emphasis of the earlier Pound had been so consistently the other way, in favour of 'technique', and of 'technique' that could be learned, that even so close an associate as Wyndham Lewis had, in *Men Without Art*, taken this to be Pound's central and distinguishing characteristic. And so, in these pages on Hardy, we see more clearly than before what a *volte-face* was involved when Pound disavowed modernist intricacy and technical sophistication in favour of a limpidity he considered 'totalitarian'. Of Hardy's generation, the last generation of British Victorian artists, Pound now says, 'they bred a generation of experimenters, my generation, which was unable to work out a code for action'. Hardy, with his insularity and his clumsiness (sometimes calculated, often not) is so much the last poet one would have expected Pound to admire, that this tribute to him gives us a new respect for Pound's generosity and open-mindedness, the genuine catholicity of his taste. Yet there is no blinking the fact that it makes nonsense of many of Pound's other professions, at this date as well as earlier. And, indeed, Pound is so discouraged by this time that he can no longer find enthusiasm for a totalitarian New Dawn. We hear again about the 'new synthesis', but Pound's heart is not in it. Instead, after acknowledging and dismissing 'the rocks anyone can throw at Hardy for romance and sentiment', Pound observes:

> Whether in a communist age we can, or will in our time be able to, concede such emphasis to the individual elegy and the personal sadness, I doubt. And if not? the transition may have been from literary to rhetorical.

'Communist' in that passage seems to refer to much more than the

Soviet Union. And if so, this is a betraying admission. Pound, for all his epic pretensions, is ready to think that in his lifetime the only true poetry will be elegiac, all else rhetoric. And indeed, the poetry that remained for him to write, like most of the poems he had written already, was to be poetry of 'the individual elegy and the personal sadness'. At least it is permissible to think so. And one does not thereby dismiss that poetry as of little worth, for the uncomfortable challenge of Hardy forces Pound in the end, after an exceptionally abject apology for obscurity, into formulating what would be the great and peculiar virtue of the Pisan and Rock-Drill cantos, as it had been of earlier work:

> I mean or imply that certain truth exists. Certain colours exist in nature though great painters have striven vainly, and though the colour film is not yet perfected. Truth is not untrue'd by reason of our failing to fix it on paper.

From 'A Song of the Degrees' in *Lustra* ('certain colours exist in nature') through to 'Le Paradis n'est pas artificiel' in the latest cantos, this is the burden of Pound's poetry at its most bracing and beautiful:

> Pull down thy vanity, it is not man
> Made courage, or made order, or made grace,
> Pull down thy vanity, I say pull down.
> (Canto 82)

'Le Paradis n'est pas artificiel', it is not man who made it.

'Paradise' is not altogether metaphorical, for *Guide to Kulchur* reveals, to many of Pound's readers if not for the first time to Pound himself, that he is a religious poet. On religion as on other matters Pound's observations veer disconcertingly between the superficial and the penetrating. On the one hand he spends many pages vindicating the Roman Catholic Church at its best against Protestantism, which latter, according to Pound, is a fundamentally usurious institution. These pages are most interesting when Pound argues, as in the Usura canto (45), that Protestant toleration of or complicity with usury infects not only its art but also its ethics and norms of conduct in the apparently unrelated field of sexual relations. But the discussion of religion becomes something better than sectarian in Chapter 17, where Pound deals (sympathetically on the whole) with Stoicism, in Chapter 39 under the head of 'Neo-Platonicks Etc.', and in Chapter 53, where Pound contends that 'our time has overshadowed the mysteries by an overemphasis on the individual' whereas 'Eleusis did not distort truth by exaggerating the individual', that 'only in the high air and the great clarity can there be a just estimation of values', that 'the Gods exist', and that 'a great treasure of verity exists for mankind in Ovid and in the subject matter of Ovid's long poem, and that only in this form could it be registered'. States of mystical exaltation 'exist in nature' (in human nature), as do, so Pound will believe, the metaphysical realities that are revealed to such states. It is notoriously difficult to embody these states and these realities in art, but this is no proof that they do not exist, for here too 'truth is not untrue'd by reason of our failing to fix it on paper'. And, in the event, Pound will rise time and again to the challenge of expressing these traditionally inexpressible experiences.

IX

The Fifth Decad of Cantos · The Chinese History Cantos ·
The Adams Cantos

It is not often observed that the art of sculpture, as traditionally
conceived, comprises two very different kinds of activity. Yeats
applauds Robert Gregory

> As he that practised or that understood
> All work in metal or in wood,
> In moulded plaster or in carven stone...

But the carving of stone and the moulding of plaster (or of clay, so
as later to make a bronze casting) are very different operations, and
profoundly different because the artist's way with his material rep-
resents in miniature his way of dealing with the whole material
world.

Some have thought that moulding and carving are not just diffe-
rent but antithetical. Adrian Stokes observed, in *The Stones of Rimini*:

> Today, and not before, do we commence to emerge from the
> Stone Age: that is to say, for the first time on so vast a scale
> throughout Europe does hewn stone give way to plastic mate-
> rials. An attitude to material, an attitude conceived... as being
> far more than the visual-aesthetic basis of Western civilization,
> can hardly survive long. The use in building of quarried stone
> must... increasingly diminish, and with it one nucleus of those
> dominant fantasies which have coloured the European percep-
> tion of the visual world. In the work of men, manufacture,
> the process of fashioning or moulding, supersedes, wherever
> it is possible, the process of enhancing or carving material, the
> process that imitates those gradual natural forces that vivify
> or destroy nature before our eyes (p.24).

And elsewhere Stokes elaborates:

In the two activities there lies a vast difference that symbolizes not only the main aspects of labour, but even the respective roles of male and female (p.110).

This last erotic analogy is several times pursued by Pound, nowhere more clearly and powerfully than in Canto 47:

> And the small stars now fall from the olive branch,
> Forked shadow falls dark on the terrace
> More black than the floating martin
>   that has no care for your presence,
> His wing-print is black on the roof tiles
> And the print is gone ·with his cry.
> So light is thy weight on Tellus
> Thy notch no deeper indented
> Thy weight less than the shadow
> Yet hast thou gnawed through the mountain,
>   Scilla's white teeth less sharp.
> Hast thou found a nest softer than cunnus
> Or hast thou found better rest
> Hast 'ou a deeper planting, doth thy death year
> Bring swifter shoot?
> Hast thou entered more deeply the mountain?

But, if the mountain is the female body ('By prong have I entered these hills'), it is also literally the mountain from which the sculptor quarries his marble block ('Yet hast thou gnawed through the mountain'), the quarrying being itself a sort of sculpture, a first stage in the carving. It is also ('Begin thy plowing... Think thus of thy plowing' – out of Hesiod in this same canto) the mountain that the farmer scores with his plough. And in *The Stones of Rimini* Adrian Stokes makes this analogy too: carving is not only like a man's way with a woman, it is also like a ploughman's way with the land. And let it not be thought that for Pound, any more than for Stokes, these analogies are fanciful; when Stokes speaks of 'fantasy' he means something as far as possible from free association – he means that in man's profoundest awareness of what he is doing, these actions are not just alike but identical. It seems clear that we should range with them that way of dealing with words which regards them, as Pound says, as 'consequences of things'; and with the other, the female role, the way of the modeller, that symbolist way with words which regards things, in the last analysis, as the consequences of the words that name them.

In Stokes's book on the Venetian use of colour, the analogous distinction in painting is between hue and tone; hue is the 'intrinsic' colour, tone that colour which is imparted to objects by the light as it strikes them this way or that, with this or that degree of intensity: and the distinctive achievement of Venetian painters, we are asked to think, lies in their attachment to hue as against tone. In Canto 52, an extremely beautiful redaction of the *Li Ki* or Chinese Book of Rites, Pound evokes in terms of ancient China a way of life that becomes ritual in its observance of the seasonable; and we learn, concerning one month in the year:

> The lake warden to gather rushes
>   to take grain for the *manes*
> to take grain for the beasts you will sacrifice
> to the Lords of the Mountains
>   To the Lords of great rivers
> Inspector of dye-works, inspector of colour and broideries
> see that the white, black, green be in order
> let no false colour exist here
> black, yellow, green be of quality

There is nothing arbitrary about introducing the inspector of dye-works. In an ideally good society his office, the keeping of colours true, is a crucial one. In the canto preceding this we have read:

> Usury rusts the man and his chisel
> It destroys the craftsman; destroying craft
> Azure is caught with cancer. Emerald comes to no Memling
> Usury kills the child in the womb
> And breaks short the young man's courting.

And this in turn has repeated Canto 45:

> Azure has a canker by usura; cramoisi is unbroidered
> Emerald findeth no Memling....

For that matter Pound years before, in 'A Song of the Degrees' from *Lustra*, had already ranged himself with hue against tone:

> I
> Rest me with Chinese colours,
> For I think the glass is evil.
>
> II
> The wind moves above the wheat –
> With a silver crashing,
> A thin war of metal.

I have known the golden disc,
I have seen it melting above me.
I have known the stone-bright place,
            The hall of clear colours.

III

O glass subtly evil, O confusion of colours!
O light bound and bent in, O soul of the captive,
Why am I warned? Why am I sent away?
Why is your glitter full of curious mistrust?
O glass subtle and cunning, O powdery gold!
O filaments of amber, two-faced iridescence!

For Pound, colour inheres in the coloured object, it is of its nature; just as the carved or hewn shape inheres in the stone block before it has been touched; just as words inhere in the natures they name, not in the minds that do the naming. Not in painting any more than in poetry will Pound agree that 'it all depends how you look at it'. Nature exists as other, bodied against us, with real attributes and her own laws which it is our duty to observe.

In Canto 46, 'The bank makes it *ex nihil*', associated with the name of William Paterson, chief founder of the Bank of England, reveals an imagination still in command of its material and giving to the distinction between carving and moulding, between stone and brick, a new slant that is totally unexpected and yet persuasive. For, as the carver strikes the block with his chisel, so the ploughman grooves the earth – in each case to draw out of nature the wealth that lies concealed in it. On the other hand, to mould a ball of clay in the hands is to draw no wealth out of that material, but to impose the wealth of significance upon it by an act of will; and this is like giving to paper money a value that is not inherent in the paper as paper. If the only reliable symbol of true wealth is the grain which the earth may be made to yield, a national currency can be a true register of wealth only when the amount of money in circulation corresponds to the wealth of the natural resources known to exist in that nation's lands and in the known aptitudes of its citizens. To create money out of nothing, in excess of natural wealth, to buy and sell money, to set money chasing after money – this is the way of the moulder and the brickmaker, not the way of stonemason and ploughman. And this is what Pound means by 'usura'.

The analogy holds, logically. Whether it can be seen at work chronologically – usurious practices in any economy reflected at once in decadence of artistic styles – this, which Pound seems to believe, is open to doubt. But at least it is not true, as is often believed, that Pound's conversion to the economics of Major C.H. Douglas and of Silvio Gesell represented a wholly new departure in his thought, which was accommodated in the *Cantos* only by distorting the emphases initially emergent and apparent; the economic doctrines arise, though unexpectedly all the more impressively, out of cardinal distinctions already made. And in Cantos 42 to 51 inclusive, which Pound called *The Fifth Decad of Cantos* (1937), the shaping hand is more than usually apparent. The measured and ominous condemnation of usury in Canto 45 has been much anthologized and much admired; but the case there stated has been argued through the three preceding cantos, which forbiddingly accumulate the necessary documentation. Our admiration and sympathy for Canto 45 is worthless because it is unscientific unless we see how the conclusions to be drawn arise unavoidably from the case in point there documented from Tuscan history – the case of the reforms instituted by Leopold, Grand Duke of Tuscany from 1765 to 1790. Righteous indignation is worse than worthless, it is a vicious self-indulgence, unless it is indeed 'righteous', unless we have earned the right to it. And so after Canto 45 the reader is forced back into the circles of Pound's hell, the snapping and snarling contradictory voices of recorded history, before in Canto 51 he has once again earned the right to join in with measured condemnation. The second immersion, as it happens, is less painful than the first, for the accidental reason that on the second time round the evidence is accumulated also from virtually unrecorded history, from the prehistory of the Mediterranean basin (Canto 47) and of ancient China (Canto 49). The evidence that reaches us, accordingly, is in the singing voice of the poet rather than the dry or snappish voice of the chronicler and diplomat.

Cantos 53 to 61 inclusive, which Pound was working at in the late 1930s, comprise the so-called Chinese History cantos, in which the most fervent of Pound's apologists have found little good. Pound's principal source for these cantos is the *Histoire générale de la Chine, ou Annales de cet empire*, traduites... par... Père Joseph-Anne-Marie de Moyriac de Mailla,[1] though Canto 56 draws also on two poems by Li Po, and elsewhere, for instance in Canto 59, there are quotations from the Latin of another Jesuit sinologist of the French

1 In 12 volumes (Paris, 1777–83).

Enlightenment, Père Lacharme.[1] In the seven lines quoted from
Lacharme in Canto 59 (they contain a phrase, *libidinis expers*, to be
quoted often in subsequent cantos), there are no less than three errors
of transcription.[2] And this is not the only evidence of extraordinary
heedlessness in these pages. To work through some of them with
Mailla's *Histoire générale* at hand is to realize how thoroughly depen-
dent Pound is on this source; but the poet's decisions about what to
take from Mailla, and what to leave behind, seem wholly arbitrary.
In Canto 53, for instance, out of the many details that Mailla gives
about the prehistoric ruler Hoang Ti, Pound chooses to emphasize
that Hoang Ti learned and taught brick-making – and we prick up
our ears. For, in line with Adrian Stokes's distinction, whereas build-
ing with stone is a case of 'carving', building with brick is a case of
the other, plastic principle, moulding or modelling; and so, in
Pound's scheme of things as it has developed to this point, the inven-
tion of brick should appear an acquisition of dubious value. Sure
enough, in a later canto, Canto 76, when Pound writes of 'bricks
thought into being ex nihil', the reference is disapproving. There
appears to be no disapproval of Hoang Ti, however. This might
not matter if the Chinese History cantos were offered as simple
narrative chronicle, in which no judgments are passed. But in fact
the non-Confucian (Buddhist and Taoist) influences on Chinese his-
tory are consistently condemned in strident language ('taozers',
'shave-heads') that recalls fisticuffs in the schoolyard and brutal and
contemptible rabble-rousing. There is no alternative to writing off
this whole section of Pound's poem as pathological and sterile.

The John Adams cantos, Cantos 62-71, are composed in the same
way as the Chinese History cantos that precede them. In favour of
the later sequence it can be said that there is more point, for most
readers, in being made to read the works of John Adams, second
President of the United States,[3] than in consulting the *Histoire générale
de la Chine*. And, indeed, Pound's pedagogical purpose is constant:
undoubtedly part of his intention in writing these cantos was to find
readers for an author who, on literary no less than historical grounds,
deserves to be read closely and often – and not just by Americans.
But even if such a pedagogical intention is legitimate in poetry (as

1 *Confucii Chi-King sive Liber Carminum*, ex latine P. Lacharme inter-
pretationis edidit Julius Mohl (Stuttgartiae & Tubingae Sumptibus J.C. Cot-
tae, 1930).
2 See Achilles Fang, in *Harvard Journal of Asiatic Studies*, 20 (1957), 213-38.
3 *The Works of John Adams*, ed. Charles Francis Adams, 10 vols. (Boston,
1850-57).

no doubt it is), it can hardly be by itself a *sufficient* reason for poetry, least of all for ten whole cantos, even in a poem on such a massive scale as this one.

Does Pound, then, do nothing by way of modifying or recreating the material that he borrows? Very occasionally he does something. For instance, in Canto 64:

SUBILLAM

> Cumis ego occulis meis
> sleeping under a window: pray for me,
> withered to skin and nerves *tu theleis* respondebat illa
> *apothanein*; pray for me gentlemen
> my prayers used to be answered, She prayed for deliverance
> 110 years of age, and some say she is over that

The tags of Greek and Latin which here juxtapose the Cumaean sybil with an old woman in New England certainly modify an anecdote from Adams's diary. But it would be wrong to say that Pound universalizes the anecdote, for the universality is in the humanity that Pound's mythopoeic treatment tends to diminish. John Adams's unaffected prose is more aghast and more compassionate, and this makes it more universal:

> Stopped at James Sullivan's, at Biddeford, and drank punch; dinned at Allen's, a tavern at the bridge. After dinner, Farnham, Winthrop, Sewall, Sullivan, and I, walked a quarter of a mile down the river to see one Poke, a woman at least one hundred and ten years of age, some say one hundred and fifteen. When we came to the house, nobody was at home but the old woman, and she lay in bed asleep under the window, We looked in at the window and saw an object of horror; – strong muscles withered and wrinkled to a degree that I never saw before. After some time her daughter came from a neighbor's house, and we went in. The old woman roused herself, and looked round very composedly upon us, without saying a word. The daughter told her, 'here is a number of gentlemen come to see you'. 'Gentlemen,' says the old antediluvian, 'I am glad to see them; I want them to pray for me; my prayers, I fear, are not answered; I used to think my prayers were answered, but of late I think they are not; I have been praying so long for deliverance; – Oh, living God, come in mercy! Lord Jesus, come in mercy! Sweet Christ, come in mercy! I used to have comfort in God, and set a good example; but I fear, etc.'
> Her mouth was full of large, ragged teeth, and her daughter

says, since she was one hundred years old, she had two new double teeth come out. Her hair is white as snow, but there is a large quantity of it on her head; her arms are nothing but bones covered over with a withered, wrinkled skin and nerves; in short, any person will be convinced, from the sight of her, that she is as old as they say, at least. She told us she was born in Ireland, within a mile of Derry; came here in the reign of King William. She remembers the reign of King Charles II, James II, William and Mary; she remembers King James's wars, etc. but has got quite lost about her age. Her daughter asked her how old she was? She said, 'upwards of threescore, but she could not tell'. (*Works*, II, 244-5.)

The most one can say for Pound's redaction is that it is, in its different way, equal to the original; and perhaps one cannot say even so much. Certainly for the most part one cannot; Pound's cuts and compressions and juxtapositions make a nonsensical hurly-burly of Adams's life, a life that was harried indeed but admirably purposeful. Adams's politicking was not senseless and desperate, like Sigismundo Malatesta's. And indeed Pound knows this. Yet his method, ruinously wasteful and repeatedly arbitrary, blurs all distinctions. An example is some lines from Canto 71 (they begin, 'I am a church-going animal'), which juxtapose snippets from an admirable letter written by Adams at the end of his life to Benjamin Rush (*Works*, IX, 635-40); the lines are pointless unless one realizes that Adams, refusing to comply with Rush's suggestion that he compose a posthumous testament to the nation, is giving examples of how malice would misconstrue any recommendations he might make. Thus Pound's redaction fails even in its intention of sending the reader to Adams's works; for Adams is far more lively, interesting, and consistent than the Adams cantos suggest. Above all Adams is more humane. Irascible and impulsive as he was, his judgments on his opponents, such as Hutchinson or Dickinson (Pound misspells the name), show up Pound's shrill interjections ('Hutchinson undoubtedly scrofulous' – Canto 64) for the infinitely dangerous simplifications of a political naïf, to whom politics appears in the black and white of abstractions. The poetic method presses to its limit the notion that all truth is in particulars; the mind behind the method is thinking in the abstract.

Cantos 52 to 71 were published early in 1940, and William Vasse, who has usefully tabulated all their numerous misspellings and apparent errors of transcription, says indulgently, 'Many are of the kind to suggest a typographical error, not caught in the proofreading, perhaps because of the rush and uncertainty of things at that time'.[1] An essay that Pound published in 1937[2] is far more illuminating than his poetry is, about how his enthusiasm for Adams and Jefferson fits in with his other enthusiasms. It does not fit very well. In the essay an extraordinary muddle supervenes as soon as Pound, having 'placed' Adams and Jefferson as heirs of the Encyclopedists, finds that in his scheme of European or world culture the Encyclopedists do not rank high; certainly not so high as he wants to rank Jefferson and Adams:

> Can we not say that the mental integrity of the Encyclopedists dwindled into bare intellect by dropping that *ethical* simplicity which makes the canonists, *any* canonist, so much more 'modern', so much more scientific than any eighteenth century 'intellectual'?

'The Encyclopedists' is one thing; 'any eighteenth century intellectual' is another. Is there no ethical simplicity in Doctor Johnson, for instance? The question is to the point, for, although John Adams could not be expected to sympathize with Johnson, the author of 'Taxation No Tyranny', yet in general Adams appeals to British precedents and British authorities and to the model of the British Constitution; and his distrust of French authorities, like the Encyclopedists, was what distinguished him most sharply from Jefferson.[3] Yet Pound says, of Jefferson and Adams alike, 'Their sanity and civilization, their varied culture and omnivorous curiosity stem from the encyclopedists. . . .' So far as Adams is concerned, this seems to be just not true.

For Pound the eighteenth century had always been a French century, almost exclusively. This appears to have come about through the influence of Gourmont, yet there was a deeper reason for it. For only in French was the century seen as the *siècle des lumiéres*, in terms of that metaphor from light that Pound had found likewise at the centre of Confucian thought, and of the thought of Dante and Cavalcanti, Richard of Saint Victor and Scotus Erigena. This is why he compares the Encyclopedists with 'the canonists' and decides that in the Encyclopedists the metaphor from light, though it persisted, was no longer taken in all seriousness:

1 'American History and the Cantos', *The Pound Newsletter*, 5 (Jan. 1955). Mr Vasse is far more generous to the Adams cantos than I can be.
2 'The Jefferson-Adams Correspondence', *North American Review*, 244 (Dec. 1937), 314-24.
3 See Z. Haraszti, *John Adams and the Prophets of Progress* (Cambridge, Mass., 1952).

They are brilliant. Bayle is robust with the heritage of Rabelais and Brantome, Voltaire a bit finer, down almost to silver point. But the idea and/or habit of gradations of value, and the infinitely more vital custom of digging down into principles gradually fade out of the picture. The degrees of light and motion, the whole metaphoric richness begin to perish. From a musical concept of man they dwindle downward to a mathematical concept. . . .[1]

But if the Encyclopedists can thus be found wanting, what of Jefferson and Adams whom Pound has agreed to regard as the Encyclopedists' transplanted heirs? In 1937 he extricates himself by asserting boldly that these American Founding Fathers had all the Encyclopedists' virtues but not their vices, having on the contrary a substantiality in their thought that goes back (he dares to think) to Aquinas:

> Their sanity and civilization, their varied culture and omnivorous curiosity stem from the encyclopedists, but they are not accompanied by the thinning, the impoverishment of mental life, which lack of structural order was to produce in a few decades.

But in a curiously modified version of this essay, which was published in 1960,[2] the emphasis is subtly different:

> The sanity and civilization of Adams-Jefferson stems from the Encyclopedists. You find in their letters a varied culture, and an omnivorous (or apparently so) curiosity. And yet the thinning, the impoverishment of mental life shows in the decades after their death, and not, I think, without cause.

Wise after the event – after, that is, the Second World War, in which Pound rested on Adams and Jefferson his conviction that he acted as an American patriot in broadcasting from Rome – Pound is prepared to think that, from the Encyclopedists or elsewhere, the canker was already in the rose, even in 1776. 'Omnivorous (or apparently so) . . .', 'and not, I think, without cause' – these are the saving clauses that make the point.

1 'The Jefferson-Adams Correspondence', *North American Review*, 244 (Dec. 1937), pp.314–24.
2 *Impact: Essays on Ignorance and the Decline of American Civilization*, edited by Noel Stock (Chicago, 1960).

In any case there was from the first a contradiction in Pound's thought, that made his eighteenth-century enthusiasms, however true to his natural temperament, anomalous in his conscious thought. It was a contradiction inherited from Gourmont. For in Gourmont and Pound alike the eighteenth-century enthusiasms cannot be squared with their enthusiasm for Flaubert and behind him for Stendhal, for 'realism' as understood by the nineteenth-century novelists, with its faith in the particular. Eighteenth-century theory (the theory much more than the practice) was, on the contrary, whether in France or in Britain, contemptuous of particulars unless they could be marshalled and abstracted into generalized maxims. And when Pound considers an English poem of the eighteenth century, Johnson's 'Vanity of Human Wishes', in some engaging and sensible pages of his *Guide to Kulchur*,[1] it is consistently enough Stendhal's strictures on eighteenth-century poetry that prevent Pound from accepting Eliot's claims for Johnson's poem. But in the essay on Adams and Jefferson, though there is a worried acknowledgment of nineteenth-century realism ('The whole gist of Flaubert was a fight against maxims, against abstractions...'), Pound cannot bring himself to press home the damaging implications of this for the case he is arguing. Indeed, how could he? For Confucius too delivers himself of maxims, though in his translations, particularly of the Analects, Pound was to go to all lengths to obscure the fact.

1 Pp.179-81, 183-4, 193.

X

The Pisan Cantos

In an interesting passage from *Modern Painters* (vol. IV, ch. xx) Ruskin speaks of 'the kind of admiration with which a southern artist regarded the *stone* he worked in; and the pride which populace or priest took in the possession of precious mountain substance, worked into the pavements of their cathedrals, and the shafts of their tombs'. Thus to regard the worked stone as 'mountain substance', and to assert that the Italians thus regarded it, is to move at once into the area of interest of Adrian Stokes and of Canto 17. And it is significant that to illustrate his point Ruskin quotes aptly from 'The Bishop Orders His Tomb in St. Praxed's Church' by the poet, Browning, whom Pound has never ceased to honour as one of his first masters -- 'pourquoi nier son père?' Taking into account some of Pound's even less fashionable allegiances, for example, to Ford Madox Ford and to Whistler, it would not be hard to trace for him a direct line of descent from Ruskin.

But this is hardly worth doing where the affinities are in any case so many and so clear. G.S. Fraser, for instance, considering Pound's position as a thinker about society, very justly sees it as Ruskinian:

> 'By their fruits ye shall know them'. There must be something right about the society that produces Chartres and something wrong that produces, say London south of the river. Men like Adams and Jefferson respect the arts, but they are not in Mauberley's sense 'aesthetes', and indeed throughout *The Cantos* Pound seems to be moving away from Mauberley's still faintly ninetyish attitude towards one more like Ruskin's in *Unto this Last*; it must be good men, in a good society, who build a good cathedral.[1]

Rather plainly Fraser feels that the relationship between healthy art and healthy society is somehow more complicated than this. And one may agree with him, while still applauding both Pound and

---

1 G.S. Fraser, *Vision and Rhetoric* (London, 1959), pp.90-91.

Ruskin for asserting that *some* connection there must be, and a close one, too. This is the less satisfactory side of Ruskin, just as, in the long run, it is the frightening and repellent side of Pound. Both men, who are very wise about trees and swans, mountains and skies and clouds, wasps and ants ('And now the ants seem to stagger / as the dawn sun has trapped their shadows' – Canto 83), and about buildings and paintings and bas-reliefs, become rather dangerously unwise – in particular, unwisely too sure of themselves – when they move, as they are right to do, to regarding the conduct of men in societies. This tragic discontinuity runs, perhaps, through the whole Ruskinian tradition; Gerard Manley Hopkins, for instance, who belongs in this tradition, is much less wise about bugler-boys than he is about highland burns and windhovers.

But in the much more persuasive matter of how they regard the world of natural beings and the world of human artifacts, Ruskin and Pound represent, each in his own period, a traditional wisdom much older than nineteenth-century romanticism. Mr Fraser goes on:

> The odd thing is that in religion Pound is a kind of eighteenth-century deist (one of his literary heroes, and an oddly assorted set they are, is Voltaire), and there must be a sense in which the cathedral, and the whole outer fabric of mediaeval life that he loves so passionately, is nothing for him but an adorable mockery or a beautiful empty shell. Critics have noted, and very rightly, the new and very moving note of religious humility in 'Pull down thy vanity' passage in the *Pisan Cantos*; but none of them have noted that the divinity not exactly invoked but hinted at here – the deity that sheathes a blade of grass more elegantly than a Parisian dressmaker sheathes a beautiful woman – is just the divinity of the Deists: Nature, or Nature's God, it hardly matters which one calls it, for it is just enough of a God to keep Nature running smoothly....
>
> (*Vision and Rhetoric*, p.91)

It was Yeats who in the 1920s struck off, in a brilliant phrase already quoted, this sympathy for the eighteenth century which is constant with Pound:

> Ezra Pound arrived the other day, ... and being warned by his wife tried to be very peaceable but couldn't help being very litigious about Confucius who I consider should have worn an Eighteenth Century wig and preached in St. Paul's, and he thinks the perfect man.[1]

1 *The Letters of W.B. Yeats*, ed. Allan Wade (New York, 1955), p.774.

Chinese thought, pre-eminently Confucian thought, was introduced to the West by representatives of the European Enlightenment, and Pound is devoted to it as were those earliest translators; partly what Pound does with it is to read back into ancient Chinese an Enlightenment scheme of things. Similarly Jefferson, together with the whole American culture that he and other Founding Fathers stand for in the *Cantos*, is for Pound an Enlightenment product; Jefferson's personality and way of life exemplify the ideals of a Goldsmith or a Montesquieu. What is more, Pound's whole philosophy of history is in the strictest sense 'Augustan'; that is to say, like Pope and Swift (but not Addison) he sees the course of human history in terms of prolonged 'dark ages' interrupted by tragically brief luminous islands of achieved civilization, for which the Rome of Augustus stands as the type. (Pound's very marked preference for the Roman as against the Greek culture is another aspect of his Augustanism). Like Pope at the end of the *Dunciad*, Pound has written and acted as if the precarious islands of achieved civility were maintained only by unremitting vigilance on the part of a tiny minority, typically a group of friends, who must continually (and in the end, always vainly) stop up the holes in the dikes against which the sea of human stupidity, anarchy, and barbarism washes incessantly. In fact, if Pound's loyalty to the Enlightenment is taken seriously, most (though not all) of his other interests and commitments fall into a rationally coherent, massive, and impressive pattern; and his 'literary heroes' will appear to be much less of 'an oddly assorted set'.

His mediaevalism, and also that element in him that may be called 'Ruskinian', look rather different if related to a prime controlling sympathy with the Enlightenment. Fraser, for instance, is very just and perceptive about the passage he refers to from Canto 81:

> The ant's a centaur in his dragon world.
> Pull down thy vanity, it is not man
> Made courage, or made order, or made grace,
>   Pull down thy vanity, I say pull down.
> Learn of the green world what can be thy place
> In scaled invention or true artistry,
> Pull down thy vanity,
>   Paquin pull down!
> The green casque has outdone your elegance.

The feeling and import of this is indeed, as Fraser suggests, very close to Pope's:

> Far as Creation's ample range extends,
> The scale of sensual, mental pow'rs ascends:

> Mark how it mounts, to Man's imperial race,
> From the green myriads in the peopled grass:
> What modes of sight betwixt each wide extreme,
> The mole's dim curtain, and the lynx's beam:
> Of smell, the headlong lioness between,
> And hound sagacious on the tainted green:
> Of hearing, from the life that fills the flood,
> To that which warbles thro' the vernal wood:
> The spider's touch, how exquisitely fine!
> Feels at each thread, and lives along the line:...

'The ant's a centaur in his dragon world' is as near as Pound chooses to come to what interests Pope centrally, the idea of a ladder and of the Great Chain of Being with never a link missing. Faithful to his manifesto in *Gaudier-Brzeska*, and along with Hopkins and Ruskin, Pound's attention has shifted somewhat from this grand design to the tight 'designs' achieved on a smaller scale, which the natural world throws up momentarily and incessantly. All the same, Nature is still seen primarily as a designer, and for just this reason is wittily described as a 'couturier' in Canto 80:

> as the young lizard extends his leopard spots
>   along the grass-blade seeking the green midge half an ant-size
>
> and the Serpentine will look just the same
> and the gulls be as neat on the pond
> and the sunken garden unchanged
> and God knows what else is left of our London
>   my London, your London
> and if her green elegance
>   remains on this side of my rain ditch
>   puss lizard will lunch on some other T-bone
>
> sunset grand couturier.

It is easy in fact to be so aware of the difference between Pope on the one hand, Ruskin and Hopkins on the other, as to miss the essential identity of their concerns. This is true at least of the Pope of the *Essay on Man*. It was the *Essay on Man* that prompted Ruskin to write of 'the serene and just benevolence which placed Pope, in his theology, two centuries in advance of his time'.[1] And it was Ruskin who memorably clinched and explained the difference

1 John Ruskin, *Lectures on Art* (Oxford, 1870), para. 70.

between his interest in nature, and Pope's: 'exactly in proportion as the idea of definite spiritual presence in material nature was lost, the mysterious sense of unaccountable life in the things themselves would be increased'.[1] As the conviction of an abiding Presence is lost, so the observer expects all the more urgently 'presences'. Pound manifests this loss of faith, as do Hopkins and Ruskin and, for that matter, Wordsworth. Nevertheless, the essential similarity with Pope remains, between 'the green midge half an ant-size' and 'the green myriads in the peopled grass'. These perceptions are possible only in an attitude of humility about the place of the human in relation to the non-human creation. And it was the shock of Pound's appalling predicament in the American prison-camp in 1945, awaiting trial for treason, that restored to him this humility, after the steady crescendo of raucous arrogance through the Chinese History and American History cantos of the years before.

It may be said that W.B. Yeats shares with the symbolist poets, and with a poet squarely in their tradition, such as T.S. Eliot, an imperious, appropriating attitude toward the perceived world. When swans get into Yeats's verse, the swan loses all its swanliness except what it needs to symbolize something in the person who observes it: 'Another emblem there!' And the poet at the end of 'Coole Park and Ballylee' says explicitly that this is also what has happened to Lady Gregory. Similarly, Frank Kermode has demonstrated how far 'In Memory of Major Robert Gregory' is concerned with Major Gregory, much less for what he is or was in himself than for what the poet chooses to make him stand for in his (the poet's) private pantheon. It is for this reason, to give an example, that Gregory's activities as a landscape painter are made so salient – so that Yeats may applaud this imperious attitude to the natural world at just the point where it would seem least likely, in landscape painting:

> We dreamed that a great painter had been born
> To cold Clare rock and Galway rock and thorn,
> To that stern colour and that delicate line
> That are our secret discipline
> Wherein the gazing heart doubles her might.

We attend to natural landscape, not for the sake of delighting in it, nor for what it may tell us of supernatural purpose or design, but

---

1 Quoted by Maynard Mack, Introduction to *An Essay on Man* (Twickenham Edition of the Poems of Pope, Vol. III-i), p.lxxv – where the context is immediately apposite and illuminating.

so that the imperious personality, seeing itself there reflected, may become the more conscious of its own power – 'the gazing heart doubles her might'. As Marion Witt was first to show, Yeats intends here to relate Gregory's practice as a landscape painter with that of Samuel Palmer and Edward Calvert, the nineteenth-century artists who, true to the Blakean tradition, which was Yeats's tradition also, reject the discipline that is the scientist's as much as the artist's, exact and intent observation, setting up instead the discipline of the visionary, who sees through the perceivable to what lies beyond.

This is a matter not of mutually exclusive categories but only of where the emphasis characteristically falls. For examples of vivid and exact observation can, of course, be found in Yeats the visionary; and conversely Ezra Pound, who characteristically sees scientific observation as not at all at odds with the poet's kind of attention, also shows himself sympathetic to the Platonist John Heydon ('Secretary of Nature, J. Heydon', in Canto 91) who attends to natural appearances only so as to read them as 'signatures' of the realm of essence. The point is best made, therefore, by quotation from Canto 83:

> and Brother Wasp is building a very neat house
> of four rooms, one shaped like a squat indian bottle
> La vespa, *la* vespa, mud, swallow system
> So that dreaming of Bracelonde and of Perugia
> and the great fountain in the Piazza
> or of old Bulagaio's cat that with a well timed leap
> could turn the lever-shaped door handle
> It comes over me that Mr. Walls must be a ten-strike
> with the signorinas
> and in the warmth after chill sunrise
> an infant, green as new grass,
> has stuck its head or tip
> out of Madame La Vespa's bottle
>
> mint springs up again
> in spite of Jones' rodents
> as had the clover by the gorilla cage
> with a four-leaf
>
> When the mind swings by a grass-blade
> an ant's forefoot shall save you
> the clover leaf smells and tastes as its flower
>
> The infant has descended
> from mud on the tent roof to Tellus,

like to like colour he goes amid grass-blades
     greeting them that dwell under ΧΤΗΟΝΟΣ ΧΘΟΝΟΣ
ΟΙ ΧΘΟΝΙΟΙ; to carry our news
     εἰς χθονίους to them that dwell under the earth,
begotten of air, that shall sing in the bower
     of Kore   Περσεφόνεια
and have speech with Tiresias, Thebae

If we say that neither Yeats nor Eliot could have written this passage, we should have in mind, not in the first place any question of poetic method or strategy, but the quality of the sensibility, the sort of attitude and attention to the natural world, that is here displayed. It is not helpful to recall Wordsworth and 'a heart / That watches and receives', for this sort of contemplation is as much an active partici- pation of the mind as are the more imperious operations of a Yeats.[1] One is reminded rather of passages in Coleridge's and Ruskin's notebooks, in some of the letters of Keats, in the essays and poems of D.H. Lawrence, above all in the writings of Hopkins. In fact, what lies behind a passage such as this (and they occur throughout the *Cantos*, though seldom at such length) is an attitude of mind that is incompatible with the symbolist poet's liberation of himself from the laws of time and space as those operate in the observable world. In order to achieve that liberation the poet had to forego any hope or conviction that the world outside was meaningful precisely insofar as it existed in its own right, something other than himself and bodied against him. There is all the difference in the world between identifying a swan with one's self, and identifying one's self with a swan. It may be the difference between Shelley's 'Ode to a Skylark' (where the lark is important because it is identified with Shelley) and a famous letter by Keats in which he identifies himself with a sparrow (where the sparrow is important because Keats can identify himself with it, and so explore an order of being other than his own). Pound identifies himself with the baby wasp as Keats with the sparrow. The wasp burrows into the earth to greet the chthonic powers of under-earth, just as Odysseus, in the *Odyssey* and time and again in the *Cantos*, must descend to the underworld to consult the Theban sage Tiresias. But at no point in the passage – not even if we remember how important for Pound, as for Lawrence, is such encountering of the chthonic powers of the loins and the libido – at

---

1 Such reliance on the special Wordsworthian case tends to blunt the point of an otherwise admirably penetrating essay by Peter Ure, 'Yeats's "Demon and Beast",' in *Irish Writing* (Dublin, 1955), which makes very much the point about Yeats that I have sought to make.

no point does the wasp become a symbol for something in Pound's predicament, or for his ethical or other programmes, or for his personality. The wasp retains its otherness as an independent form of life; it is only by doing so that it can be a source of comfort to the human observer:

> When the mind swings by a grass-blade
> an ant's forefoot shall save you

For, only if the ant is outside the human mind, can it, as we say, 'take us out of ourselves' when we observe it and try to enter into its life. This quality of tenderness, and this capacity for sympathetic identification with inhuman forms of life, make up an attitude of reverent vigilance before the natural world, an attitude which, if it is no longer the attitude of the physicist, is still surely the habit of the biologist, in the field and the laboratory alike.

These are not the terms in which Pound is usually considered, partly because these are not the terms in which he talks of himself; nor is this lineage – Coleridge, Keats, Ruskin, Hopkins – the sort of family tree that Pound draws up for himself. Moreover, it is taken for granted that, if Pound has any claim on our attention at all, it is for what he has in common with Yeats and Eliot, not for that in him which distinguishes him from his old allies, whose names are so much more respectable. Yet it should be clear that if this sort of attention is not to be found in Yeats, it is unthinkable in Eliot, as in any man whose main interest in the external world is as a repertoire of objective correlatives for his own states of mind. *Old Possum's Book of Practical Cats*, for instance, is Eliot's one venture into light verse; and the assumption behind it, that cats cannot be taken seriously in poetry, seems arbitrary when set beside the seriousness on just this subject of Christopher Smart, for instance, or Baudelaire. Pound's cat, 'Old Bulagaio's cat that with a well-timed leap / could turn the lever-shaped door handle' ('lever-shaped' – the exact observation anticipating the natural question, 'how?') is more alive, more of a cat, than any of Eliot's.

Almost from the first, sure enough, Pound has defined his poetry as radically opposed to symbolist poetry. He confesses to having learned from Laforgue and from Corbière, still more from Rimbaud; but these poets he obviously does not regard as 'symbolist'. He claims to have learned much more from the non-symbolist Théophile Gautier than even from Rimbaud – a claim that J.J. Espey, in his book on *Hugh Selwyn Mauberley*, shows to be well-founded. Pound puts it on record 'que les poètes *essentials* [as texts for English poets to study] se réduisent à Gautier, Corbière, Laforgue, Rimbaud.

Que depuis Rimbaud, aucun poète en France n'a inventé rien de
fondamental'.[1] In 1918 he writes that 'Mallarmé, perhaps unread, is
apt to be sightly overestimated...'[2] and that 'Imagisme is not sym-
bolism. The symbolists dealt in "association", that is, in a sort of
allusion, almost of allegory. They degraded the symbol to the status
of a word....' 'Moreover', he says, writing in the period of the First
World War, 'one does not want to be called a symbolist, because
symbolism has usually been associated with mushy technique'.
(*Gaudier-Brzeska*, p.97.)

Yeats and Pound were close and constant friends, and some of
Pound's remarks on symbolism are beside the point because, like
many people since, he takes Yeats as a typical symbolist; and this is
far from the truth. In the Pisan Canto 83 there are two passages on
Yeats. One of them, which follows almost immediately the page of
sympathetic identifications with the baby wasp, is Pound's hilarious
account of the life at Stone Cottage, Coleman's Hatch, Sussex, where
Yeats and Pound lived together at several periods between 1913 and
1916:

> There is fatigue deep as the grave.
> The Kakemono grows in flat land out of mist
>   sun rises lop-sided over the mountain
>   so that I recalled the noise in the chimney
> as it were the wind in the chimney
>   but was in reality Uncle William
> downstairs composing
> that had made a great Peeeacock
>   in the proide ov his oiye
>   had made a great peeeeeeecock in the...
> made a great peacock
>   in the proide of his oyyee
>
> proide ov his oy-ee
> as indeed he had, and perdurable
>
> a great peacock aere perennius
>   or as in the advice to the young man to
> breed and get married (or not)
>   as you choose to regard it

1 *Letters*, p.293 (letter to René Taupin, 1928) ... that the essential poets [as
texts for English poets to study] come down to Gautier, Corbière, Laforgue,
Rimbaud. That since Rimbaud no poet in France has invented anything
fundamental.
2 'French Poets', *The Little Review* (Feb. 1918); reprinted in *Make It New*
(1934), p.161.

at Stone Cottage in Sussex by the waste moor
(or whatever) and the holly bush
    who would not eat ham for dinner
because peasants eat ham for dinner
    despite the excellent quality
and the pleasure of having it hot

    well those days are gone forever
        and the travelling rug with the coon-skin tabs
and his hearing nearly all Wordsworth
    for the sake of his conscience but
preferring Ennemosor on Witches

did we ever get to the end of Doughty:
    The Dawn in Britain?
                  perhaps not
  (Summons withdrawn, sir.)
(bein' aliens in prohibited area)
clouds lift their small mountains
    before the elder hills

The fineness of this is identical with the fineness of the passage on
the wasp. The whole man, Yeats, is carried before us; we delight,
as the poet has delighted, in his alien mode of being. His foibles,
recorded with affectionate and amused indulgence – his way of *keen-
ing* rather than reading poetry, his 'Gothick' interests ('preferring
Ennemosor on Witches'), his preposterous snobbery ('because peas-
ants eat ham for dinner') – do not in the least detract from, they
only substantiate, the perception of his greatness. Out of this person-
ality, with all its quirky eccentricities, comes something in the splen-
did Horatian phrase 'aere perennius', more lasting than bronze, equal
in its achieved conclusiveness to the metal singing-bird of Yeats's
own 'Byzantium' and to those sonnets by Shakespeare ('the advice
to the young man to / breed and get married'), where Shakespeare
himself makes the proud Horatian claim,

    Not marble, nor gilded monuments
    Of princes, shall outlive this powerful rhyme;

It should be plain that this is very far indeed, in human terms, from
Yeats's treatment of the Gregories, the Pollexfens, John O'Leary,
Lionel Johnson, John Synge. It manifests a respect for the uniqueness
and otherness of the other person, a flexibility of feeling incompatible
with the Yeatsian private pantheon and his deliberately noble style,

even in such a splendid poem as 'The Municipal Gallery Revisited'.

The other passage on Yeats in Canto 83 is shorter, but more immediately apposite, for it considers Yeats specifically as a symbolist, and at this point not unfairly:

> Le Paradis n'est pas artificiel
> and Uncle William dawdling around Notre Dame
> in search of whatever
>   paused to admire the symbol
> with Notre Dame standing inside it
> Whereas in St Etienne
>   or why not Dei Miracoli:
> mermaids, that carving,
>
>   in the drenched tent there is quiet
>   sered eyes are at rest

'Le Paradis Artificiel' is the title of a book by Baudelaire about drugs and the beatific hallucinations they induce. Pound's rejection of the assumption behind it sounds as one of the strongest of many refrains that knit the later cantos together; it reappears, for instance, in an especially moving way in the Rock-Drill Canto 92. Pound's repeated assertion that the paradisal is *real*, out there in the real world, is a conscious challenge to the whole symbolist aesthetic. Hugh Kenner's gloss on this passage makes the essential point: 'Yeats' incorrigibly symbologizing mind infected much of his verse with significance imposed on materials by an effort of will ("artificiel")....'[1] Yeats can see Notre Dame as an artifact, a presence created in masonry and sculpture, only inside the symbol, only for the sake of what it answers to in him, not for what it is in itself. He must always arrange the perspective, and project upon the object the significance he can then read out of it. For Pound, to whom, ever since his friendship with Gaudier-Brzeska, cut and worked stone has been an especially fruitful source of presences and inscapes, this attitude is intolerable. Only when he sees stone in and for itself, the artist's working of it only a drawing out of what was latent in the stone to begin with – only then, as in the sculptures of S. Maria dei Miracoli in Venice, can it save him as the ant's forefoot could save him. Only by contemplating it thus can the 'sered eyes' (both 'seared' and 'fallen into the sere, the yellow leaf') come to be 'at rest'.

---

1 Hugh Kenner, *The Poetry of Ezra Pound* (London, 1951), p.210.

XI

Confucius

Among the papers of Fenollosa that his widow gave to Pound in 1913 was the text of a Confucian classic variously entitled, by English and French translators, 'The Doctrine of the Mean', 'Juste Milieu', 'L'Invariable Milieu', 'The Golden Medium'.[1] By 1937, Pound was calling it 'Standing Fast in the Middle'.[2] But the title he found for it when he translated it, nearly forty years after it came into his hands, was 'The Unwobbling Pivot'.[3] This work is grouped by the Chinese along with the Analects, with the work known simply as 'Mencius', and with another called *Ta Hio*, 'The Great Learning': these are 'The Four Books', which constitute an introductory course in Confucianism preparing the student for the more exacting study of other ancient scriptures called 'The Five Classics'. Pound has made formal translations of the Analects and of 'The Great Learning' (which he calls 'The Great Digest'), as well as 'The Unwobbling Pivot'. And his cantos contain extended translations, by Pound or adapted by him from others, out of Mencius and also out of the Five Classics.

Only one of these works at most, 'The Great Learning', can be regarded as the literary composition of Confucius himself, and that one only partially. His part in the Five Classics seems to have been that of a compiler or editor for the most part. As for the Four Books, the Analects were compiled by Confucius's disciples, or by the disciples of those disciples, out of anecdotes by and about the Master and sayings handed down as having come from him; the 'Mencius' records the sayings and doings of the most illustrious of Confucius's disciples, born in 372 B.C., more than a century after Confucius

1 See, on how the text came to Pound from Fenollosa, Pound's Dedication to Amiya Chakravarty, in *The Unwobbling Pivot & The Great Digest Translated by Ezra Pound* (Calcutta, 1949).

2 *The Letters of Ezra Pound, 1907-1941*, ed. D.D. Paige (London, 1951), p.384.

3 *Confucius: The Unwobbling Pivot and the Great Digest* (Norfolk, Conn., 1947). A translation into Italian had appeared in Venice in 1945.

died; 'The Great Learning' credits Confucius with only the seven paragraphs of the first chapter, the nine further chapters being commentary by a disciple; while 'The Unwobbling Pivot' is presented as a treatise by Confucius's grandson.

The Analects is the only one of these works known even by name to the common reader in the West. But very often the Confucius of the Analects is the one of 'Confucius him say', the enunciator of stupefying platitudes. And Pound's version, though he jazzed it up with slang and affected terseness, is not much more readable than any other.[1] *The Unwobbling Pivot* is a very different matter, as will be seen.

The first fruit of Pound's work on the Fenollosa manuscripts was *Cathay*; the second was his book of Noh plays; the third his edition of Fenollosa's essay 'On the Chinese Written Character as a Medium for Poetry'. It seems to have been this last that brought Chinese literature, and Confucius, into the centre of Pound's life. It was his urgency about getting this essay into print that led him to declare to John Quinn, at the beginning of 1917:

> China is fundamental, Japan is not. Japan is a special interest, like Provence, or 12th-13th Century Italy (apart from Dante). I don't mean to say there aren't interesting things in Fenollosa's Japanese stuff (or fine things, like the end of Kagekiyo, which is, I think, 'Homeric'). But China is solid. One can't go back of the 'Exile's Letter', or the 'Song of the Bowmen', or the 'North Gate'. (*Letters*, p.155.)

And within the month Pound is offering to write an essay on Confucius for Margaret Anderson's *Little Review* (*Letters*, p.161).

Of course Pound thought better of what he had written to John Quinn. His readiness to dismiss his mediaeval interests goes along with fears he had expressed in 1916 that these interests had betrayed him into Browningesque styles and into excessive archaisms of language (*Letters*, pp.138, 141). The work he was yet to do on Cavalcanti, with his essay on 'Mediaevalism', shows that thirteenth-century Italy, even apart from Dante, was in no sense for him 'a special interest'. And yet the volume in which that work appeared professed by its very title, *Make It New*, his Confucian allegiance:

---

1 Pound's translation of the Analects appeared in *The Hudson Review*, III (1950). It was reprinted as *Confucian Analects* in New York in 1951, and in London in 1956.

"In letters of gold on T'ang's bath-tub:

AS THE SUN MAKES IT NEW
DAY BY DAY MAKE IT NEW
YET AGAIN MAKE IT NEW"[1]

The mediaevalist or Romance philologist had not changed into an Orientalist, a sinologue. And yet the two lines of interest were not just concurrent; they had come together, and pointed in one direction.

This does not appear, however, from the first of the sustained Confucian translations. It was from Rapallo in 1927 that he dispatched to a small press in America the manuscript of *Ta Hio. The Great Learning. Newly rendered into the American Language.*[2] There is nothing very 'American' about this language:

> The ancient princes who wished to develop and make apparent, in their states, the luminous principle of reason which we receive from the sky, set themselves first to govern well their kingdoms; those who wished to govern their kingdoms well, began by keeping their own families in order; those who wished good order in their families, began by correcting themselves; those who wished to correct themselves tried first to attain rectitude of spirit; those who desired this rectitude of spirit, tried first to make their intentions pure and sincere; those who desired to render their intentions pure and sincere, attempted first to perfect their moral intelligence; the making as perfect as possible, that is the giving fullest scope to the moral intelligence (or the acquaintance with morals), consists in penetrating and getting to the bottom of the principles (motivations) of actions.

So far from being American, this language is quite precisely, in its structure and vocabulary, French. For it is a transliteration from the French of the nineteenth-century translator, Guillaume Pauthier.[3] And, although Pauthier doubtless is, as Pound declared, 'a magnificent

---

1 Surprisingly, there is no evidence that Pound knew of an earlier occasion when this Confucian motto had got into American literature, in Thoreau's *Walden.*
2 Seattle, 1928; also London, 1936, and Norfolk, Conn., 1939.
3 Cf. M.G. Pauthier, *Confucius et Mencius: Les Quatre Livres* (Paris, 1868), p.42.

scholar' (*Letters*, p.384) and capable moreover of elegance in his French, he is being used to poor purposes when his 'rendre leurs intentions pures et sincères' produces in Pound's English 'render their intentions pure and sincere'.

'American' figures in Pound's title for reasons that have little or nothing to do with his language. They are connected rather with what he wrote to a French correspondent in 1928:

> je viens de donner une nouvelle version du *Ta Hio* de Confucius, parce que j'y trouve des formulations d'idées qui me paraissent utiles pour civiliser l'Amerique.... Je révère plutôt le bon sens que l'originalité.... (*Letters*, p.293)[1]

And it appears that Pound only at a late stage decided not to introduce his translation with an 'acrid and querulous preface' attacking the American State Department and the administrations of President Wilson and President Harding (*Letters*, pp.289-90). In fact, what we encounter here for the first time is the strain of thought and feeling that ultimately brought the poet to face a charge of treason, and then into a mental home. This is the sinister side of Pound's interest in Confucius, and it is worth seeing what there is in the Confucian texts that can lent itself to such perilous applications as Pound was to make. Another earlier translator whom Pound has consulted and honoured (*Letters*, pp.390-91), James Legge, remarked of the *Ta Hio*:

> the execution is not equal to the design; and, moreover, underneath all the reasoning... there lies the assumption that example is all but omnipotent. We find this principle pervading all the Confucian philosophy. And doubtless it is a truth, most important in education and government, that the influence of example is very great.... It will be well if the study of the Chinese Classics should call attention to it. Yet in them the subject is pushed to an extreme, and represented in an extravagant manner. Proceeding from the view of human nature that it is entirely good, and led astray only by influences from without, the sage of China and his followers attribute to personal example and to instruction a power which we do not find that they actually possess.[2]

---

1 I have just given a new version of the *Ta Hio* of Confucius, because I find there some formulations of ideas which seem to me of use for civilizing America.... I revere good sense more than originality....

2 James Legge, *The Chinese Classics: Translated into English, with Preliminary Essays and Explanatory Notes*, Vol. I: *The Life and Teachings of Confucius* (London, 1867), p.31.

It would be laughable to find a necessary connection between Confucianism and Fascism. On the other hand, the point is not merely that the politics the Confucians envisage is necessarily authoritarian. As Legge implies, the characteristic emphasis on the exemplary function of the ruler obviously leads itself to the aggrandizing of 'the leader'. And indeed, as Legge says elsewhere, the conduct recommended in the treatise seems available, if not to no one but the Emperor himself, at least to the leader rather than to the common individual. For this reason, though for others also, one sympathizes with those Chinese who expressed to Legge 'the difficulty they felt in making the book a practical directory for their conduct'; especially with one of them who complained, 'It is so vague and vast' (Legge, p.29).

Legge raises other objections that are not so obviously just and yet are not easy to deal with. Of the paragraph that has been quoted, for instance, he remarks:

> ...we feel that this explanation cannot be correct, or that, if it be correct, the teaching of the Chinese sage is far beyond and above the condition and capacity of men. How can we suppose that, in order to secure sincerity of thought and our self-cultivation, there is necessarily [*sic*] the study of all the phenomena of physics and metaphysics, and of the events of history? (Legge, p.267.)

To see the point of this objection we need to re-read the paragraph, not in the muffled and flaccid language of Pound's first version, but from *Ta Hio. The Great Digest*, his second translation which he published along with *The Unwobbling Pivot* in 1947:

> The men of old wanting to clarify and diffuse throughout the empire that light which comes from looking straight into the heart and then acting, first set up good government in their own states; wanting good government in their states, they first disciplined themselves; desiring self-discipline, they rectified their own hearts; and wanting to rectify their hearts, they sought precise verbal definitions of their inarticulate thoughts (the tones given off by the heart); wishing to attain precise verbal definitions, they set to extend their knowledge to the utmost. This completion of knowledge is rooted in sorting things into organic categories.

'Sorting things into organic categories' (like Legge's balder version, 'the investigation of things') is very different from Pauthier's 'getting to the bottom of the principles of actions'; and it asserts, just as Legge says it does, that an inescapable preliminary to any scheme of moral self-improvement is 'the study of all phenomena of physics and metaphysics, and of the events of history'. But in Cavalcanti too, as Pound presents him to us, if the study of physics and metaphysics is not a *preliminary* to the moral improvement involved in loving truly, such study seems to be at any rate a necessary *implication* of so doing. The refusal to specialize, or to regard existing categories and fields of study as more than a working arrangement – this is not only what Pound asks us to admire in Cavalcanti, it has to be noted also as a constant and determining feature of Pound himself, as a man and as a writer. Legge's common-sensical objection to this, like the common-sensical objections to Pound's work in general and to the encyclopaedic cantos in particular, is irrefutable: the body of available knowledge has expanded so vastly since Confucius's day, or even since Cavalcanti's, that if a man wants exact and trustworthy knowledge in any field he must restrict himself to that field. However, no man does this: it is a professional rule, not a human possibility. Since the poet is not a professional among professionals, but a man who aspires to be more completely human than other men, it is he, the poet, who has a duty to break down or overleap boundaries. When Pope in *The Dunciad* mocks the natural historian of his day, such as the conchologist, common sense declares him wrong, since the event has shown that the pedestrian omnivorousness of the eighteenth-century virtuoso was necessary at that stage if scientific knowledge was to advance; but another faculty than common sense declares Pope right, since the conchologist whom he pictured had come by his specialized expertise only at excessive cost to his own humanity, by an inexcusably narrow sense of the scope of human possibilities:

> The most recluse, discreetly open'd, find
> Congenial matter in the cockle-kind.

The conchologist, as it happens, would not have been Pound's example of the narrow specialist, for he took over from Fenollosa an admiration for the scientific method as exemplified by the great naturalists such as Louis Agassiz.[1] But the same reasons that vindicate

1 See Norman Holmes Pearson, in *Shenandoah*, VII: 1 (Autumn 1955), 81-2: 'Louis Agassiz becomes a landmark. It was he in his laboratory at Harvard who trained Edward S. Morse, the Salem natural scientist who taught at the Imperial University of Tokyo and became the influential collector and curator of Oriental art . . . , not forgetting to carry over the lessons of Agassiz into the new field. And it was Morse who in turn persuaded Ernest Fenollosa, also from Salem and fresh from Harvard, to go out as instructor in rhetoric to the Imperial University, where Fenollosa's interest like that of Morse expanded to include the stimulation of Oriental culture'.

Pope against the objections of common sense, vindicate Pound also. And rather plainly the man who had consulted Grosseteste in order to understand a canzone of Cavalcanti would find attractive in Confucian thought precisely that overleaping of boundaries, that determination to regard human experience as all one, which Legge objects to as impractical. The issue is even clearer with *The Unwobbling Pivot*.

There is another observation by Legge which is more far-reaching still. This arises from the next paragraph (the fifth) of Chapter 1 of the *Ta Hio*. Legge's version of this runs as follows:

> Things being investigated, knowledge became complete. Their knowledge being complete, their thoughts were sincere. Their thoughts being sincere, their hearts were then rectified. Their hearts being rectified, their persons were cultivated. Their persons being cultivated, their families were regulated. Their families being regulated, their States were rightly governed. Their States being rightly governed, the whole empire was made tranquil and happy.

Legge observes that what Confucius offers here are the seven steps of a climax, 'the end of which is the empire tranquillized'. He goes on: 'Pauthier calls the paragraphs where they occur instances of the sorites, or abridged syllogism. But they belong to *rhetoric*, and not to *logic* (pp.29-30)'. Fenollosa might have had this comment specifically in mind when he wrote indignantly, after analyzing the nature of the Chinese written character:

> In diction and in grammatical form science is utterly opposed to logic. Primitive men who created language agreed with science and not with logic. Logic has abused the language which they left to her mercy.
> Poetry agrees with science and not with logic.[1]

But it is better to be more temperate. What Fenollosa means, as his context makes clear, is that there have been, historically, more kinds of logic than one; and that, in consequence, logic and rhetoric have not always been so flatly opposed one to the other, nor so easy to distinguish one from the other, as Legge supposes. As Fenollosa implies, and elsewhere asserts, the pioneers of the experimental

---

1 Fenollosa, *The Chinese Written Character as a Medium for Poetry* (*Square Dollar Series*, Washington, D.C., 1951). See the discussion in the present author's *Articulate Energy: An Enquiry into the Syntax of English Verse* (London, 1955), pp.33-42 and Appendix.

method in the sciences found themselves committed to a struggle among the variously competing logics of Bacon, of Descartes, and of mediaeval Scholasticism, for instance. It may be held that the subjects of the *Ta Hio*, ethics and politics, can be reliably studied only empirically, through the accumulation of specific instances closely observed and scrupulously recorded, as Pope's conchologist observed and recorded shells; and in such a case the method would properly be described as neither 'logical' nor 'rhetorical', but 'scientific'. In fact, the Confucian writings, with their constant use of the illustrative anecdote and their reliance on accumulated instances from recorded history, do seem to use such a method. (Thus, whereas Pound's first translation of this fifth paragraph had agreed with Pauthier's in being cast in the present tense, his second agrees with Legge's in using the past; and this swings it into line with the Confucian reliance on recorded instances, and generalizations from these.)

What Fenollosa maintained was that not just Confucius, but all Chinese thinkers were necessarily committed to this method, since their written language compelled it. The Chinese written character, so he maintained, had escaped or resisted the anti-scientific attentions of the logicians who had perverted the structures of Western languages. In consequence, not only was Chinese a highly, indeed essentially, metaphorical language (as English is also), but also it was a language (such as English is not) in which it was impossible for 'live' metaphors to go 'dead', a language which it was impossible to read or to write without being aware that metaphors were what you were using, what you were *thinking with*. Perhaps most readers still will think, with Legge, that a highly metaphorical discourse is likely to be rhetorical; Fenollosa argues on the contrary that its being highly metaphorical is what makes it scientific. His position, however unlikely it may seem, is a strong one; though this is not the place to examine it.[1]

As for his contention that no Chinese can read Chinese characters without being aware of how they are built up out of pictorial metaphors, most authorities now appear to disagree with him. It is in any case something that can be neither proven nor disproven. Just as most speakers of English use the word 'discourse' without being aware of the metaphor of running about concealed in its etymology, so one concedes that a slow-witted Chinese, or a sharp-witted Chinese in a state of fatigue, would not register the pictorial metaphors in the Chinese he was reading. The argument can then be pushed further only by unprofitably speculating on what is the

1 See the treatment in my *Articulate Energy*, loc. cit.

statistically normal degree of slow-wittedness or exhaustion among Chinese.

Pound at any rate was convinced by Fenollosa (though not to much purpose when he first translated the *Ta Hio*) that previous translators of Chinese had erred in not bringing out the highly metaphorical, and therefore highly concrete, nature of the original. The first sentence of the fourth paragraph shows the very interesting issues that are involved. In 1928 Pound, following Pauthier, gave for this:

> The ancient princes who wished to develop and make apparent, in their states, the luminous principle of reason which we receive from the sky, set themselves first to govern well their kingdoms....

Twenty years later, wanting to bring to life the dead, or at least somnolent, metaphor in 'luminous', he wrote:

> The men of old wanting to clarify and diffuse throughout the empire that light...

(The metaphorical force comes from 'clarify and diffuse' replacing 'develop and make apparent', more than it comes from 'light' replacing 'luminous principle'.) But in 1867 Legge had written:

> The ancients who wished to illustrate illustrious virtue throughout the empire...

And there is the light shining just as brightly as ever for any reader who knows and remembers how both 'illustrious' and 'illustrate' incorporate 'lustre', and what 'lustre' means! This suggests that, however it may be in Chinese, in English a metaphor that is dead for one reader will be live for another. I suspect there are readers of English for whom 'clarify' does not 'make clear', or not at any rate in the sense in which a day is 'clear'; and to such readers the metaphor in Pound's second version may be as 'dead' as in his first. On the other hand there may be those whose visual imagination is so prompt and lively that out of 'make apparent' in the version of 1928 they conjure up an image of an apparition glowing in light against darkness. If the second version is an improvement on the first, it is partly because nowadays, unfortunately, there are more readers of the first sort than of the second; in Legge's time things may have been different.

It is not by accident that these metaphors from the start of the *Ta Hio*, like the metaphors in Cavalcanti's 'Donna mi prega' that Pound examines in discussing that poem, are metaphors drawn from the nature, the structure, and the behaviour of light. Such metaphors are central to the Confucian experience as we encounter it in Pound's translation of the *Ta Hio* and 'The Unwobbling Pivot', just as they seem central to the experience of Cavalcanti and Dante. In a sumptuous edition of the two Confucian translations,[1] Pound prefaces them by a table of what he calls 'Terminology', presenting some seventeen Chinese characters that he considers crucial, with an English gloss on each; the gloss to the second runs:

> The sun and moon, the total light process, the radiation, reception and reflection of light; hence, the intelligence. Bright, brightness, shining. Refer to Scotus Erigena, Grosseteste and the notes on light in my *Cavalcanti*.

There can be no doubt that long before 1947, when the Confucian translations first appeared together, it was this common ground between the two areas which convinced Pound that by these two distinct avenues he was moving toward one body of insights.

The metaphors from light are even more insistent in 'The Unwobbling Pivot' than in the *Ta Hio*, as is only to be expected from a work which, as Pound says, 'contains what is usually supposed not to exist, namely the Confucian metaphysics'. Accordingly, to Legge, a Christian missionary, 'The Unwobbling Pivot' commends itself even less than the *Ta Hio* or 'Great Learning'. He finds in it

> the same combination which we found in the Great Learning, – a combination of the ordinary and the extraordinary, the plain and the vague, which is very perplexing to the mind, and renders the Book unfit for the purposes of mental and moral discipline (p.45).

The writer, he says, 'belongs to the intuitional school more than to the logical' (p.43). And as early as the fifth paragraph he finds that

> From the path of duty, where we tread on solid ground, the writer suddenly raises us aloft on wings of air, and will carry us we know not where, and to we know not what (pp.44-5).

1 *The Unwobbling Pivot and The Great Digest, translated by Ezra Pound, with Chinese 'stone' text from rubbings supplied by William Hawley, and a note on the stone editions by Achilles Fang* (Norfolk, Conn., 1951).

Legge is a sturdy thinker and a distinguished writer, as this splendidly Johnsonian cadence shows, and as Pound has insisted. When he refers to 'the path of duty', he is quoting his own translation of a term in the very first paragraph, a term that Pound translates as 'the process'. Pound here, it may be thought, is being not more concrete but more abstract than Legge (or than Pauthier, who gives '*règle de conduite morale ou droite voie* – Pauthier offers not so much translation as interpretation or concealed commentary). But a moment's thought reveals how inadequate 'abstract' and 'concrete' are as words to use in such a case; for on the one hand 'path of duty', though a metaphor, is a dead one, an inert commonplace of countless homilies, while on the other hand 'process', considered by way of its Latin etymology, releases precisely the same metaphor, thoroughly alive. The case is reversed when in the fourth paragraph Legge gives 'state of equilibrium' where Pound writes 'the axis'. Legge writes sourly, 'It is difficult to translate the paragraph, because it is difficult to understand it' (p.283 n.) And we see what he means when in his translation he has to mix his metaphors:

> This EQUILIBRIUM is the great root *from which grow all the human actings* in the world, and this HARMONY is the universal path which they all pursue.

But Pound at this point has to mix his metaphors no less:

> That axis in the center is the great root of the universe; that harmony is the universe's outspread process (of existence).

Where metaphors are thus mixed in from mechanics ('axis'), from botany ('root'), from music ('harmony'), and from travelling ('process' or 'path'), we may well feel, with Legge, that we are in 'an obscurity where we can hardly grope our way' (p.54). But if our speculations have so far have had any point at all, not just as regards the nature of the Chinese language, but as regards the nature of English also, we should have realized that metaphors *have to be* mixed, and that the prejudice against mixing them is unfounded. For, if every word of the language is metaphorical (as it is, if we learn from Fenollosa to be alert to etymology), then the metaphors released by any passage of language will hang together only in nothing less than the totality of human experience. The implications of this for poetics are revolutionary.

For the moment, however, Legge's honest confession ('It is difficult to translate the paragraph, because it is difficult to understand it') leads to something more commonplace, but more immediately useful: to the possibility that, where Pound's translation differs most strikingly from those of his predecessors, it is very often because he is at least making some sense where they make none. A good example is at the end of the very difficult Chapter XVI, where the Chinese talks of *Kwei-shin*; that is, according to Legge, 'ghosts and spirits, spiritual beings'. Pound here breaks into verse:

> Intangible and abstruse
> > the bright silk of the sunlight
> Pours down in manifest splendor,
> You can neither stroke
> > the precise word with your hand
> Nor shut it down under a box-lid.

Pauthier gives:

> Ces esprits cependant, quelque subtils et imperceptibles qu'ils soient, se manifestent dans les formes corporelles des êtres; leur essence êtant une essence réelle, vraie, elle ne peut pas se manifester sous une forme quelconque.[1]

And Legge:

> Such is the manifestness of what is minute! Such is the impossibility of repressing the outgoings of sincerity!

Where authorities like Pauthier and Legge differ so comically, the outlandishness of Pound's version turns out to be at least not gratuitous; something outlandish was called for, in order to reconcile such variants. Even so, distinctions have to be made. When Pauthier says 'elle ne peut pas se manifester sous une forme quelconque' he is after his fashion saying just what Pound says, with his talk of stroking with the hand the shutting of a box-lid; the difference comes from Pound's determination to bring over the images he sees in the components of the Chinese characters before him. Pauthier at least makes sense, and in a way the same sense as Pound. Legge on the other hand makes nonsense, because nonsense is all that he finds; as he says contemptuously, 'It is difficult – not to say impossible – to conceive to one's self what is meant by such descriptions'.[2] In the

1 These spirits, however, subtle and imperceptible though they are, manifest themselves in the bodily forms of beings; their essence being a real, true essence, it cannot manifest itself in any one form.

2 Legge, pp.292-3. Pound may have found 'abstruse' (meaning 'remote from apprehension; recondite', but also 'hidden, secret') in a rendering that Legge quotes and rejects.

context of the chapter as a whole Pound makes difficult sense where Legge makes none at all. And if Pound makes more difficult sense than Pauthier, the sense that he makes is not only more vivid; it is also more interesting. For he makes of the *Kwei-shin* not 'spooks' but embodied energies such as sunlight, informing the Creation; and for this he has the authority of some Chinese commentators whom Legge rejects even as he cites them – notably of one who asserts, 'The *Kwei-shin* are the energetic operations of Heaven and Earth, and the traces of production and transformation'.

The reader who has no Chinese can in this way read Pound, along with Pauthier and Legge, so as to assure himself that he is not at the mercy of the translator's whims. There *are* places where Pound's version seems, on this showing, wilfully eccentric – for instance, a reference to a chicken-coop in Chapter VIII; a string of epithets in Chapter XII, paragraph 1; and paragraph 14 of Chapter XX, where Pound suppresses, or transforms past recognition, something that Legge and Pauthier alike take for a recommendation about propriety in dress. But most of the time one finds with surprise that, quite apart from the greater raciness and physicality of Pound's prose, his versions reconcile the sense of Legge and of Pauthier, who differ from each other as to sense more than Pound differs from either. There are good examples of this in Chapter II and Chapter IV, in Chapter X, and also in Chapter XXIII. In the last, Pound and Legge take one view of a word, which they translate as 'shoots' in something the sense of Henry Vaughan's 'bright shoots of everlastingness'. Pauthier takes another and opposite view. Moreover, Pauthier, who is always diffuse, extends the tail of the paragraph in what looks like an inexcusable Christian-pietistic gloss, making 'change' (Pound) and 'transform' (Legge) into 'convert'. On the other hand Pauthier is more aware of metaphorical life in the original than Legge appears to be: he gives 'étant manifestés, alors ils jetteront un grand éclat' for Pound's 'manifest, it will start to illuminate' and Legge's 'From being manifest, it becomes brilliant'. As this last example shows, this is another place where the cardinal metaphor from the behaviour of light is so embedded in the original that it shows up (uncontrolledly) even in Legge.

The Unwobbling Pivot is worth this sort of effort, certainly in the context of Pound's development, but on its own account also. Legge's difficulties with it derive from what hindered him with the *Ta Hio* also: his adherence to a logic that proceeds by making sharp and final distinctions, dividing and subdividing. 'The Unwobbling Pivot' moves contrary to this habit of mind, seeking to inculcate instead a readiness to see one principle operating in metaphysics and in physics, in politics and in ethics, changing its mode of operation but not its essential nature. It sees 'sincerity', for instance, not as a specifically human quality but as the operation in a human mode of a principle that in other modes is an energy, as of sunlight, operating in the physical world. The word Legge sometimes translates as 'sincerity', he renders elsewhere as 'singleness', or 'singleness of soul'. And Pound takes off from the idea of singleness to translate it as 'the unmixed'. As such it makes its most memorable and momentous appearance at the very end of Pound's version:

> This unmixed is the tensile light, the
> Immaculata. There is no end
> to its action.

With these words Pound ends Chapter XXVI, an extremely eloquent passage which Pound presents as peroration to the whole since (as he gives notice) he does not proceed to the seven chapters remaining. The writer's excited re-creation of the plenitude of Creation ('This water is but a spoonful mid many; it goes forth and in its deep eddies that you can in no wise fathom there be terrapin and great turtles. . . .') is something that recalls the Hebrew psalmist, and its eloquence informs even the translation of Legge, whose comment is, 'The confusion and error in such representations are very lamentable' (p.311).

The word 'tensile' we encountered earlier, when it gave us trouble in the translations of the Classic Anthology of the Odes. And since the Classic Anthology or *Shi King* (Book of Songs) is itself one of the Confucian scriptures, one of the Five Classics, it is proper to return to it at this point. Indeed, it is impossible not to do so, since passages from the Odes are quoted repeatedly in both the *Ta Hio* and 'The Unwobbling Pivot'. Confucius, we are told, insisted that the Odes be studied continually; and the *Shi King* holds its place among the Five Classics because it seemed to Confucius to constitute, no less than the chronicles of ancient history, a body of recorded instances that any generalization, if it were to be useful, must draw upon and allow for.

If we start with Part III of the Anthology, as we did in our earlier consideration of the Odes, we encounter at once, in the epigraph to Poem 235 and the first couplet of that poem, verses that are otherwise translated when quoted in Chapter II of the *Ta Hio*, in juxtaposition with 'Make it new' as inscribed on T'ang's bathtub. The imagery of light running through this ode, especially as carried in words like 'splendid' and 'candour' which lose their abstractions in this metaphorically charged context, is far more meaningful when we return to it after a reading of *The Unwobbling Pivot*. The fourth strophe

('Wen, like a field of grain beneath the sun') is quoted in Chapter III of the *Ta Hio*, where Pound translates it more diffusely than in the *Classic Anthology* but at least as memorably, though to disconcertingly different effect.

As for 'tensile', this cropped up initially in poem 238:

> Thick oak, scrub oak men pile
> for fagots; order in government
> hath power, to left and right, tensile
> to zest men's interest.

And the word at least has *some* meaning after reading *The Unwobbling Pivot* where at first it had none, since even if we knew its dictionary meaning this still seemed not to fit it into this context. What we should have learned from *The Unwobbling Pivot* is that contexts are not so immutably delimited as we tend to suppose; that in a political context, as here, a word like 'tensile', a word out of physics, may still be in place, may be quite crucially in place, since it enforces the perception that the worlds of physics and of politics are not distinct but interpenetrating.

If we consult the Analects also, the relationships between Confucian poetry and Confucian prose become very intricate indeed, and present problems that are not always worth the solving. In Analects I, xv, for example, Tze-king asks Confucius what value he places on a poor man without servility, or a rich man without arrogance. Confucius replies that such characters are to be esteemed, but not so highly as 'a fellow who is poor and cheerful, or rich and in love with precise observance'. (This is Pound's version in which he agrees with Legge and with Soothill, but not with Pauthier, who alters the force of the whole anecdote.[1]) Tze-king asks if Confucius's distinction is not that made in the Odes, quoting Poem 55 from the Classic Anthology; Confucius agrees, and applauds Tze-king for making the application. The relevant portion of Poem 55 stands as follows, in Pound's translation, the *Classic Anthology*:

> Dry in the sun by corner of K'i
> green bamboo, bole after bole:
> Such subtle prince is ours
> to grind and file his powers
> as jade is ground by wheel;

---

1 Legge, op. cit.; W.E. Soothill, *The Analects* (London, 1910), also in *World's Classics* series, ed. by Lady Hosie (London, 1937); Pauthier, *Confucius et Mencius*.

he careth his people's weal,
stern in attent,
steady as sun's turn bent
on his folk's betterment
                              nor will he fail.

This is in line with Legge's note about this poem:

> ... the first of the songs of Wei, praising the prince Woo, who
> had dealt with himself as an ivory-worker who first cuts the
> bone, and then files it smooth; or a lapidary whose hammer
> and chisel are followed by all the appliances for smoothing and
> polishing (p.20).

Having followed the trail so far, we shall feel impatiently that Tze-
king hardly deserved Confucius's emphatic approval for quoting to
the point – it required no insight to do so; we shall feel this the more
sharply if we recall that in the *Ta Hio* (III.4) the same passage is
quoted, and given explicitly just the gloss that Tze-king is applauded
for. (Pound's more diffuse translation in *The Great Digest* brings out
the admirable conciseness of his *Classic Anthology* rendering). We
have to go back to Pauthier's version of the Shi-King[1] to see that in
the poem itself there is no explicit simile such as is implied by Legge's
gloss, 'had dealt with himself as. . . .' The upshot is that the point of
Analects I.xv seems to be much less the drawing of distinctions
between degrees of estimable behaviour, though the distinction is
firm enough between negative virtue and positive; rather it is an
illustration of 'how to read a poem'. But to take this point we need
to realize how far from explicit the Odes are, how they proceed
suggestively, by allusion. And this is brought home to us by neither
of Pound's versions so much as by Pauthier's.

---

1 *Chi-king ou Livre des vers traduit pour la première fois en français par G.
Pauthier* (Paris, 1872), p.280.

XII

The Rock-Drill Cantos

I have said that one may read quite a long way into the *Cantos* in the spirit of 'Lordly men are to earth o'er given' ('The Seafarer') or of 'We seem to have lost the radiant world' (as in the essay on Cavalcanti). This is the point indeed at which Pound is most clearly a man of his generation; T.S. Eliot's extraordinarily influential notion of 'the dissociation of sensibility' is only one version of the belief in a calamitous Fall, an expulsion from some historical Eden, that seems to have been an imaginative necessity as well for Yeats and Pound, for T.E. Hulme, and for Henry Adams before any of them.[1] For Pound as a young man the Fall came between Cavalcanti and Petrarch, and he seems to have persuaded Hulme to agree with him; for Yeats it came about 1550; for Eliot, some time between 1590 and 1650. Pound's position as he later developed it, however, was closer to Yeats's than to Eliot's, for he and Yeats embraced a cyclical view of historical change that permitted them to conceive of such calamities as having happened more than once, at corresponding stages in other cultural cycles than that of recorded history in Western Europe. Whereas Yeats interested himself in the cyclical theories of Spengler, Pound from about 1925 onwards pledged himself to Spengler's master, the neglected German thinker and explorer Leo Frobenius, who is accordingly drawn upon in later cantos.[2] Pound differs from all his old associates, characteristically, by choosing for his hero not a theorist but a scientist, whose conclusions are arrived at inductively from observations 'in the field'; and, in fact, since Frobenius like Louis Agassiz can be regarded as the pupil of Friedrich Heinrich Alexander, Baron von Humboldt (1769-1859), he takes his place (along with Ernest Fenollosa) in the line of succession, as Pound sees it, of the heroes of modern science. This gives to Pound's historical nostalgia an altogether sturdier and more

---

1 See Frank Kermode, *Romantic Image* (London, 1957), ch. VIII.
2 See Guy Davenport, 'Pound and Frobenius', in *Motive and Method in the Cantos of Ezra Pound* (New York, 1954).

substantial, though also a more cluttered, appearance than the nostalgias of Eliot and of Yeats.

All the same, in the case of all these men, those of their writings that rely most heavily on this pseudo-history are already tiresome. In Eliot's case little damage is done, for he mostly reserved this kind of thinking for his essays, which, having served their vast polemical purpose, are already 'dated' and outdated, as the poems are not. And in Yeats's work there are only a few poems, like 'The Statues', that seem irretrievably damaged. Unfortunately, whole tracts of the *Cantos* are laid waste in this way, because they rest, if they are to be persuasive, on an encyclopaedic knowledge of recorded history such as we know that Pound neither possesses nor could possess. The failure of the American History and Chinese History cantos can be explained in other ways; but they would have been barren in the long run, even if they had been written according to a less perverse poetic method, and by a man more in control of himself than Pound was in the 1930's. For, although they derive in one way from a genuinely scientific humility, and seek to inculcate such humility in the reader, the whole plan of them is absurdly, even inanely, presumptuous; there is simply too much recorded history available for any one to offer to speak of it with such confidence as Pound does.

It is the arrogance that is damaging, not the nostalgia, for time and again in the *Cantos* the nostalgia for a vanished Europe is controlled and personal enough to rise to the level of elegy, as it did in 'Provincia Deserta', and as it does in a recent interview, when Pound endorses the description of himself as 'the last American living the tragedy of Europe'.[1] Nothing is so mean-minded nor so wide of the mark as the common British sneer at Eliot and Pound alike that, being Americans, the Europe they speak of is a never-never land. The spectator sees most of the play, and if these Americans can see European civilization as a whole in a way no European can, that is their advantage, and something their European readers can profit from. It is abundantly possible and profitable to read the *Cantos* for the sake of the recurrent passages of elegiac lament; the landscape in Canto 20, for example, can be enjoyed in the same way as 'Provincia Deserta', whether the landscape is taken as that of Freiburg or Provence. This elegiac feeling pervades the Pisan cantos.

On the other hand, the Pisan sequence is so refreshing after the score or more of cantos that precede it largely because the poet is here content to let his mind play mournfully over the past without pretending to understand it or pass judgment on it. It is, therefore, all the more discouraging that the next several cantos to appear

1 'The Art of Poetry, V', *The Paris Review*, 28 (Summer-Fall, 1962), 51.

(85 to 89) thrust us back into Chinese and American history in a way that seems to be sadly familiar. However, it is not so familiar as it seems. The mere look of Canto 85 on the page, especially in the very beautiful Italian printing of *Rock-Drill*,[1] announces it as 'unreadable': bold black Chinese characters, in various sizes, are ranged up and down and across, interspersed with sparse print which includes Roman and Arabic numerals, Greek, Latin, French, and phonetic transcriptions of Chinese, as well as English. This is at least an advance on the Chinese History and American History cantos, which looked readable but were not. All the same, what are we to do with it? Most readers will understandably decide that life is too short, and will close the book – though reluctantly, because of the beauty in the look of it. For others, the way out is in a note at the end to the effect that 'the numerical references are to Couvreur's *Chou King*'. For, whereas the Chinese History cantos become no more readable if they are taken page by page along with their source in Mailla's *Histoire générale*, nor do the Adams cantos become readable along with John Adams's Diaries, Canto 85, which is unreadable in isolation, becomes, if not in the normal sense readable, at any rate fascinating and instructive when set beside Couvreur. What we experience then is certainly not in any normal sense a poem in the English language. On the other hand, William Blake's marginalia to Reynolds's *Discourses* are more interesting than all but the best of Blake's poems; and they require, to be appreciated fully, that we have a volume of Reynolds open before us, beside a volume of Blake. In the same way Pound's marginalia to Couvreur are more interesting than all but the best of the other cantos. The analogy breaks down, however, in that the interest of Blake's marginalia is in Blake's ideas, whereas the ideas of the *Chou King* become interesting only by virtue of the language that first Couvreur and then Pound have discovered for them. It is this that makes Canto 85 nearer to poetry as normally conceived than Blake's marginalia are.

Couvreur offers both a French and a Latin translation of his Chinese text, and his versions in both languages are very distinguished, as Pound acknowledges by reproducing so much of both. The marginal translations that Pound offers in English – 'Our dynasty came in because of a great sensibility', 'We flop if we cannot maintain the awareness', 'Awareness restful and fake is fatiguing' – emerge all the more salient and memorable from this polyglot context. But the most important of them are carefully embedded in this context so that to take the force of them we have to reconstruct, with Couvreur's volume before us, the whole linguistic situation

1 *Section: Rock-Drill, 85-95 de los cantares* (Milan, 1955).

from which they derive. For instance, between the phrase, 'not water, ôu iu chouèi', and the phrase, 'There be thy mirrour in men', there come, in column down the middle of the page, three Chinese characters, with to the right of them phonetic transcriptions of two of them and a numerical reference. We have to follow the reference to the page of Couvreur in order to unearth the ancient adage, 'Take not for glass the water's crystal, but other men' – a very important prefiguring of what will be the governing metaphor of Canto 90. Any one is at liberty to decide that he cannot afford to take this trouble. But at least Canto 85 is the logical conclusion of ways of writing that in earlier cantos were adopted sporadically and inconsistently. In particular, it represents a recognition by Pound that for him a poem could be almost as much a composition in the space of the printed page as a shape emerging out of the time it takes in the reading; and it shows him also settling with himself, as he had not settled when he wrote the Adams cantos, how far a poem made up of marginalia upon a source can stand independent of that source. Canto 85 has to be read along with its source; there is no other way to read it. Of course the ideal reader whom Pound envisages will no longer be blank in front of Chinese characters; he will have learned from *The Unwobbling Pivot* to recognize such old acquaintances as the characters for 'the total light-process' and for 'tensile light'.

However, it is in Cantos 86 to 89 that our lack of confidence in Pound as a historian does most damage. The plan and the intention are understandable enough: Canto 85 has established, being a digest of the history classic, the *Chou King*, a standard for moral judgments of historical eras; and so in the next few cantos we plunge into the time of recorded history, just as we had to do before and after the Usura canto (45). But inevitably our hearts sink as we face yet more pages of historical anecdotes capsulated and mangled, obiter dicta of past statesmen torn from their historical context, and roll-calls of names from the past. In particular, we may be mutinous when we discover that Cantos 88 and 89 draw on yet another source-book in American history, Thomas Hart Benton's *Thirty Years' View*. There are things of value and interest in for instance Canto 87, but to most readers, even devoted ones, these appear only when they glance back over these pages from the vantage point of the later cantos in the *Rock-Drill* sequence.

We seem to move, from Canto 90 onwards, into a blessedly different world from that in which Polk and Tyler and Randolph of Roanoke play their imperfectly apprehended roles on the stage of nineteenth-century America. Clark Emory defines this world by contrast with the Pisan Cantos:

In Canto 90 (and those following) of the Rock-Drill group, the myth becomes of extreme importance. We seem to be witnessing the gradual but inevitable victory of the paradisal – a victory taking place in the heart and mind of Pound himself. Throughout these cantos, Castalia appears to be the objective correlative of the place in which Pound, through prayer, humility, agony, comes to union with the process. The union –or the approach to the union – is imagized by the return of the altar to the grove, the 'substantiation' of Tyro and Alcmene, the ascension of a procession, and the upward climb of a new mythic component, the Princess Ra-Set. Where, in Canto 82, Pound was drawn by Gea Terra, and in 83 found no basis under Taishan (a holy mountain whose summit is to be achieved, as the city of Dioce is to be built) but the brightness of Hudor, in the *Rock-Drill* cantos he has moved into air, into light, and beyond. And where, in Canto 80, the raft broke and the waters went over the Odysseus-Pound, in 95 Leucothoe has pity and rescues him.[1]

What Emery calls 'the myth' might as well be called, quite simply, 'myth'. With Canto 90 we ascend from the world of history to the world of myth. It was this world to which we were introduced in the first two cantos of all, and we have never been allowed to lose sight of it altogether. Canto 47, for instance, which took us, nothing loath, from history into pre-history, by that token took us into myth – from the labour of trying to understand history into the relief of transcending it. In cantos like Canto 90, which are based on myth, the ethics that the poet commends are underpinned by metaphysical or religious intuitions, rather than by historical evidence; and yet it is the basic assumption of the *Cantos* that we have no right to our religious apprehensions unless we have taken the historical evidence into consideration.

Indeed, the myths that are useful to us, the only myths we apprehend and enter into with all seriousness, are those that raise as it were to a new power, or into a new dimension, perceptions we have already arrived at by other means. Canto 90, for example, presents as myth perceptions about the use of hewn stone by sculptor and architect, perceptions with which we are already familiar from the memoir of Gaudier-Brzeska, Canto 17, and many other passages. Hugh Kenner, it is true, in what is the most valuable account yet given of the *Rock-Drill* cantos,[2] declares that in them, 'the precision

1 Clark Emery, *Ideas into Action: A Study of Pound's Cantos* (Coral Gables, Fla., 1958), p.109.
2 'Under the Larches of Paradise', in *Gnomon* (New York, 1958).

of natural renewal has replaced the cut stone of the early cantos'.
But in Canto 90 marble plays very much the same role as in Canto 17:

> "From the colour the nature
> > & by the nature the sign!"
> Beatific spirits welding together
> > as in one ash-tree in Ygdrasail.
> > Baucis, Philemon.
> Castalia is the name of that fount in the hill's fold,
> > the sea below,
> > > narrow beach.
> Templum aedificans, not yet marble,
> > "Amphion!"

Amphion, thus invoked, stands inevitably for music and the power
of music, especially as defined in *Guide to Kulchur* (p.283):

> The magic of music is in its effect on volition.
> A sudden clearing of the mind of rubbish and the re-
> establishment of a sense of proportion.

For the Canto proceeds a few lines later to precisely 'sense of pro-
portion':

> > Builders had kept the proportion,
> > > did Jacques de Molay
> > > > know these proportions?

And the masonic associations of Jacques de Molay (accompanied
by a reference we have met before, to a shadowless room in Poitiers[1])
look forward to the achieved act, on the way to which music's
cleansing was only a necessary first stage. For the achieved act is a
stone or marble artifact:

> > The architect from the painter,
> > > the stone under elm
> > Taking form now,
> > > the rilievi,
> > > > the curled stone at the marge

From 'not yet marble' to 'the curled stone at the marge' graphs the
movement toward perfection.

---

1 See *Guide to Kulchur*, p.109.

What the architect makes, however, is in the first place an altar, as Clark Emery points out. For in between 'not yet marble' and 'the curled stone' has come, along with material familiar from earlier cantos (for instance the Adonis ritual at the mouth of the river):

> Grove hath its altar
>> under elms, in that temple, in silence
> a lone nymph by the pool.
>> Wei and Han rushing together
> two rivers together
>> bright fish and flotsam
> torn bough in the flood
>> and the waters clear with the flowing

Thus, the act is less an artistic achievement than a religious one; or rather it is a particularly solemn and worthy act of art in that it is a religious act also. For Pound's dislike of the Judaic element in Christianity stems specifically from the prohibition of graven images, since whenever religious apprehensions are not fixed in the images that an artist makes of them they are handed over instead to those who will codify them in prohibitions, and so betray them:

> To replace the marble goddess on her pedestal at Terracina is worth more than a metaphysical argument.[1]

And it is for this reason that Pound always wishes the Hellenic element in Christianity to outweigh the Hebraic:

> Tradition inheres... in the images of the gods and gets lost in dogmatic definitions. History is recorded in monuments, and *that* is why they get destroyed.[2]

It is not an uncommon attitude, but Pound's expression of it is uncommon. For instance, in an earlier passage that we encounter as we move from the music of Amphion to the architecture of the altar, the distinction between Hellenic and Hebraic is carried in two words, 'Sibylla' and 'Isis':

> Castalia like the moonlight
>> and the waves rise and fall,

1 *Carta Da Visita* (Rome, 1942); translated by J. Drummond as *A Visiting Card* (London, 1952). Cf. *Guide to Kulchur*, ch. 30.
2 *A Visiting Card.*

Evita, beer-halls, semina motuum,
      to parched grass, now is rain
not arrogant from habit,
    but furious from perception,
                  Sibylla,
from under the rubble heap
          m'elevasti
from the dulled edge beyond pain,
          m'elevasti
out of Erebus, the deep-lying
    from the wind under the earth,
          m'elevasti
from the dulled air and the dust
          m'elevasti
by the great flight,
        m'elevasti,
              Isis Kuanon
    from the cusp of the moon,
        m'elevasti
the viper stirs in the dust,
           the blue serpent
glides from the rock pool
    And they take lights now down to the water...

'Sibylla' and also 'Isis' seem to come in here out of Thaddeus Zielinski's *La Sibylle*, which argues that the Christianity of the Roman Church 'was psychologically prepared for by the cult of Eleusis, the cult of the Great Goddesses, the cult of Apollo, and the cult of Isis' (Emery, p.9). And it follows, as Emery says, 'that when Christian theologians turned from pagan teaching to Judaic, from Ovid and Hesiod to Moses and David, they falsified the true faith'.

Of course, there is much more to the passage just quoted than this cryptic allusion. And all of it – the beer-halls no less than Isis Kuanon – can be glossed without much difficulty. What needs to be noticed, however, is that, as we lend ourselves to the liturgical sway of the powerful rhythms, we do not ask for glosses because after a while we are letting the rhythm carry us over details half-understood or not understood at all. However little we like the snapped-off, jerking rhythms of the cantos that try to comprehend history, we need them to offset these rhythms of the myth that surpasses history; we need the one to validate the other, and, although Pound may have got the proportions between them wrong, some proportion there has to be.

Thus, it is not too soon to look back at one of the unattractive

cantos preceding Canto 90. We may permit 'semina motuum' in the
passage just quoted to call up 'causa motuum' from Canto 87:

> in pochi,
>> causa motuum,
>>> pine seed splitting cliff's edge.
> Only sequoias are slow enough.
>> BinBin "is beauty."
> "Slowness is beauty.":

'BinBin' conceals, maddeningly enough, the identity of Laurence
Binyon, whose 'Slowness is beauty' was applauded as a partial but
moving truth in *Guide to Kulchur*. But more than beauty is being
spoken of, for elsewhere in this canto we have heard (echoing *Guide
to Kulchur* again):

> But an economic idea will not (Mencken auctor) go into them
> in less than a geological epoch.

Thus the few who are 'causa motuum', by processes as gradual as
those by which a pine splits the edge of a cliff or by which the
sequoia grows, are men who originate ideas as well as men who
create art. But immediately after this, there comes in Canto 87 pre-
cisely the same sequence of references as those we have traced, fol-
lowing Hugh Kenner, in Canto 90. After Binyon here, as after
'Amphion!' there, come the characters for the San Ku, the Chinese
council of three which in the Tcheou dynasty had the function,
according to Couvreur, 'à faire briller l'action du ciel et de la terre'.
And then, precisely as in Canto 90, we get the unshadowed room
at Poitiers, Jacques de Molay and 'the proportion':

> to Poictiers.
> The tower wherein, at one point, is no shadow,
>> and Jacques de Molay, is where?
> and the "Section", the proportions,
>> lending, perhaps, not at interest, but resisting.
> Then false fronts, barocco.
>> "We have", said Mencius, "but phenomena."
> monumenta. In nature are signatures
>> needing no verbal tradition,
> oak leaf never plane leaf. John Heydon.
>> Σελλοί sleep there on the ground
> And old Jarge held there was a tradition,
>> that was not mere epistemology.

The identical sequence of references which, in Canto 90, takes place in the personal time of an artist proceeding to his artifact or the man of affairs to significant action, in Canto 87 takes place on the time-scale of historical epochs. The right ideas about economic morality, and with them the right ideas about artistic (architectural) practice, rise for a few years, are submerged for centuries, then show up again. This is in keeping with Canto 87 as a whole, which deals with peaks and subsequent declines in cultural traditions: the American 'paideuma' of John Adams fading through the nineteenth century; the Chinese culture transmitted to Japan; high points of Roman culture represented by Antoninus and Salmasius; of Greek by Ocellus and Justinian; of mediaeval by Erigena, Richard of Saint Victor, and Dante. Thus, the relation between 'monumenta' and 'In nature are signatures' is a wry one. The allegedly hollow monumentality of Baroque building is indeed 'a monument' to wrong thinking and wrong morality; it reveals, symptomatically, as surely as do vegetable forms, a truth, but an unpalatable one. And the phrase 'in nature' is to be understood as sardonically opposed to 'in history', which is unstated: in nature the leaf shapes, as Σελλοί (the original inhabitants of Dodona guarding the oracles of Zeus), are oracular, they signify a truth; but a phenomenon such as the Baroque style signifies the truth only by being symptomatic of its perversion.

The objections to Pound the historian remain. One may still refuse to believe that the connection between right ideas about economics and right practice in architecture can be plotted down the centuries, as Pound would have us believe. But at least we perceive that the poet is once again in command of his material, not only keeping a calculated proportion between history-material and myth-material but balancing one against the other artistically, by contriving parallels between them.

As for the altar that is raised in Canto 90, it remains to ask what god it is dedicated to. And the last page of the canto reassuringly reveals, in imagery that has been familiar ever since Canto 2, that the God is Dionysus, patron of the creatures of earth and under-earth. Thus, though Clark Emery is right to say that as we move from the Pisan cantos to *Rock-Drill*, we tend to move from the elements of earth and water into those of air and fire, yet earth and the earthy are not left behind. This is very important, and Canto 91 will explain it.

The myth of Canto 90 is not created *ad hoc* like the mythologies of William Blake. Many another before Pound had envisaged stone prodigiously shaping itself and falling into place at the behest of music. Walter Pater was one, in his 'Apollo in Picardy':

Almost suddenly tie-beam and rafter knit themselves together into the stone, and the dark, dry, roomy place was closed in securely to this day. Mere audible music, certainly, had counted for something in the operations of an art, held at its best (as we know) to be a sort of music made visible. That idle singer, one might fancy, by an art beyond art, had attracted beams and stones into their fit places.

And in 'Apollo in Picardy' Pater does what in his essay on 'Aesthetic Poetry' he had asked modern literature to do and what he had seen William Morris as doing already – that is to say, he makes play with deliberate anachronism, making the figure of Apollo out of ancient Greece reappear disguised in mediaeval France. Pater's idea that archetypal figures and archetypal situations recur in different historical epochs (a perception that in his late essay on Raphael he found embodied by that master in paint) is one that, as has been seen, governs much of Pound's writing in the Cantos, though it has been suggested that he got the idea of it from Laforgue's *Moralités légendaires*. There seems no reason why Pound should not have found it rather in these earlier experiments by Pater, for it is likely that Yeats would have pressed Pater upon his attention.

At any rate, the element of cyclical recurrence and renewal, which governs so many of Pound's ideas about history, governs also his choice of myth and his treatment of myth, in *Rock-Drill* as earlier. It informs also his understanding of science:

> The clover enduring,
>> basalt crumbled with time.
> Are they the same leaves?
>> that was an intelligent question.

Kenner comments very aptly on these lines from Canto 94:

> For one of the purposes of the poem, they are the same leaves; since the form persists, a mode of intelligence informing, as Agassiz would have said, the vegetable order. The visible is a signature of the invisible. . . .

And undoubtedly John Heydon's doctrine of signatures is one of the guide lines through these cantos; it explains, for instance, the birds and beasts reading *virtù* (the 'virtue' of the herbalists) out of the signatures of vegetable forms, at the beginning of Canto 92:

> so will the weasel eat rue,
> and the swallows nip celandine

And this is one example out of many. Yet if we see only the *paradisal* element in these cantos, if we see their structure of values as wholly Platonic (the idea of the leaf persisting behind the metamorphoses of all leafy phenomena), there is the danger that we shall murmur, 'All passion spent', and see Pound coming to rest in a well-earned quietism. And this is far from the truth; Pound is as ever, in these late cantos, strenuous, urgent, and (his own word) 'unstill'.

The reconciliation is in the idea of 'metamorphosis', for this is the idea that combines similitude in difference with an absorbed interest in the differences. And accordingly, in Canto 90 as in Canto 2, the pagan authority whom Pound wants to substitute for the tables of the Old Testament law is Ovid:

> He will... substitute for the Moses of the Old Testament the Ovid of the *Metamorphoses*, with his recognition of the vivifying personal immediacy of supernatural forces and the constant penetration of the supernatural into the natural, producing change; his good sense in maintaining a separateness of the empirically knowable from the experienced unknowable and in accepting the fact of the unknowable instead of speculating upon, generalizing from, and dogmatizing in terms of it; and his polytheistic tolerance so sharply to be discriminated from the dictatorial nay-saying which Pound finds characteristic of the Jewish scripture. (Emery, p.9.)

Hence, in the fifth line of Canto 90, 'Baucis, Philemon'. As Ovid's case of ideally harmonious human marriage they are an instance of perfect 'welding together' ('Beatific spirits welding together'), but also, as some have thought, their story represents the still point in Ovid's poem, the harmony achieved out of its flux of metamorphosis.

Canto 91 is good enough to raise again questions about the assumptions that underlie the procedures of the *Cantos* as a whole, for here many of these procedures are inventive, resourceful, and controlled as at few other places in the whole enormous work. Yvor Winters has challenged the basic assumptions of Pound's method perhaps more justly and searchingly than any other:

> There are a few loosely related themes running through the work, or at least there sometimes appear to be. The structure appears to be that of more or less free association, or progression through reverie. Sensory perception replaces idea. Pound,

early in his career, adopted the inversion derived from Locke by the associationists: since all ideas arise from sensory impressions, all ideas can be expressed in terms of sensory impressions. But of course they cannot be: when we attempt this method, what we get is sensory impressions alone, and we have no way of knowing whether we have had any ideas or not.[1]

This is admirably succinct. And it comes as a timely warning against supposing that when we have set Canto 90 against Pound's recorded ideas about the Hellenic and Hebraic components in Christianity, we have as it were broken the code of the poem, which we can now throw aside like so much packaging. Moreover – what is more important – the state, in Winters's words, of not knowing 'whether we have had any ideas or not' is an accurate description of the state of mind we find ourselves in when we have been reading the *Cantos*.

One may still turn the force of Winters's objection. For this state, of not knowing whether we have had ideas or not, may be precisely the state of mind that Pound aimed to produce – and for good reasons. Perhaps by his arrangements of sensory impressions (that is to say, of images) Pound aimed to express, not 'ideas', some of which admittedly cannot be expressed in this way, but rather a state of mind in which ideas as it were tremble on the edge of expression. Indeed, this is what we found him doing in Canto 17, when he re-created the fantasy about the nature of Istrian marble which, arguably, inspired the builders of Venice. 'Fantasy', as used by Adrian Stokes in that connection, seemed to mean precisely the state of mind in which ideas tremble on the edge of expression. What we get in Canto 17 is not quite the idea of Venice held in the mind of the Venetian builder before he began to build; rather we have expressed the state of mind in the builder immediately before the idea crystallizes. In fact, the idea crystallizes only in the process of building, and the achieved building is the only crystallization possible.

Something very like this has been claimed for another poem of our time, 'Thirteen Ways of Looking at a Blackbird', by Wallace Stevens. This poem, according to Albert William Levi, re-creates 'that moment when the resemblances of sense and of feeling are themselves fused in such a way as to point to the resemblances between ideas'.[2] And Levi quotes from Stevens himself:

1 *The Function of Criticism* (Denver, 1957), p.47.
2 'A Note on Wallace Stevens and the Poem of Perspective', *Perspective*, VII: 3 (Autumn 1954), 137–46.

The truth seems to be that we live in concepts of the imagination before the reason has established them. If this is true, then reason is simply the methodizer of the imagination. It may be that the imagination is a miracle of logic and that its exquisite divinations are calculations beyond analysis, as the conclusions of the reason are conclusions wholly within analysis.

This is hardly acceptable as it stands: to call the imagination 'a miracle of logic' is to play fast and loose with the word 'logic', just as speaking of 'concepts of the imagination' is to loosen unmanageably the meaning of concept. Yet Stevens in a blurred and extravagant way is expressing what is reasonable enough: we live (at least some of the time) in arrangements of images which, as mental experiences, have a clear connection with those experiences that the reason is subsequently to establish as concepts. And thus it seems possible that Canto 17 and Canto 91 alike illustrate, as does Stevens's poem according to Levi, 'the moment at which the ideas of sensation merge (in most un-Lockian fashion) into the ideas of reflection'.

At least twice Pound has tried to re-create such moments in his prose. In his essay on mediaevalism, which was reprinted in *Make It New*, he wrote:

> We appear to have lost the radiant world where one thought cuts through another with clean edge, a world of moving energies *'mezzo oscuro rade'*, *'risplende in se perpetuale effecto'*, magnetisms that take form, that are seen, or that border the visible, the matter of Dante's *Paradiso*, the glass under water, the form that seems a form seen in a mirror....

And the reference to magnetism connects this with a passage from *Guide to Kulchur* (p.152):

> 'I made it out of a mouthful of air', wrote Bill Yeats in his heyday. The *forma*, the immortal *concetto*, the concept, the dynamic form which is like the rose pattern driven into the dead iron-filings by the magnet, not by material contact with the magnet itself, but separate from the magnet. Cut off by the layer of glass, the dust and filings rise and spring into order. Thus the *forma*, the concept rises from death....

Here too 'concept' is used loosely. For it is plain that, speaking at all strictly, the *forma* and the concept are distinct. In the first passage, for instance, the *forma* evoked is something common to any number of mediaeval concepts; the one form can be, as it were, separated out into several distinct concepts, some belonging to physics, some to metaphysics, some to psychology, and so on. The one pattern informs all these different manifestations. And the point to be made is that Pound in the *Cantos* characteristically aims at re-creating not the concept, any or all of them, but rather the *forma*, the thing behind them and common to them all. By arranging sensory impressions he aims to state, not ideas, but the form behind and in ideas, the moment before that 'fine thing held in the mind' has precipitated out now this idea, now that.

The image of immaculate conception ('I made it out of a mouthful of air' – and the pun on conception is central to Pound's poetry) relates the passage from *Guide to Kulchur* to one from Canto 91, on virgin birth:

> Merlin's fader may no man know
> Merlin's moder is made a nun.
> Lord, thaet scop the dayes lihte,
> 　　all that she knew was a spirit bright,
> A movement that moved in cloth of gold
> 　　into her chamber.

But the images of these passages from the prose – especially those of glass and water, and of glass under water – pervade the whole canto. It begins with two lines of music in archaic notation set to words in Provençal; and continues:

> that the body of light come forth
> 　　from the body of fire
> And that your eyes come to the surface
> 　　from the deep wherein they were sunken,
> Reina – for 300 years,
> 　　and now sunken
> That your eyes come forth from their caves
> 　　& light then
> 　　　　as the holly-leaf
> 　　　　qui laborat, orat
> Thus Undine came to the rock,
> 　　　　　　by Circeo
> and the stone eyes again looking seaward.

The lines of music make the important if obvious point that at the level of the *forma*, the artists of a period are at one with the conceptual thinkers; the *forma* is behind and in the music of the thirteenth century just as it is behind and in Grosseteste's work on the physics of light.

And indeed, when Pound in *Guide to Kulchur* wants to illustrate how 'the *forma*, the concept rises from death', his example is from art, from the history of European song. In Canto 91 the example is the same; and even a casual reader of Pound will recognize it as the stock example. The mediaeval *forma* that Pound particularly values is re-created whenever the tradition of song (originating, Pound thinks, in Provence) is momentarily recovered, for instance by Henry Lawes in England in the seventeenth century. It is for this reason that Pound's version of the 'Donna mi prega' is dedicated 'to Thomas Campion his ghost, and to the ghost of Henry Lawes, as prayer for the revival of music'. The whole of Canto 91 is, from one point of view, just that prayer repeated. The 'queen', the *forma*, has been lost 'for 300 years' – three hundred years since the heyday of Henry Lawes, the cryptic reference thus taking up the archaic music at the head of the page.

But it is important to realize that what is lost, according to Pound, is not just one technique of musical composition nor even one attitude toward such composition; what has gone is not a knack nor an expertise, but a *forma*. It is important to grasp this, because this determines what we mean by saying that it (the *forma*, the tradition) is 'lost'. Pound has protested indignantly at people who credit him with re-creating a lost sensibility.[1] It is lost in one sense, but in another it never can be lost. In the poem Pound says that it is 'sunken'; and this is no mere poeticism, it is more precise than 'lost' would be. This is proved by the prose passages we glanced at. The *forma* when it is manifest to thinkers and artists, informing their activities, is like 'glass under water'; when we say that it is 'lost', we do not mean that it is mislaid (in which case strenuous search would recover it) nor that it is gone for good, but that the glass has sunk back under the water so far that it can no longer be seen. The metaphor is more precise than any formulation in prose. The prayer, accordingly, is for the *forma* to rise through the waves again, not right to the surface but to just under the surface – 'Thus Undine came to the rock'. At the same time the thinkers and artists must be looking for it; eyes must again look seaward. They are stone eyes because the waiting upon the *forma* must be a ritual ceremonious act, the invocation of a spirit or a god; and the waiting must also be an act of art, because this is the only ceremony that can be trusted – the stone eyes are, for instance, those of the marble goddess replaced on her pedestal at Terracina. The eyes are of stone because they are the eyes of stone statues raised, as by the Greeks, to express man's ceremonious waiting upon the elemental energies of air and water. It may be objected

1 Introduction to *La Martinelli* (Milan, 1956).

that we are given here not glass under water, but eyes under water; but eyes have most of the properties of glass (a man may for instance see himself mirrored in the pupils of another's eyes), together with an active *virtù* in themselves. The *forma* is an active and activating principle; and eyes under water is therefore a more precise ikon that the glass under water that Pound offered earlier in his prose.

The matters remaining to be explained from these lines are those which most clearly relate Canto 91 to other cantos. Thus, the lines 'that the body of light come forth / from the body of fire' take up the imagery of the previous canto; here it is sufficient to note the obvious analogy between light, lambent air, coming clear out of fire, and the eyes coming clear as they rise through the water. More important are the lines 'as the holly leaf / qui laborat, orat'. Obviously the distinction between the eternal *forma* and its manifestations temporarily in art, concept, and artifact is in many ways like the Platonic distinction between the unchanging Idea of a table and its temporal manifestations in this table and that one. Hence the relevance here of a matter much canvassed in other cantos of this sequence, always in images of foliage; the neo–Platonic doctrine of 'signatures', by which every particular holly leaf vouches for an indentical *forma* reduplicated endlessly as every holly leaf in its generation grows and withers. The holly leaf, simply by being itself, celebrates a spiritual order, just as, by an old compassionate doctrine, the simple man simply fulfilling his proper vocation makes thereby an act of piety – 'qui laborat, orat'.

There follow several lines making up one of Pound's characteristic rolls of honour, naming those who seem to him to have stood for this truth or for aspects of it: Apollonius of Tyana, Pythagoras, Ocellus the Pythagorean philosopher, and Justinian the law-giver. An odd name out is that of 'Helen of Tyre'. The locution links Helen of Troy with that of Eleanor of Castile and other Eleanors of crusading and Provençal times;[1] and we know from the earliest cantos of all that Pound has used the recurrence of this name, and of feminine beauty going along with it, as a witty or fanciful analogy to the great theme of an idea (in the Platonic sense), or a *forma*, fitfully manifested at moments in history. Hence the point of renewed reference to the Platonic signatures, 'from brown leaf and twig'.

---

1 George Dekker, *Sailing After Knowledge* (London, 1963), pp.200-201, points out that the Provençal line set to archaic music at the head of this Canto 'appears to be Pound's own pastiche of lines taken from Bernart de Ventadorn & Guillem de Poitou'; and that it was Eleanor of Aquitaine 'to whom Bernart's song was directed across the English Channel'.

The poem continues:

> The GREAT CRYSTAL
> doubling the pine, and to cloud.
> pensar di lieis m'es ripaus
> Miss Tudor moved them with galleons
> from deep eye, versus armada
> from the green deep
> he saw it,
> in the green deep of an eye:
> Crystal waves weaving together toward the gt/
> healing
> Light *compenetrans* of the spirits
> The Princess Ra-Set has climbed
> to the great knees of stone,
> She enters protection,
> the great cloud is about her,
> She has entered the protection of crystal
> convien che si mova
> la mente, amando
> XXVI, 34
> Light & the flowing crystal
> never gin in cut glass had such clarity
> That Drake saw the splendour and wreckage
> in that clarity
> Gods moving in crystal

This writing, unlike the opening passage, is uneven in quality. As against the incomparable compression of 'doubling the pine, and to cloud', there is, in 'green deep of an eye', an apparently unintended echo of a line from Yeats quoted facetiously in the Pisan sequence, and the remembered facetiousness does harm. However, the meaning continues to be reasonably clear. Water (doubling the pine by reflecting it, and transformed to cloud by evaporation) is now invoked as 'the Great Crystal', and the Elizabethan seaman Drake, no less than the queen 'Miss Tudor' who protected him, is conceived as entertaining, in his seafaring, some fantasy of this kind, of sea water as the signature of transcendent clarity. Since a cloud is nothing but sea water moving in the sky, the Princess Ra-Set who climbs into cloud (her hieroglyph is over the page – a barge or gondola on water) is rapt into the clarity just as Drake is when he puts to sea. These illustrations, Drake and Ra-Set, are chosen from a multitude of other possibilities; we should attend, not to seeing how they fit in, but seeing what they fit into, the re-creation in terms of constellated images of the fantasy held in the mind by any man who wants to act or to speak or to think with clarity. The poet is restoring to life the dead metaphor in the cliché 'crystal clear'. Working with the three elements of water, air, and fire, he builds up, in each of them and compounded out of all of them, the image of the crystal-clear as the ultimate, or nearly ultimate, good. Pound wants to restore to the expression, 'crystal clear', and to the fantasy behind it, the imaginative urgency and power that will inspire men to realize the fantasy in act and artifact.

After a brief snatch of roll-call (Apollonius, Ocellus, John Heydon), comes a passage about 'the golden sun-boat'. This seems to be a description of Ra-Set's hieroglyph, from which we gather that she was herself a goddess, or more appropriately a priestess, of the sun; the phrase loops over intervening lines to hook on to 'Ra-Set over crystal' and her hieroglyph. This sets the key for what is the main business of these lines, the movement from sea water to sun, or rather the extension of the fantasy of the one to unite with the fantasy of the other; if we were to lift the experience from the level of fantasy to the level of concept (a lifting which, as we have seen, it is essential for Pound *not* to make), we could say that the idea of crystal clarity is being brought into harmony with the sun-derived ideas of vigour, fecundity, and ardour. If it is remembered how often Platonic thought has lent itself to strenuous asceticism, and to a crude opposition of supposedly pure spirit to allegedly impure flesh, we shall realize how necessary it is to guard against such mis-understanding by bringing in ideas of fertility and vigour. It is for just this reason that Pound, as in Canto 90, makes the presiding divinity in these matters not Minerva (say) but Zagreus-Dionysus-Bacchus. And this explains why the missing element, earth, had to join in the dance of the other elements at the end of Canto 90.

None of this is at all new. The concluding passage of Canto 90, evoking 'the great cats approaching', the leopards attending Dionysus answering the ritual call, is only the latest of many passages in the *Cantos* making the point that any invocation of the spirits of air, of perceptions more than usually delicate and subtle, must also be an invocation of the chthonic powers, the spirits of earth and under-earth. Thus it is that at this stage in Canto 91, when the new context has been prepared for them, we encounter themes long familiar from points earlier in the poem. This continual taking up of certain thematic references, each time seen differently because each time in a new context, is one of the peculiar glories of the *Cantos*, and of the poetic method they exemplify. So here:

> "Tamuz! Tamuz!"
> They set lights now in the sea
>   and the sea's claw gathers them outward.
> The peasant wives hide cocoons now
>   under their aprons
>   for Tamuz

The cult of Tamuz, especially the local cult that centres upon the ochreous stain appearing at a certain season on a river of the Middle East (the stain on the waters being taken by the worshipper for the blood of Tamuz yearly slain afresh) has been drawn upon repeatedly at earlier stages of the poem, and in words ('the sea's claw gathers them outward') hardly different from the words used here. The watching of the estuary for the fearful sign is plainly related to that watching of the waters already evoked in connection with Undine and with Drake; but since Tamuz is a fertility god, and his cult a fertility cult focussed on the equinox, the one reference makes the necessary bridge from sea to sun, from clarity to fecundity. The cocoons hidden under the aprons to help Tamuz by sympathetic magic have also appeared before, and have been manipulated in several ways. To take one instance, in Canto 77 and elsewhere this has been played off against a sort of parody-ritual in a society based on money values rather than on natural fecundity:

> "Trade, trade, trade..." sang Lanier
> and they say the gold her grandmother carried under
> her skirts for Jeff Davis
>   drowned her when she slipped from the landing boat.

(Whether these lines in isolation are poetry or prose is a pedantic question; the relationship between these lines and others from elsewhere is a poetic relationship.)

At this point in Canto 91, between 'hsien' on one side and 'tensile' on the other, appears a Chinese character. With these clues to guide us it does not matter if we do not recognize the character; we can realize that Pound is appealing to Confucian authority. And again, whether the appeal can be sustained (we are told that Pound's translations of Chinese are idiosyncratic) does not concern us. We can take Confucius provisionally on Pound's terms, for the sake of Pound's poem; and if we do so, we perceive the same bridge being built from the other end – the sun standing in Confucian sensibility for fertility indeed but also for the clarity of tensile light. Pound would maintain – and this is his justification for printing Chinese characters – that the Chinese ideogram can override unnecessary distinctions in a way our writing cannot. Here, for instance, it is not a case of fertility *but also* clarity; it is on the contrary a matter of fertility and clarity together as two aspects of one thing, which is precisely the notion that Pound wants to establish.

Drake now reappears ('That Drake saw the armada'), and after Ra-Set with her hieroglyph, we continue:

> in the Queen's eye the reflection
> & sea-wrack –
> > green deep of the sea-cave
> ne quaesaris.
> > He asked not
> nor wavered, seeing, nor had fear of the wood-queen, Artemis
> > that is Diana
> nor had killed save by the hunting rite,
> > > sanctus.
> Thus sang it:
> > Leafdi Diana, leove Diana
> > Heye Diana, help me to neode
> Witte me thurh crafte
> > whuder ich maei lidhan
> > to wonsom londe.

The Queen of the first line is the 'Reina' who was besought to return at the start of the canto. She stands for the *forma* that is sunken. But she is also Drake's queen, Miss Tudor, and it seems that Drake was reintroduced to make this plain. Elizabeth, of course, was celebrated by innumerable poets as Diana. But in any case Diana, at once the moon goddess of the skies and the sylvan goddess of the chase, is yet another bridge – as Tamuz was, and the Chinese character – between the clarity of light ('the Great Crystal') and 'the furry assemblage', the woodland beasts of the powers of earth. The elements of fire and water, air and earth have by this stage been drawn together into 'the Great Crystal'; and this means (if once again we raise to conceptual level what Pound so resolutely keeps below it) that to attain the ideal clarity in act, thought, or artifact, makes demands on all men's faculties, the earthiest as well as the most refined. The archaic language of the renewed invocation to the lost Queen – this time in her capacity as a goddess of earth, of woods, and of the chase – looks forward to the only slightly less archaic language of the lines about the birth of Merlin, which follow almost immediately. But it has the more important function of presenting, not as an idea but manifested concretely in words, that medieval sensibility in which the *forma* was present and operative as in the modern sensibility it is not.[1]

It follows that such exegesis as has just been attempted is necessarily wide of the mark and wrong-headed, for, since it proceeds by raising to the explicitness of ideas matters that the poet goes to great lengths not to make thus explicit, the reading that exegesis offers is necessarily a travesty of what the poetry means and is. Perhaps this is true of all poetry whatever, but it is true to such a degree of the *Cantos* that Pound seems to have had before him, as one main objective, the baffling and defeating of commentators and exegetes. If so, he has succeeded, for the *Cantos* defeat exegesis merely by inviting it so inexhaustibly. The self-defeating exercise nevertheless may be undertaken to make a point – in the present case to rebut a case made by Yvor Winters. Winters maintains that Pound's procedure is based on the fallacy that, since all concepts arise from sense impressions, all concepts can be expressed in terms of images. Pound may hold this view, or he may have held it once. But since, in the *Cantos*, he seeks to create or re-create not concepts but the *forma* behind and in concepts (or, in Adrian Stokes's terms, fantasies that precede conceptualizing as they precede artistic endeavour), it follows that the erroneous post-Lockian view, if he holds it or has ever held it, does not damage or invalidate his poem.

When 'ideas' do come into this poetry, the poetry immediately goes to pieces around them. This happens in Canto 91 in a passage printed in abusive slang, which is as despicable in diction and style as the despicable ideas it promulgates – 'and, in this, their kikery functioned'. After this disastrous lurch of tone comes a long passage in which the structure of the images comes close to what Winters describes as 'more or less free association, or progression through reverie'. It should be clear that the structure of the lines so far considered does not answer to this description. That much of the *Cantos* does answer to it is undeniable. But this looseness of organization over long stretches is deliberate. For only if we are presented with references thus disorganized can we appreciate the drama of their gradual drawing together toward the high points of the poem, where

---

1 Noel Stock, in *Poet in Exile: Ezra Pound* (Manchester, 1964) points out (pp.25-6) that for Pound religious rites originate with the hunting tribes, worshipping Diana as goddess of the chase, whereas primitive shepherd cultures, fattening for the kill, do not rise to religious perceptions of any fineness.

what began as random associations are seen to organize themselves into constellations ever more taut and brilliant, and ultimately into the *forma*. This gradual clarifying and drawing together (which has an analogue in social organizations – see Canto 93, 'Swedenborg said "of societies" / by attraction') can be seen taking place not just inside a canto but over a sequence of many cantos.

The weight of Winters's objection falls elsewhere, however; and, surprisingly, Pound appears to have foreseen it and guarded against it. In one of his latest pieces of criticism, an introduction to reproductions of paintings by Ceri Martinelli, Pound has censured what he sees as a new orthodoxy derived from misunderstanding of a painter, Percy Wyndham Lewis, whom Pound had championed many years before:

> Lewis said something about art not having any insides, not meaning what several misinterpreters have assumed. I had a word in the early preface to some studies of Cavalcanti. Frate Egidio had already written against those who mistake the eye for the mind.

Mistaking the eye for the mind is precisely what Winters accuses Pound of doing. The early preface to Cavalcanti is presumably the essay on mediaevalism, containing a passage that is indeed, as we have seen and as Pound implies, sufficient of itself to disprove Winters's contention. 'Frate Egidio' appears in the notes to Pound's version of 'Donna mi prega'; he is Egidio Colonna, an orthodox commentator suspicious of the heterodox Cavalcanti. And he appears also in Canto 94, which starts with several references to John Adams and what followed him in American thought about civics. It continues:

> Beyond civic order:
> >   l'AMOR.
> Was it Frate Egidio – 'per la mente'
> >   looking down and reproving
> "who shd/ mistake the eye for the mind".
> Above prana, the light,
> >   past light, the crystal.
> Above crystal, the jade!

A hierarchy is established among kinds of creditable activity. The setting up and maintaining of civic order, exemplified by John Adams, is one sort of praiseworthy activity. Beyond this comes activity under the aegis of love. Beyond that comes 'the light', beyond that 'the crystal', beyond that 'the jade'. What is meant by 'the crystal' we have seen from Canto 91; it is the wooing into awareness, and the holding in awareness, of the *forma*. What lies beyond or even above this is 'the jade'. And a clue to what this may be is provided perhaps by an essay on Brancusi, which dates from as far back as 1921:

> But the contemplation of form or of formal-beauty leading into the infinite must be dissociated from the dazzle of crystal; there is a sort of relation, but there is the more important divergence; with the crystal it is a hypnosis, or a contemplative fixation of thought, or an excitement of the 'subconscious' or unconscious (whatever the devil they may be), and with the ideal form in marble it is an approach to the infinite *by form*, by precisely the highest possible degree of consciousness of formal perfection; as free of accident as any of the philosophical demands of a 'Paradiso' can make it.[1]

If this indeed is the right gloss on 'the jade', it seems that last as first Pound is taking his bearings from the art of sculpture. But it is from sculpture seen in its aspect of carving, as making manifest what is extant. In the Brancusi essay Pound is insistent – what Brancusi gives is 'not "his" world of form, but as much as he has found of "the" world of form'. In the last analysis the art that comes of a marriage between the artist and nature is still, for Pound, superior to the art that comes by immaculate conception, self-generated – 'I made it out of a mouthful of air'.

---

1 *Literary Essays of Ezra Pound*, ed. T.S. Eliot (London, 1954), p.444.

XIII

Women of Trachis · Thrones · Conclusion

It has been asserted – in passing, as if it required no argument – that Pound's mind and temperament have always been fundamentally authoritarian.[1] It would be more plausible to detect in him from first to last a consistent *gamin* compulsion to cock a snook at authority. The pained tut-tutting of Chinese pundits over Li Po is echoed for instance in the reactions of some professional classicists to one of Pound's latest translations, of the *Trachiniae* of Sophocles.[2] Frederic Peachy, while admiring much, deplores 'occasional orneriness, vulgarity, and desire to *épater, ou plutôt se foutre du bourgeois, et du professeur*', and he objects in particular to 'Pound's continuous cheapening, through choice of words, of his heroine'. For that heroine, Peachy says, 'is a lady, something which Pound refuses to comprehend'. And Richmond Lattimore concurs: 'Deianeira, once the gentle lady though nobody's fool, talks through this version like a brassy, cocksure guttersnipe which, in this version, she seems to be. And all the other characters talk the same way'.[3]

Peachy expects his protest – 'Deianeira is a lady' – 'to provoke an outburst of obscenity from some'. It should not, for it honestly brings into the open what for some readers is an insurmountable obstacle between Pound and themselves, while for others it is a positive attraction in him, and for others again it is unimportant one way or the other. This is the tone that Lattimore calls 'brassy, cocksure', a tone that is very common in Pound's writing quite apart from *Women of Trachis*, though more prominent later than earlier.

All the same, it is hard to sympathize with Peachy or Lattimore. 'Deianeira is a lady' – can we believe this? Can Peachy ask us to believe that Sophocles' idea of regal and matronly dignity in any

---

1 See Martin Seymour-Smith, letter to Editor, in the *New Statesman*, 31 May 1963.
2 *Hudson Review*, VI: 4 (1954); and *Women of Trachis* (London, 1956).
3 Both these opinions are cited from *The Pound Newsletter*, 5 (Berkeley, 1955).

way comports with what British or American usage of the present day understands as 'ladylike'? (Lattimore's expression – 'once the gentle lady' – gives us another sort of lady, the *gentildonna* of Cavalcanti perhaps, or of Chaucer; but this is just as incredible, since Sophocles was no more a mediaeval Italian than he was a twentieth-century Briton; and to Pound the mediaevalist *gentildonna* may have presented itself as an attractive gloss which he deserves the more credit for eschewing.) As a matter of fact, Pound does at times come dangerously near presenting Deianeira as Mrs Miniver:

> Something's gone wrong, my dears, awfully,
> terribly wrong, and I'm scared…;

and once at least this tone carries over from her to Likhas, who momentarily becomes a character from Terence Rattigan or from Eliot's *Cocktail Party*:

> And I was most awfully surprised
> and cheered by it.

It is more understandable to object that Deianeira is too ladylike than that she is not ladylike enough.

The trouble is that 'tone', which is an indispensable term of literary criticism, inevitably carries, for some people more than others but for all to some extent, associations of class and social status. This confusion is especially current and damaging in relation to Greek and Latin literature, because in the English-speaking world those literatures have been the basis for the education of a governing elite. This is why it is impossible for some readers to realize that when Pound calls Odysseus a 'little runt who finally has to do all the hard work', he is not 'cheapening' or debunking him but on the contrary relishing and applauding both the character as created and the art that created him. It is this uneasiness with language, not as literary vehicle but as symptom of social stratification, that leads Lattimore to the extraordinary judgment that Pound's version of Sophoclean dialogue, though 'brilliant', is unintentionally comic; for the well-established notion that proletarian idiom can appear only in comedy, and to comic effect, is an obvious overspill from language as a symptom of class into language as literary vehicle. In fact, when Pound goes for cadence and vocabulary to the argot of the proletariat, he means this as a heightening of tone, not as a cheapening; and it is not difficult to see, if only one can forget about language as a badge of class, that in strictly literary terms this indeed is how it works.

The classicists who wrote in *The Pound Newsletter* (to whom, and still more to those who invited their opinions, one must be grateful for this invaluable experiment in audience reaction) differed interestingly about just what language Pound had used for his version. Sir Maurice Bowra spoke of 'the colloquial American in which it is written'. F.R. Earp, whose opinion Pound is known to value highly, spoke more cautiously of 'slang, or what seems so to an Englishman who has not been in the United States since the end of the last century'; and T.S. Eliot, of 'English and American slang, some of which is already out of date'. On the other hand Sir Maurice Bowra and Professor Earp agree that Sophocles' language is 'artificial'. And so, it seems, is Pound's; as Richmond Lattimore realizes, it is 'a special dialect, part hillbilly, part city-tough, part purely Pound colloquialism....' Thus Eliot's implication that Pound has misjudged – 'some of which is already out of date' – is beside the point. Pound is translating Sophocles not into colloquial American, but into a special dialect that corresponds to the special artificial Greek of the original. As in other translations Pound uses archaisms, so here he uses slang. Argument must turn, not on his having put together a special poetic diction, but on whether he has put it together out of the right materials; and there is certainly point to Earp's contention that Pound would have had more excuse for slang in translating either Aeschylus or Euripides than Sophocles.

It had been Aeschylus in fact, rather than Sophocles, who had provoked Pound's interest down the years. And Chapter 12 of *Guide to Kulchur*, telling how Pound tried in vain to render Aeschylus' *Agamemnon*, doubtless gives an accurate idea of how, decades later, he worked at the *Trachiniae*:

> I twisted, turned, tried every ellipsis and elimination. I made the watchman talk nigger, and by the time you had taken out the remplissage, there was no play left on one's page.

The interesting thing is that Pound does not suppose that his and others' failure with Aeschylean language in any way casts doubt on Aeschylean *drama*. Even before he translated the Noh plays, as early as the chapter on Lope de Vega in *The Spirit of Romance* (which incidentally provides some very attractive translation from Lope's Spanish), Pound had shown himself possessed of the Aristotelian insight that in drama language is very much a secondary consideration. For others as well as for Pound this Aristotelian position was restated with singular and valuable intransigence by Cocteau in the 'twenties; and in *Women of Trachis*, as earlier in *Guide to Kulchur*, Pound honours Cocteau both for this theoretical *rappel à l'ordre* and

for Cocteau's own versions, which show the theory in practice.[1]
One might even square with Aristotle – with his idea of *anagnorisis*
or 'recognition' – Pound's contention that the art of drama (as of
the novel also) is an art of 'scenario':

> Neither prose nor drama can attain poetic intensity save by
> construction, almost by scenario; by so arranging the cir-
> cumstance that some perfectly simple speech, percepton, dog-
> matic statement appears in abnormal vigour.[2]

It is this that lies behind Pound's isolating of one line of the *Trachiniae*
– 'What splendour, it all coheres' – as 'the key phrase, for which the
play exists'; and he deals similarly with Cocteau's *Antigone*.[3]

It follows, in any case, that in drama dialogue matters more than
lyric chorus or set speech. And yet, whereas the dialogue of *Women
of Trachis* has been appreciated only (very justly) by Denis Donoghue
(Ch. 13), the choruses have been generally admired. And it is not
hard to see why:

> What mournful case
>   who feared great ills to come,
> New haste in mating threatening her home,
> Who hark'd to reason in a foreign voice
> Entangling her in ravage out of choice.
> Tears green the cheek with bright dews pouring down;
> Who mourns apart, alone
> Oncoming swiftness in o'erlowering fate
> To show what wreck is nested in deceit.

Not only is the level of the diction here proper and acceptable in
class terms, but the syntactical ellipses can be decoded easily into
orthodox poetic grammar, and – what is more remarkable – the
meter is nearer to iambic pentameter than Pound had permitted
himself to come in forty years. Moreover, there is rhyme, internal
as well as terminal echoes ('case' with 'haste'), and sometimes rhyme
quite luxuriously intertwined, as at the start of this same chorus:

> OYEZ:
> Things foretold and forecast:

1 See Francis Fergusson, *The Idea of a Theater* (Princeton, 1949); and Denis
Donoghue, *The Third Voice* (Princeton, 1959).
2 *Make It New*, p.289.
3 Pound declares in *The Paris Review*, 28 (Summer-Fall, 1962), p.26: 'The
Trachiniae came from reading the Fenollosa Noh plays for the new edition,
and from wanting to see what would happen to a Greek play, given that
same medium and the hope of its being performed by the Minorou company'.

Toil and moil.
God's Son from turmoil shall
– when twelve seed-crops be past –
be loosed with the last,
            his own.
Twining together, godword found good,
Spoken of old,
            as the wind blew, truth's in the flood.
We and his brood see in swift combine,
            here and at last that:
Amid the dead is no servitude
            nor do they labour

The 'oy' of 'oyez' linking on through 'toil and moil' with 'turmoil',
'blew' linked with 'truth's' leading to 'brood' and chiming into a
close on 'servitude' – no wonder that Pound, here as elsewhere in
the choruses specifies musical accompaniment: 'low cello merely
sustaining the voice'. Orchestration of this richness cannot, how-
ever, be sustained in the normal syntax of modern English, and in
this passage there is some very gnomic grammar that might well
recall for some readers 'The Seafarer' of forty years before. Probably
it comes not from Old English but from Old Chinese, for it is in
the Confucian Odes, which Pound was translating at the same time
as *Women of Trachis*, that we find similar grammatical forms in the
service of a similarly intricate harmony of chime and assonance.[1] In
the Odes, however, Pound seldom permits himself such bravura
pieces as in the Sophoclean choruses.

In 1960 Cantos 96 to 109, which had appeared in ones and twos in
the magazines, were published together as *Thrones*.[2] *Thrones* got a
good press, and this was surprising since even a loyal reader might

1 See W.A.C.H. Dobson, *Late Archaic Chinese* (Toronto, 1959): 'One of
the most distinctive linguistic features of L[ate] A[rchaic] C[hinese]...[is]
the non-obligatoriness of the use of many of its grammatical devices....
Statements are made with the minimum of grammatical indications consis-
tent with clear statement....It might seem to those accustomed to the
obligatory grammatical indications of Indo-European languages that such
selectivity in their use would make for ambiguity or lack of clarity, but in
practice this is rarely so....' Quoted by W. McNaughton, *PMLA*, LXXVIII
(March 1963), 144-5.
2 Cf. Pound in an interview in *The Paris Review*, 28 (Summer-Fall, 1962),
49: 'The thrones in Dante's *Paradiso* are for the spirits of the people who
have been responsible for good government. The thrones in the *Cantos* are
an attempt to move out from egoism and to establish some definition of an
order possible or at any rate conceivable on earth'.

feel a sinking of the heart as the *Cantos* moved into their second century. Besides, the *Rock-Drill* cantos had seemed in some ways to be foreshadowing a full close to the whole poem. Insofar as the poem had some sort of affinity with the *Divine Comedy* (as Pound had intimated), it had seemed with the *Rock-Drill* cantos that we were moving at last out of Pound's Purgatorio into his Paradiso, since there were passages and whole cantos of an unprecedented serenity, carried in Dantesque imagery of light and flame and the crystal. And it was true that in some of the new group, notably Cantos 102 and 106, the same paradisal quality was clear and haunting. Also it informed and buoyed the Confucian ethics of Canto 99, where the Confucian tradition was distinguished (yet once more) from those other Oriental traditions, Buddhism and the Tao. But Pound much earlier in the poem had jeered at 'you who think you will / get through hell in a hurry', and even in *Rock-Drill* it had been clear that the Paradiso was not going to be uniformly paradisal. As for *Thrones*, that title, though it had been foreshadowed in earlier cantos, becomes clearer with Canto 97:

> Mons of Jute should have his name in the record,
>   thrones, courage, Mons should have his name in the record.

And when, six lines later, we hear that 'When kings quit, the bankers began again', we know what we are in for. We are still going to hear about the iniquities of high finance, which only a monarch can control. And, in fact, we hear about this, not only in Canto 97, but in 96, which is mostly about the disintegration of Rome and the rise of Byzantium; in 100, which deals with European economic history in the eighteenth and nineteenth centuries; in 101, mostly about the American Civil War; and in 107 to 109, which have to do with English history from the standpoint of the great jurists Littleton and especially Coke. It is this last material, much of it quarried from Catherine Drinker Bowen's *The Lion and the Throne*, which is most disquieting, partly because it seems late in the day to have this wholly new field opened up, but more grievously because some of it is wretchedly written:

> and that slobbering bugger Jim First
>   bitched our heritage
> OBIT, in Stratford 1616, Jacques Père obit,
>   in 33 years Noll cut down Charlie
> OBIT Coke 1634 & in '49
>   Noll cut down Charlie

Elsewhere the old master is still in evidence: as imagiste ('the sky's glass leaded with elm boughs', Canto 107), as coiner of maxims ('And who try to use the mind for the senses / drive screws with a hammer'), and, supremely perhaps, as the paradisal lyrist of controlled synaesthesia:

> stone to stone, as a river descending
> the sound a gemmed light,
>   form is from the lute's neck
>   (Canto 100)

But no amount of the old accomplishment can make up for the insanely pointless jocularity of Jim and Noll and Charlie for James I, Cromwell, and Charles I, or for the Baconian or worse bee that is apparently buzzing in Pound's bonnet about Shakespeare. In fact, one cannot read *Thrones* without remembering that the author had spent twelve years in a hospital for the insane. The best one can do is to remember Christopher Smart's *Rejoice in the Lamb*, with which *Thrones* has some things pathetically in common, as when a cat, because it says miaow, is said to 'talk...with a greek inflection' (Canto 98). *Rejoice in the Lamb*, though plainly the product of a mind unhinged, is none the less a work of genius and somehow a great poem.

In a long and bitter comment of 1945,[1] William Carlos Williams declared of Pound, 'He really lived the poet as few of us had the nerve to live that exalted reality in our time'. If this is true, as it seems to be, the implications are demoralizing. For if the conception of the poetic vocation, of living the poet, is indeed an exalted one, it was anything but exalted when the conception was realized in the life of Pound, at least from 1939 onwards:

> When I think of the callousness of some of his letters during the last six or seven years, blithe comments touching 'fresh meat on the Russian steppes' or the war in Spain as being of 'no more importance than the draining of some mosquito swamp in deepest Africa', 'Hitler the martyr' and all that – I want to forget that I ever knew him. His vicious anti-semitism and much else have lowered him in my mind further than I ever thought it possible to lower a man whom I once admired. (Williams, quoted by Norman, pp.412-14.)

1 Quoted by Charles Norman, *Ezra Pound* (New York, 1960), pp.412-14.

And, from another point of view, what reality is more squalid than that of Pound still mischievously consorting with rabble-rousers, and refusing to withdraw any of his rabble-rousing opinions, while he is haled home to face a charge of treason, found unfit to plead, held in a mental hospital, and mercifully released when the charge against him is dropped? When, in February 1949, the first Bollingen prize for poetry was awarded to *The Pisan Cantos*, and the award was upheld through the storm of protests that followed on the floor of Congress and elsewhere, this was enormously to the credit of American society, but it did nothing to vindicate the exalted reality of living the poet's life. For what it meant in effect was that American society accepted and recognized an absolute discontinuity between the life of the poet and the life of the man. Ever since, in British and American society alike, this absolute distinction has been sustained, and upheld indeed as the basic assumption on which society must proceed in dealing with the artists who live in its midst. Undoubtedly, at the present moment of history it is the most humane, and to that degree the most civilized arrangement possible. Still, the privilege that it extends to the artist is the privilege of the pariah; and it is not at all such a solid or exalted platform as some people thought when from that vantage point they fulminated righteously at Russia over the case of Pasternak's Nobel prize. In Russia the artist was found fit to plead, whereas in Britain and America he is found unfit: which conception of the artist is more exalted? In the event, of course, the Russians, though with a bad grace, decided to agree with the Americans that the artist is, or is likely to be, a political imbecile; whereupon Western observers forgave them for having entertained more exalted ideas of a poet's wisdom and responsibility.

And for much of this Pound is to blame. To be sure, he was out of his mind. But American society has refused to see him as therefore a special case. Nor is this unjust, for madness is one of the risks that the poet runs:

> We Poets in our youth begin in gladness
> But thereof come in the end despondency and madness.

From now on, the poet may take that risk, but society will not take it for him. To be on the safe side, society will treat him from the first as pathologically irresponsible in everything beyond mere connoisseurship and expertise in his craft. For Giorgio Bocca's question to Pound is unanswerable:

> How is it that you who merited fame as a seer did not see?[1]

1 Quoted by Norman, p.461.

Pound has made it impossible for any one any longer to exalt the poet into a seer. This is what Pound has done to the concept of the poetic vocation; and, challenged with it, all he can say is, 'I'll split his face with my fists' (Norman, p.465).

Pound's arrogance ('he always felt himself superior to any one about him and could never brook a rival'[1]) has over-reached itself not only for him but for all poets. Poets can no longer believe what they have believed ever since the romantic movement, that arrogance was not just a privilege of their vocation, but a duty. Charles Olson in the fifth of his *Mayan Letters* declares that Pound's egotism, the fact that Pound recognizes only Confucius and Dante as his betters, 'creates the methodology of the Cantos' wherein, 'though the material is all time material, he has driven through it so sharply by the beak of his ego, that he has turned time into what we must now have, space and its live air'. And so, because Pound's egotism in the *Cantos* 'destroys historical time', Olson decides that it is 'beautiful'. Perhaps not many will find the egotism beautiful, on these or any grounds; and Olson himself sees that, beautiful or not, it is neither useful nor true. For, comparing Pound with his contemporary Edward Dahlberg, Olson points out: 'they never speak, in their slash at the State or the Economy, basically, for any one but themselves. And thus, it is Bohemianism', for which it is 'much too late'. Just so. Bohemia is that privileged pariahs' field from which arrogance may be tolerated precisely because its originating there declares it to be irresponsible, necessarily. And so when Olson further objects to Pound that 'the materials of history which he has found useful are not at all of use', he ought to mean that the materials are useless because the stance from which the poet regards them is necessarily distorting and untrustworthy, the stance of the Bohemian. Whatever the original reason for the division between the poet's life and the life of society, whether the blame should rest historically on the poets or on the societies they were born to, the gulf between them is now so wide that, out of the Bohemia he is condemned to, the poet cannot truthfully see or investigate public life at all.

This is what justifies a post-Poundian poet such as Charles Olson in wishing to 'destroy historical time' and to rule out of poetry any treatment of 'the direct continuum of society as we have had it'. Whatever more long-term effect Pound's disastrous career may have on American and British poetry, it seems inevitable that it will rule out (has ruled out already, for serious writers) any idea that poetry can or should operate in the dimension of history, trying to make sense of the recorded past by redressing our historical perspectives.

1 Williams, quoted by Norman, pp.412-14.

The poet may one day be honoured again as a seer. Within the time-span of the individual life, his insights may be considered as not just beautiful but also true; and so they may, when they operate in the eschatological time-span of religion, or even in the millennia of the archaeologist and the geographer. But the poet's vision of the centuries of recorded time has been invalidated by the *Cantos* in a way that invalidates also much writing by Pound's contemporaries. History, from now on, may be transcended in poetry, or it may be evaded there; but poetry is not the place where it may be understood.

Thus it may be true that in the *Cantos*, wherever Pound deals with history successfully, he does so in an elegiac, not epic, spirit. But it is almost inevitable that it should seem so, for history caught up with Pound and passed him even as he wrote his poem. We no longer hope to understand the past through a poem about it; and so the poem can move us only when, in the course of trying to understand the past, it elegiacally celebrates and mourns it. Moreover, in a paradoxical way the elegiac poet annihilates historical time or at least historical succession. To the elderly prisoner gazing from his cage beside the Viareggio-Pisa highway, the Provence of Bernart de Ventadour was no more remote than the London before 1914 in which he had known W.H. Hudson and Cunninghame Graham, Newbolt and Binyon. Both were equally past and gone, and appear so in the Pisan cantos. This seems to be hardly what Charles Olson had in mind when he praised the *Cantos* for transforming 'time material' into 'space and its live air', yet it makes sense in those terms. And Pound's ranging of his poetry across as well as down the printed page of the *Cantos*, no less his choosing at times to take his poetic bearings from the spatial art of sculpture – these suggest that to talk of 'space', or at least of spaciousness as against sequaciousness, is relevant to what Pound attempted and achieved in the best pages of his poem.

Yet it is unsatisfactory if it is pressed at all far. For a poem's existence in real or imagined space can never be on a par with its existence in time, since a poem's existence in time, which brings poetry near to music, is a fact of another order altogether:

> Ezra Pound is one of the most competent poets in our language, possessed of the most acute ear for metrical sequences, to the point of genius, that we have ever known.[1]

Despite its incautiousness, this brings us down to earth on the word

1 Williams, quoted by Norman, pp.412-14. Williams goes on: 'He is also, it must be confessed, the biggest damn fool and faker in the business'.

'sequences'. Poetry is an art that works sequentially, by its very nature, therefore, it inhabits the dimension of time quite literally. Charles Olson realizes this, as any one must realize it who praises Pound for the fineness of his ear:

> Let's start from the smallest particle of all, the syllable. It is the king and pin of versification, what rules and holds together the lines, the larger forms, of a poem. I would suggest that verse here and in England dropped this secret from the late Elizabethans to Ezra Pound, lost it, in the sweetness of meter and rime, in a honey-head.

This claim for Pound – that he recovered for English verse something lost to is since Campion or at least since Waller – may get more general agreement than any other. And Olson is surely right to point to this achievement as rooted in something altogether more basic and less conspicuous than, for instance, the luxurious orchestration of the choruses in *Women of Trachis*. It is something that has to do with the reconstituting of the verse-line as the poetic unit, slowing down the surge from one line into the next in such a way that smaller components within the line (down to the very syllables) can recover weight and value. When Pound is writing at his best we seem to have perceptions succeeding one another unusually slowly. But succession, in any case, is what is involved – succession, sequaciousness. To slow the pace at which syllables present themselves is not at all to escape from the time dimension; on the contrary, it is to emphasize it in a way we are unused to, for only when the pace is slowed do variations of pace register insistently.

The last quotation was from Charles Olson's manifesto, *Projective Verse*, which is the most ambitious and intelligent attempt by a poet of today to take his bearings, and plot his future course, by his sense of what Pound's achievement amounts to – Pound's and also Williams's. The basic distinction in Olson's essay is between the open or projective verse that he is pledged to, and closed verse. By 'closed verse' he means (taking I suspect a leaf from the book of H.M. McLuhan), 'that verse which print bred and which is pretty much what we have had in English and American, and have still got, despite the work of Pound and Williams. . . .' We still have it indeed, and in the work of Pound himself. For it appears that the Pound whom Charles Olson honours is the Pound of the *Cantos*, certainly not the Pound of the Confucian Odes, of that 'totalitarian' poetry to which he vowed himself in *Guide to Kulchur*. Such at least seems to be the burden of Olson's poem 'I, Mencius, Pupil of the Master. . .':

the dross of verse. Rhyme!
when iron (steel)
has expelled Confucius
from China. Pittsburgh!
beware: the Master
bewrays his vertu.
To clank like you do
he brings coolie verse
to teach you equity,
who layed down such rails!

Who doesn't know a whorehouse
from a palace (who doesn't know the Bowery
is still the Bowery, even if it is winos
who look like a cold wind, put out their hands
to keep up their pants

   that the willow or the peach blossom
   . . . Whistler, be with America
   at this hour

   open galleries. And sell
   Chinese prints, at the opening,
   even let the old ladies in –

   let decoration thrive, when
   clank is let back
   into your song
     when voluntarism
   abandons
   poetic means

Noise! that Confucius himself
should try to alter it, he
who taught us all
that no line must sleep,
that as the line goes so goes
the Nation! that the Master
should now be embraced by the demon
he drove off! O Ruler

  in the time of chow
  that the Soldier
  should lose the Battle!

that what the eye sees,
that in the East the sun untangles itself
from among branches,
should be made to sound as though there were still roads
on which men hustled
to get to paradise, to get to
Bremerton
shipyards!

II
that the great 'ear
can no longer 'hear!

o Whitman,
let us keep our trade with you when
the Distributor
who couldn't go beyond wood,
apparently,
has gone out of business
let us not wear shoddy
mashed out of
even the Master's
old clothes, let us bite off Father's
where the wool's
got too long (o Solomon Levi

in your store on Salem Street,
we'll go there to buy our ulsterettes,
and everything else that's neat

III
We'll to these woods
no more, where we were used
to get so much, (Old Bones
do not try to dance

go still
now that your legs

the Charleston
is still for us

You can watch

It is too late
to try to teach us
    we are the process
    and our feet

        We do not march

We still look
    And see
        what we see
        We do not see
        ballads
other than our own.

This is a poem like Shelley's 'Peter Bell the Third', in which the pupil (Mencius, Olson) honours his master (Confucius, Pound) at the same time as he castigates and disowns him. Rhyme, the poem says, is 'the dross of verse', mechanical; and at the very time when China under Communism has mechanized herself, Pound mechanizes Confucian wisdom into rhyme, to present it to an American metropolis of mechanization, Pittsburgh. The metallic clank of rhyme is wittily exemplified in the comical echo of 'vertu' in 'you do'. 'Who doesn't know' may be a rhetorical question, or it may be (in a way familiar from the syntactical ellipses of the *Cantos*) a relative clause qualifying the unstated subject, 'Pound'. Similarly, 'that the willow' may introduce either another object for 'doesn't know' or else, in a way again familiar from the *Cantos*, the beginning of a prayer meaning 'Would that...', or 'Let....' This dismemberment of the verseline acts so as to drain away the impetus with which a sentence drives through its verb from subject to object; nevertheless, the impetus is never so sapped that the language acts on us in any way but sequentially, in time. Olson's invocation of Whistler, a mocking invocation, asserts that the Orientalism fostered and catered to by Pound's translation of the Odes is as insignificant as the enthusiasm of half a century ago that produced, in both Britain and America, the vogue for willow pattern and for *Madame Butterfly*. And the echo of Shakespeare's 'Let copulation thrive' says that this is a way of debauching taste. For 'Confucius' in what follows we read 'Pound', who has (so the poem says) abandoned the cause of open or projective verse at just the time when the battle for it seemed to be won. 'What the eye sees', together with the two lines following, is a specific allusion to Fenollosa's essay on the Chinese written character, in which Fenollosa analyses a Chinese ideogram into a picture of the sun tangled among branches; it is alleged that Pound in his translations of Chinese poems has betrayed just that 'ideogrammatic method' to which his first endeavours with Chinese had led him. And the men who hustle to get to Paradise recall Pound's jeer at those who think they will get through hell in a hurry. In the second section the invocation of Whitman, as another whose cause Pound is said to have betrayed, seems to allude specifically to Pound's 'A Pact' from *Lustra*:

> I made a pact with you, Walt Whitman –
> I have detested you long enough.
> I come to you as a grown child
> Who has had a pig-headed father;
> I am old enough now to make friends.
> It was you that broke the new wood,
> Now is a time for carving.
> We have one sap and one root –
> Let there be commerce between us.[1]

In Olson's poem Whitman is associated with wood, whereas the 'clank' of rhyme is connected rather with metal, partly because Pound had made the association in this early poem, but partly because of what Olson says in *Projective Verse* when he recommends what he calls 'objectism':

> ... 'objectism' a word to be taken to stand for the kind of relation of man to experience which a man might state as the necessity of a line or a work to be as wood is, to be as clean as wood is as it issues from the hand of nature, to be as shaped as wood can be when a man has had his hand to it.

In the third section of Olson's poem, quite apart from the specific borrowing from the Pisan cantos ('we are the process'), the spacing across and down the page, if it is noticeably less resourceful than in the *Cantos*, is plainly derived from there. The poem censures one body of Pound's recent poetry, the translations of the Confucian Odes, in a form which by its own procedures honours other writing by Pound, the writing of the *Cantos*.

Olson's poem, by adopting these procedures, achieves a witty compactness, but it lacks intensity to just the degree that it lacks

1 In 1913 the poem read 'I make a truce' for 'I make a pact'. See Roy Harvey Pearce in *The Continuity of American Poetry* (Princeton, 1961), where there is a valuable exegesis of a Whitmanesque passage in the Pisan Canto 82. Pearce's essay is reprinted in *Ezra Pound. A Collection of Critical Essays*, ed. Walter Sutton (Englewood Cliffs, N.J., 1963), pp.163–77.

what its author most values in theory, the weighing of syllables in the line and the leading on of the reader's breath from one syllable to the next. As for the case made against the versions in the *Classic Anthology* – that by using rhyme they align themselves with the closed poetry of print and not with the open poetry of the speaking breath – the obvious retort is that, although in these poems Pound often rhymes, he writes them in free verse, and in a free verse where the syllables are weighed, and the varying pace controlled, as scrupulously as in anything else he has written. The freedom is earned and justified by the poet's acceptance of this responsibility, a responsibility more onerous than any incurred by the writer in regular meter. And the verse is accordingly irregular and gnarled and yet sappy, far more like growing timber than like steel rails. As for the rhyme, these are poems that characteristically celebrate the decorous in private and public life, and the verse must be in keeping; rhyme, when it occurs, is one of several concessions to decorum. But there seems no room for any notion of the decorous in Olson's 'objectism', any more than there is room for it in the lawless world of the *Cantos*, or in Pound himself when he is without a master to translate, whose example makes him surpass himself. When we turn from the *Rock-Drill* cantos to the *Classic Anthology*, something is lost but much is gained. And the *Classic Anthology* shows, therefore, that Williams was in the right when, to close his sour and justifiably contemptuous statement of 1945, he wrote:

When they lock the man up with Jim and John and Henry and Mary and Dolores and Grace – I hope they will give him access to books, with paper enough for him to go on making trans-lations for us from the classics such as we have never seen except at his hands in our language.

First published by Oxford University Press (New York), 1964.

The Cantos:
Towards a Pedestrian Reading

Pound appears the most crucial case, at least among poets writing in English, of those whose poetry – for those who value it – has to survive a self-evidently and perilously wrong understanding of history, and hence of politics. And yet, as may be seen from the cardinal importance he attaches to a Herodotean term like the *periplus*, Pound can be invoked by poets for whom the natural subject-matter is topographical rather than historical, or at any rate historical only so far as history is checked against, and embodied in, and qualified by, topography. This indeed is the burden of Pound's own poem, 'Near Perigord', which argues that the puzzle of a particular poem by Bertrand de Born – a historian's puzzle about the reasons for certain historically recorded events – is to be solved only by realizing the strategic implications of the location of Born's own fortress of Hautefort. At a time when Pound was principally a student of Provençal poetry, he appears to have been as good as his word, and to have travelled on foot over the terrain in question. This seems to have been, at least in part, the motive behind a walking-tour which Pound took in 1911, of which we learn in chapter 16 of his *Guide to Kulchur*, written twenty years later:[1]

> If a man can't afford to go by automobile, and if he is content with eating and architecture, the world's best (as I have known it) is afoot from Poitiers, from Brives, from Perigord or Limoges. In every town a romanesque church or chateau. No place to stay for any time, but food every ten miles or fifteen or twenty. When I say food, I mean food. So, at any rate, was it. With fit track to walk on.

This experience is referred to many times in the Cantos:

1 But see also Dorothy Shakespear Pound, *Etruscan Gate* (Exeter, 1971), p.20: 'After the first world war we escaped from London to the S. of France ... took two walking tours centred on Brives'.

The valley is thick with leaves, with leaves, the trees,
The sunlight glitters, glitters a-top
Like a fish-scale roof
            Like the church roof in Poictiers
If it were gold.

                                        (4/14:18)

And a quarter-century later, in the Pisan cantos, when the poet is imprisoned in the American Army detention-camp at Pisa, these are among the memories which come back to him most poignantly. In Canto 74 for instance, there are lines which allude to the Magdalenian cave-paintings discovered at Lascaux and elsewhere in this region of Perigord and Limousin:

and at Limoges the young salesman
bowed with such french politeness "No that is impossible."
I have forgotten which city
But the caverns are less enchanting to the unskilled explorer
        than the Urochs as shown on the postals,
we will see those old roads again, question,
                            possibly
but nothing appears much less likely

                                        (74/428:455)

And in Canto 76, altogether more plangently:

But to set here the roads of France,
            of Cahors, of Chalus,
        the inn low by the river's edge,
    the poplars; to set here the roads of France
    Aubeterre, the quarried stone beyond Poitiers

                                        (76/455:482)

It seems to have been this last line which caused the editors of the *Annotated Index to the Cantos of Ezra Pound* to provide one of the few pieces of misinformation in that admirable work. For they give, against 'Aubeterre', 'A church just outside Poitiers, France'.[1] In fact the Aubeterre that Pound means is Aubeterre-sur-Dronne not in Poitou at all but southward, in Perigord. The proof is in the very beautiful early poem, 'Provincia Deserta':

At Chalais
    is a pleached arbour;

1 Misinformation repeated by K.K. Ruthven, *Guide to Ezra Pound's Personae (1926)*, (Berkeley and Los Angeles, 1969).

> Old pensioners and old protected women
> Have a right there –
>   it is charity.
> I have crept over old rafters,
>   peering down
> Over the Dronne,
>   over a stream full of lilies.
> Eastward the road lies,
>   Aubeterre is eastward,
> With a garrulous old man at the inn.
> I know the roads in that place:
> Mareuil to the north-east,
>   La Tour,
> There are three keeps near Mareuil,
> And an old woman,
>   glad to hear Arnaut,
> Glad to lend one dry clothing.

Anyone who opens before him Carte Michelin No. 75, can see the places named, related just as Pound says: Chalais, on the main line from Paris to Bordeaux; Aubeterre in the valley of the Dronne, twelve kilometres to the east; then thirty kilometres north-eastward a little place called La Tour Blanche; and perhaps fifteen kilometres further, just on the edge of the map, Vieux-Mareuil. The Michelin guide to Perigord will reveal a castle either preserved or in ruins at each of these places, though one would need to go off the map to Mareuil-sur-Belle, as well as Vieux-Mareuil, to identify all the three donjons which Pound speaks of in that vicinity. Equally, one needs to have walked these roads oneself if one is to locate 'the inn low by the river's edge'. That inn is what Pound always remembers of Aubeterre, for instance in Canto 80:

> and at Ventadour and at Aubeterre
> or where they set tables down by small rivers,
> and the stream's edge is lost in grass.
>   (80/509:544)

And yet that inn, the Hotel de Perigord, being set down by the Dronne, is on the outskirts of Aubeterre. For Aubeterre is a hill-town, set on a chalky cliff above the river (whence the name – Aubeterre, Alba Terra). I suspect that Pound never went further into Aubeterre than this inn, and one needs to have walked in his footsteps from Chalais to Aubeterre to see how he could well have done this, skirting the hill, stopping for perhaps a mid-day meal in the inn, and then pushing on at once for La Tour Blanche. If he did this, Pound missed a great deal, for Aubeterre is one of the most beautiful and delightfully peaceful places in the whole of old Aquitaine. (In the days of Bertrand de Born, Aquitaine of course was a province of the English crown; Eleanor of Aquitaine, the princess whose marriage to an English King brought this about, is one of the *femmes fatales* of the Cantos; and Richard Coeur de Lion, trying to make good his claim to all this part of France, was killed at Chalus – a place in this area to which the Cantos refer repeatedly in connection with the King's death.)

If Pound in this way did bypass Aubeterre, he missed something after his own heart. For one of the curiosities of Aubeterre is a church in the form of an artificial cave hewn in the face of the chalk cliff. The Michelin Guide to the *Côte de l'Atlantique* says that this eerie and impressive cavern, which communicates by a passage through the cliff to the château on the summit, was probably made in the twelfth century to shelter the relics of the Holy Sepulchre at Jerusalem brought back from a Crusade by Pierre II of Castillon, who at that time held the château. Now Pound has interested himself a great deal in the order of the Templars, to which Pierre of Castillon belonged. In fact it is the Templars, some of whose ritual survives in the practices of modern Freemasonry, who account for Pound's interest in Poitiers, one of their principal centres. In the thirteenth century the King of France, abetted by a weak Pope, very brutally suppressed the Order of Templars and appropriated their enormous wealth. The Grandmaster of the Order at this time was Jacques de Molay. And that name, Jacques de Molay, is evoked by Yeats in Section VII of his 'Meditations in Time of Civil War':

> 'Vengeance upon the murderers', the cry goes up,
> 'Vengeance for Jacques Molay'. In cloud-pale rags, or in lace,
> The rage-driven, rage-tormented, and rage-hungry troop,
> Trooper belabouring trooper, biting at arm or at face,
> Plunges towards nothing, arms and fingers spreading wide
> For the embrace of nothing; and I, my wits astray
> Because of all that senseless tumult, all but cried
> For vengeance on the murderers of Jacques Molay.

Yeats learned about Jacques de Molay in Thomas Wright's *Narratives of Sorcery and Magic* (1851). Pound's source, on the other hand, was almost certainly chapter 6 of *The Law of Civilization and Decay* (1896) by Brooks Adams, Henry Adams's brother. In Canto 90 we read:

> to the room in Poitiers where one can stand
> casting no shadow,

> That is Sagatrieb,
>   that is tradition.
> Builders had kept the proportion,
>   did Jacques de Molay
>   know these proportions?
> and was Erigena ours?

Mr Noel Stock, who speaks as one who had Pound's confidence in recent years and was in daily contact with him, explains that this passage derives from a hint thrown out by Jessie L. Weston in her *From Ritual to Romance*, to the effect that the charges of heresy brought against the Templars were not wholly unfounded, since some of the practices of the Eleusinian mystery-cults from the Pagan Near East survived in the heart of Christendom in the rituals of the Templars, a survival to be traced in literature in the stories and poems about the quest of the holy grail.[1] *From Ritual to Romance* came out in 1920, and was a new book when T.S. Eliot borrowed from it for *The Waste Land*, thus making it permanently famous; Pound could not have known of it in 1911, but if he had then visited the Templars' cavern-church in Aubeterre he could hardly have failed to remember it in the light of Jessie Weston's argument. Certainly in recent years Pound's interest in mystery-cults has been more than antiquarian; in 'was Erigena ours?' he asks whether the philosopher Scotus Erigena was one of the Eleusinian brotherhood, and 'ours' can be given full weight – Noel Stock goes so far as to claim (op. cit. p.22) that some of the obscurity of these later Cantos is deliberate and arcane – 'he writes about them as an initiate in words that are both "published and not published"....'.

Fascinating as this is, it is surely with relief that we return from thus checking printed source against printed source, cross-referring and tentatively identifying, to the open air of 'the roads of France'. And indeed I would insist on this: the first requirement for a study of Pound is a set of maps (preferably half an inch to the mile) of at any rate certain regions of France, Italy and England; the second requirement is a set of Michelin Green Guides for France and Italy, and (if one is American) similar guides to the South of England. In this, the case of Pound is no different from other writers, or it is different only in degree. Yet, oddly, the only authors for whom we are ready to make this provision nowadays are the Irish ones, Joyce and Yeats. Everyone knows that a Street Directory of Dublin is essential to the reading of Joyce. There would be general agreement

---

1 Noel Stock, *Poet in Exile* (Manchester, 1964). See *From Ritual to Romance* (Doubleday Anchor Books, 1957), p.187.

that maps of County Sligo and County Galway are essential aids to the study of Yeats. And perhaps most people qualified to judge would concede that there comes a time early in any study of Joyce where the student has to beat the Dublin streets on foot. Similarly no one who has attended the Yeats Summer School in Sligo will deny that the seminars and lectures are less profitable than driving to Glencar, or Gort, and walking in those places, or wandering in the demesne of Lissadell and under the shoulder of Ben Bulben. And yet we are shamefaced about this. It smacks of the Dickensian Society making pilgrimages to Rochester and Dover and Yarmouth; or of 'poetry-lovers' haunting Grasmere and Coniston Water. Perhaps it does. But I incline to think that our grandfathers and grandmothers were in the right of it, and that no one can claim to understand Wordsworth who has not been to Hawkshead and Ambleside. The reason why we are embarrassed to admit this is that we have lived in an age when the self-sufficiency, the autonomy of poems has been elevated into dogma. Poems *can* be self-sufficient, leaning on no reality outside themselves other than the history and usage of the words out of which they are made. But in every age there have been poets who were uninterested in thus cutting their poems free of any but a linguistic reality, poets who are 'realistic' and 'mimetic' in the most straightforward senses of those two complicated words. In our age Pound, far more than Eliot or Yeats, is such a poet. And yet we have seen that the topography of Sligo (to which one should add the topography of at least one part of London, Bedford Park) is illuminating for the reader of Yeats. And who is to say that the topography of the Somerset village of East Coker is unimportant to a reading of Eliot's *Four Quartets*? And yet how few of us have made that pilgrimage!

Chalais and Aubeterre figure at least once in the Cantos that Pound has written more recently. In Canto 101, which was published in the volume *Thrones* (1960) we read:

> Finding scarcely anyone save Monsieur de Rémusat
>   who could understand him
> (junipers, south side) M. Talleyrand
>   spruce and fir take the North
> Chalais, Aubeterre
>   snow-flakes at a hand's breadth, and rain.
> Trees line the banks, mostly willows
>   (101/722:75)

Here only the place-names refer to France; the junipers, the spruce and fir, and the falling snow are taken over by Pound from a landscape at the other side of the world. So are 'the willows'.[1] What is amusing and significant about this latest reference to 'the roads of France' is the name of Talleyrand. For Charles Maurice de Talley-rand-Perigord, Bonaparte's grand chamberlain, is one of several new heroes who have appeared in the Cantos written since 1945. He appears once or twice in earlier cantos, but not flatteringly; whereas in Canto 105 for instance we are told, by no means persuasively:

> Talleyrand saved Europe for a century
> France betrayed Talleyrand;
> > Germany, Bismarck.
> And Muss saved, rem salvavit,
> > in Spain
> > > il salvabile.
> > > > (105/746:98)

('Muss' is Mussolini.) Now, the Talleyrand-Perigords have, as their name implies, been mighty lords in Perigord since the early Middle Ages, and in the early poem 'Near Perigord' Talleyrand is one of the powerful and menacing neighbours whom Bertrand de Born has to play off one against another, thus earning (so Pound's poem suggests) the title which Dante gives him in the *Inferno*, 'sower of strife'. The château of Chalais has been a stronghold of the Tal-leyrands from that day to this, and when Pound in recent years read about Napoleon's grand chamberlain, notably in the memoirs of Madame de Rémusat (a principal source for Canto 101),[2] this new association with Chalais re-activated his memories of that place, which accordingly is named afresh, bringing 'Aubeterre' with it, but in a quite different tone and spirit from 'to set here the roads of France'. The trees that 'line the banks, mostly willows' are still there, and there are places in the town of Chalais crouched underneath its château, where Pound might still creep over old rafters in search of 'a stream full of lilies'. Pound seems to have misremembered, how-ever, for at Chalais the river is not the Dronne but a smaller stream, the Tude. And although the Tude has plants in its waters, I am reluctant to believe that any of them are lilies; for Chalais has suffered from the twentieth century as Aubeterre has not, and the Tude is polluted whereas the Dronne runs clear.

Already in 1915 Pound was making this mistake about the rivers, for in 'Near Perigord', which he published in that year, he declares:

1 See J.F. Rock, *The Ancient Na-Khi Kingdom of Southwest China* (Cam-bridge, Mass: 1947) Vol. I, p.270; Vol. II, pp.281, 298.
2 *Memoirs of Mme. de Rémusat*, translated by Mrs Cashel Hoey and John Lillie 2 vols. (London, 1880).

Chalais is high, a-level with the poplars.
Its lowest stones just meet the valley tips
Where the low Dronne is filled with water-lilies.

A map could have put Pound right, as it can put us right. But no map, nor guide book either, can vindicate for us, 'Chalais is high, a-level with the poplars'. To confirm this we have to pause and look back from the road to Aubeterre as it climbs the eastern slope of the valley of the Tude, just as Pound must have paused in 1911; and then we see that, whereas the modern town of Chalais is in the river bottom, old Chalais, a manorial village grouped round the gate of the château, does indeed stand on the ridge behind, so that the tops of the tallest poplars by the river wave just below the walls of the château.

Some poetry is 'true' in just this literal fashion. And in the case of a poet like Pound, who presses upon as as 'truths' so many readings of history which in fact are dangerous errors, truths like these are precious. To take one last example, when we read in Canto 101 (and many other places) about 'Mont Ségur', the gloss we need is in the Michelin Guide to the Pyrenees, where we learn that the Château of Mont Ségur saw the last stand of the Cathars or Albigensians, another heretical movement of the Middle Ages which is mysteriously connected with the quest of the grail. But I feel sure that only by going to St Bertrand de Comminges (another name that crops up in the Cantos), and from there to Mont Ségur, shall we see the point of: 'at Mont Ségur the chief's cell / you can enter it sideways only' (101:725:77). Place and spirit of place is the inspiration of more poetry than we nowadays like to admit; and to do that poetry justice, the critic needs to turn himself into a tourist.

Paideuma I : 1 (Spring-Summer 1972); reprinted in *The Poet in the Imaginary Museum*, ed. Barry Alpert. Manchester: Carcanet New Press, 1977.

Six Notes on Ezra Pound

I Ezra among the Edwardians

If I wanted to be pretentious, I might call this paper an investigation
of the sociology of literature. It is at any rate a sketch of what might
be involved in restoring a writer – in this case, the young Pound –
to the highly specific social milieu, that of Edwardian England, in
which he moved and on which he impinged. It is thus a contribution
to biography, not to criticism.

  Among Pound's associates in that vanished world, the most
instructive figures, I'm inclined to think, are Frederic Manning and
Allen Upward; but unfortunately we're still very far from recovering
from oblivion the lineaments of either of these men. (Recovering
them is a matter of great urgency; and a start has been made, but
there's a long way to go – especially with Upward, whom oblivion
has enveloped with a completeness that is startling and significant.)
Since Manning and Upward are in this way for the moment denied
us, I shall make do with two other names: Maurice Hewlett and
Laurence Binyon. And Hewlett is the one to start with, probably
the best peg on which to hang a necessarily rash characterization of
that literary world of late-Edwardian England which Fred Manning
entered from Australia, and Pound from the United States.

  Not that Hewlett was a representative figure, if by that we mean
a sort of undistinguished average. On the contrary he was taken to
be something of a maverick and flutterer of dovecotes. Or so it
appears from the valuable memoirs of Mrs Belloc Lowndes, in chap-
ter nine of her *Merry Wives of Westminster*:

> On the whole he had a poor opinion of human nature, and he
> felt an angry contempt for politicians. Indeed he was apt to
> take violent prejudices against certain men and women in pub-
> lic life with whom he was not personally acquainted. On many
> a winter morning I jumped out of bed and put a letter of his
> in the fire, feeling it would be wrong to allow it to survive;
> and when some years ago I was asked by a distinguished man
> of letters if I could help him to write an account of Maurice

Hewlett, I rashly said I would send him some of the letters I had received from him. But when I looked over those I had kept, I decided I could not do so.

If many of Hewlett's correspondents felt as Mrs Lowndes did, this explains why Hewlett's letters as edited by Laurence Binyon (1925) make such unexciting reading; she herself records that of the three hundred letters printed by Binyon there was only one 'which I felt to be characteristic of the man I knew so well'. Binyon's volume does however bear out quite touchingly one point that Mrs Lowndes makes: that Hewlett's ambition was to be known as a poet rather than novelist, though it was his historical romances in Wardour Street prose that brought him fame and money. (And some of those romances were set in medieval Aquitaine of the troubadours – which certainly constitutes one common interest that drew Pound and Hewlett together.)

Hewlett and Mrs Lowndes moved in the same influential circles. And Pound was not above using his connection with Hewlett so as to get entry to those circles. Thus in a letter to his father of 3 June 1913, all the names are of people who figure in Mrs Lowndes's memoirs:

> We had a terribly literary dinner on Saturday. Tagore, his son and daughter-in-law, Hewlett, May Sinclair, Prothero (edt. *Quarterly Rev.*) Evelyn Underhill (author of divers fat books on mysticism), *D*. and myself.

The name to give us pause here is that of G.W. Prothero. For Prothero is the demon-king of the Poundian pantomime, ever since Pound cast him for this role by printing, at the end of his essay on De Gourmont – originally in the *Little Review*, then in *Instigations* (1920) – the letter which Prothero wrote him in October 1914:

> Dear Mr. Pound,
>   Many thanks for your letter of the other day. I am afraid that I must say frankly that I do not think I can open the columns of the Q.R. – at any rate, at present – to any one associated publicly with such a publication as *Blast*. It stamps a man too disadvantageously.
> Yours truly,
> G.W. Prothero
>
> Of course, having accepted your paper on the *Noh*, I could not refrain from publishing it. But other things would be in a different category.

And Pound understandably gets all the mileage possible out of the
ill-starred history of '*QR*':

> I need scarcely say that *The Quarterly Review* is one of the most
> profitable periodicals in England, and one of one's best "con-
> nections", or sources of income. It has, of course, a tradition.
>
>   "It is not that Mr. Keats (if that be his real name, for we
> almost doubt that any man in his senses would put his real
> name to such a rhapsody)" – wrote their Gifford of Keats'
> *Endymion*. My only comment is that the *Quarterly* has done it
> again. Their Mr. A. Waugh is a lineal descendant of Gifford,
> by the way of mentality. A century has not taught them man-
> ners. In the eighteen-forties they were still defending the
> review of Keats. And more recently Waugh has lifted up his
> senile slobber against Mr. Eliot. It is indeed time that the func-
> tions of both English and American literature were taken over
> by younger and better men.
>
>   As for their laying the birch on my pocket, I compute that
> my support of Lewis and Brzeska has cost me at the lowest
> estimate about £20 per year, from one source alone since that
> regrettable occurrence, since I dared to discern a great sculptor
> and a great painter in the midst of England's artistic desolaton.
> ("European and Asiatic papers please copy.")

Waugh's 'senile slobber' against Eliot – he as good as called Eliot 'a
drunken helot' – has been remarked on several times, notably in his
son Evelyn's autobiography, *A Little Learning*.

  Prothero the demon-king has never bounded on to the stage more
sulphurously than in Hugh Kenner's *The Pound Era*:

> Abstract and remote though the contents of *Blast* might be,
> the establishment had bared its fangs and invoked its ultimate
> weapon, the boycott. To men who lived on what they could
> pick up from articles and reviews, the ultimate weapon implied
> more than lack of a showcase: it implied starvation....Prothero
> was snarling like a guilty thing surprised. Of what was he
> guilty? Of reverence for death, or perhaps decorum.... The
> long-term psychic damage Pound underwent is beyond calcu-
> lation. On the continent men were soon killing each other. A
> third of a million Frenchmen died in the first five months....

Hugh Kenner doesn't need to be told how much I admire *The Pound
Era*. Accordingly I ought to be able to say that at this stage his
comments seem to me beside the point, or more exactly in excess

of it. What with all this baring of fangs and of ultimate weapons, these snarlings and 'long-term psychic damage', how is one to protest mildly that Prothero is – with an engagingly archaic elegance ('stamps a man too disadvantageously') – telling Pound that he needn't wast his time submitting manuscripts to the *Quarterly Review* for the time being? Would it have been more honourable for Prothero to let Pound go on submitting, when there was no hope of his being accepted? It helps, I think, to take note of Conrad Aiken on 'Ezra Pound: 1914' (*Ezra Pound: Perspectives*, ed. Stock, 1965):

> But it was typical of Pound's kindness, even to a potential enemy or rival, that he should have so persisted in trying to give me the right contacts.
>
> Contacts: yes, these, as I was to discover, were of prime importance: they were part of the *game*. And for Pound it *was* a game, a super-chess game, and not without its Machiavellian elements. For example, this was the summer of the famous *Blast* dinner for the Vorticists, in which Wyndham Lewis was of course much involved. Pound sent me a card, which I still have, naming place and date, and saying, rather peremptorily, "I think you had better take this in." This put my back up. I had no intention then, or ever after, of joining any group or "movement" and I therefore sidestepped the Vorticists just as I sidestepped both the Imagists and the Amygists. I didn't attend the dinner, for which in a way I'm now sorry, and Pound never forgot or forgave. Nineteen years later, in an angry letter from Italy about some review I'd written which began: "Jesus Gawd Aiken, you poor blithering ass" he concluded by saying: "I've never forgotten that you wouldn't go to the *Blast* dinner."

It was a game, which Pound had played trickily and with zest. When he joined in with *Blast*, he miscalculated and overplayed his hand. And just that, nothing more, is what Prothero is telling him. If the game was for high stakes, if Pound's livelihood was at stake, the more reason for playing the game circumspectly. He didn't; and he paid the price. What is there in this to evoke the shades of a third of a million dead Frenchmen? Or to make a Lucifer figure out of G.W. Prothero?

It could be argued that *Blast* was a miscalculation all round, even for Wyndham Lewis. Certainly it was for Pound. And Violet Hunt, loyally selling copies at half-price in her drawing room, confesses in her memoir *I Have This to Say* that she was at a loss to explain why the damned were damned, and the blest were blest. Among the blest, 'Lady Aberconway was put in to please me', and 'Madame Strindberg, who ran the Club of the Golden Calf for the sake of the set, could hardly escape a favourable mention....' But 'Mrs Belloc Lowndes felt, I am sure, that she needed no blessings from anyone but her Church'. On the other hand, among those blasted, if one understood well enough about 'Rabindranath Tagore, from whose recitations ad infinitum we all suffered a great deal about this time', why pick on Thomas Beecham, who at this time with the backing of Lady Cunard was embarking on a lifelong crusade for English opera? Hugh Kenner veers unexpectedly into the idiom of the British schoolboy: '*Blast* should have been a great lark'. But even a schoolboy's jape is supposed to have some ascertainable point; and *Blast* had none.

As for Hewlett, how far he knew that he was being 'used' by Pound is what at this point no one can determine. I'd guess that he knew, and didn't resent it. For 'the game' was one that everyone played, and that was all right so long as you took your losses without squealing. In any case it didn't preclude, on Pound's part, genuine affection. As we see from Canto 74:

> Lordly men are to earth o'ergiven
> these the companions:
> Fordie that wrote of giants
> and William who dreamed of nobility
> and Jim the comedian singing:
> "Blarney castle me darlin'
> you're nothing now but a stOWne"
> and Plarr talking of mathematics
> or Jepson lover of jade
> Maurie who wrote historical novels
> and Newbolt who looked twice bathed
> are to earth o'ergiven.
>
> (432:459)

Later in the *Pisan Cantos* (80/515:550) we read of 'that Christmas at Maurie Hewlett's' – Christmas 1911 in Hewlett's fifteenth-century house outside Salisbury – to which Pound was driven from Southampton across a tract of Hardy's Wessex which his imagination peopled with phantoms out of *Under the Greenwood Tree*. Henry Newbolt was at this time Hewlett's neighbour in Wiltshire, and it seems to have been at this Christmas time that Hewlett took Pound to see Newbolt, who figures elsewhere in Canto 80:

> "He stood", wrote Mr Newbolt, later Sir Henry,
> "the door behind" and now they complain of cummings.
>
> (507:541)

But the Pisan ordeal had shocked Pound into recovering a compassion and tenderness which we look for mostly in vain in the Pound of the years preceding. And in the 1930s he had been unforgiving towards these friends of his youth. In 1939, for instance, in an obituary of Ford for *The Nineteenth Century and After*, he had written of 'the stilted language that then passed for "good English" in the arthritic milieu that held control of the respected British critical circles, Newbolt, the backwash of Lionel Johnson, Fred Manning, the Quarterlies and the rest of 'em'. And this echoed a letter of 1937 to Michael Roberts, extolling Ford and saying, 'The old crusted lice and advocates of corpse language knew that *The English Review* existed'. In *Ezra Pound: The Image and the Real*, Herbert Schneidau reasonably enough names three of the 'crusted lice' as Henry Newbolt, Frederic Manning, and G.W. Prothero, and with a proper scrupulousness he notes that all these 'were treated with great deference in Pound's early letters and writings'.

Schneidau follows Pound's own broad hints by tracing his gradual alienation or liberation from these early admirations according as Ford's demands for a prosaic strength in verse writing gradually won Pound over from the Wardour Street language of his own early poems (such as 'Canzone: The Yearly Slain', written in reply to Manning's 'Korè'). The story is an intricate one, as Herbert Schneidau acknowledges; and Pound's holding out against Ford for the Dantesque principle of a 'curial' diction (see his introduction to the poems of Lionel Johnson) represents to my mind an objection that can still be raised to Ford's principles of diction, salutary as Ford's polemics undoubtedly were for Pound at this time. Moreover Prothero, a historian, perhaps had no ideas about poetic diction one way or the other; Pound, as we have seen, thought himself victimized by Prothero not for anything to do with writing but for having championed Lewis the painter and Gaudier the sculptor. All the same Schneidau's argument is just and illuminating, so far as it goes.

But does it go far enough? It is worth looking again at Pound's letter to Michael Roberts, strident though it is. Pound there, it is plain – for instance, in his comment on Hilaire Belloc – is as unwilling as any Marxist to abstract a question like the proper language for poetry from the whole social matrix and milieu in which such a subject may get itself debated. Pound speaks of the 'order of a pewked society'. And indeed it is, for us too, evasive and misleading to abstract the manageably limited issue from the larger one. For instance, nothing is more likely than that Prothero, when he said that association with *Blast* 'stamped a man too disadvantageously', had in mind among other things Ford's connection with the magazine and the scandal of Ford's relations with Violet Hunt – a scandal that had already made a breach between Violet Hunt and the cruelly timorous Henry James, as told painfully in *I Have This to Say*.

This is where Mrs Belloc Lowndes is so illuminating. She writes well, though carelessly. And in *The Merry Wives of Westminster*, knowing just what she is doing, she recreates a world as exotic as that of the Andaman Islanders: the world of cultured Edwardian London. I am not concerned to defend that world; I am merely trying to understand it, and the rules by which it lived. Some features of that world are nowadays entirely inscrutable – notably, what it was in Frederic Lowndes's self-effacing position on *The Times* which gave him and his wife access to a society of international aristocracy and even royalty, and to the inner circles of the cabinet, as well as the society of novelists and playwrights. What is clear is that this was all *one* society, in which the wives – like Mrs Lowndes herself – wrote books or maintained salons, while their husbands were functionaries, some of them much in the public eye as ministers of the Crown, others – like Frederic Lowndes – no less influential and esteemed for operating under wraps, as grey eminences. Barrie and Arnold Bennett, Hewlett and Henry James, were free of this society whenever they chose. It was 'the establishment', or one very thick and influential layer of it; but it certainly was not made up of stuffed shirts and Colonel Blimps along with their twittering wives. Indeed, if we can suppress the automatic 'liberal' prejudice which indexes 'Newbolt, Sir Henry (1862-1938)' as 'English imperialist poet' (in *Ezra Pound. Penguin Critical Anthology*, ed. Sullivan), we have to acknowledge that it was in many ways an attractive society, and an admirable one. That we are dealing with a privileged élite goes without saying; as also that it depended on the institution of domestic service. But there appears not to have been, for instance, any of that sterile rivalry between man and wife which is now the bane of middle-class society with any claims to cultural or intellectual interests; plainly Mrs Lowndes and the young matrons who were her friends did not seethe resentfully at having their intellectual and imaginative capacities shackled to kitchen and nursery, whereas their husbands could exercise theirs in the great world. Moreover – and more to the point – if as literary intellectuals we feel frustrated at having no channel of access to the figures who exercise decision-making power in our societies, Mrs Lowndes shows us a society in which literary intelligence had direct access to such centres of power, by way of the conjugal bed as well as over the dinner table. Pound – thanks to Hewlett probably more than anyone else – had, at the time of his dinner party for Hewlett and Prothero and the rest, the chance of moving into that society. His espousal of *Blast* closed to him just those doors that were on the point of opening; and twenty years later, when he desperately wanted such access to the power-wielding centres of society, he was condemned to the world of fantasy in which he thought he could influence United States policy by way of such unlikely intermediaries as Senators Borah and Bankhead, and Italian policy by way of Ubaldo degli Uberti.

(This is not to say that Pound's decision was wrong. For Eliot, who chose the other way, earned entry into nothing more seriously influential than the circles of Bloomsbury, where the Edwardian pattern survived only in an attenuated and largely illusory version.)

If we ask what it was about this society which made Pound and also Lewis affront it more or less deliberately, to ensure that its doors were closed to them, I think only one answer is possible: it was ineradicably vowed to the idea of the artist as the amateur. It is true that Arnold Bennett, for one, refused to conform to that stereotype; and doubtless one could find other exceptions. But it is plain than in Mrs Lowndes's society, writing, for instance, was conceived of as typically a spare-time activity. It could not be otherwise if literary intelligence was to make itself available in drawing-rooms to administrative and political decision making. That English tradition of the amateur is of course a long one, and by no means ignoble, reaching back as it does through John Morley to Walter Bagehot, to Burke, to Addison, and so all the way to Philip Sidney and the Renaissance all-round man. But both Pound and Lewis were American or Americanized enough to have on the contrary a *professional* attitude to their respective arts, in the quite precise sense that they saw the continuity of art traditions ensured by the *atelier*, the master instructing his prentices. The renegade or maverick Englishmen with whom they allied themselves – Ford, and at another level A.R. Orage – shared this un-English conviction and habit. And this difference between them and such initially sympathetic Englishmen as Hewlett and Newbolt went very deep; for ultimately it meant that, when the question arose whether the artist's first responsibility was to his art (his *trade*) or to his society, Pound and Lewis and Ford would opt for the first alternative, Hewlett and Newbolt for the second – as indeed we soon see them doing when both of them answer the call of First World War patriotism by writing morale-building poems and stories. It is not hard to see that in *Homage to Sextus Propertius* Pound is centrally concerned with just this question, and is defending his own scale of priorities against Hewlett's or Newbolt's.

Something had certainly gone wrong – gone soft and mawkish – with the English tradition of the amateur, when we find Hewlett on facing pages of Binyon's volume of *Letters*, writing in 1916 to

E.V. Lucas, 'My Dear Lad, That will be jolly indeed', and to J.C. Squire, 'Dear Squire, I am very glad to have your quire of poetry... which is in jolly type and on jolly paper....' It is not thus, one cannot help feeling, that the serious artist addresses a fellow practitioner. And even before the War, though Hewlett in correspondence with Harold Monro and Newbolt could give and take hard knocks by way of semi-technical criticism, yet it is enveloped and emasculated by similarly anxious camaraderie. Still, Newbolt at any rate was able to understand something of what was at stake. In his 'A Study of English Poetry', which ran in *The English Review* from March to June 1912, Newbolt refers to Pound as 'a critic, who is himself a poet, and whom I always read with great interest'. Those who think of Pound as a great liberator from stiff and hidebound conventions will be disconcerted to find that Newbolt on the contrary treats him as an academic formalist. Newbolt says:

> The vast majority of what are generally called well-educated persons in this country have, in the very process of their education, been impressed with the belief that metre is an arrangement of language which can be judged by the application of a mechanical test, and that the poet who produces a line which does not answer to the test is a fit subject for correction by any critic who can point out the discrepancy. It is true that we are more enlightened than we were; there is a public which has learnt to smile at the reviewer who declares that a line 'will not scan', or that it contains a 'trochee' where it should have had an 'iamb', without considering whether it was ever intended to 'scan', or whether there is anything in English verse which can be treated as the absolute equivalent of a Greek or Latin trochee. But... the fallacy does appear, in much subtler forms. In the *Poetry Review* for February, 1912, a critic, who is himself a poet, and whom I always read with great interest, speaks of the struggle 'to find out what has been done, once and for all, better than it can ever be done again, and to find out what remains for us to do".... But if every work of art is simply the expression of the artist's intuition, it is evident that an absolute or complete pattern would be useless, since the intuitions of two different minds could never be expressed by the same form: nor can anything in art be said to have been "done once for all", since if it were "done again" by another hand – used, that is, to express the intuition of another spirit – it would be no longer what had been done before.

Newbolt's attitude is still very common – not only among the British

(especially those who have come under the influence of F.R. Leavis),
but also among American free versifiers who think they are an avant-
garde and who are muddled enough to think that they have Pound's
authority to back them. Whether they know it or not, they are in
fact endorsing Henry Newbolt against Pound! All the same, there
is by and large a crucial difference here between British and American
attitudes, and one that is today every bit as marked as it was in 1912.
For on nearly every American campus there is an *atelier* in the shape
of a 'Creative Writing programme', whereas on no British campus
is there any such thing, and indeed the British scoff at the mere
possibility – on precisely the grounds that Newbolt here puts for-
ward.

Pound's exasperated bewilderment before the spectacle of British
loyalty to the amateur, and British readiness to pay the price in
tolerance of the amateurish, is nowhere so evident as in his lifelong
esteem for Laurence Binyon, the editor of the Hewlett *Letters*.

According to Noel Stock's *Life*, Pound first met Binyon in the
second week of February 1909, and early in March he found 'in-
tensely interesting' a lecture by Binyon on European and Oriental
art, for which the lecturer had sent him a ticket. Some time that
year there occurred a famous meeting at the Vienna Café, in New
Oxford Street near the British Museum, when Pound as Binyon's
'bulldog' met Wyndham Lewis as the 'bulldog' of T. Sturge Moore.
This, nearly forty years later, was celebrated in Canto 80:

> Mr Lewis had been to Spain
>   Mr Binyon's young prodigies
> pronounced the word: Penthesilea
>   There were mysterious figures
> that emerged from recondite recesses
>   and ate at the WIENER CAFÉ
> which died into banking, Jozefff may have followed
> his emperor.
> "It is the sons pent up within a man"
> mumbled old Neptune
>   "Laomedon, Ahi, Laomedon"
> or rather three "ahis" before the "Laomedon"
>   "He stood" wrote Mr Newbolt, later Sir Henry,
> "the door behind" and now they complain of cummings.
> So it is to Mr Binyon that I owe, initially,
> Mr Lewis, Mr P. Wyndham Lewis. His bull-dog, me,
>   as it were against old Sturge M's bull-dog,

> Mr T. Sturge Moore's
>   bull-dog, et
>   meum est propositum, it is my intention
> in tabernam, or was, to the Wiener cafe
> you cannot yet buy one dish of Chinese food in all Italy
> hence the debacle
> "forloyn" said Mr Bridges (Robert)
> "we'll get 'em all back"
> meaning archaic words. . . .
>
> (506:540)

For 'prodigies' ('Mr Binyon's young prodigies') surely we ought to read 'protégés'; and then it becomes possible to wonder whether the jocularity about bulldogs doesn't mark a wistful or resentful sense that Binyon and Sturge Moore ('old Neptune') might have done more with their respective protégés than merely set them to sniff and snarl at each other's heels; to question whether the two senior writers could not have established themselves – at least for some purposes – as masters of *ateliers* in which the two young hopefuls might have enrolled as apprentices. Instead, the outcome of what seems to have been an uncomfortable occasion was merely that Pound and Lewis took that much longer to find out that they were natural allies.

It was probably on this occasion that Binyon said something that Pound, misdating the event 1908, recalled in the postscript to a letter to Binyon in 1934:

> I wonder if you are using (in lectures) a statement I remember you making in talk, but not so far as I can recall, in print. "Slowness is beauty", which struck me as very odd in 1908 (when I certainly did not believe it) and has stayed with me ever since – shall we say as proof that you violated British habit; and thought of it.

Who thought of it? Binyon, or Pound? Hugh Kenner is no doubt right to suppose that it was Pound who had been thinking of it. For it crops up in the *Rock-Drill* Canto 87, in the 1950s:

> Only sequoias are slow enough.
>   BinBin "is beauty."
> "Slowness is beauty."
>
> (572:608)

The mingled exasperation and admiration that Pound felt for

Binyon are nowhere so explicit and appealing as in what he wrote for *Blast* (July, 1915), so as to introduce into that inappropriately vociferous context nine quotations from the demure prose of Binyon's *The Flight of the Dragon. An Essay on the Theory and Practice of Art in China and Japan* (London, 1911):

> We regret that we cannot entitle this article "Homage to Mr Lawrence (sic) Binyon," for Mr Binyon has not sufficiently rebelled. Manifestly he is not one of the ignorant. He is far from being one of the outer world, but in reading his work we constantly feel the influence upon him of his reading of the worst English poets. We find him in a disgusting attitude of respect towards predecessors whose intellect is vastly inferior to his own. This is loathesome (sic). Mr Binyon has thought; he has plunged into the knowledge of the East and extended the borders of occidental knowledge, and yet his mind constantly harks back to some folly of nineteenth century Europe. We can see him as it were constantly restraining his inventiveness, constantly trying to conform to an orthodox view against which his thoughts and emotions rebel, constantly trying to justify Chinese intelligence by dragging it a little nearer to some Western precedent. Ah well Mr Binyon has, indubitably, his moments. Very few men do have any moments whatever, and for the benefit of such readers as have not sufficiently respected Mr Binyon for his, it would be well to set forth a few of them. They are found in his "Flight of the Dragon", a book otherwise unpleasantly marred by his recurrent respect for inferior, very inferior people.

It isn't hard to see here, once again, Pound's baffled exasperation that, instead of setting up shop as *maître d'école*, 'the very learned British Museum assistant' should resolutely duck back into doing such a worthy and humane but undoubtedly over-modest activity as editing such of the letters of his old friend Hewlett as could not conceivably give offence. Yet Binyon knew the unformulated rules of the society that he moved in, and played the game consistently as the amateur that that society required him to be. It is true to this day in England that, if one has learning, one must wear it so lightly that it is unnoticeable.

It would be tedious to quote and consider every one of the tributes that Pound paid to Binyon. One is at the end of *Gaudier-Brzeska* (1916); another is in a *Criterion* article of 1937, 'D'Artagnan Twenty Years After'; in that year appeared *Polite Essays*, which includes Pound's review of Binyon's translation of the *Inferno* (originally in *The Criterion* for April 1934); there are two tributes to Binyon in *Guide to Kulchur* (1938); in 1948 at St Elizabeth's Pound was still pressing Binyon on the attention of Charles Olson; and as late as 1958 he took the opportunity of *Pavannes and Divagations* to get back into print his appreciative note on *The Flight of the Dragon*.

None of these items is without interest. But 'Hell', the review of Binyon's *Inferno*, is particularly important; for it may well be one of the most careful and illuminating acts of criticism that Pound ever performed. It includes this passage:

> I do not expect to see another version as good as Binyon's... Few men of Binyon's position and experience have tried or will try the experiment. You cannot counterfeit forty years' honest work, or get the same result by being a clever young man who prefers vanilla to orange or heliotrope to lavender perfume.
>
> "La sculpture n'est pas pour les jeunes hommes."
>   (Brancusi)
>
> A younger generation, or at least a younger American generation, has been brought up on a list of acid tests, invented to get rid of the boiled oatmeal consistency of the bad verse of 1900, and there is no doubt that many young readers seeing Binyon's inversions, etc., will be likely to throw down the translation under the impression that it is incompetent.
>
> The fact that this idiom, which was never spoken on sea or land, is NOT fit for use in the new poetry of 1933–4 does not mean that it is unfit for use in a translation of a poem finished in 1321.

Pound may be right or wrong about the merits of Binyon's version, as about the sorts of language that are acceptable in verse translation; what is certain is that he's here applying to diction a sort of sliding scale or set of variable standards such as Ford's principles didn't allow for.

At any rate, Pound's enthusiasm for Binyon's version had led him to re-open correspondence with Binyon. And a letter of 30 August 1934 is particularly interesting, since it is rather plainly a reply to protests from Binyon about Pound's contemptuous treatment of Rubens. Pound's humility under Binyon's supposed rebuke is very striking:

> Dear L.B: When one has finally done the job and found the *mot juste*, I dare say violent language usually disappears. Rubens' technique (at least in one painting about 4 ft. square)

is not stupid. I dare say I damned him, for the whole grovelling imbecility of French court life from the death of Francois Premier to the last fat slob that was guillotined..... And my use of "idiotic" is loose. You are quite right about that. Have always been interested in intelligence, escaped the germy epoch of Freud and am so bored with *all* lacks of intelletto that I haven't used any discrimination when I have referred to 'em....

If, as I'm inclined to believe, this unwonted willingness to kiss the rod represents one last offer by Pound (at this time, aged forty-eight!) to enrol in Binyon's seminar if Binyon would only call it into being, Binyon once again knew better than to understand what Pound was driving at.

Oddly enough, the last word – though a mournful one – can be with Maurice Hewlett. For in 1920, when Binyon began work towards his version of the *Inferno*, he exchanged letters with Hewlett, who had translated the first canto years before, and now urged Binyon to shorten his measure to tetrameters, pointing out that this was what he himself had done in his 'Song of the Plough', a long poem in terza rima in which he had invested a great deal. Hewlett remarked: 'Another thing: putting in eights compels the terseness of Dante, wh. amounts sometimes to a vice in him. Still, there it is, and you must reproduce it'. How could Binyon have failed to remember this, when Pound complimented him by saying, 'He has carefully preserved all the faults of his original'? In *Guide to Kulchur* (chapter 30) Pound was to say, again with Binyon's translation specifically in mind, 'Honest work has its reward in the arts if no other where'. How one would like that to be true! But turning over the pages of poor Hewlett's unreadable but honest 'Song of the Plough', one wonders about that. One does indeed.

II Ezra Pound Abandons the English

Ezra Pound's long love affair with England, and his angry and
wounded turning against her in 1917 or 1918, cannot of course bulk
so large in an American's sense of him as in an Englishman's. It is
an American, Herbert Schniedau, who has asked:

> Can any man who identifies himself with the British world of
> letters, however independent and tolerant he may be, write a
> fair-minded book about Pound? What Pound did to English
> literature and British sensibilities doesn't seem forgivable, and
> I really think that the English were more offended by Pound's
> political obsessions than were the countrymen he ostensibly
> betrayed.

This is fair comment; and the last clause in particular is, surprisingly,
manifestly true, explain it how we may.

And yet an Englishman's relation to English culture and its trad-
itions may be more tormented than Schniedau allows for, especially
if the Englishman in question defines himself as, or aspires to be,
an English *artist*. Such a one may feel that Pound's 'writing off' of
England, his abandonment of her – physically in 1920, in imagina-
tion some years earlier – was abundantly justified, to the extent
indeed that it was not so much his justified rejection of her, as *her*
unjustifiable rejection of *him*. And yet such an Englishman must
wonder: Was there once virtue in England, which subsequently went
out of her? If so, when did this happen? In the casualty lists from
the Battle of the Somme? (Or is that merely rhetoric?) And can the
virtue that thus went out of the spiritual reality called England ever
be restored? Has there been such a restoration, since 1920? If so,
when did it happen? And if not, when will it ever happen? When,
and how?

These are serious and painful questions. At all events there are
Englishmen who find them so. To take one example out of many, the
native Englishman D.H. Lawrence reached just the same conclusion

as Pound at just the same time, and Lawrence's letters record it; he concluded, just as Pound did, that England after the First World War was, for the artist, uninhabitable. The names of Robert Graves, W.H. Auden, and Christopher Isherwood may serve to remind us of English writers who seem to have reached the same dismaying conclusion over the years since.

However that may be, there are reasons for thinking that the abandonment of England, and of any hopes for her, was not much less momentous for Pound than it is for his English readers. After all, Pound had *married* England – not figuratively, but literally, in the person of Dorothy Shakespear; and Ben Hecht in 1918 reported that Pound was 'a doting monogamist'.[1] It didn't last; his alienation from England seems to have coincided with an alienation from Dorothy, for within five years he had a child by Olga Rudge. And this is not altogether surprising; for Dorothy Pound seems to have been English in a singularly entire and uncompromising fashion. The daughter of Olivia Shakespear, who had been briefly Yeats's mistress and had bought Wyndham Lewis's canvases and Gaudier's drawings, Dorothy told Hugh Kenner in 1965, 'I read poetry only with difficulty. I never did much care for it'.[2] She said also, recalling Pound translating Noh plays on their honeymoon at Stone Cottage in Sussex, 'I was not then preoccupied with plays and characters. I was trying to make out what sort of creature I was going to be living with'. Moreover, Dorothy's Englishness was centuries old: among her cousins was one Charles Talbot – 'one of the Shakespear names', she said – who owned a medieval abbey, 'and once Ezra and I crawled over the roof in a turret to see a copy of the Magna Charta, kept there in a glass case'. In 1945, in an American prison camp near Pisa, Pound remembered that (Canto 80):

> To watch a while from the tower
>   where dead flies lie thick over the old charter
> forgotten, oh quite forgotten
>   but confirming John's first one,
>   and still there if you climb over attic rafters;
> to look at the fields; are they tilled?
> is the old terrace live as it might be
> with a whole colony
>   if money be free again?
> Chesterton's England of has-been and why-not,

1 Quoted by W.K. Rose, 'Pound and Lewis: the Crucial Years', in *Agenda* Wyndham Lewis Special Issue (1969-70), 130.
2 Hugh Kenner, 'D.P. Remembered', *Paideuma* 2 : 3 (1973), 486-93.

> or is it all rust, ruin, death duties and mortgages
> and the great carriage yard empty
>   and more pictures gone to pay taxes
> When a dog is tall but
>   not so tall as all that
>   that dog is a Talbot
>   (a bit long in the pasterns?)
> When a butt is ½ as tall as a whole butt
> That butt is a small butt
>   Let backe and side go bare
> and the old kitchen left as the monks had left it
> and the rest as time has cleft it.
>
> (Only shadows enter my tent
>   as men pass between me and the sunset)...

If, as Hugh Kenner believes, Pound never ceased to love Dorothy even while he loved Olga, this is surely part of what he loved in her, an aspect of what she meant to him; and so Pound's feelings for and about England were, right to the end, not much less tormented than any English reader's can be. And the English reader who does not understand that the punning on 'Talbot' is painful and all but hysterical, like the punning of Shakespeare's Hamlet, does not understand Pound at all. As for Dorothy's loyalty, it proved equal to any occasion; and in particular through the years of Pound's incarceration in St Elizabeth's her devotion was exemplary. Certainly she was no philistine, but a graphic artist herself. And yet... 'I read poetry only with great difficulty. I never did much care for it'. It is at any rate possible that in her a certain ethical rightness and decency coexisted with aesthetic stiffness and suspicion. It was a not uncommon combination in a certain breed of Englishman and Englishwoman – a breed perhaps now vanished, which is not to say, improved upon.

As for Canto 80, it continues, and closes upon, 'the matter of England':

> beyond the eastern barbed wire
> a sow with nine boneen
> matronly as any duchess at Claridge's
> and for that Christmas at Maurie Hewlett's
> Going out from Southampton
> they passed the car by the dozen
>   who would not have shown weight on a scale
>   riding, riding

                              for Noel the green holly
           Noel, Noel, the green holly
           A dark night for the holly

     That would have been Salisbury plain,
          and I have not thought of
             the Lady Anne for this twelve years
                  Nor of Le Portel
     How tiny the panelled room where they stabbed him
                  In her lap, almost, La Stuarda
             Si tuit li dolh ehl planh el marrimen
                  for the leopards and broom plants

     Tudor indeed is gone and every rose,
     Blood-red, blanch-white that in the sunset glows
     Cries: 'Blood, Blood, Blood!' against the gothic stone
     Of England, as the Howard or Boleyn knows.

     Nor seeks the carmine petal to infer;
     Nor is the white bud Time's inquisitor
     Probing to know if its new-gnarled root
     Twists from York's head or belly of Lancaster;

     Or if a rational soul should stir, perchance,
     Within the stem or summer shoot to advance
     Contrition's utmost throw, seeking in thee
     But oblivion, not thy forgiveness, FRANCE.

     as the young lizard extends his leopard spots
          along the grass-blade seeking the green midge
                  half an ant-size
     and the Serpentine will look just the same
     and the gulls be as neat on the pond
     and the sunken garden unchanged
     and God knows what else is left of our London
                  my London, your London
     and if her green elegance
          remains on this side of my rain ditch
          puss lizard will lunch on some other T-bone

     sunset grand couturier.

'That Christmas' (not that it matters) was Christmas 1911, which
Pound spent as a guest of Maurice Hewlett's at the Old Rectory,

Broad Chalke, Salisbury – a house which had once been a nunnery, dating back to 1487.[1] Hewlett, author of *The Queen's Quair*, brings to mind another writer who had similarly concerned himself with Mary Queen of Scots ('La Stuarda') – that is to say, Swinburne in his *Mary Stuart*. Swinburne is alluded to, here as elsewhere, by the place-name 'Le Portel', where – so Pound seems to have believed (wrongly, for the name is 'Yport') – Swinburne on a famous occasion was saved from drowning by French fishermen. At Holyrood House in Edinburgh one is still shown the room where Rizzio was stabbed 'in her lap almost'. The line in Provençal is from Bertran de Born's 'Planh for the Young English King', which Pound had translated splendidly as early as 1909. The 'leopards and broom plants', Plantagenet emblems, signify the dynastic reasons for which Henry the young king was killed, as were Rizzio and Mary's husband Darnley centuries later.

Anyone is free to decide that life is too short for such unriddlings; others (I speak from experience) may develop a taste for them. A more important point is that passages of this sort, spliced as they are with images like the lizard from the immediate foreground of Pound's tent inside the wire-mesh cage of the prison camp, do not come into being out of the free associations of idle reverie, though in these Pisan cantos Pound exploits the illusion of that, as Joyce did in *Ulysses* when he pretended to transport himself and us into the mind of Leopold Bloom. The reason we are reminded of these historical episodes, rather than any of a hundred others, comes clear only with the surprising and congested line that closes the quatrains about the Wars of the Roses: 'But oblivion, not thy forgiveness, FRANCE'. The England that Pound mourns the loss of is, as it had been for him from the first, an integral province of western Europe, sharing a common culture with France and always reaching out, through France, to the shores of the Mediterranean.

This emphasis will not commend itself to the English reader whom Herbert Schniedau envisages. Such a reader is likely to define his Englishness as precisely that which continental Europe is not. And in fact, of recent years Dickens's Mr Podsnap has walked again, cherishing insularity as a patriotic duty. But of course there are other things in this passage which will put English teeth on edge. Colonel Blimp today is likely to be a Roundhead colonel, in his professed sentiments a Leveller, though not of course in his practices. And his egalitarianism will be offended by 'the great carriage yard empty', and by 'more pictures gone to pay taxes'. Especially as voiced by an

1 Noel Stock, *The Life of Ezra Pound* (London, 1970), p.108. See also p.222 above.

American who had disloyally taken the wrong side in a war just successfully completed 'for democracy', the sentiments must have seemed – in 1948, when *The Pisan Cantos* appeared – nothing short of shameless! An English writer who went into self-exile just when Pound and Lawrence did, Ford Madox Ford, had always been denied serious consideration (as he is denied it still), in part for having, in *No More Parades* at the end of a previous war, envisaged the England he was leaving in just such manorial terms: and if the Englishman could not be forgiven, how forgive the American? (Lawrence, it is true, envisaged the England *he* was relinquishing very largely in the image of Garsington Manor; but then, Lawrence's origins are so impeccably proletarian that the aberration can be overlooked!)

And then there is the insolence of the last line: 'sunset grand couturier'. Isn't that the giveaway? It will certainly seem so to the Englishman (as I take him to be), who found in the 'Envoi' to *Hugh Selwyn Mauberley* – Pound's most explicit farewell to England, as he prepared to leave her in 1918 – 'externality: an externality which, considering what *Mauberley* attempts, is utterly disabling'.[1] This is the same reader who, having decided that the 'Envoi' is '*literary*, in a limiting sense', is provoked by the word 'magic' in the middle stanza into deciding that 'the term "literary" becomes a good deal more limiting, for the term "aesthetic" rises to our lips, and so, perhaps, does "American" '. And there we have it! For this sort of Englishman, 'externality' – to things English – is what any American is condemned to; and per contra 'inwardness' – with things English – is what an Englishman quite simply has, painlessly, as a birthright. From this point of view, the only good American is one who stays shamefacedly mute about his English cousins, however many years he may have lived among them. The same rule does not hold, it will be noticed, when there is any question of Englishmen talking about Americans.

The comment I have been quoting from appeared in 1965. The vocabulary is different from the comments of fifty years earlier which wounded and infuriated Pound, and drove him out of England,[2] but the sentiments are identical. And indeed even the vocabulary is

1 A.L. French, 'Olympian Apathein...', *Essays in Criticism* (1965). Reprinted in *Ezra Pound: a Critical Anthology* ed. J.P. Sullivan (Penguin, 1970), pp.326–42.
2 See particularly the last pages of 'Remy de Gourmont: A Distinction', (in Pound, *Instigations*, 1920). Here we find quoted G.W. Prothero of *The Quarterly Review* in 1914 refusing to print Pound in those august pages because of Pound's association with the Vorticist magazine, *Blast* – 'It stamps a man too disadvantageously'. More strikingly, a letter from de Gourmont in 1915 wonders none too politely if his writings could ever be acceptable to American readers; and Pound reproducing the letter reflects tartly that they certainly couldn't be acceptable to the English!

sometimes the same. The horrifying thing about, for instance, Robert Nichols's review in the *Observer* for 11 January 1920 – 'Mr Pound, indeed, serves his lobster à l'Américaine' – is that it could perfectly well have appeared in the *Observer* last Sunday.

It is entirely possible to think that if 'literary' and 'aesthetic' are words that go naturally with 'American' but not with 'English', so much the worse for the English. Ah, but we mean 'literary' – presumably 'aesthetic' also 'in a limiting sense'. Yet from those English lips which utter this face-saving locution, one has yet to hear the words uttered in any sense that is *not* 'limiting'. And from a set of preconceptions like that there is no way into Pound's universe at all. As regards 'externality', for instance, Pound may be thought to admit the charge, and to glory in it. For he applauded Wyndham Lewis's alter ego in *Tarr*, when the latter explained that it is a condition of art '*to have no* inside, nothing you cannot see. It is not something impelled like a machine by a little egoistic inside'; and again, 'deadness, in the limited sense in which we use that word, is the first condition of art. The second is absence of *soul*, in the sentimental human sense. The lines and masses of a statue are its soul'.[1] Between a *limiting* sense (for 'literary') and a *limited* sense (for 'deadness'), we are here navigating in light and tricky airs. And Pound had later to explain what he meant, and what he did *not* mean, by his endorsement of Lewis. After all, he was later to applaud Hardy's poetry for having precisely, 'the insides'. Yet he never retracted this avowal; nor – given what he meant by it – did he need to. The clue to what he meant is the last sentence from Lewis: 'The lines and masses of a statue are its soul'. That 'inwardness' so prized by some English readers, and characteristically found by them (implausibly) in Lawrence, is an attention directed so far 'inward' that it can never come to the surface for long enough to notice how the sunlight breaks upon the edges and volumes of a piece of sculpture; and that is why indeed such readers cannot use the word 'aesthetic' except 'in a limiting sense'.

Accordingly, the most instructive gloss on 'externality' is to be found where we might expect it, in Pound's 1916 memoir of the sculptor, Gaudier-Brzeska, where he writes of Gaudier and Lewis and other 'vorticists', painters, and sculptors:

> These new men have made me see form, have made me more conscious of the sky where it juts down between houses, of the bright patterns of sunlight which the bath water throws up on the ceiling, of the great "Vs" of light that dart through

1 Pound, *Instigations*, p.223.

the chinks over the curtain rings, all these are new chords, new
keys of design.

It is in this profoundly grateful and reverent sene, certainly not with
any heartless flippancy, that forty years later in the prison stockade
Pound greets the sunset as a designer – 'grand couturier'. Plainly
the man who wrote this was the man who in *Hugh Selwyn Mauberley*
took as his model and master Gautier, who described himself
proudly as a man 'pour qui le monde visible existe'. But the English
reader has a label ready to tie on to Theophile Gautier; and by this
time we can guess what is written on it – 'arid aestheticism'.[1]

When Schniedau says, 'What Pound did to English literature and
British sensibilities doesn't seem forgivable', he doubtless has in
mind certain passages from *How to Read*, which was originally
addressed to the American readers of the *New York Herald Tribune
Books* on 13, 20, and 27 January 1929. For instance:

> The Britons have never shed barbarism; they are proud to tell
> you that Tacitus said the last word about Germans. When
> Mary Queen of Scots went to Edinburgh she bewailed going
> out among savages, and she herself went from a sixteenth-
> century court that held but a barbarous, or rather a drivelling
> and idiotic and superficial travesty of the Italian culture as it
> had been before the debacle of 1527. The men who tried to
> civilize these shaggy and uncouth marginalians by bringing
> them news of civilization have left a certain number of trans-
> lations that are better reading today than are the works of the
> ignorant islanders who were too proud to translate.

Whereupon Pound applauds, as he had done before and was to do
again, Gavin Douglas's translation of Virgil and Arthur Golding's
and Marlowe's translations of Ovid. Again (where Pound's addres-
sing himself to Americans is especially evident):

> We are so encumbered by having British literature in our fore-
> ground that... one must speak of it in disproportion. It was
> kept alive during the last century by a series of exotic injections.
> Swinburne read Greek and took English metric in hand; Ros-
> setti brought in the Italian primitives; Fitzgerald made the only
> good poem of the time that has gone to the people; it is called,
> and is to a great extent, a translation or mistranslation.
>
> There was a faint waft of early French influence. Morris

1 A.L. French, op. cit.

translated sagas, the Irish took over the business for a few years; Henry James led, or rather preceded, the novelists, and then the Britons resigned *en bloc*; the language is now in the keeping of the Irish (Yeats and Joyce); apart from Yeats, since the death of Hardy, poetry is being written by Americans. All the developments in English verse since 1910 are due almost wholly to Americans. In fact, there is no longer any reason to call it English verse, and there is no present reason to think of England at all.

This is unfair? Yes, of course it is. Elsewhere in *How to Read* Pound remembers Landor and Browning, and has to make special provision to exempt them from these strictures. Moreover, when Pound revised and expanded *How to Read*, to make *ABC of Reading* (1934), he obliquely admitted the unfairness of these passages. But they are not *manifestly* unfair; there is a case to answer. We English have never answered the case, because we have refused to recognize that the case was ever made. And so the case against us has gone by default. Among serious writers and readers in the United States (as distinct from shallow and modish Anglophiles mostly around New York), it is taken for granted that Pound's caustic dismissal of us in 1929 was justified, and that nothing has happened in the forty-five years since to alter that picture significantly. Hugh Kenner, for instance, in a work of massive scholarship, *The Pound Era* (1971), can write: 'By the mid-1920s a massive triviality, a failure of will on a truly forbidding scale, was allowing English culture to lapse into shapes characterized by childishness, self-indulgence, utter pre-dictability'. And throughout Kenner's book 'English' is taken to imply arrogant obtuseness, complacent inertia, and effeminate ener-vation. If we resent this (as we should), we ought to realize that it is we who are to blame for it. For neither Kenner nor Pound is a professional or obsessive Anglophobe. Both men are reporting what seem to them the facts of the case, and they are the more confident about doing so because no Englishman has arisen to rebut their arguments. For us to respond with sneering anti-Americanism is the merest childishness.

After this, Pound's relations with England and the English were for the most part an aspect of his relations with that one of his erstwhile protégés who had become, surprisingly, a pillar of the English establishment – Eliot, editor of the *Criterion*. And these negotiations are mostly conducted in a tone of high comedy; after 1930 Pound's anger is virtually monopolized by Roosevelt's USA, and English culture is for him just something that he can't take seriously. This does not prevent him from honouring English writing when it is honourable; for instance Binyon's Dante, Rouse's Homer, the early books of Adrian Stokes, and the poems of Basil Bunting. But the preferred tone is one of indulgent banter. (And at the risk of labouring the obvious, let it be said that Pound is often a very *funny* writer, in verse and prose alike.) If the English reader doesn't like this, let him ask himself if Housman's *Name and Nature of Poetry*, or – touching as it is, and as Pound acknowledges – the career of Harold Monro, is not treated with as much compassionate indulgence as possible in the *Criterion* articles by Pound which he reprinted in *Polite Essays* (1937).

Still more to the point is another essay in that volume, 'Mr Eliot's Solid Merit' (originally in the *New English Weekly* for 12 July 1934). Considering that this was written at a time when Pound's reputation was eclipsed as Eliot's rose towards the zenith, the generosity of this essay, its lack of rancour, is admirable. And Pound's generosity towards Eliot did not fail through subsequent decades, when nothing was more common among the English intelligentsia, especially the academic part of it, than to assail Pound with weapons picked from Eliot's armoury. This strategy is still in high favour among us. It consists of making categorical and systematic certain distinctions made, and preferences expressed, by Eliot in his essays; and then dismissing Pound merely because he writes with a measure of respect of certain writers (Swinburne is one example) on whom Eliot, the arbiter of taste, is supposed to have conclusively turned down his thumbs. At its most ludicrous, this makes the 'Envoi' to *Hugh Selwyn Mauberley* suspect, or worse than suspect, simply because it alludes to Edmund Waller, whereas the okay authors from Waller's period, among pedestrian readers·of Eliot's essays, are taken to be Donne and Marvell. Eliot, needless to say, never countenanced these devious manoeuvres.

We should now be in a position to answer Herbert Schniedau's question: 'Can any man who identifies himself with the British world of letters... write a fair-minded book about Pound?' The answer is: Yes, this can be done, and it *has been* done – by G.S. Fraser, for one. If the English writer stops short of uncritical adulation, and also has a longer memory than the Americans for the loathsome politics that Pound was infected by, that is all to the good. There *are* British Poundians, and they are among the best. If there are few of them, we have seen why. It is because trying to give credit to this great poet commits a patriotic Englishman (or Scotsman for that matter – Fraser is a Scot) to very tormenting and unwelcome questions and reflections about the spiritual state of England or Scotland today, and over the last fifty years. It is therefore inevitable that our Poundians will be exceptions, and that majority opinion for the foreseeable future will be more or less hysterically hostile to Pound. This would not matter so much if Pound had not been a great technical innovator in verse writing. Because the British world of letters as a whole has refused, and still refuses, to consider Pound temperately, it refuses to acknowledge – indeed, it cannot even *understand* – the poetic forms that Pound invented, or the principles of form which he enunciated. And in saying this, one has in mind not the *Cantos* but the much more straightforward and generally serviceable forms which Pound put into currency in collections like *Ripostes* (1912) and *Lustra* (1916). One thinks, for instance, of imagism, and of the treatment which the *TLS* meted out to Peter Jones's anthology of imagist poetry. In short, what happens is that in England – and here one *does* mean England, rather than Scotland or Ireland – the non-academic makers and moulders of literary opinion are judging poetry by standards which are sixty years out-of-date. The rest of the world surveys this spectacle with amused disbelief.

Poetry Nation (Manchester) no. 4 (1975).

If we look at Pound in 1927 and 1928, when he instituted from or through Paris his periodical, *The Exile*, and sustained it through four issues, we get the impression of a man yawing about without direction, as at no time either earlier or later in his career. The very pages of his own magazine express the discernibly patronizing indulgence that it seems the American expatriate community extended to him. Robert McAlmon, writing reportage in *The Exile* number 2, noted: 'At the Stryx, I found Ezra Pound talking to an English girl, and describing America as it never was, is not, and never will be. I was glad to see Ezra, because what biased attitudes he has are so biased that he manages to be, all round, a more generous-minded and discriminating person that others who spread their capacity for bias over their entire mental outlook'. This is certainly not the language that one uses of a resident sage or recognized 'master'; and it seems that in Paris at that time there was in fact no one who esteemed Pound in either of those ways.

For just this reason the issues of *The Exile*, though they provide only conflicting evidence about Pound's acumen as an editor, are very instructive about the cast of his sensibility. Particularly interesting is the fact that, after backing so many winners, Pound in *The Exile* backed unmistakably at least one loser. This was Ralph Cheever Dunning, whose 'Threnody in Sapphics' appeared in *The Exile* number 2, and was strenuously defended by Pound in number 3:

> My present feeling is that any one who cannot feel the beauty of their melody had better confine his criticism to prose and leave the discussion of verse to those who understand something about it. . . . It still seems to me that the acting critics of poesy are for the most part incapable of looking for more than one thing at a time, having got started about 1913 (I mean a few of 'em got started about 1913 and a lot have started since) to look for a certain plainness and directness of speech and simple order of words; and having about 1918 got started

looking for Mr Eliot's rather more fragile system (a system excellent for Mr Eliot but not very much use to any one else), they now limit their criticism to inquiring whether or no verse conforms to one or other of these manners, thereby often omitting to notice fundamentals, or qualities as important as verbal directness and even more important than "snap".

The meaning of 'snap' in relation to Eliot's 'rather more fragile system' is at this date, I suppose, irrecoverable; but the general drift of these remarks is clear.

And this is not the only place in *The Exile* where Pound shows himself restive inside the image of himself that had been built up among initiates by his propaganda of fifteen years before, when he had taken over 'imagism' and championed Ford Madox Ford's ideas about a diction for poetry that should be 'plain' and 'direct'. At the end of this same issue of *The Exile* there appears from Pound a page headed 'Desideria':

> Quite simply: I want a new civilization. We have the basis for a new poetry, and for a new music.

But this ringing declaration is no sooner issued than it has to be qualified virtually out of existence. In the first place,

> I say "new" civilization, I don't know that I *care* about its being so very different from the best that has been, but it must be *as good* as the best that has been.

And secondly, much more to our present purposes:

> (Parenthesis. No, dearie, when I say, the basis for a new poetry, I don't mean the vers libre movement as it was in the year 1912.)

Of course the most cursory glance at Dunning's 'Threnody in Sapphics' (not to speak of more miserable performances like 'Isabelle of Hainault' in *The Exile* number 3) shows that Pound had, as it were, no alternative; there was no way to vindicate Dunning by imagist principles. He could not be vindicated by any other principles, either. But before we jump to the conclusion that Pound had simply had a brainstorm, or had been trapped by misplaced compassion for Dunning as a lame duck, we ought to consider another possibility – that imagism, and Pound's endorsement of Ford's insistence on 'the prose tradition', had never been for him more than an aberration, though in the short term a very profitable one, from a

way of feeling that impelled him always toward the *cantabile*, a pro-
clivity that would, in the interests of melody, tolerate notably eccen-
tric diction. It is thus that he declares himself for Dunning's sapphics,
flashing out at 'any one who cannot feel the beauty of their *melody*'
(my italics). And within six years, wanting to register (in *The Criter-*
ion for 1934) the distinction of Binyon's version of the *Inferno* despite
its consistent inversions of prosaic word order, Pound found himself
in the same situation, having to contend with those who had learned
too well or too inflexibly the lessons he himself had taught them:

> Before flying to the conclusion that certain things are "against
> the rules" (heaven save us, procedures are already erected into
> RULES!) let the neophyte consider that a man cannot be in
> New York and Pekin at the same moment. Certain qualities
> are in OPPOSITION to others, water cannot exist as water
> and as ice at the same time.

Moreover these were the years when Pound was writing Canto 30:

> Compleynt, compleynt I hearde upon a day,
> Artemis singing, Artemis, Artemis
> Agaynst Pity lifted her wail:
> Pity causeth the forests to fail,
> Pity slayeth my nymphs...

and Canto 36:

> I have no will to try proof-bringing
> Or say where it hath birth
> What is its virtu and power
> Its being and every moving
> Or delight whereby tis called "to love"
> Or if man can show it to sight.

To be sure, both of these cantos are special cases – as was, we may
suppose, the 'Envoi' to *Hugh Selwyn Mauberley*, written many years
before. Yet in one sense the circumstances of any and every poem
are 'special'; and at any rate all these instances show that, in his own
writing as in the writing of others, Pound was prepared to recognize
circumstances which justified departing very far indeed from Ford's
and the imagists' precepts about diction, indeed flying in the face of
them.

But what, then, are we to make of it when, in 1939, writing an
obituary of Ford, Pound lumped together two old associates of his,

Fred Manning and Henry Newbolt, and excoriated them for con-
tinuing to use the 'poetical' diction from which Ford's timely
polemics had weaned Pound himself? Is this inconsistency? Is it
worse – positive dishonesty? And what's to be said of his declaration,
as late as 1964 (in *Confucius to Cummings*, the anthology he put
together with Marcella Spann), that Ford's insistence on 'the limpid-
ity of natural speech, driven towards the just word, not slopping
down... into the more ordinary Wordsworthian word' was 'the
most important critical act of the half-century'? How could Pound
continue to proclaim this, when his own writing for decades before
had belied it? (For undeniably, the cantos are not *limpid*; much of
them isn't 'speech' at all, but 'song'; and of the parts that are speech,
by no means all are 'natural'.) Have we convicted Pound of incon-
sistency, or worse?

I think not. Pound knew enough of his own gifts, and of the
protracted strenuousness of his apprenticeship, to know that what
was safe for him was not safely available to others, least of all to
those he called 'the neophyte'. He knew too that the poem he was
engaged upon, *The Cantos*, was unprecedented and (he must have
thought) *sui generis*. (He was not to know that Charles Olson, after
next to no apprenticeship at all, would recklessly try to emulate
him.) But in any case, the best proof of the pudding is in the eating
– by which I mean that any one who has tried to help young poets
over the years, whether in Britain or America, knows that Ford's
and the imagists' precepts about diction are what most of them most
need to learn – no novelty, after all, since they can learn the same
lessons from the preface to *Lyrical Ballads*, if they choose to. What
they learn in such a case is, of course, only a rule of thumb; for if
criticism sometimes has to be prescriptive, its prescriptions are never
applicable except 'by and large'. Rules of thumb are the only rules
there are, in the *atelier*. But experience has taught me that this is the
rule of thumb that can be most profitably proposed and acted upon.
I dare to go further: some of the most gifted and earnest among my
contemporaries – I think of Edgar Bowers in the United States and
Geoffrey Hill in the United Kingdom (though I except Hill's won-
derful *Mercian Hymns*) – fall short of pleasing me as they might,
because they seem not to have followed this rule of thumb, and their
language is habitually for my taste a shade, or several shades, too
grandiloquent or 'literary'. I conclude that Ford's 'critical act' was
indeed (by and large, always by and large) the most important of
the first half of this century, and that it is, moreover, irreversible.

When was Pound in Sicily? How many visits did he pay to the island? What particular cities and districts did he visit? For which of these excursions was he in the company of Yeats? Presumably from the Pound papers now at New Haven it would not be hard to come up with answers to these questions. But in the meantime the printed sources are hazy, if not quite contradictory. According to Noel Stock (*The Life of Ezra Pound* [1970], p.251), 'about the middle of February 1923 the Pounds went to Sicily with Yeats and his wife'. On the other hand, in Joseph Hone's *W.B. Yeats, 1865-1939* (1942, p.367) we read that the Yeatses went to Sicily in November 1924 and stayed for two months, 'the attraction there being, besides the sunlight, the presence of Ezra Pound on the island, and the Byzantine mosaics of Monreale and the Capella Palatina at Palermo'. Certainly Pound was writing from Taormina in December 1924, and writing to Joyce from Syracuse on 21 January 1925 (*Pound/Joyce* ed. Forrest Read, 1967). And Richard Ellmann, in *New Approaches to Ezra Pound* (1969), names *1925* as the year in which the two poets, with their respective wives, were together in Sicily. All one can say with any certainty is that the Pounds (and probably the Yeatses also) paid at least two visits to Sicily in these years, and that on at least one occasion – probably on more than one – they stayed there for some weeks, if not months.

If we look in *The Cantos* for traces left by this experience, we are surprised to find how few they are, and how meagre. We might think that 'Naxos' in Cantos 2, 24, and 78 is the place of that name beneath Taormina, the site (lately and partially excavated) of the earliest Greek colony in Sicily, and thereafter the port whence the teams from all the Sicilian Greek cities made a ceremonial departure to compete in the Olympic Games; but the *Annotated Index* is doubtless right to identify Naxos, on the contrary, with an island in the Aegean. Apart from that, we have (at 25/115) 'that serene Lord King Frederic of Sicily' – which is to say, Frederick of Aragon (1272-1337), who was Frederick II, king of Sicily (1296-1337). At 27/129, we hear of 'the earthquake in Messina' (28 December 1908), but this is merely incidental to the vast *blague* perpetrated by Romains, Vildrac, and others in Paris – to be nostalgically remembered years later in the Pisan Canto 80 (see Richard Sieburth in *Paideuma* 2, p. 280). At 77/467 and again at 80/512, reference to the 'quai' or 'quais' at or of 'Siracusa' seem not much less adventitious, in the sense that location in the Sicilian city of Syracuse seems, at first sight anyhow, not to be significant. Rather more arresting is 80/503:

> hurled into unstillness, Ixion
> Trinacrian manxman

– where 'Trinacria', the ancient Greek name for Sicily, is related to the legend of how Vulcan the divine smith, somewhere in the island, solved the problem of perpetual motion, by a wheel with three dogleg spokes, its never ceasing to roll recalling the wheel that was the hellish and interminable torment of Ixion. (The same three-spoked wheel is the heraldic emblem of the Isle of Man.) There remains the joke, at 82/524, on the name of Frederic W. Tancred, a member of the Hulme-Flint circle (*c.* 1909), chiming with that of Tancred, Norman king of Sicily (d. 1194). This is a poor harvest from those weeks or months that the Pounds spent in Sicily; and indeed it is no harvest at all, since none of these allusions depends in any way on the poet's having been physically present in the island.

The same is true of a passage in the *Rock-Drill* Canto 94 (640-41):

> Acre, again,
>   with an Eleanor
> who sucked the venom out of his wound,
>   and came up via Padua,
> for a balance of wine & wool,
>   distraint and tolls not unbridled
> and in 1288 a thunderbolt passed between them
>
>   this wd / be in the time of Federico Secondo,
> Alfonso, St. Louis, and Magnus of Norway
> and two years later she died and his luck went out,
> Edwardus, who played Baliol against the Bruce
>   and brought the stone down to London
>   where it is seen to this day
>   PACTUM SERVA
>   Be Traist.

Here the Sicilian reference, in itself a very slight one but worth pointing out for reasons that will emerge, is in 'Federico Secondo', who is identical with the 'Frederic' of canto 25, glossed above. It is essential not to confound him with the greater Frederick II (Hohenstaufen), holy Roman emperor from 1215 to 1250, and before that (1198–1212) king of Sicily as Frederick I. For this great figure, author of *The Book of the Falcon* and a hero for Dante as well as Pound, is to figure portentously in the Thrones cantos to come as we shall see. By the same token, we have to keep a watch on dates so as to see that this Eleanor is *not* Eleanor of Aquitaine, but her great-great-granddaughter, Eleanor of Castile, wife of Edward I of England. The possibility of confusion is very great; for just as Eleanor of Castile landed at Acre in 1270, accompanying Edward on the seventh crusade, so Eleanor of Aquitaine had landed there 120 years before, accompanying *her* husband (that is, her first, Louis VII of France) on *his* crusade – which is presumably what Pound means by 'Acre, *again*'. (This 'rhyme in history' between namesakes is doubtless meant to strengthen the already well-established conflation of these Eleanors with their near namesakes, Helen of Troy and Helen of Tyre.) Most of the details about Eleanor and her relations with Edward, including his attempts to subjugate Scotland, symbolically signified by his removing the Stone of Scone to London, are found in the first volume of that small classic, Agnes Strickland's *Lives of the Queens of England* (1864).

At 97/681–2, we get:

PUER APULIUS

       "Fresca rosa" sang Alcamo.
Of Antoninus very little record remains

That he wrote the book of the Falcon,
Mirabile brevitate correxit, says Landulph,
     of Justinian's Code.

And here is the other Frederick, the Hohenstaufen emperor, he who wrote *The Book of the Falcon (The Art of Falconry, being the De Arte Venandi cum Avibus*, tr. C.A. Wood and F. Marjorie Fyfe, 1943). He appears under the name he was given in his orphaned youth – the Boy from Apulia. And with him comes Ciullo d'Alcamo, whose 'Rosa Fresca aulentissima' was translated by D.G. Rossetti: 'Thou sweetly-smelling fresh red rose / That near thy summer art....' This poem, and its author, figure in *The Spirit of Romance*, as showing that Italian poetry taking up from Provence originated not in Tuscany but Sicily. Though Ciullo by Rossetti's reckoning composed the poem in the 1170s, at least twenty years before Frederick Hohenstaufen came to the throne of Sicily, Pound in *The Spirit of Romance* juxtaposes the two names, presumably as 'an instigation' – though to what, it is not easy to say. Fifty years later, in *Thrones*, this is still the best he can do – juxtaposing the two authors, and the two compositions, as here, so also at 98/689, 100/719, and 103/736. If significance is supposed to accrue with each repeated conjunction, it fails to do so for me.

However, at Canto 106/753-54 (there is a brief allusion at 104/745 to the mosaics at Monreale), we do at last find a Sicilian allusion in the context of writing that we can recognize as distinguished:

>   That the goddess turn crystal within her
> This is grain rite
>   Luigi in the hill path
>   this is grain rite
> near Enna, at Nyssa:
>   Circe, Persephone
> so different is sea from glen that
>   the juniper is her holy bush
> between the two pine trees, not Circe
>   but Circe was like that
>   coming from the house of smoothe stone
> "not know which god"
>   nor could enter her eyes by probing
>   the light blazed behind her
>   nor was this from sunset

Enna, traditional location of the rape of Persephone (see Milton), is in mid-Sicily. But the location is, as it were, accidental, and contributes nothing to the tension between Circe and Persephone as it has been teased out, in this passage along with others, by Guy Davenport (see his 'Persephone's Ezra', in *New Approaches to Ezra Pound*).

In Canto 107, the Sicilian references suddenly come quite thick and fast, spliced into numerous quotations from Sir Edward Coke. This makes sense to the degree that one of the legal authorities whom Coke most often cites is Bracton (Henry de Bracton, *De Legibus et Consuetudinibus Angliae*), who dies in 1268, having flourished under Henry III of England and during the minority of Henry's son, the future Edward I. Moreover Edward and Eleanor spent the winter of 1270-71 in Sicily, en route to the Holy Land, and returned there in 1272 for Edward to learn that, his father having died, he was king of England. These are frail reasons, but the best I can find, for canto 107 to begin with a flourish of Sicilian place-names:

           The azalea is grown while we sleep
In Selinunt',
                    in Akragas
Coke, Inst. 2.,
                    to all cathedral churches to be
                        read 4 times in the yeare
                    20. H. 3.

Like so much else in these cantos, the last line is midleading, since
it suggests it was by an edict of Henry III that the Magna Charta
was sent to all cathedrals and read four times a year, whereas Coke's
Institutes make it clear that this was on the contrary an enactment of
Edward I. 'Selinunte' and 'Akragas' (the old name of Agrigento)
are ancient Greek cities in Sicily. Later in the canto (107/757-58) we
come upon:

           OBIT Coke 1634 & in '49
                        Noll cut down Charlie
           Puer Apulius... ver l'estate
           Voltaire could not do it;
           the french could not do it.
                        they had not Magna Charta
           in ver l'estate, Queen of Akragas
           resistent,
                    Templum aedificavit
                        Segesta

I think I know what this might mean, or what it might be *made* to
mean.[1] But I can hardly care. For this is wretched writing by any
standards. I said as much when *Thrones* first came out, remarking
on the insanely pointless jocularity of 'Noll' for Oliver Cromwell
and 'Charlie' for Charles I. Harsh words! But I repeated them in
Ezra Pound: Poet as Sculptor, and nothing that has come to my notice
since, including an erudite and adulatory article on these cantos by
David Gordon in *Paideuma* 4 (1975), has made me want to retract
my words or change my mind. Those of us who want to champion
Pound do him no service at all when we try to excuse the inexcusable.
And writing like this, if not indeed the writing of *Thrones* in general,
I take to be inexcusable. Moreover the style faithfully mirrors the

1 The meaning that might be ferreted out would identify the 'it' that Vol-
taire and the French 'could not do' with *Concord*. At any rate, that – Concord
– is the best I can suggest as 'Queen of Akragas', this on the admittedly
dubious grounds that the temple said to be 'of Concord' is the most perfect
of the temples surviving at Agrigento. As for the last two lines, the fascist
regime *did* re-erect some fallen columns in the temple at Segesta.

puerility of the content: to think that the barons who faced King John at Runnymede were anything like the Cokes or Hampdens who challenged the royal prerogative of the Stuarts in the seventeenth century, or that these in turn had much or anything in common with Sam and John Adams or Tom Paine, is to adopt the notorious 'Whig interpretation' of English history in a sort of parody version for grade school.

At 107/759, lo and behold, yet *another* Eleanor! In fact she has made a cryptic entrance already in the fifteenth line of this canto: '... of Berengar his heirs was this Eleanor'. This points to Eleanor *of Provence*, Edward's mother and consort of Henry III, whose reputation is as bad as that of Eleanor of Castile is good – though not for David Gordon, who seems to think that because she's said to be 'of Provence', this puts her above suspicion. At any rate, this identification is now confirmed:

> & this Helianor was of the daughters, heirs
> of Raymond Berengar
> and sister of Arch. Cantaur

'Cantaur' should of course be 'Cantuar', the Latin abbreviation by which the primate of England signs himself. For we read in Agnes Strickland: 'The death of St. Edmund, archbishop of Canterbury, furnished Henry with a further opportunity of obliging Eleanor, by obtaining the nomination of her uncle Boniface to the primacy of England'. Pound, it will be noticed, gets the kinship wrong, as well as the spelling. If there were not this evidence that at this point he is only hazily in command of what he is doing, we might ask – though to no purpose, I think – whether Eleanor's fiddling of her uncle into the see of Canterbury is presented to us for our approval, or the reverse. I don't believe Pound knows any more than we do.

And so to the last of the Sicilian references, 109/774:

> Clear deep off Taormina
>   high cliff and azure beneath it
> form is cut in the lute's neck, tone is from the bowl
> Oak boughs alone over Selloi
>   This wing, colour of feldspar
>   phylotaxis

And doesn't this give us – faintly indeed, but unmistakably – just what we've looked for in vain in all the other Sicilian allusions: that's to say, evidence that when Pound was in Sicily he didn't go around with his eyes closed, his ears and nostrils stopped? For that surely is the disconcerting, downright depressing, reflection that this sorry catalogue must leave us with. Sicily for Pound never but once had any existence that wasn't either *verbal* (as in the wordplay on 'Trina-cria' or the Eleanors), or else *notional*, ideological (as providing a sort of slender mnemonic crutch for a tendentious reading of history). The contrast with Yeats is instructive, and it doesn't work in Pound's favour. The effect of the Sicilian experience on Yeats is disputed by Yeats scholars, but it is generally agreed that some effect there was. Certainly, when Yeats chaired the Irish Senate committee that commissioned the Irish coinage (so wonderfully handsome as it turned out to be), it was photographs of Sicilian Greek coins that went out to prospective designers to show them what the committee had in mind. In Pound, on the other hand...are we to believe that he, the long-time admirer of Pisanello, when he was in Syracuse never visited the unrivalled collection of ancient coins in the museum there? Apparently we must believe that; at least there is no evidence that, if he did visit the collection, it impinged on his consciousness. And indeed what evidence is there that Sicily as a physical presence, a quite insistent presence as generations of travellers have found it, ever modified Pound's sensibility in the least? We are not looking for additions to the canon of 'sacred places'. We can accept that by 1923 or 1924 the sacred places had been settled on, and there were quite enough of them. What we seek is merely evidence that Pound didn't go to Sicily with a closed mind. Pound was to mock Yeats indulgently for seeing in Notre Dame not a physical presence in worked stone, but only a symbol; yet in Sicily Pound's seems to have been the mind that was *symbologizing*.

I do not like being forced to this conclusion. It pushes back, to a disconcertingly early period in Pound's life, the first signs of that aridity, that closing of the doors of perception, which – drastically arrested and reversed though it was, at Pisa and through the first years at St Elizabeth's – reasserted itself and wreaked the desolation of *Thrones*. Does not the use of the Na-Khi material in those cantos tell its own tale? This was material which the poet did not and could not *perceive*. Between the verbal and the notional, the perceived and perceptible were dropped out of his world. When he wrote in the last fragments

> "That I lost my center
>> fighting the world" –

this was the centre that he had lost. And when he wrote 'Tho' my errors and wrecks lie about me', I believe that cantos like 107 and 108 were those that he had in mind; and that he was right to judge them thus harshly.

V Two Kinds of Magnanimity

'Olson saved my life'. Thus Pound in January 1946, in his first days at St Elizabeth's, appealing in terror at the prospect of losing whatever sanity remained to him. How that life was saved we can now know, thanks to Catherine Seelye who has put the story together, mostly out of Olson's posthumous papers at the University of Connecticut.[1] Her tact and scrupulousness are beyond praise, and the book she has made cannot be recommended too urgently – even (perhaps especially) to those who have no special interest in, or liking for, either Charles Olson or Ezra Pound. What to do in a democratic society with the errant or aberrant citizen of genius – this question, fumbled at or glossed over by everyone who has written on Pound's case (jurists and psychiatrists, as well as biographers and critics), is here posed more starkly, and explored more searchingly, then ever before. We might have guessed that Olson would do it, if any one could. . . .

And yet this probably is the first point to make. To take the force of this testimony that none of us deserves to avoid, it's not necessary to like either Olson or Pound, but it is necessary that we *respect* them. And it's not always easy to respect the author of *The Maximus Poems*, marred as they are on nearly every page by solecisms and gaucheries, by arbitrary coarseness in diction, punctuation, syntax, lineation. This endemic failure at the level of execution is counterbalanced, for those who are patient and sympathetic, by the audacity and grandeur of the conception. But for the moment, that's not the point – which is rather that those who have been, legitimately or at least understandably, affronted by the pretensions of Olson as poet should not therefore write him off as anything but what he was: an exceptionally earnest and magnanimous man, and a man moreover who knew, as few poets since John Milton have known, what the polity looks like from the point of view of those who administer it

1 *Charles Olson and Ezra Pound. An Encounter at St. Elizabeth's*, ed. Catherine Seelye (New York, 1975).

day by day. It's because of this – the magnanimity even more than the political expertise – that Olson's appalled and self-questioning reflections on Pound's arraignment and incarceration make all others seem puerile at best.

By 'magnanimity' the last thing one means is a willingness to forgive and forget. On the contrary Olson is to be praised in the first place for the relentless hostility with which he presses the charge home:

> Pound can talk all he likes about the *cultural lag* in America... but he's got a 200 year *political lag* in himself. It comes down to this: a rejection of the single most important human fact between Newton and the Atomic Bomb – the sudden multiple increase of the earth's population, the coming into existence of the MASSES. Pound and his kind want to ignore them. They try to lock them out. But they swarm at the windows in such numbers they black out the light and the air. And in their little place Pound and his kind suffocate, their fear turns to hate. And their hate breeds death. They want to kill. And, organized by Hitler and Mussolini, they do kill – millions. But the breeding goes on. And with it such social and political change as they shall not understand.

Pound's admirers will protest at this, but they will be wrong. If they ask for proof, let them look into their own hearts. Do they not find there (I know I do) just that suffocation Olson speaks of? Just that panicky fear, always on the verge of turning into hatred until we shamefacedly choke it back? The Masses! How can we not fear them, and fearing them, how not hate them? Olson, in several ill-written but splendidly honest verse diatribes against MUZAK, showed that he knew that fear and hatred as well as any of us. For we cannot feel what we know we *ought* to feel – that 'the masses' are 'just folks'. (It isn't true anyway.) The fear and the incipient hatred are something that we impenitent elitists must learn to live with, not anything we can deny. For this is part of what 'democracy' means, or has come to mean. And yet we haven't come to terms with that. Which is partly what Olson meant when, linking Pound with Julius Streicher, he declared:

> Our own case remains unexamined. How then shall we try men who have examined us more than we have ourselves? They know what they fight against. We do not yet know what we fight for.

That is as true now as it was in 1945, when Olson wrote it.

What Olson drives at in Pound is his Fascism, not his anti-Semitism. Of the latter he gives horrific examples, which sicken him and enrage him (though as much in Mrs Pound's genteel English version as in Pound's red-necked American). But he always treats the Fascism and the anti-Semitism as two separate heads on the bill of indictment; and this I think (again I speak for myself) is what most of us stopped doing long ago. We act as if the anti-Semitism comprehended the Fascism – which would be true only if all Fascists were anti-Semites (they aren't), and if all anti-Semites were Fascists (even less true). Hatred of Jews is something that the Fascist is especially prone to, but it isn't a necessary consequence of his Fascism, and in any case it's only a symptom, certainly not the root cause of his disease. (In Italian Fascism it showed up only quite late, as Giorgio Bassani may remind us.) When we denounce the anti-Semitism and let the Fascism take care of itself, we are fastening on what is pre-political or sub-political, and refusing to engage ourselves on the plane of politics where, as Olson insists, we're required to vindicate our own sorts of polity against the Fascist sorts. What we gain from this is obvious: our own consciences are clear, and we're no longer implicated. Or if we are implicated a little (since doubtless some Gentiles and even some Jews have anti-Jewish feelings that they're ashamed of), the implication I would guess is altogether more manageable than what happens when – Jew and Gentile alike, black as well as white – the educated elite is forced to confront its feelings about 'the Masses'. And Olson won't let us squirm off the hook – for him the anti-Jewishness is symptom, not cause:

> There it is. It stops you. You feel him imagining himself as the last rock of culture and civilization being swept over by a wave of barbarism and Jews (communism and commercialism), the saviour of more than the Constitution, the saviour of all that has been culture, the snob of the West. For he is the AESTHETE, as I had Yeats speak of him. All – his pride in his memory, his sense of the internationale of writers, painters, musicians, and the aristocrats, his study of form as technique (no contours, no edges, intellectual concepts, but rounding, thrusting, as a splash of color, as Yeats described his aim in the Cantos...) it is all a huge AESTHETICISM, ending in hate for Jews, Reds, change, the content and matter often of disaster, a loss of future, and in that a fatality as death-full as those for whom the atom bomb is Armageddon, not Apocalypse.

Again, Pound's admirers will protest; and they will be right, insofar as Yeats's account of the *Cantos* isn't so definitive as Olson takes it to be. But the main thrust of Olson's argument is unaffected, and it can't be set aside: this great American poet (and Olson knows that Pound is all of that) was a Fascist, profoundly, and no amount of talk about his affinities with Whitman will save him for democracy, nor will any attempt to treat his anti-Semitism as an unrelated pathological aberration.

Another escape hatch that Olson slams shut upon us is the device of distinguishing between Pound-the-man and Pound-the-poet. The trouble with this manoeuvre is that it cannot help but demote poetry. And Olson will have none of that:

> Can any man, equipped to judge, find Pound other than a serious man? Can any writer honestly argue with those who shall, do, call him a crank? It's no good, that business. Around his trial you will hear it again and again. Just one of those goddamned writers. They're crazy. A Bohemian. There are writers who are such, but not Pound, despite all the vomit of his conclusions.

Pound was a serious man, and never more serious than when he was writing poetry; and his poetry drives towards just those unpalatable conclusions that Olson forces us to look in the face. If, on the other hand, from some consciousness of immaculate rectitude, we follow Allen Ginsberg in giving Pound a kiss of forgiveness – and it is in effect what David Heymann does towards the end of *The Last Rower* – it is poetry that we are presuming to forgive, not the man but 'the-man-as-poet'. How deep one has to go, to distinguish not 'the man' from 'the poet' but 'the-man-who-is-the-poet', appears from Olson's splendid essay of 1949, 'Granpa, Goodbye'. It is impressionistic? You bet it is impressionistic, and would that we had more such 'impressions':

> His power is a funny thing. There is no question he's got the jump – his wit, the speed of his language, the grab of it, the intimidation of his skillfully-wrought career. But he has little power to compel, that is, by his person. He strikes you as brittle – and terribly American, insecure. I miss weight, and an abundance. He does not seem – and this is a crazy thing to say in the face of his beautiful verse, to appear ungrateful for it – but I say it, he does not seem to have inhabited his own experience. It is almost as though he converted too fast. The impression persists, that the only life he had lived is, in fact, the literary, and, admitting its necessity to our fathers, especially

to him who had such a job of clearing to do, I take it a fault.
For the verbal brilliance, delightful as it is, leaves the roots
dry. One has a strong feeling, coming away from him, of a
lack of the amorous, down there somewhere.

Wait. I think I've got it. Yes, Ezra *is* a tennis ball, does bounce
on, off, along, over everything. But that's the outside of him.
Inside it's the same, but different, he bounces, but like light
bounces. Inside he is like light is, the way light behaves. In
this sense he is light, light is the way of E.P.'s knowing, light
is the *numen* of him, light is his way.

Maybe now I can get at this business of *amor* as of Ezra, and
get at it right. It isn't a lack of the amorous, perhaps, so much
as it is a completely different sense of the amorous to that
which post-Christian man contains, to that which . . . the likes
of Duncan, say, or myself may feel.

Of the likes of Bill W.? I am struck by the image of "fire" in
"Paterson." Maybe fire is the opposite principle to light, and
comes to the use of those who do not go the way of light.
Fire has to consume to give off its light. But light gets its
knowledge – and has its intelligence and its being – by going
over things without the necessity of eating the substance of
things in the process of purchasing its truth. Maybe this is the
difference, the different base of not just these two poets, Bill
and E.P., but something more, two contrary conceptions of
love. Anyway, in the present context, it serves to characterize
two different personal *via*: one achieves its clarities by way of
claritas, the other goes about its business blind, achieves its
clarities by way of what you might call *confusio*.

And this would be the point from which to look back at Olson, as
Catherine Seelye wants us to, and to regard *The Maximus Poems* as
embodying 'the way of *confusio*'. Which would raise the further
question whether this way, as practised by Olson, and by Williams
in *Paterson*, isn't so unlike the ways of poetry as we have known it
that to call their works 'poems' doesn't merely confuse the whole
issue. But that wouldbe a strictly literary question; and it's for raising
quite other questions that this book is momentous and irreplaceable.

New York Review of Books, 1975.

VI   Ezra Pound and the English

I have the impression that the novels of Phyllis Bottome are now little read, though I remember my mother borrowing them from the local library in Barnsley in the 1930s, and speaking of them with respect. They are too good to be forgotten, or some of them are. The one that in its day attracted most attention was *The Mortal Storm*, about the Nazis: though Phyllis Bottome herself seems to have preferred *Old Wine*, set in Vienna. The book of hers that stayed with Pound was *Private Worlds*, which he reviewed in the *New English Weekly* in 1935, and referred to twice in *Guide to Kulchur*.

Pound had known Phyllis Bottome between 1905 and 1907, when they were fellow students at the University of Pennsylvania, and it's not clear whether it is that early association, or a period later when she had caught up with him in London, that Phyllis Bottome had in mind when she wrote of how Pound tried to transform her as a writer from a talented amateur into a professional:

> I had successfully entered, at seventeen, precocious, and without a standard, the market of a profession which was, at the time I stormed it, financially profitable rather than intellectually exacting. Ezra provided me with a standard; and gingered me into an attempt to train towards it.

Certainly it is the Pound of the London years, who had profited from Ford Madox Ford's pronouncements on diction, that Phyllis Bottome must have had in mind when she wrote:

> The concrete image, unruffled by an adjective, *was* a thing Ezra would willingly have died for. *Rhetoric* was a thing he would gladly have murdered; and he had already carried out his theory of honest thinking at the expense of considerable financial and perhaps emotional sacrifices. His passionate and austere sincerity acted like a torch upon the young intellectuals of his day. He cast off his home and his country because he

was disgusted by its slovenliness of intellectual outlook, although he was certain (with his gifts) of success and reputation had he remained in his own land; and he was wholly unknown and unsupported when he attempted to browbeat London.

'His passionate and austere sincerity acted like a torch. . . .' This emphasis is significantly different from what it is nowadays common form to acknowledge – Pound's kindness and generosity to other writers, particularly in his London years. Behind the geniality and the ebullient showmanship, something 'passionate and austere' – I know of no other testimony which strikes that necessary note so firmly. And yet this testimony is little known.

It's to be found in *From the Life* (1944): one hundred sheets of wartime austerity paper to which Phyllis Bottome commits 'six studies of my friends' – that's to say, Alfred Adler, Max Beerbohm, Ivor Novello, Sara Delano Roosevelt, Ezra Pound, and Margaret MacDonald Bottome (this last the writer's American grandmother who in her forties became an influential evangelical orator). The pages on Pound are not the only ones worth reading. In particular the essay on Beerbohm is startlingly good: temperate, appreciative, sympathetic, yet in the end unsparing. And it is worth dwelling on that, to the extent of calling into evidence another of Bottome's books, *The Gaol* (1962), p.240:

> Ezra would have liked to see more of Max Beerbohm, whom he at least partially admired for his wit, although of course he could not have tolerated his philosophy of life. But although they lived as the only intellectual representatives of their own language in so small a place as Rapallo, they were not destined to decrease each other's mental loneliness.
>
> I found that Max Beerbohm, having once met Ezra, declined to enlarge their acquaintance. "I do not really see Ezra Pound in Rapallo," Max Beerbohm told me. "He seems out of place here. I should prefer to watch him in the primeval forests of his native land, wielding an axe against some giant tree. Could you not persuade him to return to a country in which there is so much more room?"

The consummate *silliness* of Beerbohm's sneer, quite apart from showing just how brittle and thin was that famous 'wit' of his, has alas a representative significance also, as we see when we put beside it Maurice Bowra, another famous 'wit', saying of Pound that he was 'not just a bore, but an *American* bore'. Such frightened insolence about Americans is still to be found in England, and among what the English regard as their intellectual and artistic elite. Often enough it takes the same form as with Beerbohm: the affectation of an anachronistic ignorance about what life in North America is like. And it shows, in Beerbohm and Bowra and as it survives today, how inevitable it was that Pound should have abandoned England and the English just when he did. He had no alternative; had he remained in London after 1920, the antagonism to him could only have got more obdurate and more brutal.

This is something that the Anglo-American Phyllis Bottome, writing in England in wartime, finds hard to accept:

> ...I like to think he will be forgotten as the belligerent sycophant of Fascism and remembered as what he was when I first knew him, in the years before our little war of 1914, when he was trying to take London by storm.

> Foreigners always find that a difficult process – in fact only one of them made a real success of it – and Disraeli possessed what Ezra had been denied – the elasticity and toughness of a good Jew.

> Ezra had neither toughness nor elasticity: he was as rigidly intelligent as a Plymouth brother; and as vulnerable as a sea-anemone.

> His unquiet personality could not outface the somnolent arrogance of the greatest city in the world.

> Yet Britain needed the youthful Ezra, almost as much as Ezra needed the thickly padded hide of this favoured country...

Or again:

> ...Had Jonah been less indigestible how can we be sure that the whale would have expelled him? Yet it was, I think, a tragedy for both parties that the whale of London could not keep down this nimble Jonah who distracted, but so well stimulated, her lethargic stomach. From the moment Ezra left the Anglo-Saxon world he began to suffer more and more from the isolation of his intellectual exile. This wild and wayward child of the Prophets – "a Daniel come to Judgment" – needed the thick padded hide of the antediluvian monster, whose maw he had so precipitately fled from.

One thinks rather the better of Phyllis Bottome for wanting to believe that what *had* to happen could in fact have been averted. But it should be clear to us now that the English hide which she thought so 'thickly padded' was in fact morbidly sensitive – certainly as long ago as Beerbohm's spitefulness in the 1930s, and perhaps as long ago as Robert Nichols's inexusable review of 'Homage to Sextus Propertius' in 1920. If Pound had been different...? He would have had to be as different as T.S. Eliot; and there's an end of *that* speculation! (For Bottome herself says: 'No one could write better than Ezra when he was not trying to score off T.S. Eliot by writing as badly as he knew how....')

What Phyllis Bottome wants to do – what, in 1944, she *needs* to do – is to shift the blame for Pound's Fascism on to something other than the heedless impetuosity of Pound himself. On the one hand she makes a speculative diagnosis of him, out of Adlerian psychology; on the other hand she half believes – but can't quite bring herself to say – that the blame lies with England, for virtually expelling him a quarter-century before. Even as she offers her diagnosis, she very touchingly envelops it in a renewed insistence on how he was still, in 1935, 'passionate and austere':

> Even as a young man, Ezra had always taken a determined stand on general decencies. It was not licence he wanted; alas! not even freedom – his goal was the forcible enlightenment of mankind....

> Even as a good Fascist Ezra found it hard to swallow the persecution of the Jews. He got away from the subject when I pounced upon it. The Teutonic mind, he said quickly, was no favourite of his: Mussolini, he implied, did not particularly dislike the Jews.

> It is necessary to turn back to Ezra's childhood to find a key to that dire impatience which has led him into so strange a spiritual home as Fascist Italy. It is, alas, the spoiled and wilful child who makes whips and bloodshed take the place of wisdom and social interest!

> Nevertheless in Ezra we are dealing with a creative artist who never – however impatient he was – sold his birthright for a mess of pottage. Ezra can be mistaken – more thoroughly mistaken than most people – but he has never been venal. He is one of the few people I have ever met who has never been either inflated or deflated by personal possessions. There is

practically no limit to his asceticism for any purpose – other
than asceticism. He lived in 1935 (when I last saw him) in the
utmost simplicity, although if he had been a little more con-
ciliatory he could always have earned enough for his comfort
– and his wife's; but he never valued anything that money
could buy as he valued the integrity of his sharp-shooting
mind.

Elsewhere in this memoir there is more that is notable – both of
documentation and diagnosis. In 1944 it took courage to write so
favourably about Pound; and it may even be that Phyllis Bottome
foresaw, and was trying to guard against, the peril that Pound would
be in as soon as hostilities should be over. In any case, what she
produced was something generous, anxious, and grateful. It should
be remembered, and she should be honoured for it.

I do not forget that my subject is Ezra Pound, not Max Beerbohm.
Yet the circumstance of the two writers being noncommunicating
neighbours in Rapallo is too piquant not to be instructive. And so
I think it is worth recalling what W.H. Auden wrote of Beerbohm
in 1965:

> Greatly as I admire both the man and his work, I consider Max
> Beerbohm a dangerous influence – just how dangerous one
> must perhaps have been brought up in England to know. His
> attitude both to life and art, charming enough in him, when
> taken up by others as a general cultural ideal becomes some-
> thing deadly, especially for the English, an intelligent but very
> lazy people, far too easily bored, and persuaded beyond argu-
> ment that they are the *Herrenvolk*. One may be amused –
> though not very – that after living in Italy for forty-five years
> Max still could not speak Italian, but such insularity is not to
> be imitated. "Good sense about trivialities", he once wrote,
> "is better than nonsense about things that matter." True
> enough, but how easily this can lead to the conclusion that
> anyone who attempts to deal with things that matter must be
> a bore, that rather than run the risk of talking nonsense one
> should play it safe and stick to charming trifles. . . .

This, remember, is W.H. Auden, whom for many years some people
in England have regarded as himself too anxious not to bore, too
anxious always to amuse. If this suggests that there are other sorts
of English people than the sort Auden has in his sights, on the other
hand it lends point and force to his censure of Beerbohm, and of
what Beerbohm stands for in English life. Auden goes on:

As it is, he slyly suggests that minor artists may look down their noses at major ones and that "important" work may be left to persons of an inferior kennel, like the Russians, the Germans, the Americans, who, poor dears, know no better. The great cultural danger for the English is, to my mind, their tendency to judge the arts by the values appropriate to the conduct of family life. Among brothers and sisters it is becoming to entertain each other with witty remarks, hoaxes, family games and jokes, unbecoming to be solemn, to monopolize the conversation, to talk shop, to create emotional scenes. But no art, major or minor, can be governed by the rules of social amenity. The English have a greater talent than any other people for creating an agreeable family life; that is why it is such a threat to their artistic and intellectual life. If the atmosphere were not so charming, it would be less of a temptation. In postwar Britain, the clothes, accents, and diction of the siblings may have changed, but, so far as I can judge, the suffocating insular coziness is just the same.

Here, as often with the author of *Thankyou, Fog*, we may well suspect that Auden generalizes about English life too much on the basis of his own late-Edwardian childhood in a comfortable rentier household. And yet I wouldn't dismiss out of hand Auden's claim that what he says of our family life holds as true of Coronation Street as of Lowndes Square. In any case, enveloped though it is in ingratiating compliments to us on how charming we are in the bosoms of our families, the indictment is quite firm and it is unsparing: 'Suffocating insular coziness'. Most of all worth remembering is the trenchant declaration: '. . . no art, major or minor, can be governed by the rules of social amenity'. It was because Pound behaved always in the spirit of this remark that he could not fail to offend Englishmen of the type of Beerbohm and Bowra, and that he continues to offend their likes and their successors (in all social classes) at the present day, as, for instance, his confrere T.S. Eliot did not and does not. On this issue indeed the comparison with Eliot is inescapable. Eliot very early learned and bowed to the English rule that social amenity must not be disturbed – alike in his life-style and, after *Poems 1920*, in his poetic style also, he observed this rule punctiliously. Pound saw him doing it, and chuckled indulgently; it was what he meant by dubbing Eliot 'the Possum' (opossum, the creature that escapes danger by shamming dead). And when we remember what Eliot did with the gibe, taking it over in the title of *Old Possum's Book of Practical Cats*, that collection of whimsical fireside charades in verse, we may well think again about Auden's comment that in English family life 'it is becoming to entertain each other with witty remarks, hoaxes, family games and jokes'. Is it perhaps true that for many of the English, poetry has never been anything else but a superior parlour game? We might begin to think so if we reflected that in parlour games the rules never change, and then noticed that this year the most accomplished of our poets in their forties published, sixty years after Pound's *Lustra* and Eliot's *Prufrock*, an ambitious poem in the shape of fifteen interlinked pentameter sonnets.

However, a safer and a wiser idea is to take up what I began with: Phyllis Bottome telling how Pound, when they were both young, tried to turn her as a writer from an amateur into a professional. It was, of course, what he tried to do with everyone that he thought worth the trouble. And once again it was this unrelenting professionalism in Pound that set, and continues to set, Englishmen's teeth on edge. For in our national tradition, in the arts as until recently in sports, it is the amateur who is most admired; and Auden's charming joker by the Christmas hearth is only a particular version of the amateur. He observes the prohibition against 'talking shop', whereas Pound through his London years seems never to have talked anything else. (Once again Eliot knew, or soon learned, better.) And the most Anglophobe of Pound's books is, appropriately, the one that is most full of shoptalk – though of shoptalk of a special kind, the talk of the master to his apprentices in the shop that is a workshop, the *atelier* where the talk that goes on is the vehicle by which an artistic tradition is transmitted, not in conceptualizing, and tendentious readings of history, but where it is *concrete*, in tricks of the trade and rules of thumb and words to the wise. I have in mind *How To Read*, a disastrously misnamed little treatise, since its real subject is How to Write, and it is addressed to what Pound called (with the engagingly dated Edwardian elegance that he never wholly shed) 'the neophyte' – that is to say, to the young American writer who wants to know as soon as possible, though at the expense of considerable exertion which he is prepared for, how to assemble his kit of tools for the job in hand and others that he can dimly foresee. When Pound revised and expanded this to make *The ABC of Reading* (the title is *still* a misnomer), he winkled out of it most of the anti-Englishness that had been present in the first version, when Pound was still smarting from what he took to be England's rejection of him eight years before, in 1920. I have argued elsewhere that Pound was prepared to take instruction, as well as to give it; that when he first came to London in 1908, he was looking for masters to whom he might apprentice himself; that he found them in the Irishman W.B. Yeats and the maverick Englishman Ford Madox Ford (whose professionalism about writing still denies him in England the recognition that he gets abroad); and (so I have speculated, though I know it cannot be proved) that Pound sought the same relationship with another Englishman, Laurence Binyon, who was too cagey to go along with the idea. Before we leave this topic, with some doubtless well-received witticisms about the American *ateliers* that are called Schools of Creative Writing, let us ask ourselves how an artistic tradition *is* transmitted from generation to generation in England, if it is not transmitted in the way that Pound took for granted. And let me assist such reflections by reporting that a gifted and earnest English poet of thirty-two, whom I met this very summer, not only confessed that he had never read through Basil Bunting's *Briggflatts*, but quite plainly saw no reason why he ever should.

We can stage a little comedy for ourselves if we pick out two expressions that I used in my last paragraph, and imagine ourselves presenting them to the startled and unwelcoming gaze of Max Beerbohm. They are the expressions 'kit of tools' and 'job in hand'. We may doubt that Beerbohm had the acumen or the catholicity to respond to this provocation as conclusively as he should. But in that case, let us do it for him. The conclusive objection to 'kit of tools' or 'job in hand' as appropriate expressions when we talk of poetry, is in some late lines by Eliot:

> Because one has only learnt to get the better of words
> For the thing one no longer has to say, or the way in which
> One is no longer disposed to say it.

It is the occasion which determines what figurations of language are appropriate to it, and no one poetic occasion duplicates any other. To this extent and in this way the English distrust of the professional writer can and must be vindicated. It was what Pound found out the hard way, when the recurrent occasions of *The Cantos* compelled him time and again, not infrequently, to go against the precepts that he had promulgated himself when he was the fugleman for imagism and vorticism – for instance (and it *is* only the most obvious instance), the prohibition against archaic diction. What's more, though it seems not to be generally realized, Pound recognized what had happened and acknowledged it; he did so in the public welcome he gave to Binyon's translations of Dante, which employ a very archaic and convoluted diction indeed. And this was not the only occasion on which he protested, in the 1920s and 1930s, at having the precepts that were formulated to meet the special conditions of 1914 taken as absolute and binding for all poetic situations at all times. He does not, however, retract his proposal that the precepts of the imagist manifesto *are* still the best rules of thumb for 'the neophyte', the beginner in his 'prentice-work; and for what it is worth my own experience in the workshop certainly bears that out. The notion that we crucially need, I think, to do justice to the conflicting claims of the amateur and the professional in these matters, is the idea of *thresholds*. In verse writing, as in virtually any other human activity we may think of, there are thresholds to be reached and crossed: below a certain threshold of practice and expertise, the attitude of the amateur produces only work that is 'amateurish' (and heaven knows, we see plenty of that all around us); above a certain threshold of facility, the attitude of the professional produces work that is glib, facile, heartless, and academic – and we see plenty of that, too. Though I think neither Eliot nor Pound explicitly used the idea of 'the threshold', the idea is surely implicit in the criticism of both men; and it is an implication that in our own criticism, and our own practice as verse writers, is almost universally ignored.

At any rate, in this way if in no other, the English ideal of the artist as amateur has a continuing validity – and one that it behoves us, as Poundians, to acknowledge more often than we do. It is an idea – the idea that the practice of our art should *ideally* be an avocation rather than a vocation – which has a distinguished and ancient lineage, to be traced back through the English bourgeois idea of 'the gentleman' to the Italian aristocratic idea of 'the courtier'. Yeats's poem, 'In Memory of Major Robert Gregory', is centrally concerned with this, as when he associates Robert Gregory with that paradigm of the English courtier, Philip Sidney. And during the years when Pound was most under Yeats's influence, Pound too embraced this ideal – as when in 1912 he went with Yeats and some others to pay an act of homage to one of the last English representatives of the type, the Sussex squire Wilfred Scawen Blunt:

> But to have done instead of not doing
>   this is not vanity
> To have, with decency, knocked
> That a Blunt should open
>   To have gathered from the air a live tradition
> or from a fine old eye the unconquered flame
> This is not vanity.
>   Here error is all in the not done,
> all in the diffidence that faltered.

However, we know from Yeats's letters even more than his poems that he thought the last possibility for aristocratic ease in the arts had disappeared when Robert Gregory was shot down over France in 1915. And I think it could be maintained that when Pound left

England in 1920, it testified to a similar recognition by him that the amateur ideal in the arts, however admirable in the abstract, and however rich its achievements under earlier structures of society, under the conditions of mass democracy could mean only amateurishness in technique, and thin-skinned insolence in debate. Who is to say that Yeats and Pound were wrong? Not I, certainly.

What is important to realize is that for Yeats certainly, and I think at times for Pound also, the only alternative open was a sorry second best. Yeats in a letter specifically invoked the name of Wilfred Scawen Blunt on one of many occasions when he girded in rage against the 'unnatural labour' that verse writing had become for him, with the disappearance of the less egalitarian society that Gregory and Blunt stood for. Professionalism in writing was what Yeats resentfully found himself condemned to; but he didn't like it, and he never pretended to. Obviously, the same cannot be said of Pound. On the contrary, as I have insisted, one indelibly American thing about Pound from the day when he first reached London was his, as it must seem to us, excessive faith in know-how, in a communicable 'bag of tricks'. And yet there is his tribute, as late as the Pisan years, to Blunt; there is the fact that his friendship with Yeats did not end except with Yeats's death; and there is above all the fact that his disenchantment with mass democracy kept pace with Yeats's, and culminated for him as for Yeats in the false alternative of Fascism. I believe a close examination of his recorded opinions, and of the idiom in which those opinions were expressed (an idiom, even to the end, as much British as American), would show that Pound too was not insensible to the ideal of the aristocratic amateur in the arts, and was at least sometimes resentful, just as Yeats was, that political and socio-economic developments had made that attitude to the arts impracticable and sterile. If so, we English Poundians, even as we castigate our countrymen for clinging to the norm of the amateur in an age when that norm is unserviceable, may well spare more than just wistful nostalgia for this ideal that survives among us only in a debased and anachronistic version.

One reason for insisting on this possibility is to prevent us from being too complacent and self-congratulating about what we are engaged in, here and now. We should beware of supposing that, if Pound from the shades is looking at this present occasion, he is unreservedly gratified by what he sees. Weekend conference and seminar and study group, doctoral dissertations, and communally compiled working papers toward another *Annotated Index* – we may agree, as I do, that in present historical conditions these are the best or the only ways of responding to the achievement of a very great, though of course imperfect, poet. We may even feel, as certainly

I do, that some of the later cantos are of such a nature that it's hard to conceive in *any* age of a way of encountering them other than the way we're here embarked upon. And yet we need to remember – Pound, I think, would have wanted us to remember – what a late-come development this is in the relations between a poet and his readers, how recent this is, and, in the perspective of history, how bizarre. We may surely placate the shade of Max Beerbohm sufficiently to acknowledge that the danger we run in approaching poetry this way is indeed the danger of one sort of professionalism – specialized and therefore blinkered, inflexible, and humourless. I suspect that Pound is rueful at best when he looks down and sees us industriously annotating out of Sir Edward Coke Canto 107, without noticing that the English language is in that canto handled with none of the sensitivity that would make those labours worthwhile.

What I am saying is that a lot of the common English objections to Ezra Pound have substance, and would be worth taking seriously, if only we could be sure that they were advanced in good faith, in humility, and with compassion. Unfortunately the tone in which they are expressed, and the language they are couched in, prevent our taking them in that way, and recall for us rather the heads of Auden's indictment: 'lazy... too easily bored... persuaded beyond argument...' Accordingly, an assembly such as this in England – and let me remind you there have been earlier ones, at Sheffield and Keele – is an act of homage to a great and greatly maligned poet; but it is also, and cannot help but be, a patriotic demonstration against 'suffocating insular coziness'.

Paideuma 7 : 1-2 (1978). This was originally a lecture to a London conference of Pound studies in 1977.

Virgil's Presence in
Ezra Pound and others

Most considerations of Virgilianism in our modern poetry have concentrated on, have been perhaps mesmerized by, the figure of T.S. Eliot. This is natural: the exceptionally influential eminence that Eliot achieved through the second half of his life, together with his almost explicit (though characteristically demure) donning of the Virgilian mantle himself,[1] have made it inevitable. And Eliot is still the massive figure that must be circumvented if we are to see Virgil as having exerted a powerful influence on our modern poetry in ways more partial, devious and oblique than Eliot allowed for.

For Eliot was intransigent. Like the less diplomatically suave authority, Theodore Haecker,[2] whom Eliot was at times glad to call on, the author of *Four Quartets* and editor of *The Criterion* required us to take Virgil as, above all, the author of the Fourth Eclogue, the pagan poet who prophesied Christianity, whose vision of human history must accordingly be seen as completed and vindicated by *The Divine Comedy*. Eliot, it seemed, would have us take Virgil on his terms, or not at all. And his terms were unyielding. They were the same terms which Dante and the mediaeval jurists insisted on: Virgil was great, was perpetually relevant and in that sense 'a classic' (if not, more exactly, the one indisputable 'classic'), because in him could be found what Dante teased out of him – the vision of Empire, of the divinely appointed *imperium*, which must be reconciled (this way and that, for the reconciling was not easy) with the no less divinely intended *ecclesia*. The Holy Roman Empire, of Charlemagne, of the Ottonian emperors, through to the Hohenstaufens, was to be seen in all seriousness as the legitimate heir of 'the Augustan peace': a dispensation which, though seldom or never actualized through the last five centuries, must be held in mind as the one and only imaginable harmonizing of Church and State, of religion and politics, at least throughout Europe. Nothing less than that potentiality

---

1 See especially *What Is a Classic?* (London, 1944).
2 *Virgil, Father of the West*, tr. A.W. Wheen (London, 1934).

could, so Eliot seemed to suggest, give order and significance to the otherwise squalid and meaningless turbulence of the middle decades of the present century.

The vision was grand and, in its intransigence, breath-taking. But how it could be brought to bear on specific political decisions that had to be taken in for instance the 1930s – this was far from clear even to Eliot himself, if we judge from the dryly disenchanted tone of many of his editorial pronouncements and observations in *The Criterion*. Others before Frank Kermode, in his suave and erudite but ultimately acidulous *The Classic* (New York, 1975), had protested that as a framework inside which real political decisions and actions could be taken, Eliot's Virgilian-Dantesque perspective was not just useless but dangerous. After all, had it not led Eliot into seeming to endorse the anti-semitic French royalism of Charles Maurras?

In recent years the one English voice that has seemed to reiterate the Eliotic thesis in anything like its entirety has been the voice of C.H. Sisson:

> The case of Virgil is a crucial one... For anyone for whom literary education – like any other – is an exploration of the meanings we have and live by, so far as we do live by meanings, Virgil and Dante are connecting rooms... To talk of getting the full charge of the Divine Comedy – or more modestly and exactly, the fullest charge the particular reader is capable of getting – while treating Dante's master as an irrelevance, is nonsense;...[1]

This is part of a polemic (reluctant, because in other contexts and on other grounds Sisson venerates Pound) against Ezra Pound's treatment of Virgil: '.... there are such absurdities in Pound as the assertion that Gavin Douglas's excellent *Aeneidos* is "better than the original", together with other devaluings of Virgil'. For Eliot and Sisson it is unthinkable that one can venerate Dante without venerating Virgil, and *vice-versa*; whereas Pound was firmly pro-Dante, and yet often raucously dismissive of Virgil. The divergence is important, perhaps crucial, because Pound and Eliot, American expatriates of roughly the same generation, in the London of the second decade of this century made common cause and thereafter – despite ever wider ideological disagreements – remained friends, mutually respectful and mutually supporting, until Eliot's death in 1965. Even today the two-headed chimera 'Pound-Eliot' (not in

---

1 'Pound's Literary Programmes', in *Agenda* 17: 3–4 and 18: 1 (1980), 206–07.

all ways chimerical) still stalks at large in literary discourse.

Some part of Sisson's censures must surely be conceded: whatever esteem we have and should have for Gavin Douglas's translation of the *Aeneid*, we can hardly believe that the Philadelphian Ezra Pound was any more at ease than most of us with Bishop Douglas's six-teenth-century Scots. And some of Pound's many tributes to Doug-las admit as much. Pound's championing of Douglas had much to do with a polemic, in itself just and timely, against the presumed and unearned superiority of metropolitan English over the dialects of the British Isles, and of the English-speaking world. At any rate it should not surprise us that when Virgil most startlingly irrupts into Pound's *Cantos* (rather late – it is in Canto 78), he should be heard speaking in the Caledonian accents of Gavin Douglas.

The question can still be raised whether Pound had any access to Virgil except through translation. Pound, following a polemical strategy which served him well in the short run (but which later back-fired) deliberately provoked the academic classicists of his day; and his use of his sources, classical and other, was always both hasty and high-handed. And so there are still to be found Latinists who think that the hilarious mistranslations in his *Homage to Sextus Propertius* (1919) were inadvertent rather than mischievously delib-erate. Accordingly the point must be made that the young Pound, as a doctoral student grounded quite rigorously in the Romance languages, certainly could and did read Virgil in the Latin. Evidence of this is in the play he makes with the Virgilian *aether* and *patet* (*Aeneid* 6, 127, 130) in the puzzling but impressive Canto 16. But even more telling is the negative evidence that, with the confessedly eccentric exception of Gavin Douglas, none of Virgil's translators have left their footprints on *The Cantos*. Particularly conspicuous by his absence is that verse-translator of Virgil who is generally held (in my view, rightly) to have set a standard that no other can equal, except momentarily; that is, Dryden. One commentator has indeed thought he found an echo of Dryden's translation of *Aeneid* 2, 417-20, in the opening lines of Canto 4; but I am persuaded by later scholars that the case is untenable.[1] This conspicuous absence of Dryden, though it helps to show that Pound needed no intermediary in his traffic with Virgil, also exposes a dispiriting limitation to Pound's taste, so catholic as he meant it to be: he never stretched his originally late-Victorian conditioning so far as to appreciate the masters of the English heroic couplet. So in his late anthology,

---

1 See Bradford Morrow, in *Paideuma* 3 : 2 (1974), 245-6; and cf. Christine Froula, *To Write Paradise* (New Haven & London, 1984), p.47n.

Confucius to Cummings (New York, 1964, with Marcella Spann), he explicitly preferred George Chapman's Homer to Pope's, even though he had admitted that Chapman is unreadable, except for a few pages at a time. And we cannot help but contrast the generous appreciation of Dryden by Eliot, who might have been expected to be temperamentally less in tune with him.

There is a more telling comparison. Thomas Hardy, of an older generation, had implicitly claimed to be, and in the event had proved to be, a profoundly Virgilian poet.[1] Hardy was self-educated. But his self-education had been very thorough, so that he turned himself into a good Latinist and a good Grecian also, as Pound in *Confucius to Cummins* acknowledged. It is the more remarkable that Pound, no more than any one else for fifty years after Hardy died, pondered the Virgilian epigraph that Hardy put at the head of his 'Poems of 1912-13', originally in *Satires of Circumstance*, (London, 1914). The epigraph is *Veteris vestigia flammae* from *Aeneid* 4, 23, where Dido confesses to her confidante that the love she once felt for her now dead husband is about to renew itself for Aeneas. The same phrase had been translated and mordantly placed by Dante in Canto XXX of the *Purgatorio*; and so, when Hardy in these poems confronts the shade of his recently deceased and estranged wife Emma, not only does Aeneas in *Aeneid* 6 confront the reproachfully haughty ghost of Dido, but Dante's pilgrim confronts for the first time the shade or apparition of his lost Beatrice. In fact the original eighteen poems of the Hardy sequence, (in the *Collected Poems* of 1919, he damagingly extended it by three extra pieces) tell a story of the poet's pilgrimage to his and Emma's early haunts, matching the stages of the journey there and back to specific stages of Aeneas's journey, in *Aeneid* 6, to the abode of the blest. It thus represents, on the part of the supposedly non-modernist Hardy, a stratagem often taken to be definitively modernist: the use of an ancient fable to structure and resonate with a twentieth-century narrative, as the *Odyssey* structures and resonates with James Joyce's *Ulysses*. Yet so firmly established is the image of Hardy as a rustic provincial that Virgil rates not a single entry in the index to J.O. Bailey's 700-page *Poetry of Thomas Hardy. A Handbook and Commentary*, (University of North Carolina, Chapel Hill, 1970). Hardy undoubtedly read Virgil in the original; yet we know that long before he taught himself Latin his remarkable mother gave him (on his eighth birthday) a copy of Dryden's translation of the *Aeneid*. And so there is reason to look

---

1 See my *Hardy's Virgilian Purples*, originally in *Agenda* 10: 2-3 (1972); reprinted in *Arion* (1974), and in *The Poet in the Imaginary Museum* (Manchester, 1977).

in Hardy's poetry not just for allusions to Virgil's Latin but for echoes of Dryden's English. The only scholar as yet to have followed this scent is Tom Paulin in his *Thomas Hardy: The Poetry of Perception* (Totowa, New Jersey, 1975). Paulin for instance considers some lines from *Aeneid* 11, in which Dryden makes Diomede say, of the war dead:

> Transform'd to Birds, my lost Companions fly:
> Hov'ring about the Coasts they make their Moan;
> And cuff the Cliffs with Pinions not their own.

The masterly masculinity of 'cuff' may be thought to belong with Dryden's conception of the grand style more than with Virgil's. There is nothing exactly comparable in the poem by Hardy which Paulin brings into comparison, 'The Souls of the Slain' (1899, about the dead of the Boer War), but whether or not Dryden was the intermediary, the conceit and fable of the poem undoubtedly derive from this moment in Virgil:

> Soon from out of the Southward seemed nearing
>   A whirr, as of wings
>   Waved by mighty-vanned flies,
>   Or by night-moths of measureless size,
> And in softness and smoothness well-nigh beyond hearing
>   Of corporeal things.
>
> And they bore to the bluff, and alighted –
>   A dim-discerned train
>   Of sprites without mould,
>   Frameless souls none might touch or might hold –
> On the ledge by the turreted lantern, far-sighted
>   By men of the main.

Hardy's diction here is certainly pre-modernist, though in matters other than diction Hardy was more of a modernist than we commonly suppose. At any rate such verses prevent us from supposing that only with modernism could fruitful contact with Virgil be resumed, or that late-Victorian Virgilianism was the perquisite of Alfred Lord Tennyson. The Virgilianism of Hardy cries out for further investigation.

Pound greatly admired Hardy the poet – as Eliot did not, nor Yeats either. But if Hardy's Virgilianism had been pointed out to Pound, this would not have counted in Hardy's favour. For Pound's *animus* against Virgil was deep-seated and virulent from the first,

and it persisted. Already in 1914 he was exhorting the readers of
Poetry (Chicago):

> Let us choose: Homer, Sappho, Ibycus, Theocritus' idyl of the
> woman spinning with charmed wheel; Catullus, especially the
> *Collis O Heliconii*. Not Virgil, especially not the Aeneid, where
> he has no story worth telling, no sense of personality. His hero
> is a stick who would have contributed to *The New Statesman*.
> He has a nice verbalism. Dante was right to respect him, for
> Dante had no Greek, and the Aeneid would have stood out
> nobly against such literature as was available in the year 1300.[1]

And three or four years later, in an essay that is still valuable inasmuch
as it is a *catena* diligently culled from curious reading, Pound urges
readers of *The Egoist* to pay attention to Ovid rather than 'the more
Tennysonian Virgil'.[2] In 1916 Pound recommends to the neophyte,
Iris Barry, readings in Catullus, Propertius, Horace and Ovid, but
warns her against trafficking with Virgil (or Pindar).[3] Most tellingly,
in his *Homage to Sextus Propertius* (1919) he coerces Propertius into
avowing anti-Virgilian sentiments that in fact Propertius did not
profess. From a different position, independently arrived at and
much less troubling, the animus was to be shared lifelong by Robert
Graves.[4] The grounds of Pound's hostility show up much more
respectably than in any of his slashing prose in a passage of verse
that has seldom been remarked. It is in Canto 7 (originally 1921):

> Dido choked up with sobs, for her Sicheus
> Lies heavy in my arms, dead weight
> > Drowning, with tears, new Eros,
>
> And the life goes on, mooning upon bare hills;
> Flame leaps from the hand, the rain is listless,
> Yet drinks the thirst from our lips,
> > solid as echo,
> Passion to breed a form in shimmer of rain-blur;
> But Eros drowned, drowned, heavy, half dead with tears
> > For dead Sicheus.

1 'The Renaissance', in *Literary Essays of Ezra Pound*, ed. T.S. Eliot (London, 1954), p.217.
2 'Notes on Elizabethan Classicists', ibid., p.235.
3 *Selected Letters*, ed. D.D. Paige (New York, 1951), p.138.
4 See Robert Graves, *Oxford Addresses on Poetry* (London, 1962). Graves's
charge was familiar: Virgil was a toady, the Emperor's lickspittle.

> Life to make mock of motion:
> For the husks, before me, move,
>   The words rattle: shells given out by shells.

The passage, even when returned to context, will obviously abide more interpretations than one. (For good or ill, it is the poet's strategy that it should.) Having lived with the passage for years, I am persuaded that it represents – based, as it plainly is, on *Aeneid* 1, 341ff., and 4 – a response to *veteris vestigia flammae* drastically at odds with Hardy's response (which, as we have seen, Pound had apparently not noticed in any case). '*New* Eros' – carried as it is on an elaborately established sobbing and languorous rhythm, the word 'new' denies itself. How can the erotic stirring for Aeneas be 'new', when it is explicitly saturated with sentiment for the old, the dead, for 'Sicheus'? Dido's sobbing for her old lover even as she lies in the arms of her new one – this melancholy, which Virgil, and following him Hardy, responded to with such sympathy, is for Pound deathly, it precludes the genuinely 'new', which he urgently wants to find and to celebrate. The Canto as a whole, whatever its incidental obscurities, is plainly concerned with the phenomenon of 'the living dead', focussed in part, as Ronald Bush has invaluably pointed out, on the old men, Clemenceau, Lloyd George and Woodrow Wilson, legislating at Versailles for a future they had no part in.[1] (They were thus represented in Maynard Keynes' *Economic Consequences of the Peace*, which Pound had read by 1920.) The lines quoted, for instance, lead directly into a portrait of Alessandro de Medici as a personification of *abuleia*, with more than one indication that it will serve also as a portrait of Henry James:

> And the tall indifference moves,
>   a more living shell,
> Drift in the air of fate, dry phantom, but intact.
> O Alessandro, chief and thrice warned, watcher,
>   Eternal watcher of things,
> Of things, of men, of passions.
>   Eyes floating in dry, dark air, . . .

There are gradations among the living dead. Some shells are more living than others; some – Alessandro, Henry James – carry off their condition of living death with a dignity that compels admiration. Nevertheless, shells is what they are, husks, as earlier in this Canto:

1 Ronald Bush, *The Genesis of Ezra Pound's Cantos* (Princeton, 1976), pp.272–73.

> Thin husks I had known as men,
> Dry casques of departed locusts
>   speaking a shell of speech...
> Propped between chairs and table...
> Words like the locust-shells, moved by no inner being;
>   A dryness calling for death;...

What has failed in them is Eros; wherever erotic stirring in them seems to be new, it is nothing of the sort but a reminiscence of a stir that once was. If Pound had attended to Thomas Hardy's marriage to Florence Emily Dugdale within two years of the death of his first wife, Emma, there can be little doubt that this is the verdict he would have passed on the transaction.

The break that Pound thus makes, not just with Hardy and James (his two acknowledged mentors – one English, one American), but with a succession of revered masters reaching back to Virgil, is momentous. What he denies is not just *veteris vestigia flammae* but what Racine makes his Phèdre say, in appalled awareness of her own condition: *C'est Vénus tout entière à sa proie attachée.* In that incomparable verse Racine surely articulates the classical and terrible conception that underlies also Virgil's treatment of Dido: sexual passion, the erotic, understood as one undifferentiated energy running wild, fastening itself seemingly at random on this person or that one, and switching from one to another in a way that discredits all human vows of constancy. This was Hardy's conception also, as we see from poem after poem and story after story. But of course the erotic can be conceived quite differently, as it was by Pound. For him it was a matter of great moment, for he was one of those artists who hold that the energy of artistic creation is itself erotic, indeed (in his most extreme formulations) positively *genital*. As the child that comes or may come from a sexual encounter between a man and a woman differs from the child born from that man and some other woman (or from the same man and the same woman on another occasion), so every genuine poem is the unique product of one unrepeatable encounter between the artist and an unearthly partner who may be called 'Muse' or 'goddess'. 'Make it new!' was notoriously Pound's cry. Though every responsible artist must know the annals of his art (no one more than Pound insisted on that), still every artwork that is worth anything not only can be but has to be *new*, unprecedented. For Pound, alike in his sexual and artistic life, 'Make it new' was incompatible with 'Here we go again' (if that vulgarity be permitted). Those who know the life of P.B. Shelley, or of many another, will undoubtedly reflect that a man with this exalted view of the erotic life commonly makes a less reliable consort than one with more modest expectations. And it is true that whereas on the whole Pound managed his amorous career with more decorum than Shelley, still the pattern was, so far as we can discern, not very different.

It seems that on the basis of Canto 7 we can explain Pound's hostility to Virgil very simply indeed: it was precisely Virgil's melancholy, the *lacrimae rerum* which endears him to so many, that Pound could not stomach, so sanguine as he was and so determined to remain so. In this stubborn bent towards the hopefully open-ended (which he lost before the end), Pound may legitimately seem to us more indelibly American than his fellow expatriate, Eliot. But anyone who is tempted to affect an Old World condescension to the New ('a *young* nation', and similar self-servings) should consider again the date at which Canto 7 was written. Because Pound was not a combatant, and because he resolutely resisted making easily patriotic and self-righteous gestures (this is what *Homage to Sextus Propertius* is about, very largely), the impact upon him of the First World War is under-estimated. Yet he was to say that the entire enterprise of *The Cantos* was undertaken so as to uncover the reasons why war happens, so as to preclude its happening again. In 1919, as the old men negotiated at Versailles, hope did not come easy, yet imposed itself as an unavoidable necessity. After the four years of murderous deadlock on the Western Front – most of Canto 16 is concerned with that – 'Here we go again' or 'Plus ça change' expressed a sentiment that was intolerable. The new, the really new, had to be possible, since all the old wisdoms had proved themselves ineffective. The hopefulness of Canto 7 is desperate.

Moreover, even if we allow 'America' to mean only the United States, the Old World needs to remember that there are more Americas than one. Pound speaks for one, Eliot for another. In many ways they differ, these two Americas, but they are alike in never having known defeat. There is another America which neither of them knew, except tangentially: the America of the Old Confederacy which *had* known defeat, and was committed to living with that knowledge. To the citizens of that America, Virgil's story in the *Aeneid* could have a painful immediacy. Hence, Allen Tate's 'Aeneas at Washington' (1933):

> I myself saw furious with blood
> Neoptolemus, at his side the black Atridae,
> Hecuba and the hundred daughters, Priam
> Cut down, his filth drenching the holy fires.
> In that extremity I bore me well,
> A true gentleman, valorous in arms,

Disinterested and honourable. Then fled:
That was a time when civilization
Run by the few fell to the many, and
Crashed to the shout of men, the clang of arms:
Cold victualing I seized, I hoisted up
The old man my father upon my back,
In the smoke made by sea for a new world
Saving little – a mind imperishable
If time is, a love of past things tenous
As the hesitation of receding love.

Here the first four lines are a translation, and surely a fine one, of
Aeneid 2, 499-502. But the city that goes down, the civilization 'run
by the few' which 'fell to the many', is not Ilium but Richmond or
Montgomery or Atlanta, any one of the cities of the Confederacy
finally sacked by Grant or Sheridan or the specially hated Sherman,
generals of the victorious Yankee North. The association is pressed
home when the action resumes. The destroyed South is named in
'Blue Grass', byword for Tate's native Southern state of Kentucky,
rammed hard against 'Troy' in controlled synaesthesia that identifies
conflagration with fruition:

> I saw the thirsty dove
> In the glowing fields of Troy, hemp ripening
> And tawny corn, the thickening Blue Grass
> All lying rich forever in the green sun.
> I see all things apart, the towers that men
> Contrive I too contrived long, long ago.
> Now I demand little. The singular passion
> Abides its object and consumes desire
> In the circling shadow of its appetite.
> There was a time when the young eyes were slow,
> Their flame steady beyond the firstling fire,
> I stood in the rain, far from home at nightfall
> By the Potomac, the great Dome lit the water,
> The city my blood had built I knew no more
> While the screech-owl whistled his new delight
> Consecutively dark.
> Stuck in the wet mire
> Four thousand leagues from the ninth buried city
> I thought of Troy, what we had built her for.

There is plenty of *lacrimae rerum* here, and one may legitimately wish
for a touch of Dryden's bluffness or of Pound's impatient suspicion

of the elegiac note. This is a comment not just on poetic style, but on the substance of the political alternative that Tate and some fellow Southerners were in these years trying to put together, to challenge the industrial capitalism of the restored Union. Certainly Tate is not prepared to see the Federal capital, Washington, as a restored Richmond, as Virgil's Aeneas sees Rome as a second Troy.

Accordingly the phrase 'a new world' is mordantly, if a little cheaply, ironical. The same irony is enriched and plangently deepened in another fine poem by Tate of the same year, in which once again the many Virgilian echoes point to a deeper affinity – with the fable of the *Aeneid* as making more sense than he can find anywhere else, for the historical predicament that the American Southerner has inherited and must make sense of. This poem, now entitled 'The Mediterranean', was originally called 'Picnic at Cassis', and that first title invaluably brings out the occasion of the poem – that is to say, a holiday excursion by boat taken by expatriate Americans along the coast of Southern France. The last three of its nine pentameter quatrains read thus:

> Let us lie down once more by the breathing side
> Of Ocean, where our live forefathers sleep
> As if the Known Sea still were a month wide –
> Atlantis howls but is no longer steep!
>
> What country shall we conquer, what fair land
> Unman our conquest and locate our blood?
> We've cracked the hemispheres with careless hand!
> Now, from the Gates of Hercules we flood
>
> Westward, westward till the barbarous brine
> Whelms us to the tired land where tasseling corn,
> Fat beans, grapes sweeter than muscadine
> Rot on the vine: in that land were we born.

It is not outlandish to see in these verses a modern American so estranged from modern American society – its wastefulness ('Fat beans...Rot on the vine'), its heedlessness ('with careless hand'), and its enervation (its land is 'tired', its conquest of that terrain 'unmanned') – that he would like if he could to unravel the threads of history, and become again a citizen of that Old World which his ancestors should never have left. In that case the last clause – 'in that land were we born' – is no patriotic bugle-note, but rather a flat acknowledgement of what cannot be helped. Even if this is only one of possible readings, these stanzas and the poem as a whole surely represent an extraordinarily searching and painful exploration of what may be involved, for people of today, in the Virgilian *pietas*.

Despite his metrical conservatism (his strenuous handling of the pentameter is surely surprising and admirable) and his unfashionable addiction to the grand manner and the high style, Allen Tate was certainly a modernist; that is what he was thought to be, and it is how he conceived of himself. However, his allegiance to the cause and principles of international modernism never comprehended an allegiance to Ezra Pound as a modernist master. Given Tate's deep-seated and as it were forefated Virgilianism, it hardly could. Eliot was his master, and in some measure Yeats. Yeats divagated into Virgil's territory only when, in 1915, he wrote *Per Amica Silentia Lunae*, going for that title to *Aeneid* 2, 255: *A Tenedo tacitae per amica silentia lunae*. But no one has ever thought that Yeats's temperament was Virgilian, and characteristically, in this momentous book of verse and prose mixed, he glimpsed Virgil momentarily only through the spectacles of – of all unlikely people – Paul Verlaine.[1] However, the poem that opens the volume, *'Ego Dominus Tuus'*, is in the form of an inconclusive dialogue between two persons 'Hic' and 'Ille', who it is generally agreed might as well be named at certain points as 'Ez' and 'Willie'. These identifications will not hold good throughout the poem, precisely because the two poets were so intimate, and would remain so: each could and did 'internalize' the other, in the sense that within Yeats there was a voice that spoke the sentiments of Pound, and within Pound a voice that spoke like Yeats. One of the things they seem to have agreed about, among innumerable disagreements, was the irrelevance of Virgil to their concerns.

Not all the commentators on *The Cantos* have remarked how conspicuous is the absence of Virgil's name and presence, among the numberless names and presences which jostle on Pound's pages. Peter Makin for instance, in general one of the very best such commentators, misleads when he glosses a passage from Canto 23 by remarking: 'Troy was the citadel of a culture, and when it fell... the priest-king Aeneas (guided by the chthonic deities) took the heritage to Italy, where his descendants planted Rome...'.[2] All quite true of course, but it has little or nothing to do with the passage in question, whoch focuses very markedly not on Aeneas but on his father Anchises:

> And that was when Troy was down, all right,
>> superbo Ilion...
> And they were sailing along

1 See Lawrence Lipking, *The Life of the Poet* (Chicago, 1981), p.57.
2 Peter Makin, *Pound's Cantos* (London, 1985), p.297.

Sitting in the stern-sheets,
Under the lee of an island
And the wind drifting off from the island.

"Tet, tet...
   what is it?" said Anchises.
"Tethnéké.". said the helmsman, "I think they
"Are howling because Adonis died virgin."
"Huh! tet..." said Anchises,
   "well, they've made a bloody mess of that city."

"King Otreus, of Phrygia,
"That king is my father."
   and saw then, as of waves taking form,
As the sea, hard, a glitter of crystal,
And the waves rising but formed, holding their form.
No light reaching through them.

In a passage like this (and there are several very like it, as we shall see), Pound's interest in Aeneas is limited to the matter of his semi-divine birth, how he was conceived by Aphrodite after she had assumed human form so as to lie with Anchises. The source is not Virgilian, but the fifth of the so-called Homeric Hymns, 'To Aphrodite'. Aphrodite's lie about a non-existent human father, 'King Otreus, of Phrygia', is designed to conceal her divinity from her human mate, who is applauded for seeing through the fiction because of something uncanny in his bed-mate's bearing – sometimes specified as her gait, her way of walking. Anchises is the hero, not Aeneas. And he is the-hero-as-artist, who is called upon to make just such recognitions, of the divinely eternal through the veil of the quotidian. The last lines quoted, which are also the last lines of the Canto, reveal this clearly for those who know *The Cantos*: the paradoxical coupling of the fluid (the waves) with the fixed (the crystal) is what Pound regularly sees as the essence of the authentic artifact. Pound here is very close to Yeats who is, for instance in his great sonnet 'Leda and the Swan', fascinated similarly by the moments when the inhuman – it may be bestial, it may be divine, subhuman or superhuman hardly matters – invades the human. To neither Pound nor Yeats did it seem that Virgil had much or anything to say about this matter which so preoccupied them.

More than twenty years later, at the end of World War Two, Pound, in a prison-stockade awaiting trial for treason, was still celebrating Anchises in the same strain, and for the same reason:

each one in his god's name
as by Terracina rose from the sea Zephyr behind her
and from her manner of walking
as had Anchises
till the shrine be again white with marble
till the stone eyes look again seaward
(Canto 74)

Or again, in Canto 76:

or Anchises that laid hold of her flanks of air
drawing her to him
Cythera potens, Κύθηρα δεινα
no cloud, but the crystal body
the tangent formed in the hand's cup
as live wind in the beech grove
as strong air amid cypress

The 'tangent... in the hand's cup' has to do with the legend that the shapes of the finest Greek vases were replicated from the contour of the divinely beautiful woman's breast, as cupped in her lover's hand and thereafter imprinted on his mind – obviously a powerful emblem of how the impulse to artistic manufacture is erotic. For present purposes the point is that such passages, which because of the name 'Anchises' may seem Virgilian, are nothing of the kind.

Accordingly, when the Virgilian voice *does* irrupt into these relatively late Cantos, it does so with all the more force for being unheralded. It speaks Scots, as we have intimated:

"Who *says* he is an American"
a still form on the branda, Bologna
"Gruss Gott", "Der Herr!" "Tatile ist gekommen!"
Slow lift of long banners
Roma profugens Sabinorum in terras
and belt the sitye quahr of noble fame
the lateyn peopil taken has their name
bringing his gods into Latium
saving the bricabrac
"Ere he his goddis brocht in Latio"
"each one in the name"
in whom are the voices, keeping hand on the reins
Gaudier's word not blacked out
nor old Hulme's, nor Wyndham's...

This is Canto 78, another of those composed in the Pisan prison-stockade while their author awaited transportation and trial for treason. The opening lines of Gavin Douglas's *Eneados* (printed 1553) read:

> The batellis and the man I will descrive,
> Fra Troys boundis first that fugitive,
> By fait to Itale coyme and coist Lavyne;
> Our land and see cachit with mekle pyne,
> By force of goddis abuif, fro every steid.
> Of cruell Juno throw ald ramembrit feid.
> Greit pane in batell sufferit he also,
> Or he his goddis brocht in Latio,
> And belt the ciete, fra quhame, of noble fame,
> The Latyne peple takin hes thair name...[1]

The commentator who has done most justice to this appeal to Virgil by way of Gavin Douglas is the South African, Anthony Woodward.[2] But even Woodward fails to bring out how surprising it is (as well as how the line *Roma profugens Sabinorum in terras*, has been enigmatically inserted in the preceding Canto 77). Pound in this passage recollects how, late in the war, he set out with borrowed boots and haversack from Rome, already doomed to fall to the advancing Allied armies, for the Italo-Austrian domicile of his natural daughter, Mary,[3] and how, hiking and hitch-hiking, he encountered much kindness from Germans and Italians alike. What strikes him of a sudden, as he remembers this experience, is how it had been foreseen and marmoreally recorded by Virgil: as Virgil's Aeneas left doomed Troy, carrying his household and ancestral gods, so Pound leaves the doomed Rome of fascist Italy, carrying in his haversack *his* gods – books by Henri Gaudier-Brzeska and T.E. Hulme and Percy Wyndham Lewis. For a poet so hostile to Virgil to discover that *in extremis* only Virgil had foreseen and foresuffered his predicament, and thereby eased it – this surely constitutes a very poignant moment in literary history, and in a history rather larger than 'literary' may suggest.

1 I take my text from Charles Tomlinson's noble *Oxford Book of Verse in English Translation* (Oxford & New York, 1980). In the version that Pound printed in his own anthology, *Confucius to Cummings* (New York, 1964), the orthography is eased.
2 Anthony Woodward, *Ezra Pound and the Pisan Cantos* (London, 1980), pp.49-54.
3 See Mary de Rachewiltz, *Discretions* (Boston, 1971).

Virgil in a Cultural Tradition, eds R.A. Cardwell & J. Hamilton. University of Nottingham, 1986.

Eliot, Williams and Pound
in the Twenties

Harold Monro, writing in the London *Chapbook* in February 1923, observed of T.S. Eliot's *Waste Land* that 'in England it was treated chiefly with indignation or contempt', whereas in America *The Dial* had awarded the author its annual prize of $2,000. But the implied contrast is misleading. Allowing for the conventions of sedate amenity that governed American reviewing (as for the most part they still do), one can detect in the American reviewers of Eliot's *Poems* (1920) and of *The Waste Land* (1922) the same recalcitrance that the British reviewers expressed more cheekily. Louis Untermeyer, Robert Frost's correspondent who was to be an influential anthologist, wrote of *Poems* (*The Freeman*, 30 June 1920) that 'Eliot cares more for his art than he does for his attitudes'; and that 'the exaltation which is the very breath of poetry – that combination of tenderness and toughness – is scarcely ever present in Eliot's lines'. When *The Waste Land* appeared, Untermeyer had become more irate: 'The *Dial*'s award to Mr T.S. Eliot and the subsequent book-publication of his *The Waste Land* have occasioned a display of some of the most enthusiastically naive superlatives that have ever issued from publicly sophisticated iconoclasts'. The poem itself he found 'a pompous parade of erudition', and he decided that 'were it not for the Laforgue mechanism, Mr Eliot's poetic variations on the theme of a super-refined futility would be increasingly thin and incredibly second rate' (*The Freeman*, 17 January 1923). Obviously a writer who is happy with 'super-refined' (elsewhere he says that Eliot's 'Portrait of a Lady' is 'extraordinarily sensitized') is not a critic worth pausing on for long; and yet when Untermeyer cites all too patent imitations of Eliot's 'Sweeney Among the Nightingales' in quatrains by Osbert Sitwell and Herbert Read and Robert Nichols, one can see good reason for him to think that Eliot's reputation, achieved so fast on such a slender body of work, was no more than modish. And indeed it asks no great exertion of the historical imagination to recognize that, at a time when 'the Sitwells' were taken to be 'modernists' equal with Eliot and Pound, modish was just what Eliot's reputation was. The achievement was quite otherwise; but it would be several years before that could be perceived, and the perception validated.

For this no one in American deserves more credit than Edmund Wilson. He wrote, in *The Dial* for December 1922, the most emphatically welcoming and apparently influential review of *The Waste Land*, and although this reads a little quaintly now because Wilson took very seriously Eliot's supposed debt to Jessie L. Weston's *From Ritual to Romance* (which later criticism has taken lightly), his piece had the great virtue of conceding valid points to the opposition:

> It is true his poems seem the products of a constricted emotional experience and that he appears to have drawn rather heavily on books for the heat he could not derive from life. There is a certain grudging margin, to be sure, about all that Mr Eliot writes – as if he were compensating himself for his limitations by a peevish assumption of superiority. But it is the very acuteness of his suffering from this starvation which gives such poignancy to his art.

However, it was more than three years later (*The New Republic*, March 1926) that Wilson brought Eliot's poetry home to the bosoms of his countrymen. He did so, having 'The Hollow Men' before him, by insisting on the extent to which Eliot was indelibly American:

> Mr Eliot has lived abroad so long that we rarely think of him as an American and he is never written about from the point of view of his relation to other American authors. Yet one suspects that his real significance is less that of a prophet of European disintegration than of a poet of the American Puritan temperament. Compare him with Hawthorne, Henry James, E.A. Robinson and Edith Wharton: all these writers have their Waste Land, which is the aesthetic and emotional waste land of the Puritan character and their chief force lies in the intensity with thich they communicate emotions of deprivation and chagrin.

It is not at all incongruous that Wilson, who thus insisted on Eliot's Americanness, should a few years later, in his pioneering classic *Axel's Castle* (1931), insist on Eliot's Frenchness, thus giving substance and weight to Untermeyer's too glib acknowledgement of 'the Laforgue mechanism'. By taking seriously Eliot's debt to the French *symbolistes* (as before him only Allen Tate had done, in *The New Republic*, 30 June 1926), Wilson was still stressing Eliot's Americanness by showing at any rate how un-British he was. Not surprisingly,

though deplorably, British and also many American readers con-
tinued to ignore Eliot's French affinities, following instead the hints
that Eliot had dropped for their benefit in his criticism, implying
his kinship with such solidly English writers as Donne and Webster.
As Tate remarked austerely, 'His Eliabethanism has indubitably been
too ingenuously appraised by some critics'.

If we chronicle not how Eliot's reputation was advanced, but how
Eliot's poetry (and all modern poetry) came to be understood, the
part played by Allen Tate bulks very large and honourably. He was
among the first to champion Eliot. Already as a young man of
twenty-four he had pressed Eliot's claims upon his seniors, John
Crowe Ransom and Donald Davidson, in the circle of the Nashville
'fugitives'; and this initially provincial dispute was played out on a
national stage as early as 1923 when, in the *New York Evening Post
Literary Review*, Ransom, with the courtly composure that was to
be his hallmark, tried to promote Robert Graves before Eliot, only
to be taken to task in the same columns by his younger associate.
The exchange shows neither Ransom nor Tate at his best. But both
were themselves poets, and by that token were concerned more
urgently than other commentators, even Edmund Wilson. From
1927 onwards, as the consequences of Eliot's baptism into the
Anglican church showed up in the imagery of 'Journey of the Magi',
'A Song for Simeon', 'Animula', and most conspicuously 'Ash-
Wednesday' (1930), Tate, open to the solicitations of Christian belief,
took up the running on Eliot's behalf from the non-believer Wilson.

It was not easy. Tate, an ambitious poet whose few irreplaceable
poems were yet to come, was by 1927 in animated correspondence
with two poets, Yvor Winters (1900-1968) and Hart Crane (1899-
1932), who were at one, if in little else, in their certainty that Eliot's
fame and Eliot's precedent were bad news for American poetry.
Already in 1926 (*The New Republic*, 30 June) Tate was obliged –
faced with the aridity in diction and imagery of 'The Hollow Men'
– to concede that 'It is possible that he has nothing more to say in
poetry'. Yet this admission was not so grievous for Tate as it would
have been for others. For Tate's very distinguished criticism, then
and afterwards, was always more concerned with the socio-cultural
conditions for poetry than with poetry itself. And so it was not with
any special disappointment that Tate envisaged how Eliot's message,
his distinctively American apprehension of Europe, might thereafter
be conveyed less in poems than in his conduct of *The Criterion*, the
magazine he had begun to edit in 1923:

> Going home to Europe, Mr Eliot has had to understand
> Europe; he could not quite sufficiently be the European simply

to feel that he was there; he has been forced to envisage it with a reminiscent philosophy. And it is not insignificant that the quarterly of which he is the editor is the first British journal which has attempted to relate the British mind to the total European mind; that has attempted a rational synthesis of the traditions of Roman culture; that has, in a word, contemplated order.

And Tate proceeded to cite, with equanimity and approval, some of the non-English writers whom Eliot had solicited for *The Criterion*, or else had approved there: Charles Maurras, Paul Valéry, Henri Massis, Oswald Spengler – several of whom would not unjustly, though with the benefit of hindsight, be condemned later as Fascist or proto-Fascist.[1]

But in any case there was a grave difficulty. For if Eliot's debt to the French poets went beyond an easy charting of 'influences', or the neat and better than neat adaptation of French lines (for instance, from Laforgue) into English, it could only have meant an elimination from poetry of any notion of 'message'. 'Message' was precisely what French poetry, at least since Mallarmé if not before, had set its face against. But alike in the British and the American traditions the expectation that the poet would have a message was so ingrained that even by those readers most alert to and informed about Eliot's French connections *The Waste Land* was still thought to deliver an urgent signal – usually about the bankruptcy of the European, or the Western, cultural and civic traditions.

In this dilemma, Eliot was less than helpful to his apologists. The editor of *The Criterion*, from 1923 and more insistently from 1926, revealed himself as a writer with indeed a message, of a very bleak and uncompromising sort, affronting at almost every point the suppositions of secular liberalism. And it was asking too much of readers that they should insulate Eliot the editor and editorialist from Eliot the poet; so that they should read 'Ash-Wednesday' without feeling that they were being nudged into the Roman Catholic or the Anglo-Catholic church –

> At the first turning of the second stair
> I turned and saw below
> The same shape twisted on the banister
> Under the vapour in the fetid air
> Struggling with the devil of the stairs who wears
> The deceitful face of hope and of despair.

1 See C.K. Stead, *Pound, Yeats, Eliot and the Modernist Movement* (London, 1986), pp.203-04.

At the second turning of the second stair
I left them twisting, turning below;
There were no more faces and the stair was dark,
Damp, jaggèd, like an old man's mouth drivelling, beyond repair.
Or the toothed gullet of an agèd shark.

At the first turning of the third stair
Was a slotted window bellied like the fig's fruit
And beyond the hawthorn blossom and a pasture scene
The broadbacked figure drest in blue and green
Enchanted the maytime with an antique flute.
Blown hair is sweet, brown hair over the mouth blown,
Lilac and brown hair;
Distraction, music of the flute, stops and steps of the mind
                over the third stair,

Fading, fading; strength beyond hope and despair
Climbing the third stair.

Lord, I am not worthy
Lord, I am not worthy
          but speak the word only.

It is perfectly true that there is nothing conclusively in the poem to make us identify the first stair with Dante's *Inferno*, the second with his *Purgatorio*, the third with *Paradiso*; as there is not (a more piercing uncertainty) anything to determine for us whether 'the broadbacked figure drest in blue and green', with his 'music of the flute', is an image of what must be renounced in order to achieve Paradise, or else an image of how terrestrial life can most nearly attain the paradisal. But no one will seriously maintain that the verses do not have a design upon us; that they do not promulgate a message – the message that all secular explanations of human life are vain and inadequate. That the alternative religious explanation should still not know what value to put on 'music of the flute' – this will be experienced by some as a cruel disappointment, by others as a welcome acknowledgement that dogmatic certainty on the large scale can comprehend uncertainties on the small. But in either or any case these verses must surely confound the French theorists: the poem as a construction of words must be – at least when the words come from such a charged area of human experience as these do – a construction also of sentiments and ideas. The poem does convey a message, though the message cannot be at every point decoded.

Allen Tate rose to this challenge. His essay on 'Ash-Wednesday'

(*The Hound and Horn*, January–March 1931) has been anthologized many times, and rightly. It is a masterpiece of literary criticism, precisely by being much more than that; under its surface is the furious rejection by Tate, now consciously an alienated Southerner and impenitent Confederate, of the scientific humanism of Yankee America. Tate saw clearly the point at issue: 'Mr Eliot's critics are a little less able each year to see the poetry for Westminster Abbey; the wood is all trees'. And his retort, masterfully bold though disingenuous, is that 'in a discussion of Mr Eliot's poetry, his doctrine has little to command interest in itself'. Of 'Ash-Wednesday' Tate said, among much else that was penetrating:

> These six poems are a brief moment of religious experience in an age that believes religion to be a kind of defeatism and puts its hope for man in finding the right secular order. The mixed realism and symbolism of 'The Waste Land' issued in irony. The direct and lyrical method of the new poems creates the simpler aesthetic quality of humility. The latter quality comes directly out of the former, and there is a nice continuity in Mr Eliot's work.

Before he is through, Tate is claiming that 'Ash-Wednesday' represents 'probably...the only valid religious poetry we have', and he isolates two features of the writing which lead him to think this. One, which need not concern us, has to do with imagery. The other emerges when he remarks in the opening lines 'the regular yet halting rhythm, the smooth uncertainty of movement which may either proceed to greater regularity or fall away into improvisation'. This perception is picked up later, more than once, as Tate moves through the poem: 'subtly and imperceptibly the rhythm has changed...', 'there is constant and sudden change of rhythm...', 'a broken and distracted rhythm'. If we read 'Ash-Wednesday' through with Tate's commentary at our elbow, we see at any given point what he means: he has a good ear, as we might expect from his own poems (which are however metrical, as 'Ash-Wednesday' isn't). And we may agree that what binds together the six parts of 'Ash-Wednesday' is in large part something rhythmical. It remains true that in Tate's criticism and since (for no advance has been made in this quarter) 'rhythm' and 'movement' are wholly impressionistic – you hear what the critic is talking about, or else you don't. This is one area where modern criticism has notably failed. To be sure, the vocabulary for defining such rhythmical effects is yet to seek; but should not critics apply themselves to seeking and finding that vocabulary, instead of pursuing semantic and allusive niceties? In all the many thousands of words that have been expended on Eliot's achievements, this crucial matter – his alertness to, and exploiting of, the rhythms of the English verse-line – remains a vacuum, occupied only by unsupported and insupportable appeals to 'the ear'.

In 1927 Tate's correspondents Winters and Crane had been discussing between themselves not Eliot but William Carlos Williams (1883-1963). On 19 March that year Crane told Winters that 'Williams probably means less to me than to you', and then proceeded to a hesitant account of how he felt about this one of their older contemporaries:

> – There is no doubt of the charm of almost all of W's work. I except the Paterson and Struggle of Wings lately published in the Dial. I think them both highly disorganized. But in most of Williams' work I feel the kind of observations being 'made' ... seem to me too casual, however delightfully phrased, to be especially interesting...[1]

Later in the letter, considering apparently a different sort of poem written by Williams, Hart Crane confesses:

> Personally I often delight in some of these excursions of W's – but I won't 'approve' of them. They are too precious, insulate to all but – at least I fancy – a few 'choice spirits', and even then rather toylike. I don't mean that I'm a democrat. But I don't believe in encouraging the fancy – as long as there is imagination.

It is impossible to recognize in the poet thus characterized – 'precious', 'insulate', 'toylike' – the William Carlos Williams whom American opinon over the last thirty years has promoted as a respectable, and better than respectable, counterweight to Eliot. For one thing, the poet thus extolled has been presented as above all poetically 'a democrat'. Yet Crane's assessment of Williams still has its validity, as is apparent if we consider (wearily, for it is the instance always cited) Williams's 'The Red Wheelbarrow'. The British poet Charles Tomlinson has cited this piece to enforce his contention that 'There is no occasion too small for the poet's celebration'. But is this, in any case, true? Commonsense, not without distinguished endorsement from past centuries, thinks as Hart Crane did that it is not true

1 Thomas Parkinson (ed.), *Hart Crane and Yvor Winters. Their Literary Correspondence* (University of California Press, 1978), pp.69-70.

at all; that on the contrary there are occasions too trivial, too lacking
in dignity or resonance, to deserve the ceremoniousness that, as
Tomlinson perceived, verse-writing always brings with it. The
unfortunate effect in such cases is portentousness; and 'The Red
Wheelbarow' is surely in this way *portentous*:

> so much depends
> upon
>
> a red wheel
> barrow
>
> glazed with rain
> water
>
> beside the white
> chickens.

'So much depends', says the little squib (for it is nothing more), on
the wheelbarrow, the glaze of rain, the chickens. But just how much
does depend? The momentousness of the sparsely furnished scene is
blankly asserted, not proved. Or rather it *is* proved – by sleight of
hand; for if the little scene is not momentous, how did it come to
be framed, in all its sparsity, by so much white paper? The reverential
hush is thus not only demanded, but enforced. The poet cannot lose;
whatever claims he makes for the momentousness of his subject-
matter are vindicated simply by the way those claims are made.

Such poetry is invulnerable, existing in a self-sealed and self-
justifying realm called 'aesthetic', from which no appeal is allowed,
or can be made, to other realms like the ethical or the civic. The
literary histories invite us to associate such a belief in the unbreach-
able autonomy of art with haughty and disdainful decadents of the
1880s and 1890s. The achievement of Williams, of his followers and
admirers, has been to show that the most secure haven for such
doctrines is on the contrary in an ideology that is aggressively egalitar-
ian, and also secular. For the belief that 'there is no occasion too
small' is naturally at home in a society that resists any ranking of
certain human and civic occasions below or above certain others.
And thus it seems that liberal social democracy cossets and protects
the aesthete as no other form of society does. Williams's 'It all
depends' asserts and takes for granted the absence of any agreed
hierarchies, hence the freedom of any individual to establish and
assert his own hierarchy, without fear of challenge. 'Spring and All',
a more substantial and widely praised poem, follows the same pro-
cedure as 'The Red Wheelbarrow' with the added spice of *faux-naïf*

cuteness (announced in the very title, and taken up in epithets like
'twiggy'). One hopes that that is not what Crane had in mind when
he credited Williams's poems with 'charm'.

Williams had certainly written better poems than these, and doubt-
less Yvor Winters had those others in mind when, in *Poetry* for May
1928, he wrote of 'the most magnificent master of English and of
human emotions since Thomas Hardy, William Carlos Williams'.
Significantly, this was in a review mostly concerned to deplore
Eliot's influence on poetic style. At that time hardly anyone but
Winters would have named Williams in the same breath as Eliot,
and it is characteristic of Winters's perversity (or his independence)
that thirty years later, when it had become usual to set Williams up
against Eliot, Winters's opinion of Williams had long been much
less favourable. However, he never ceased to admire a poem like
'The Widow's Lament in Springtime':

> Sorrow is my own yard
> where the new grass
> flames as it has flamed
> often before but not
> with the cold fire
> that closes round me this year.
> Thirtyfive years
> I lived with my husband.
> The plumtree is white today
> with masses of flowers.
> Masses of flowers
> load the cherry branches
> and color some bushes
> yellow and some red
> but the grief in my heart
> is stronger than they
> for though they were my joy
> formerly, today I noticed them
> and turned away forgetting.
> Today my son told me
> that in the meadows
> at the edge of the heavy woods
> in the distance, he saw
> trees of white flowers.
> I feel that I would like
> to go there
> and fall into those flowers
> and sink into the marsh near them.

This must be the sort of writing that Crane had in mind when he applauded Williams (still rather grudgingly, however) for some-times attaining 'the classic manner of the old Chinese poets'. Cer-tainly the deliberate naïveté here is not in the least false, but has the limpid directness of some of the Chinese poems that Pound had marvellously transfigured in *Cathay* (1915). And so it was reasonable for Crane and Winters, who in the twenties was reaching for this style in his own poems, to call such writing 'imagist'. (Williams however in such a poem beautifully weaves the syntax of the sentence into and over his verse-lines – which is not a resource that most imagists were aware of.) Certainly this limpidity is not within Eliot's reach even when he is trying to be limpid, as in 'Ash-Wednesday'; and of course the experience of a simple person enduring a common-place and unavoidable sorrow – is such as Eliot could never manage, early or late. It has to be pointed out, to those who are sure that Eliot is a great poet, what vast tracts of human experience are never touched on in his poetry.

Williams himself had entered the lists against Eliot, saying of Eliot's early poetry (and Pound's also):

> It is the latest touch from the literary cuisine, it adds to the pleasant outlook from the club window. If to do this, if to be a Whistler at best, in the art of poetry, is to reach the height of poetic expression, then Ezra and Eliot have approached it and *tant pis* for the rest of us.

And Williams jeered:

> I do not overlook De Gourmont's plea for a meeting of the nations but I do believe that when they meet Paris will be more than slightly abashed to find parodies of the middle ages, Dante and Langue D'Oc foisted upon it as the best in United States poetry.

This was in *The Little Review* for May 1919, where Williams was taking issue with praise of Eliot by one of Pound's British friends, Edgar Jepson; but Williams's hostility to British culture ran deeper than that, and was to be a permanent feature of his outlook. His malevolence towards Pound, his friend since their college days in Philadelphia, is extraordinary; and when in 1920 he amplified this piece in the prologue to his *Kora in Hell*, Williams compounded the offence by quoting selectively from a private letter that Pound had written him. Astonishingly, Pound did not break off relations. Instead he was provoked, in a letter, into one of the most illuminating and betraying comments that he ever made, on Eliot, Williams and himself:

> There is a blood poison in America; you can idealize the place (easier now that Europe is so damd shaky) all you like, but you haven't a drop off the cursed blood in you, and you don't need to fight the disease day and night; you never had to. Eliot has it perhaps worse than I have – poor devil.
>
> You have the advantage of arriving in the milieu with a fresh flood of Europe in your veins, Spanish, French, English, Danish. You had not the thin milk of New York and New England from the pap; and you can therefore keep the environment outside you, and decently objective.
>
> (*Selected Letters*, ed. D.D. Paige, p.158)

Pound here anticipates, and paints in a blacker hue, Edmund Wilson's recognition that Eliot is 'a poet of the American Puritan temperament', and Pound claims to be tarred with the same brush himself. One must mind one's manners (and one's metaphors – tarring with brushes, for instance!) when venturing on to the territory that Pound opens up with his reflections on the ethnic mix of the American population, and the distinction that he makes between the older stock (Eliots and Pounds) and the relative late-come immigrants (Williams's stock on both sides). Moreover Pound's anti-Semitism, later so notorious, certainly casts a sinister light on his readiness to broach these issues. Yet these matters, it has been suggested, lie deep – indeed, *unutterably* deep – in every American psyche; and it is good that from time to time the unutterable be uttered – it is, one might say, one of the things that we look to poets for. There can be little doubt for instance that the doubtfulness or downright hostility felt towards Eliot by some Americans, particularly in recent decades, derives from the *sort* of American Eliot was – and remained, long after he had taken British citizenship. Eliot hailed from St Louis, but the Eliots there seem to have regarded themselves as Bostonian and Unitarian missionaries to that mid-western Philistia. The poet did not share this sense, he actively disliked it, but he could not escape – not even in Europe – from what he saw as the balefulness of that inheritance. He was what we have learned to call a WASP, and his lifetime coincided with the process, not yet quite completed, by which that caste – white Anglo-Saxon protestants of the northeast – was supplanted from the position of privilege that they had enjoyed from the first days of the Republic. That privilege, and the airs and presumption that went with it, are still resented; and some of the resentment has rubbed off on the poet.

Pound's case is by no means so clear-cut. At least one of his grandparents had made a career on the frontier; and in *The Cantos* this forebear, Thaddeus Coleman Pound, makes several entries, always with an encouraging flourish on the drums. It is the more remarkable that Pound in his letter to Williams should diagnose himself as suffering from a milder form of Eliot's disease; most of the time, alike in his life and his poetry, he seems to be denying it by strenuously over-compensating. Only once, late in life when he made as much of an excuse as he would ever make for his anti-Semitism, did Pound ever again enter the plea for himself that he suffered from the cultural anaemia of growing up in a suburb of an Eastern seaboard city. As for Williams, who had an English father, it would be easy to explain away his hostility to England; but the sorrier likelihood is that he saw quite justly the baleful mixture of timidity and arrogance which characterized literary London in his lifetime. However, Pound's diagnosis of Williams's condition was surely perceptive: Williams could abide American reality (where Pound and Eliot had to flee from it) because, as in the admirable 'To Elsie' ('The pure products of America / go crazy'), he remained the immigrant, the outsider looking in on the behaviour of the nation that he had been, by the sheerest accident, born to.

Yvor Winters, eschewing lurid and unstable metaphors of blood-poisoning and leukaemia, applied the discipline of intellectual history to isolate the virus that for him too disabled American literature of the north-east. It was, he decided, Emersonianism – a disease (if that is what it is) which is certainly no less rife now than it was when Winters made his diagnosis fifty years ago. This investigation was part of the wholesale scrutiny and revaluation that Winters was shocked into by the suicide of Hart Crane in 1932. In that revaluation, whereas Pound held his modest but respectable place, Williams was drastically demoted with Eliot rising in the scale against him. Winters in California perhaps thought himself securely distant from the seat of the infection; he never visited Europe, still less was he tempted to expatriate himself.

Pound's forbearance towards Williams remains astonishing, the more when we realize that Williams's challenge to him came when he was remarkably uncertain and at sea about his own talents and the direction in which he should go. Bowled over by the originality and assurance of Joyce's *Ulysses*, which was being sent to him by the author in typescript section by section, Pound was between 1920 and 1922 dismantling the several hundred lines of *The Cantos* that he had written and published, and recasting them radically, using some of the same material but trying for a less personalized presentation. Moreover Pound had reached Williams's conclusion about literary London, and in 1920 left for Paris, whence in 1924 he moved to Rapallo. His acrid and accusing farewell to London was *Hugh Selwyn Mauberley* (1920). But the poem of his that he most needed reassurance about was *Homage to Sextus Propertius* (1919), and for that he had to wait a long time. When Eliot in 1928, loyally reciprocating services rendered, edited Pound's *Selected Poems*, he insisted on excluding the Propertius poem, and it was not until 1932 that Basil Bunting wrote, already retrospectively, 'In my considered opinion, "Propertius" was the most important poem of our times, surpassing alike "Mauberley" and "The Waste Land".' This was in *The New English Weekly*, a London journal of very limited circulation; there appears to have been no comparable acknowledgement in the poet's native land. Bunting, who respected Eliot, applied himself first to rebutting the reasons which Eliot gave, in his Introduction to *Selected Poems*, for omitting this long and elaborate poem:

> It is impossible to understand why Eliot should have excluded the 'Propertius' from his selection of Pound's work. The plea of its difficulty will not hold, for as a consummation is always simpler than a beginning, the 'Propertius' is certainly much simpler than some of Pound's shorter earlier works whose content is sometimes elusive, tenuous, evanescent...
> ... The question of the relation of Pound's poem with the book of Propertius's elegies does not arise, except for the literary historian. There is no claim that this is a translation. The correspondence, the interpenetration of ancient and modern, is Pound's, not Propertius's...[1]

Half a century later, such commentary as there is on Pound's poem is still for the most part concerned with this question that for Bunting 'does not arise'. When he goes on to justify his high estimate of the poem, Bunting specifies:

> The beautiful step of the verse, the cogent movement of thought and feeling throughout, the sensitive perception of the little balanced in the great and their mutual dependence, the extraordinary directness, here and there quite naked, achieved in spite of the complexity of the whole conception; ...

Some of these claims can be considered, and either allowed or disallowed, only by looking at the work as a whole; others can be at least understood after reading only a few lines:

1 Carroll F. Terrell (ed.), *Basil Bunting, Man and Poet* (National Poetry Foundation, 1981), pp.253-4.

My cellar does not date from Numa Pompilius,
Nor bristle with wine jars,
Nor is it equipped with a frigidaire patent;
Yet the companions of the Muses
                    will keep their collective nose in my books,
And weary with historical data, they will turn to my dance tune.

Happy who are mentioned in my pamphlets,
        the songs shall be a fine tomb-stone over their beauty.
    But against this?
Neither expensive pyramids scraping the stars in their route,
Nor houses modelled upon that of Jove in East Elis,
Nor the monumental effigies of Mausolus,
                        are a complete elucidation of death.

Flame burns, rain sinks into the cracks
And they all go to rack ruin beneath the thud of the years.
Stands genius a deathless adornment,
                    a name not to be worn out with the years.

Noting in passing how conclusively the 'frigidaire patent' rules out any notion of a translation of Propertius (unless it were a translation in the sense of a raucous travesty or 'put-down' – and indeed some academic latinists did misconceive Pound's poem in that way), some early readers were understandably disconcerted by the inversions of conversational or prosaic word-order – 'Happy who', 'Stands genius' – especially from a poet who some years before had seemed to polemicize for just that rule about word-order which he here flouted. But these inversions were quite different in purpose and effect from those that Pound had practised indiscriminately in his earliest collections, and thereafter castigated; these were not poeticisms, but indications that he was addressing a sophisticated urban intelligentsia, that of Great War London, just as Propertius had addressed the sophisticates of Augustan Rome. The clue is in the diction, which gives 'are a complete elucidation of', for 'clears up' or 'makes clear'. The poet writes for, and gives a voice to, people whose privileged education has closed off for them the possibility of speaking as limpidly and directly as the speaker of 'The Widow's Lament in Springtime'. A special pathos is achieved when the poetry acts out the predicament of people whose all too expert command of language debars them (paradoxically) from expressing a common human sorrow – mortality, the fear of it, and its conclusiveness – as limpidly as could Williams's 'widow'. In the end the speaker of *Homage to Sextus Propertius* wins through to articulating that common plight as memorably as Williams's speaker does – with, as Bunting says, 'extraordinary directness . . . quite naked'. But Pound's speaker, so far from naïve, has had to struggle through to that desired but unfamiliar nakedness; and Pound's verse enacts the struggle.

It may seem that when Bunting speaks of 'the beautiful step of the verse, he is gesturing into a void not much less than Allen Tate when he wrote of the 'rhythm' and the 'movement' of Eliot's 'Ash-Wednesday'. But in fact the metaphor 'step', implying tread, implies also volition and direction. More important, since Pound's use of indentations conveys visually the effect of the verse-lines being 'stepped' down the page, to speak of 'step' shifts attention from what rhythmically happens between the start and end of a line to how the poet manages to turn from one line to another. (And 'verse' from *versus*, means precisely 'turn'.) To be sure, this is still rudimentary and indefinite. But certain writings by Pound, Bunting and a couple of others can take us a little further. What all of them contend is that the auditory effect of *all* English-language verse can only in a schematic and starveling fashion be pin-pointed by applying the only two measurements that traditional scansion recognizes: on the one hand the number of syllables, on the other the number of occurrences of *ictus* or 'stress'. One feature of English verse that is scanted by this method, or can be acknowledged only incidentally, is one that every careful reader knows from his or her experience: *tempo*, the speeding up or slowing down of enunciation, and therefore of apprehension, as we read through a line or through several lines in sequence.

This seems to be intimately connected with another principle, which is more radical and therefore more important: that of *quantity*, of syllables as being, in relation to their contiguous syllables, either long or short. The variation between English-language speakers about what syllables, in effect what vowels, they treat as long or short, is so great that there can be no question of imposing on English verse a quantitative metre such as was used for ancient Latin (doubtless with some strain for those who spoke classical Latin with dialectal variations as to quantity). This granted, it remains true, as anyone's experience of his own and others' speech-habits will confirm, that some English vowels are experienced and expressed as relatively long, others as relatively short. Not just unmetrical poets like Pound (for the most part) and Bunting, but also a strictly metrical poet like the later Yvor Winters, came to think that the finest auditory effects in English-language verse were attained by those poets who attended to the quantitative elements in British or American speech as an incalculable dimension super-added to the recognized and calculable dimensions of syllable-count and stress-count. Quantity in this sense, *duration*, is what musicians and musical composers are continually concerned with; and so it is not surprising that poets of this way of thinking, like Pound and Bunting, show themselves avidly interested in poetry which has been, not at a level of theory but as a fact of performance, intimately associated with music: poetry that has been set, or has been written in the hope of being set, to music. It is notable that it was Bunting, in his generation the only British emulator of Pound, who was most confident and insistent that in these matters Pound's immediate master was American, the Walt Whitman of 'Out of the Ocean Endlessly Rocking'. It is in any case certain that for years before *Homage to Sextus Propertius* Pound had been studying, not for their content chiefly but as models of musical form, the poems in quantitative metre of ancient Greece. (His British predecessor in such technical study had been Thomas Hardy; but that is another, and difficult, topic.)

These matters are important because they explain how Pound and Eliot, who had campaigned as a team and would help each other for many years to come, radically differed not just in themes and attitudes (of which something will be said hereafter) but at this deep level, in the not altogether conscious interstices of their craft. Fortunately Eliot declared himself unequivocally, in an essay, 'Reflections on *Vers Libre*: '. . . the ghost of some simple metre should lurk behind the arras in even the "freest" verse; to advance menacingly as we doze, and withdraw as we arouse'. This is what Pound could never have said. When, infrequently, he wanted to write in 'some simple metre', he did so; but when more often he wanted to get away from standard metres, he left them behind altogether, no ghost of them lurking behind his arras. The difference between the two poets corresponds (not quite exactly, because the nature and history of French verse differs so greatly from English) to the distinction that the French make between *vers libre* and *vers libéré*; between, we may say, free verse and freed verse. Eliot's practice, as his remarks just quoted make clear, was always 'freed' verse: verse freed indeed from the constraints of traditional prosody, yet rather constantly recalling to the reader's ear one of the traditional patterns it was departing from. (Hence, notably in 'Gerontion', Eliot's ability to approximate and even conform to Jacobean blank verse, yet to depart from it smoothly when he pleased.) Pound's verse on the contrary was, at least after *Homage to Sextus Propertius*, free, not 'freed': the rhythms that he sought and attained either had never appeared before in the language, or else had not appeared there for many centuries. His departure was much more radical. And yet he was not doctrinaire about it, having declared on the contrary (as early as 1917, significantly in a review of Eliot's *Prufrock and Other Observations*):

Unless a man can put some thematic invention into *vers libre*, he would perhaps do well to stick to 'regular' metres, which have certain chances of being musical from their form, and certain other chances of being musical through his failure in fitting the form.

The one who *was* doctrinaire was Williams, who regarded the iambic measure as a chief curse of the English legacy from which American poetry must free itself if it was ever to stand on its own. However, Winters was to decide that Williams was 'wholly incapable of coherent thought', and when Williams tried to explain his own rhythmical procedures he invented 'the variable foot' – which is, as has been remarked, the equivalent of a rubber inch. Williams had a good ear, and since his death some of his admirers have made more sense of his procedures than he could ever make for himself, but the lamentable effect of his example has been to lead poets to trust their ear implicitly, thus discrediting the very notion of *measure*.

The closeness of Pound's and Eliot's collaboration when they were young did not become clear until 1972. In that year comparisons of Eliot with Pound were stimulated, and exacerbated, by the publication of what were called the 'drafts and transcripts' of *The Waste Land*; that is to say, the heterogeneous packet of typescripts and manuscripts which Eliot had dumped on Pound in Paris, out of which Pound had helped Eliot to extricate the poem that for forty years had been known under that title. In most ways this book reflected great credit on both poets, and was affecting evidence of their mutual trust, of how their common dedication to the poetic calling had precluded any taint of rivalry or wounded *amour-propre*. On the other hand the material which Eliot had put into Pound's hands turned out to be so inchoate that many readers were led to wonder how far the poem as they had had it all these years was in any authentic sense Eliot's at all. To be fair to him, he had repeatedly hinted that, when the evidence was in, it would show that Pound's contribution went far beyond the mere passing of judgement on particular passages; and indeed it turned out that the very structure of the poem had been extricated by Pound, rather than conceived and composed by the poet whose name appeared on the title-page. This was disconcerting, to say the least. It was not easy to think of a precedent, and one could be forgiven for concluding that the notorious obscurity of the poem came about not by the author's design but accidentally, because the work was the product not of one mind but of two. The poem, we might say, is in two minds about itself and its own meaning.

But that is not the whole story. For Pound undoubtedly made the poem more obscure by asking for the excision of some transitional and bridging passages where the language was not at full pressure, but on the other hand he caused to be removed some extended sections which, being plainly extraneous, could only have added to readers' bafflement. Moreover in some important respects Pound was more old-fashioned than Eliot. As his later disastrous interventions in politics would make clear, he was a realist in quite a simple-minded sense, one who was concerned for public life, and believed (like activists of the Left) that a poet had the right and the duty to act in and upon that life quite directly; whereas the oddly distant weariness of Eliot's political pronouncements, even when he was most *engagé* as editor of *The Criterion*, revealed a man for whom the psychological reality of private torments took priority over any reality which announced itself as social and public. Thus Pound was quite ready, and became eager, to deliver a message, though with more obliquities and delays than the impatiently moralistic reader could see reason for; whereas Eliot, true to his inheritance from French *symbolisme*, was sceptical and chary of conveying in poetry any message at all. (Pound had studied some of the same French poets, notably Laforgue and Rimbaud, but he had profited by them in a quite different way from Eliot, and he was averse to the central thrust of the *symboliste* endeavour, to which indeed the imagist or *imagiste* movement which he had sponsored had been intended as a challenging alternative.)

The difference between the two of them showed up in *The Waste Land* drafts. For among the rather few objections by Pound that Eliot paid no attention to were one or two which would have required him to make consistent, in terms of locality and historical period, some of his references to London life. Eliot seems to have ignored these suggestions because for him the physical and social landscape of London was no more than a screen on which to project a phantasmagoria that expressed his own personal disorders and desperations (partly sexual, as one might expect, and as the drafts make clear); whereas Pound seems to have supposed that the subject of the poem was London in all its historical and geographical actuality, much as the city of Dublin was from one point of view the subject of Joyce's *Ulysses*. Quite independent of Pound, most admiring commentators have read the poem more nearly as Pound read it than as Eliot intended. They could always have maintained of course that, whatever the poet's intentions, the poem as an achieved entity answered to their interpretations. But critics of the twenties, knowing nothing of Pound's part in the poem, and ignorant also of Eliot's private sufferings through his wretched first marriage, saw no need to go so far around, to support their conviction or assumption that *The Waste Land* was a poem with a message.

What was known about Pound's association with Eliot did Pound's reputation no good at all. The insufferable Untermeyer in 1923 castigated the texture of *The Waste Land* as 'that formless plasma which Mr Ezra Pound likes to call a Sordelloform'; and in the same year in London, Clive Bell, the voice of 'Bloomsbury', said of Eliot that 'no aesthetic theory can explain his indiscreet boosting of... the lamentable Ezra Pound'. But the most vicious discriminiation had come in the previous year, from Edmund Wilson, who applauded the structure of *The Waste Land* by contrasting it to 'the extremely ill-focused Eight Cantos of his imitator Mr Ezra Pound, who presents only a bewildering mosaic with no central emotion to provide a key'. Eliot, distressed, wrote to Wilson and to another of his champions, Gilbert Seldes, protesting that he did not want to be praised at Pound's expense since he was indebted to Pound (as indeed his dedication to Pound as *il miglior fabbro* had elegantly acknowledged). Eliot told Wilson and Seldes that 'I sincerely consider Ezra Pound the most important living poet in the English language'.[1] But the damage had been done, and Wilson's elevation of Eliot at Pound's expense was to be echoed time and again for at least thirty years, and indeed is still to be heard even today. Pound suffered immediately, in his pocket-book. Always short of money, Pound in the twenties found one outlet after another closed to him and had great difficulty making ends meet. He seems not to have whined, and his only complaint, posthumously recorded by Bunting in his obituary of Pound, is drily judicious: he 'said in the Thirties that Eliot had got stuck because he could not understand Propertius [i.e. Pound's *Homage*] and all the rest had got stuck a few books earlier still'.

How early Pound came by this perception is not clear, but certainly he had no illusions from the first that his *Cantos*, building as they did on the rhythmical and thematic procedures of *Homage to Sextus Propertius*, would be found readily acceptable. In 1922 he explained in a letter:

> Perhaps, as the poem goes on I shall be able to make various things clearer. Having the crust to attempt a poem in 100 or 120 cantos long after all mankind has been commanded never again to attempt a poem of any length, I have to stagger as I can.
> The first 11 cantos are preparation of the palette. I *have to get*

1 Noel Stock, *The Life of Ezra Pound* (London, 1970), pp.249–50; quoted by Michael Grant in *T.S. Eliot, The Critical Heritage* (London, 1982), I, p.20.

down all the colours or elements I want for the poem. Some
perhaps too enigmatically and abbreviatedly. I hope, heaven
help me, to bring them into some sort of design and architec-
ture later.   (*Selected Letters*, p.180)

Excusably perhaps, neither Edmund Wilson nor any one else could
understand, or could credit, the scale on which Pound was working:
120 cantos, and by the time Pound died in 1972, the poem had fallen
only just short of that. In a poem designed on such a scale (and this
evidence of 'design' on such a scale from the first is astonishing) it was
obviously illegitimate to look, as Edmund Wilson did, for emotional
or affective unity in each or any Canto in isolation. As Pound confessed
in another letter in 1933: 'Most Cantos have in them "binding matter",
i.e. lines holding them into the whole poem and these passages don't
much help the reader of an isolated fragment... More likely to con-
fuse than help'. Pound was in all seriousness embarked on an epic
poem (which he defined, following of all unlikely authorities Rudyard
Kipling, as 'the tale of the tribe'); he could not and did not expect
understanding from readers who supposed that the epic poem had
died in the seventeenth century if not before, whose expectations
therefore were conditioned by their experience of the brief or else
extended lyric. There are lyrical passages or interludes in *The Cantos*,
as in any epic poem, but to excerpt these for applause while deploring
their context is to fudge the issue, and evade the challenge of the
poem as a whole. The scale on which Pound was working was not
clear even to the poet himself; so that the eleven cantos which he
originally designated as 'preparation of the palette' are now by
responsible commentators considerably extended – to the extent that
the first thirty cantos, which are all that the twenties knew of the
poem (*A Draft of XVI Cantos* (Paris, June 1925); *A Draft of the Cantos
17-27* (100 copies, September 1928); and *A Draft of XXX Cantos*
(210 copies, August 1930)), are now often regarded as laying out on
the painter's palette the hues that only in subsequent cantos would
be combined to polemical and imaginative purpose. Certainly only
in the next batch of cantos (post-1930), which began with extended
excerpts from the founding fathers of the Republic, would the scale
of magnitude of the poem become apparent, also its topicality and
its Americanness. Of the first thirty cantos by themselves, no
account is more plausible than that of a writer in the *New York Herald
Tribune Books* for 9 January 1927, who decided: 'Mr Pound is
avowedly writing a history of the Mediterranean basin'.[1] The writer

---

1 Brita Lindberg-Seyersted (ed.), *Pound/Ford. The Story of a Literary
Friendship* (London, 1982), p.86.

was Ford Madox Ford, who was among the most loyal as he had
been among the first of Pound's friends; in the twenties he was as
penurious and as out of fashion as Pound.

It is easy to cheat when quoting from these early cantos: either
by imposing a seeming self-closure on passages that are in fact open
at both ends, or (and as well) by presenting a lyrically appealing
passage as typical of the whole. Any quotation must in any case be
extensive:

> So that the Xarites bent over tovarisch.
> And these are the labours of tovarisch,
> That tovarisch lay in the earth,
> And rose, and wrecked the house of the tyrants,
> And that tovarisch lay then in the earth
>   And the Xarites bent over tovarisch.
>
> These are the labours of tovarisch,
> That tovarisch wrecked the house of the tyrants,
> And rose, and talked folly on folly,
> And walked forth and lay in the earth
>   And the Xarites bent over tovarisch.
>
> And that tovarisch cursed and blessed without aim,
>   These are the labours of tovarisch,
> Saying:
>   'Me Cadmus sowed in the earth
>   And with the thirtieth autumn
> I return to the earth that made me.
> Let the five last build the wall;
>
> I neither build nor reap.
> That he came with the gold ships, Cadmus,
> That he fought with the wisdom,
> Cadmus, of the gilded prows. Nothing I build
> And I reap
> Nothing; with the thirtieth autumn
> I sleep, I sleep not, I rot
> And I build no wall.
>   Where was the wall of Eblis
> At Ventadour, there now are the bees,
> And in that court, wild grass for their pleasure
> That they carry back to the crevice
> Where loose stone hangs upon stone.
> I sailed never with Cadmus,
>   lifted never stone above stone.'

'Baked and eaten tovarisch!
'Baked and eaten, tovarisch, my boy,
'That is your story. And up again,
'Up and at 'em. Laid never stone upon stone.'

'The air burst into leaf.'
'Hung there flowered acanthus,
'Can you tell the down from the up?'

As 'tovarisch' quite raucously announces, Pound here in Canto 27 reflects on the October Revolution in Russia in 1917. And not only the Xaritès (or Charitès, the Greek Graces) bend some solicitude over the unnamed revolutionary comrade, so does the poet – for indeed in 1930 Pound's desire for an authoritarian leader in politics was as ready to fix on Lenin as on Mussolini. Rather plainly the poem decides, as others have decided before and since, that the revolution's humble heroes, revolution once accomplished, did not know what to do with the liberation they had achieved. One needs Ford Madox Ford's emphasis on 'the Mediterranean basin' to understand that 'tovarisch' is being dignified by having his exploits measured against the myths of ancient Greece – for instance, that of Cadmus, founder of Thebes, who sowed dragon's teeth from which sprang warriors which fought among themselves until only five remained. Pound has no recourse to that staple of anti-Russian propaganda in every generation (some of it was being aired in these years in Eliot's *Criterion*) according to which the Russian is 'asiatic', outside the confines of Europe. What will disconcert readers who come to Pound after Eliot, what they will find either refreshing or exasperating, is the literalness of Pound's imagination. When he has tovarisch say, 'Nothing I build', this is to be understood not allegorically but literally: working of stone, either architecturally or sculpturally, was for Pound the register of culture – a conviction which he shared in his lifetime with few except the British art-critic whom he knew and esteemed, Adrian Stokes. Thus the reference to the ruined walls of Eblis, in Aquitaine, is not gratuitous; and we know from other passages that Pound's refusal in the last resort to take seriously Russia's contribution to European culture was grounded in his notion that Russia had never produced an indigenous tradition of stone architecture.

On the other hand, when in the ruined court of Eblis the bees find 'wild grass for their pleasure', that is good too. For human building (art) and the processes of germination (nature) are not in this vision opposed, as alternatives we must choose between. The one mirrors the other, and is nourished by the other. To build is as natural as to procreate. Accordingly tovarisch condemns himself not only because 'nothing I build', but also because 'I reap/Nothing'; the failure in the one capacity implies a failure in the other. The identity of the two activities is asserted, with a succinctness that only the build-up has made possible, in 'flowered acanthus' (*acanthus*, a classical motif of architectural sculpture, is also the stylized representation of specific foliage), and also in 'Can you tell the down from the up?' (for there is no way of deciding whether 'nature' is the 'up' and 'art' the 'down', or vice-versa). This sanguine trust in the unity and coherence of the universe is as far as possible from 'the American Puritan temperament', as Eliot suffered it and articulated it. And nearly half a century later, when *The Cantos* would tail off (not discreditably) in 'Drafts and Fragments', Pound would still be purveying the same message, in terms of 'the gardens of Proserpine', the mineral and metallic gardens that Proserpine according to the myth created in the underworld, to duplicate as 'art' the springing herbage that she inspired in spring and summer through her six months in the overworld. No one in the twenties could have divined this over-arching design, nor did Pound suppose that anyone would.

How any of this was relevant to twentieth-century America was precisely the question that Williams had raised when he jeered at 'parodies of the middle ages, Dante and Langue D'Oc' being presented as 'the best in United States poetry'. And it is true that Williams was aware of creative work in American photography and painting, as Pound in his self-exile could not be. But Pound with his invaluable naïveté really believed that the United States was 'a land of opportunity'; that his nation's glory was all in the future, and would be achieved if only Americans would sort out those achievements of European culture (and of non-European cultures also) which were worth their emulating and trying to surpass.

The New Pelican Guide to English Literature, ed. Boris Ford. Harmondsworth: Penguin, 1988.

Pound as Critic

Pound belongs in that sub-class of the species 'critic', which we call 'poet-critic'. So does Eliot of course, so does William Empson; not to speak of Dryden, Johnson, Coleridge, Arnold. Yes, but unlike Eliot and Empson, Pound – by the abrupt, brusque and aphoristic way in which he delivers his critical judgements – insists that we understand them as immediately spun off from the imaginative work, thrown over his shoulder, as it were, as he hurries from one part of the workshop to another. In this, of the great poet-critics of the past the one he most nearly resembles is Dryden, whose criticism virtually always comes before us as the preface to a volume of original imaginative writing – including translations which, in this too like Pound, Dryden considers no less 'original' than poems he has made up for himself. Eliot and Empson take off their poet's hat, and wear a critic's hat – that at least is the decorous illusion which, by their style and procedures, they try to maintain; Pound and Dryden on the contrary wear the poet's hat all the time, even when they criticize. To some this seems presumptuous. Perhaps some of Dryden's early readers objected to this presumption in him; there is no doubt that many of Pound's readers have felt affronted, and feel affronted still, by the authority he claims, the impatiently magisterial tone of much of his criticism. For the abrupt, hasty manner of Pound's criticism seems to some readers to carry the implication (to which Pound in fact did not subscribe) that no critic is worth listening to unless he has laboured at the maker's workbench; that all worthwhile criticism of stories comes from story-tellers, that only poets are worth listening to about poems.

In the 1930s critics so variously and widely influential as Allen Tate, Yvor Winters and F.R. Leavis each in his own way considered Pound's criticism, or some of it, and then instructed their readers that that criticism could safely be ignored. An instance, and a momentous one, is Tate's review in *Poetry* for November 1932, of Pound's *How To Read*:

> The real criticism of Mr Pound is not to be directed against his theory as such, but rather at the hasty headlong fashion

in which he presents it, at the logical confusion of his intellect when it is not performing the task which is specifically his own, that task being poetry. The justification of Mr Pound's thesis in *How To Read* is not his arguments, but his poetry.

Leavis, who countered *How To Read* with a booklet, *How to Teach Reading*, and Winters, who declared in 1937, 'Mr Pound resembles a village loafer who sees much and understands little', told the same story as Tate: Pound was a *naif*, an imagination and sensory apparatus that consistently performed better than it knew, in ways that the maker's own discursive intelligence failed to comprehend or measure up to; in Winters's memorable and mordant judgement of 1943, 'a sensibility without a mind, or with as little mind as is well possible'. Take Pound the poet (though in strictly limited dosages, if you listened to Leavis or Winters), and ignore Pound the critic – the message was loud and clear, and it was attended to.

The damage this did to our criticism was as nothing compared with the harm it did to our poetry. Tate, so devoted to Eliot's precedent, appears to have dismissed as amiably perfunctory the respect that Eliot, not quite consistently but repeatedly, accorded to Pound's prose-writings and Pound's literary opinions; and – so it might be argued, though this is not the place for it – Tate's own verse, and the verse of those he influenced, were the worse for having taken note of Eliot's precedent without attending equally to Pound's. (For the two sensibilities were radically different.) As late as the 1960s the translations and imitations of Robert Lowell, who had sat at Tate's feet, were widely supposed to have been validated by Pound's precedent in this kind of writing, whereas in truth Lowell's *Imitations* allowed themselves liberties such as Pound would never have condoned. Moreover, the advice that in 1932 Tate implicitly offered – 'Read Pound's poetry, and ignore his criticism' – was disingenuous. For it turned out that Pound's poetry – *The Cantos* certainly but much of the earlier work also – could be understood and enjoyed only by those who had attended to Pound's criticism enough to grasp what it was that Pound was trying to do, or conceived himself to be doing, in his poetry. And it was 1952 before that road was taken – by Hugh Kenner; it was only then that responsible criticism of Pound became possible – everything before that belongs, as it were, in pre-history.

Because Pound the critic seems to be always in his shirt-sleeves sparing a few distraught hours or minutes from the more serious business of writing poems or translating them, his criticism is dispersed, though there is much more of it than we are likely to remember. Much of it indeed – art criticism and music criticism as well as criticism of literature – still languishes in the files of defunct magazines, from which no one seems anxious to rescue it. For the rest, his exceptionally loyal publisher, James Laughlin of *New Directions*, exerts himself to keep in print as much as possible. But there is no one book, not even any two or three books, that can be pointed to as constituting the corpus or the canon of Pound's criticism.

The chronologically first and formally most decorous of his critical books, *The Spirit of Romance* (originally 1910), can very profitably be used – I speak from experience – as a manual for able undergraduates; especially if taken along with *Confucius to Cummings*, the anthology that many decades later Pound compiled along with Marcella Spann. *The Spirit of Romance* is undertaken on the principle that Pound never ceased to hammer home, notably in *How To Read* and *The ABC of Reading*: the principle that no one can understand the history of poetry in English unless he or she takes note of poetry in, or responsibly translated out of, other languages than English. Perhaps no one would deny this; but as each generation of students arrives more defiantly or hopelessly monoglot, as a whole new discipline (called 'Comparative Literature') has come into being to cater for those exceptional persons who can read more languages than one, the need for a classroom manual to redress this state of affairs becomes ever more urgent. And yet, to the best of my knowledge, *The Spirit of Romance* and *Confucius to Cummings* have no competitors. It is entirely typical of Pound that he should want his criticism to be immediately useful – to, as he says, 'the neophyte'. And not just students but their teachers would do well to acknowledge themselves neophytes. It is true that Pound does not readily conceive of a reader who is not also an aspiring writer – something that led Leavis astray when he tried to retort to *How To Read*; but there is no harm, and much profit, in letting the student of the history of poetry suppose that he or she is in due course going to write poems.

A very different book, much more idiosyncratic in its structure and its procedures, is the one of 1938 called in the American printing *Culture*, and in the London edition *Guide to Kulchur*. This is not a work of criticism though it contains much criticism along the way, and of the first order – for instance, Pound's respectful demurrer from the high valuation that Eliot had put on Johnson's *Vanity of Human Wishes*. *Guide to Kulchur* gives us Pound at his most personal, at his most deliberately vulnerable; it is here that we find him wondering aloud, for instance, if the body of his work to that date could be mentioned in the same breath with Thomas Hardy's.

Three years before this, Yale University Press had brought out in a very handsome volume called *Make It New* seven essays representing Pound's criticism at its most scholarly, on such recondite

topics as Cavalcanti, and Elizabethan Classicists, and early transla-
tions of Homer. Pound's point, of course, in these essays reprinted
from magazines and from earlier collections like *Pavannes & Divisions*
(1918) or *Instigations* (1920), is that these matters that we think of as
recondite should not be so regarded. Perhaps no one has been per-
suaded of this except those – a growing number, after all – who find
that knowledge in these areas is indispensable for the understanding
of *The Cantos* and of Pound's later translations, for instance from
Sophocles. But the thrust of these essays is not so special, nor so
self-serving; those who nowadays gird at 'the canon', as an array of
allegedly classic masterpieces in literature, their classic status
imposed as an instrument of cultural oppression, need to take
account of how in these essays Pound challenged the canon, requir-
ing that it be revised. Arthur Golding's translation of Ovid's
Metamorphoses may not yet be 'canonical'; but it is a lot nearer to
being so because Pound campaigned for it. The canon may or may
not be oppressive: it is not inert, as Pound's revisions of it prove.

Fortunately, most of the essays in *Make It New* were brought back
into print in 1954, when Eliot edited *Literary Essays of Ezra Pound*.
Of the many loyal services that Eliot did for his old comrade-in-
arms, this may be the most notable. Given the dispersed profusion
of Pound's criticism, neither the choice of what to reprint, nor the
arrangement of it when chosen, can have been easy. And Eliot lets
us know that he had to argue with Pound, who wanted in some
items that Eliot excluded, and wanted out some items on which
Eliot insisted. In the event, Eliot's selection and his arrangement are
admirable; and undoubtedly a sure sense of what is great and irre-
placeable about Pound as critic can be gained from this one volume.
In his Introduction Eliot declares roundly: 'Pound's critical writings,
scattered and occasional as they have been, form the *least dispensible*
body of critical writing in our time'. The italics are Eliot's. Those
who have read him know how seldom he declares himself thus
roundly and emphatically. And in 1954 Eliot's influence and author-
ity were unparalleled. Yet this criticism which he declared indispens-
able has by and large been dispensed with, since 1954 as earlier. It
is not easy to understand why. But it is charitable to assume that it
has something to do with the *kind* of critic that Pound is. And about
this Eliot is again uncharacteristically emphatic, as well as eloquent.
Pound, Eliot says,

> would cajole, and almost coerce, other men into writing well:
> so that he often presents the appearance of a man trying to
> convey to a very deaf person the fact that the house is on fire.
> Every change he has advocated has always struck him as being

of instant urgency. This is not only the temperament of the teacher: it represents also, with Pound, a passionate desire, not merely to write well himself, but to live in a period in which he could be surrounded by equally intelligent and creative minds. Hence his impatience. For him, to discover a new writer of genius is as satisfying an experience, as it is for a lesser man to believe that he has written a great work of genius himself. He has cared deeply that his contemporaries and juniors should write well; he has cared less for his personal achievement than for the life of letters and art. One of the lessons to be learnt from his critical prose and from his correspondence is the lesson to care unselfishly for the art one serves.

This is a noble tribute. And yet it ends by striking a note that is not altogether happy, nor altogether adequate to what Eliot had said earlier. 'To care unselfishly for the art one serves...' – that is right, of course, and no more than just. But in Eliot's earlier sentences we have been told of Pound's serving not 'art', but artists; of his being concerned that they should each realize his or her full potential, so that the *level* of accomplishment (in 'letters' as well as 'art') should be raised all round. In that way, so Eliot has suggested, Pound made himself responsible for a whole 'period', the period of his lifetime, anxiously impatient that it too lift itself to a higher level. If this is so, then it seems that for 'the art one serves' one might as well read: the *culture* one serves, the *historical period* one serves, even the *society* one serves (perhaps an international society). In short, Eliot has delineated a critic who recognizes public or civic responsibilities; and unless we are very careful, to say of this critic that he 'serves his art' may seem a rather sudden cramping and diminution of the claims made for him. The same thing happens when, later in the essay, Eliot defines the limitation of Pound's kind of criticism (for 'any kind of criticism has its limitations'): 'The limitation of Pound's kind is in its concentration upon the craft of letters, and of poetry especially'. To move from 'art' to 'craft' is rather plainly a further contraction, or diminution: and it will be radically misunderstood unless we remember that for Pound the level of craftsmanship (not just in letters, but in supposedly humbler trades also) is a register, a thermometer-reading, of the good or ill health of a period or of a society. (His most categorical assertions of this are in *Guide to Kulchur*.)

It is just here, I suspect, that we – many of us – are 'turned off'. In the first place, this is Pound at his most old-fashioned. John Ruskin, it might be said, was the last considerable figure before Pound to hold in all seriousness, as Pound did, that the level of craftsmanship and artistry in a society was the one infallible measure of that society's moral and civic health. And many of us, I dare say, have tacitly (perhaps wistfully) consigned Ruskin's views to the ash-can of history, along with other Utopian systems put together in the nineteenth century which the desolate history of our own century has made no longer tenable. Moreover, when we consider the courses that Pound was led into by his conviction of the civic responsibility of the man of letters – his money pamphlets of the 1930s, his desperate visit home in 1938 to keep the USA out of war with Italy, particularly his wartime broadcasts over Rome radio – we have some right to conclude either that the artist has no civic responsibility at all, or else that that responsibility can safely be discharged only in his art and nowhere else. Understandable as it is, this reaction is plainly not altogether reasonable. For Pound may have been wrong in selecting Fascist Italy as the modern society than came nearest to satisfying his Ruskinian demands, and yet right in thinking that societies should be judged according as they met, or failed to meet, that standard. That he went grossly wrong in applying the standard does not mean that the standard as such was inapplicable. However, most of us either no longer want to believe in the Ruskinian and Poundian relation between craftsmanlike performance and civic health, or else we tell ourselves (perhaps with Pound's fate before us as a cautionary tale) that we can no longer *afford* to believe it. We are only just beginning to recognize that if we take this attitude, we are denying to arts and letters, and to the criticism of them, any bearing at all on public life – including, for instance, public education. At any rate, though we would most of us like to maintain that Pound's Fascism is a quite distinct issue from Pound's poetry and his criticism, it is plain that we cannot do this. His anti-Semitism may be a separate issue (though many of course will deny even that); but his Fascism cannot be, since it represents a disastrously false judgement made in the course of following through a conviction *not* self-evidently false – about there being a connection between the health of letters and the health of the commonweal.

It so happens that this troublesome question, or complex of questions, is not raised by the piece in Eliot's selection that I shall take to represent Pound's criticism at its irreplaceable best. This is the brief article (less than five printed pages) which originally appeared in *Poetry* for February 1918, under the title, 'The Hard and Soft in French Poetry'. The title alone is enough to show that this piece, if it avoids giving offence in the ways just glanced at, will offend none the less. For hardness and softness in relation to poetry – where have these qualities been defined? Does Pound define them? No, he does not, except circuitously and by implication. However, he begins, after a fashion that is less rare with him than is commonly supposed, by apologizing for the impressionism that supplies him with the terms he needs:

> I apologize for using the semimetaphorical terms 'hard' and 'soft' in this essay, but after puzzling over the matter for some time I can see no other way of setting about it. By 'hardness' I mean a quality which is in poetry nearly always a virtue – I can think of no case where it is not. By 'softness' I mean an opposite quality which is not always a fault.

Annoyed as we may be at having the cardinal terms left thus undefined (for Pound proceeds no further towards defining them), we are compelled to see that this criticism is not of the chalk-or-cheese, sheep-and-goats variety; the discrimination proposed is more subtle – between a quality in poetry that is 'nearly always' a virtue ('I can think of no case where it is not'), and an opposite quality that is 'not always' a fault. This is a critic who uses sliding scales, not one fixed Procrustean rule. The bluffly categorical manner is misleading; Pound is always ready to concede that 'circumstances alter cases'.

One reason why Pound's scales must 'slide' is that nowhere in his criticism does Pound forget chronology – literary history and literary criticism are for him two aspects of one unified act of attention. But there is more to it than that. For Pound all dates are important but none more so than the date on the calendar above the critic's desk. This is what Eliot means by insisting: 'It is necessary to consider Pound's literary pronouncements in the light of the circumstances in which they were written...' This sounds defensive, even apologetic. But Eliot doesn't mean it so, as we see from the notorious case that he cites in illustration:

> A great writer can have, at a particular time, a pernicious or merely deadening influence; and this influence can be most effectively attacked by pointing out those faults which ought not to be copied, and those virtues any emulation of which is anachronistic. Pound's disparagement of Milton, for instance, was, I am convinced, most salutary twenty and thirty years ago; I still agree with him against the academic admirers of Milton; though to me it seems that the situation has changed.

In Eliot's view, the circumstances have changed so greatly over thirty years since 1924 that what was rightly said of Milton in that year cannot rightly be said of him in 1954. This is relativity with a vengeance, and many of us have felt than in a case like this the scales that

Eliot measures by are not so much sliding as slithering. In this instance Pound, we notice, stood firm. But he was nearly as ready as Eliot to insist that all critical judgements and pronouncements are relative – relative, above all, to the date at which they are made. Already in 1928 he was protesting that his own pronouncements at the time of the Imagist manifesto were tailored to the specific needs of 1914, and should not be taken as binding fourteen years later. To minds of absolutist temper like Leavis and Winters, this was contemptible; and undoubtedly it is next to impossible to establish criticism as an academic discipline on grounds so sandy and shifting. But perhaps the moral we should draw is that criticism is not, and cannot be, such a discipline (though literary history is, or may be). A great mystery is why Eliot, who was more of a relativist than Pound, should have been accepted by the academic establishment whereas Pound was not.

Instead of defining 'hardness' in poetry, Pound rapidly cites three poets where he finds the quality in question: Gautier, Hérédia, Albert Samain. He distinguishes among them, cursorily, as he cites them in order. Turning to English (where, he assures us, the quality is much harder to come by), he reviews the claims of a Ben Jonson lyric, of George Herbert, Christina Rossetti and Lionel Johnson. He by no means dismisses the claims of these poets, but gently and respectfully sets them aside – 'I do not feel that they have much part in this essay. I do not feel that their quality is really the quality I am seeking here to define'. Why, then, are they named? For a very good reason. Pound says, in effect: 'If your French isn't good enough to go where the quality is both defined (metaphorically) and exemplified, i.e. in Gautier's "L'art" specifically and in his *Emaux et Camées* as a whole, or in the work of followers like Hérédia and Samain, then remind yourself, or re-experience, what it is like to read George Herbert and Christina Rossetti and Lionel Johnson. Ask yourself what these three poets in your experience of them have in common, and in answering that you will *get near* to the quality I am trying to isolate.' Nothing, after all, could be more scrupulous; this is how a truly empirical criticism proceeds and must proceed. An array of instances, almost of specimens, is set before us; and we are invited to make our own observations, inferring from them as much as they will bear. This was, Pound believed (and with good reason), the method of a great biologist, Louis Agassiz; and when pressed Pound was ready to call the procedure not just 'empirical' but 'scientific'. What is likely to strike us, however, is the compliment that Pound pays us; his courteous confidence in our disinterestedness, our patience and eagerness, and our capacity to experience what is on the page before us, whether in French or English, without needing to have him constantly at our elbows, nudging us and crying, 'Can't you *see*?' No aspect of Pound is more widely misunderstood. It is rightly said of him that he was always a pedagogue, but he is a pedagogue in the courtly nineteenth-century mode of Professor Agassiz, who sets up the controlled experiment and invites us to participate in it, not in the hectoring and charismatic mode of the star of the lecture-hall.

Meanwhile Pound has proposed an English poet who is more nearly an analogue to Gautier than any so far mentioned, a nearer analogue and yet still not wholly trustworthy because he is 'from poem to poem, extremely uneven'. This is Walter Savage Landor; and this short article explains why Landor figures repeatedly, and always with respect, not just in *The Cantos* and in Pound's later criticism, but in Yeats's poetry and prose also. Probably not in this essay as such, but in that area of Pound's conversation of which this essay is a distillation, we find the reason – so I believe – why Yeats said admiringly of Landor in 1917: 'He had in his *Imaginary Conversations* reminded us, as it were, that the Venus de Milo is a stone.' And I submit that out of this same background – conversations with Pound – comes that surprising coupling of names with which Yeats ends 'To a Young Beauty' (1918):

> There is not a fool can call me friend,
> And I may dine at journey's end
> With Landor and with Donne.

What we are groping for, what Pound (we now see) is inciting us to grope for, what Yeats is laying claim to, is that effect in writing which an earlier criticism knew as 'lapidary': that is to say, the effect or the illusion of words as not written or printed on a page, but as incised on a stone block. The aspiration after this effect is very ancient, as we know from the Greek derivation common to both 'epigram' and 'epitaph'. Certainly the aspiration is not limited in modern times to those who have read *Emaux et Camées*, the French book that Pound respectfully pillaged for *Hugh Selwyn Mauberley*; it is to be found in all modern poetries known to me, Russian and Polish as well as French, and (more faintly) in British and American. In short, what this has to do with modern poetry is very clear; what it has to do with modern criticism is not clear at all, since that criticism has, as we have seen, no vocabulary for dealing with it, and moves further and further from finding such a vocabulary, the more it takes its lead from linguisticians like Saussure and Jakobson.

After he has made his first claim for Landor, Pound writes two paragraphs of the sort that have provoked near-apoplexy, because they have not been taken in the spirit that Pound intended:

We have in English a certain gamut of styles: we have the good Chaucerian; almost the only style in English where 'softness' is tolerable; we have the good Elizabethan;... and the bad, or muzzy, Elizabethan; and the Miltonic, which is a bombastic and rhetorical Elizabethan coming from an attempt to write English with Latin syntax. Its other mark is that the rich words have gone: *i.e.*, words like *preluciand*, which have a folk tradition and are, in feeling, germane to all Europe: *Leuchand, luisant, lucente*: these words are absent in Miltonism, and purely pedantic words, like *irriguous*, have succeeded them.

We have Pope, who is really the Elizabethan satiric style, more or less born out of Horace, and a little improved or at least regularized. And we have Landor – that is, Landor at his best. And after that we have 'isms' and 'eses': the pseudo-Elizabethanism – *i.e.*, bad Keats; the romantics, Swinburnese, Browningese, neo-celticism. And how the devil a poet writing English manages to make or find a language for poems is a mystery.

No, Professor X, Pound does *not* say that Landor, or Landor at his best, is better than Keats; and no, sir, he does *not* say that Chaucer is better than Milton. He is concerned with 'the Miltonic', with 'Miltonism', not with Keats but with '*bad* Keats', not with Browning but with 'Browningese'. He is not talking about any one of these great writers (his devotion to Browning was well advertised) but about, in Eliot's words, the 'pernicious or merely deadening influence' that 'a great writer can have, at a particular time'. A great writer's idiom is, by himself when he nods and more certainly by his epigones who emulate and copy him, rigidified and adulterated. And the more idiosyncratic his genius (this is the case of Milton, surely), the more likely it is that what will be copied is his mannerisms. If it be objected that no beginning writer shops around in this way among the idioms handed down to him from the past, the evidence is that certain beginning writers *do* shop around in just this way; Ezra Pound was one of them, and he is by no means so exceptional as is supposed. For such a beginning writer in such a situation, it may well turn out that a minor master like Landor is more fruitfully instructive than a major master like Milton or Keats: and if it does turn out so, one has a certain debt of honour that must be paid to the past master by whom one was liberated.

Two-thirds of the way through his essay, Pound apologizes again: 'If this seem an over-long prologue...' And we are astonished. It had not occurred to us that this ranging survey of the idioms of English and incidentally French verse had been no more than a 'prologue' – and to what, for heaven's sake? But Pound has not forgotten what his assignment is. He believes, or he *chooses* to believe, that in Chicago or somewhere else there were readers of *Poetry* magazine in 1918 who zealously and in all seriousness wanted to know what French poets of that time they might profitably read, and what in the broadest terms they should look for in each of them. And so the last page or so is given over to French names: Corbière and Jammes and De Regnier; Tailhade and Romains; Vildrac, Spire and Arcos – poets who at the present day have few readers even among the French. Pound has been conned by French reputation-making? Not at all; good writing is so infernally difficult that even the most modest achievement (and Pound's claims for some of these poets are modest indeed) should not go unacknowledged. Pound was to acknowledge some of them, all over again, years later in the *Cantos*. And meanwhile, what courtesy to the readers of Poetry! How confident he is, or affects to be, about their disinterestedness, their alertness, the range of their sympathies, the use that they will make of the gentlest hint or nudge! That deference towards the well-disposed reader is hard to find in later criticism – for good reason, no doubt.

Well, but – so some readers may be saying or thinking – what about the *content* of these so numerous poems? What are they saying, these poets, French and English? Pound seems to have no interest in that. Is it not the case that George Herbert and Christina Rossetti and even Lionel Johnson are devoutly Christian poets, whereas Pound is militantly non-Christian? And if Pound so blithely over-looks that difference, doesn't that mean that we have in him a critic who attends to form, to style, at the expense of what that form and that style are used so as to convey? Don't we have in him a formalist, in fact an aesthete? This is the brickbat that has been thrown at Pound from the first, and is thrown at him still, because of his unswerving attention to what makes poetry poetry, and not some other sort of discourse versified. It was the accusation, or the self-accusation, that Pound wrestled with in *Hugh Selwyn Mauberley*, and settled not wholly to his own or any one else's satisfaction. In 'The Hard and Soft in French Poetry' Pound confronts the issue very early, and deals with it to my mind conclusively. This is when he discriminates Hérédia from Gautier:

> Heredia is 'hard', but there or thereabouts he ends. It is perhaps that Gautier is intent on being 'hard'; is intent on conveying a certain verity of feeling, and he ends by being truly poetic. Heredia wants to be poetic *and* hard; the hardness appears to him as a virtue in the poetic. And one tends to conclude that

all attempts to be poetic in some manner or other defeat their own end; whereas an intentness on the quality of the emotion to be conveyed makes for poetry.

To go for the lapidary effect as such is sterile; one tries for the lapidary because, if achieved, it is a guarantee of the verity of one's feeling – Christian or non-Christian, as the case may be. Aestheticism, *l'art pour l'art*, is identified, and impaled, in Hérédia (though with a beguiling hesitancy – 'perhaps', 'one tends to conclude'); to aim for the poetic ends up in something other than poetry, or else in inferior poetry.

In conclusion, and to end near to our starting-point, we should look at Pound's second apology. In context, the effect of it is hardly apologetic at all:

> If this seem an over-long prologue, think how little discussion there is of these things. Only a few professors and their favourite students seem to have read enough to be able to consider a matter of style with any data at their disposal – these and a few poets of the better sort...

'With any data at their disposal' – the terminology puts us back into Louis Agassiz' laboratory. And is it not a true bill, now as in 1918? Who would assert with confidence that there now are more professors with 'data at their disposal' than there were in 1918? And of such professors, how many would rest content with the conclusion that Pound reached in 1918: 'A critic must spend some of his time asking questions – which perhaps no one can answer. It is much more his business to stir up curiosity than to insist on acceptances.' Pound as critic cuts the critic down to size; which is, one may think, a pressing need, now, in 1984.

Adapted from *The Sewanee Review*, 92: 3 (1984).

Pound and the Perfect Lady

Pound's Artists: Ezra Pound and the Visual Arts in London, Paris and Italy, introduced by Richard Humphreys. London: Tate Gallery Publications, 1985.

Ezra Pound and Dorothy Shakespear: Their Letters 1909-1914, edited by Omar Pound and A. Walton Litz. Faber, 1985.

Thanks to Clive Wilmer among others, an exhibition of paintings, sculptures, photographs and printed material bearing on Pound's interests in 'the visual arts' was mounted for the Cambridge Poetry Festival on 14 June, and could be seen in Cambridge's not sufficiently renowned Kettle's Yard Gallery until 4 August; it will now be at the Tate from 11 September to 10 November. Humphrey Carpenter's report on the exhibition for the *TLS* of 28 June will hardly choke the turnstiles. The show has, he said, 'something of the air of a school reunion about it', and with a few exceptions 'it is the Pound business much as usual'. No one, he thinks, who is unfamiliar with 'Pound's P.T. Barnumising for the visual arts' will know what to make of it. This tone is intolerable, and augurs very ill for Carpenter's biography of Pound, said to be in the works. No one who reads the three solid essays in what is described as the catalogue of the exhibition (though it isn't quite that) can think that 'Barnumising' in any way describes Pound's ardent response to painting and sculpture, photography and architecture, first in London 1908-1920, then in Paris 1920-1925, and thereafter in Italy. Carpenter, predictably, finds the three essayists – Richard Humphreys, John Alexander and Peter Robinson – 'taking a rather solemn approach to the whole thing'; whereas, he assures us, Pound's exertions on behalf of these arts partook 'more than a little of the amiable joke'. Before it is through, Pound's centenary year will bring on indigestion in even the most devoted Poundians. But whether his artistic life was, as a few think, exemplary, or, as rather more think, a fearsomely cautionary fable, it is at all events a matter of some solemnity, and the amused weariness of we-have-heard-it-all-before will not serve in 1985 as it did in 1920 or 1940 or even, scandalously, as late as fifteen

years ago. We have *not* heard it all before, unless we have read, as
few of us have, Harriet Zinnes's compendium *Ezra Pound and the
Visual Arts*, which all these essayists draw on very heavily. Amiable
joking was never what Pound intended, and only a total insensitivity
to his tone of voice could lead one to think otherwise.

Solemn? 'Sedate' is a better word for these essays. And two of
them might be called even pedestrian. No harm in that: pedestrian
documentation is what there is a call for – Pound himself, and his
admirers emulating him, have been so sprightly for so long that they
have persuaded people they, and he, cannot be in earnest. All the
same, John Alexander's piece on the Paris period would have made
livelier and easier reading if he had not, like Richard Humphreys
on the London years, limited himself so self-effacingly to the
documentation, necessary though that is. The problem, for instance,
of Pound's admiration for Brancusi, and of how that fits or does
not fit with his other proclivities and principles, cannot for much
longer be left where Alexander leaves it. On the other hand, his
account of Pound's attitude to Fernand Léger is new to me, and
fascinating. Peter Robinson's essay on Pound and Italian art is quite
another matter: altogether more ambitious and probing. Out of
D.S. Chambers and Michael Baxandall and some Italian scholars
Robinson measures up Pound's ideas about the right relation
between artist and patron against what we know of how patronage
in fact worked in the ducal fiefs of Renaissance Italy; and when he
deals with the closeness of Pound's views on this and related matters
to Ruskin's ideas (a theme common to all these essayists), Robinson
dares to broach the too long forbidden topic of the poet's antagonism
– inertly received, so some would say, rather than considered – to
Christian faith and Christian ethics. Ruskin's espousal of a crafts-
manly aesthetics, Robinson points out, is grounded in Christian
convictions about the humility proper to a fallen creature: lacking
such grounds, Pound's holding to the craftsmanly not only seems
arbitrary and unargued, it is as often presumptuous as humble. It's
Peter Robinson, too, who won't stay content with ritually shocked
head-shaking at Pound's Fascism. When Pound in an early Canto
includes among a hero's conversational topics

> And men of unusual genius,
> Both of ancient times and our own,

Robinson detects 'a severe confusion of categories and contexts',
and he asks: 'Might we not distinguish in kind between literary
promotion, such as Pound's for Joyce, in war or peace, and advocacy
such as Pound's for Mussolini in war rather than peace?' Well, so we

might, but we might also think that 'literary promotion' is an inadequate description of Pound's sustained and inventive activities on behalf of his notably non-reciprocating Irish colleague. In any case, Pound has the centuries on his side when he equates a genius in statecraft – Jefferson if not Mussolini – with a genius in an art or in speculative thought. In fact, the equation is more challenging the other way round: Pound thinks Joyce a phenomenon deserving equal attention with Mussolini – a temperate judgement that the years may be thought to have vindicated. Art is at least as important as politics, whether in peace or war, and it is Pound's intransigent conviction of this that brings out the philistine in others beside Peter Robinson. The statesman as artist – God knows it is a dubious and dangerous idea, but to get rid of it probably involves demoting statesmen and aspiring statesmen from the privileged position that they still enjoy in public estimation.

Omar Pound, with Walton Litz of Princeton, has edited the letters that his parents exchanged through their protracted courtship, and their publishers have made of this a very pretty book. This is appropriate, for the story that the letters not so much tell as adumbrate comes through with a wistful fragrance that is very affecting if one reads slowly. Omar Pound must know the full story, but rightly I think, though surely austerely, he has left it for us to piece together. And some of the nuances are lost on us, or left hanging as possibilities. Was Frederic Manning, for instance, the Australian who would later write *Her Privates We*, in love with Dorothy, and wounded when she preferred Pound? We are not told. This is not to say that the letters can be left to speak for themselves. On the contrary, the two young persons communicate in a jokily affectionate private language, often about people in a not undistinguished but certainly restricted circle of acquaintants and Shakespear connections, who lived according to social codes now utterly unremembered. Accordingly, even those who have learned some of the relevant names from Pound's biographers would be quite at sea if the editors had not marshalled, deftly and compactly and sometimes wittily, some very out-of-the-way information. Even so, the world that we have to enter – the world of the solidly professional bourgeoisie and minor gentry of pre-1914 England – is so remote from us, so exotic, that we can't always keep our bearings. One is astonished, for instance, at how the daughter of Olivia Shakespear, no ordinary mother, was restricted, even in the arty society that she and Olivia frequented, by the still rigid conventions that wheeled her, uncomplaining but always chaperoned and often bored to tears, through a round of pointless visitings. Dorothy Shakespear, one sometimes feels, was not much less imprisoned than Elizabeth

Barrett had been, and in not much less need of a poet-errant to liberate her. Neither the captive nor her would-be liberator wasted much time complaining: these were the rules of the game, and the two of them could only be patient.

Patience is not what we associate with Pound, and from time to time he seems to have kicked over the traces (at least once to be ticked off for it by Dorothy): yet we see all over again that the young Pound was well content with Edwardian England, was hopeful of it and ready to abide by its rules in everything that mattered. Of course, where Dorothy was concerned, that was his only strategy if he wanted to secure her in the end. And in fact that is one of the affecting things: the story that we read is undoubtedly a love-story. One had doubted this. Our information about the later phases of the Pound marriage is certainly imperfect. (And why should it not be? So Omar Pound might legitimately ask.) But such information as we have undoubtedly reflects more credit on Dorothy than on Ezra. One was forced to envisage the possibility that Ezra courted Dorothy, not cynically indeed, but abstractedly, impulsively, without due consideration. This corrspondence, though Dorothy figures in it more prominently than Ezra, I believe puts paid to such suspicions. By 1913 Pound is confiding in his fiancée as, we must believe, he did to no one else. In their private code Yeats, who was to marry Dorothy's cousin and best friend Georgie Hyde-Lees, figures as 'the Eagle'. And in 1913 we have Pound writing of Yeats, who had just published 'The Grey Rock', that the latter is 'very fine, but his syntax is getting obscurer than Browning's', then confessing: 'I wonder which is worse, to die in the aromatic subtlety of a disappearing cadence (*à la* ME) or to stodge one's nobility into an incomprehensible narrative, *à la* The Eagle'. (The allusion to Pope's 'Essay on Man' is one of the few that the editors pass over.) This is very astute criticism of Yeats: but more to the point is that Pound here confesses self-doubts such as he would have concealed from anyone he did not trust absolutely. As we read the correspondence we seem to see Dorothy growing out of the gushing flibbertigibbet that she was in 1909 into a person altogether more substantial. But this is almost certainly an illusion: as she becomes surer of her hold on the affections of her poet, so she becomes surer of herself, can dispense with affectations, and dares to speak with a certain authority about compositions that her lover sends to her – animadversions that the poet in turn receives quite humbly.

Although students of Pound will fasten with delighted alacrity on such passages as the one just quoted about Yeats, and on one or two similar passages (for instance, one of January 1914, where he speaks with hostility about symbols and symbolism), still this book doesn't really belong with other Poundiana. Its place is at least equally with *The Diary of an Edwardian Lady*, or even, since through long months the lovers are at opposite ends of Italy, with E.M. Forster's *Room with a View*. Its fragrance is real, and penetrating: but it does not release itself at the first casual opening of the pages.

And yet the fact must be faced: however much patient sympathy we bring to our reading, we close the book feeling frustrated. For Dorothy is still not in focus, and one begins to think that she never will be, even if the correspondence of the Pounds' later years is some day published. Dorothy, one suspects, was always too much 'the perfect lady', and schooled too thoroughly in the pre-1914 code of proud reticence (a code which incidentally her husband also adhered to), for her to escape the role of 'poor Dorothy' that some recent writers have cast her in. Certainly she could not compete on anything like equal terms with Hilda Doolittle, the poet H.D. who, having mythologised her relations with Pound in a *roman à clef* many years ago, did it all over again just before her death in *End to Torment*, a supposed 'memoir' which people seem disposed to take literally, though in its scattiness it may well be as fictionalised as the novel had been. It does not help, I'm afraid, now when American cultural chauvinism wants to reclaim Pound, that Dorothy was an English-woman whereas Hilda, the childhood sweetheart from Bethlehem, Pa., was *echt*-American. H.D., nicknamed 'the Hama-dryad', is the subject of much high-spirited comedy in the letters that Ezra and Dorothy exchanged, and this ought to provoke second thoughts in those who want to take Hilda's account at face-value: H.D. may have honestly persuaded herself that she was the great (though vir-ginal) love of Pound's life, but it's unlikely that Pound thought so, nor need we. Dorothy however remains, not nebulous exactly, but enigmatic. The odd anecdote – for instance, James Laughlin's of 1965 about how she advanced his education in Rapallo by reading to him the stories of Henry James – brings her momentarily into focus, but then she disappears again behind a smokescreen of gra-cious good breeding. The loss is grievous. For when the Pisan deten-tion-camp in 1946 compelled the poet to breach, though guardedly, the barrier of his reticence, he certainly wrote about the women he had loved; and if Dorothy is of that company (as she must be, surely), we need to know just where she figures, and on what terms. It is the reader of moving and extraordinary but cryptic poetry who needs to know this, not the perhaps nosey biographer.

Polemic

'Res' and 'Verba'
in Rock-Drill and After

Pound's preference for res over verba is so notorious, and has been reiterated so insistently by the master himself (from the resounding Thomist declaration 'Nomina sunt consequentia rerum', in the Gaudier memoir of 1917, through to his preferring on just these grounds in *The Pisan Cantos* Ford's conversation to Yeats's) that, when it comes to a choice or a show-down between a mimetic view of how language relates to reality and a structuralist view, it seems clear that Pound must stand with the conservative and nowadays somewhat embattled champions of *mimesis*. And yet, as people are beginning to notice, Pound's own practice in *The Cantos* (throughout, but more markedly in the later sequences, *Rock-Drill* and *Thrones*) lends itself more readily to explanation in structuralist than in mimetic terms – to the extent that there is at least *prima facie* justification for Massimo Bacigalupo's charge that Pound was culpably naïve in not realizing how his own practice went beyond his own mimetic theory. To be blunt about it, Pound's transitions seem to be frequently from *verbum* to *verbum* (by way of often translingual puns, fanciful etymologies, echoings of sound) with no appeal over long stretches to the *res* supposedly under discussion; Pound moves often from signifier to signifier, leaving the signified to take care of itself. The most obvious example, first appearing very early in *The Cantos* and thereafter insistent enough to be a sort of structural principle, is Pound's taking over from Aeschylus the pun on the name of Helen (*helandros, helenaus, heleptolis*) and extending it to apply to other Helens or Eleanors, principally Eleanor of Aquitaine, but also Eleanor of Castile, Eleanor of Provence, and others. This is obviously, and has duly been called, 'word-play'; and I incline to think that the most pressing dilemma facing Pound's admirers today is whether such 'play' can be considered responsible (as most structuralist theories would agree that it can be), or else must be declared irresponsible (as most mimetic theories have regularly judged it).

If this seems to suggest that, whatever Pound's own asseverations to the contrary, structuralist assumptions give us more access to

The Cantos than a mimetic approach, there are nevertheless difficul-
ties in the way of the structuralist. First of these is the assumption,
made by most structuralists though not all, that there is a radical
breach between 'the modern' and all previous centuries of verse-
writing. Typical is John Steven Childs (*Paideuma*, 9 : 2, pp.289-307):
'it is not the interactions of characters which afford meaning in Mod-
ernist literature; it is the mental character of the writer/narrator him-
self which orders events and feelings' (p.290). Or again, 'Modern
poetry, eschewing directly social or didactic functions, is based on
the exploitation of non-referential discourse' (p.293). Both of these
dicta plainly go against the bent of Pound's temperament, so imbued
with *pietas* towards the recorded and inherited past, so ready to risk
the didactic, and so vowed – until the Pisan experience in some
degree compelled otherwise – to avoid the overtly and unashamedly
'subjective'. Moreover, in the one case we have so far considered,
Pound might vindicate his word-play by appeal to a precedent so
far from modern as Aeschylus. Or else, if this should seem only a
debating-point, consider another of Pound's ancient masters, Ovid,
who as Edgar M. Glenn points out (*Paideuma*, 10 : 3, pp.625-34)
indulged just the same word-play in the *Metamorphoses* with the
name of the nymph Coronis, a pun on the names for raven (*corvus*)
and for crow (*cornix*). Structuralist criticism, it seems, must be ready
to offer revisionist readings of Ovid, no less than of a 'modern' like
Pound. And indeed it's entirely possible that through the many cen-
turies when Ovid has been admired, a mimetic or pre-structuralist
understanding of language, and of how language traffics with real-
ity, has failed to do justice to the power and vitality of Ovid's mind;
though poets like Dryden have delighted in Ovid's *logopoeia* (his
'turns'), one is familiar with apologetic scholarly comments to the
effect that this regrettable proclivity in Ovid is a price we must pay
for his more solid virtues.

In any case *The Cantos* pose some real difficulties for that tradi-
tional criticism which I shall continue to call, somewhat loosely,
'mimetic'. A very bold and clear example is what Michael Alexander
makes of some lines from Canto 95:

> I suppose St. Hilary looked at an oak-leaf.
> (vine-leaf? San Denys
>   (spelled Dionisio)
> Dionisio et Eleutherio.
> Dionisio et Eleutherio
>   "the brace of 'em
> that Calvin never blacked out
>   en l'Isle.)   (95/647)

To Michael Alexander it is quite clear that this is 'not...serious'. And he remarks sharply:

> The suppositiousness here is pretty marked. Though it may well be true that free love is commoner in Paris than in Geneva, this is not a consequence of the etymology of the names of Saints Hilary and Denis; nor is it easy to see how Calvin could have been able to black it out.... In this mood, Pound might have been just as happy to play with the names of Calvin and Charles le Chauve. The passage is a harmless example of playful free association yet suggests a weakness for seeing historical significance in convenient verbal coincidence. There is no reason to suppose St. Hilary of Poitiers was particularly cheerful or particularly sensitive to nature, pleasant though it is to think that he was.[1]

The bluff common sense of this is refreshing. Yet the difficulties it runs us into are surely obvious; the transition or glissade from Hilary to *hilaritas*, or from Denys to Dionysus (for which Pound has a pre-modern precedent, Walter Pater's 'Apollo in Picardy') is not at first sight any different from the 'convenient verbal coincidence' that has many times in earlier cantos linked Helen, or various Helens, with various Eleanors. If a difference is to be found, it can be found only by appealing in all these cases from *verbum* to *res* – and pointing out for instance that as a matter of historical record Eleanor of Aquitaine did destroy men and ships and cities, just as did Aeschylus's legendary Helen; whereas, as Alexander points out, the historical record concerning St Hilaire is just not full enough for us to predicate about him so certainly. And it's notable that Edgar Glenn, when he discusses Ovid's glissades among Coronis and *corvus* and *cornix*, seems in the end to justify them by a similar appeal to *res*: '...although this is word play, the identifications are operative in the tale because all three are betrayers and all three are punished' (p.631). The *res* here, however, is much more dubious, for there is no question of appeal to any historical record other than the fabulous history that Ovid chooses to tell, and so the *res* turns out to be nothing other than the internal necessities and structural principles of Ovid's verbal artifact. The *res* in fact *is* structure; which is just what structuralism claims. In precisely the same way the necessities and principles of Pound's poem require that Denys and Hilary and Calvin be given the significances that in this passage he demands

1 Michael Alexander, *The Poetic Achievement of Ezra Pound* (London & Boston, 1979), p.215.

for them. It seems, therefore, that to be consistent Michael Alexander would have to deny the plea that Edgar Glenn enters for Ovid.

Alexander says that this passage, though it 'suggests a weakness', is all the same 'harmless'. It is hard to see how this can be true; for anything that diminishes a reader's confidence in his poet cannot help but be harmful to that poet and his poem. And one need not go all the way with Michael Shuldiner in his ambitiously schematic treatment of *hilaritas* in relation to *sinceritas, caritas* and *humanitas* (*Paideuma*, 4 : 1, pp.71-81) to feel uneasily sure that from the Pisan Cantos onwards hilarity, or *hilaritas*, is being asked to carry a lot of weight, in a way that demonstrably irresponsible play with St Hilary cannot help but weaken. The point at issue is surely much more crucial than Michael Alexander wants to admit, and it follows that if Pound's word-play in this passage *can* be vindicated, that vindication should be spelled out.

To that end we may consider a passage from Canto 92 that is superficially dissimilar:

> But in the great love, bewildered
> farfalla in tempesta
> under rain in the dark:
> many wings fragile
> Nymphalidae, basilarch, and lycaena,
> Ausonides, euchloe, and erynnis
>
> (92/619)

I dare say many readers have been content to suppose (hazardously however, for we should know by now that Pound is a tricky poet who for instance neologizes) that the six splendidly resonant nouns in the last two lines name species or families of butterflies; but there may have been others like me who only lately, after knowing the lines for many years, chose to check that hunch against Alexander B. Klots' *Field Guide to the Butterflies of North America, East of the Great Plains* (1951). Klots' Index does indeed list five of these six names, along with others (e.g. 'Dryas' and 'Dione') which have cropped up in *The Cantos* in contexts where butterflies seemed not to be in question. Having thus linked these *verba* with the *res*, butterfly, one has perhaps achieved something; but certainly one has not achieved meaning, significance, where before there was none. On the contrary, a range of significance has been rather grievously contracted from the time when, in ignorance of Alexander Klots, one mused happily over etymologies, linking 'euchloe' with the Greek *euchloos*, with its sense of 'making fresh and green'; or recognizing in 'erynnis one form of the Latin word for the Furies, the Greek Eumenides; discovering too from the Latin dictionary that the one name missing from Klots, 'Ausonides', is poetical for *Ausonii*, Italians. As for 'basilarch', that thunderous compound of the Greek roots for 'king' (basileus) and for 'ruler' (arkhon), one feels positively let down by the discovery in Klots that it names the Viceroy butterfly, so named because for protective purposes it seems to mimic in colours and markings the inedible Monarch butterfly. Further, I can recall from rather long ago the almost mutinous disappointment with which I discovered that 'farfalla' is common Italian for 'butterfly', thus not ruling out, but certainly muting, a translingual pun that I thought I detected, between 'farfalla' ('in tempesta') and an English expression: 'far fallen'. Do I stand convicted of having been a frivolous, an irresponsible reader? Or was it my poet who was frivolous when he exploited an apparently unearned resonance from the word 'basilarch', applied to a *res* that seemed not to merit such a trumpet-note? Or is it not the case, rather, that neither Pound nor I was being frivolous when we refused to let the multivalent potencies of the *verba* be channelled into the narrow duct of a single and highly specialized 'meaning'? Supposing that, I am forced to suppose that structuralist criticism has indeed much to offer readers of *The Cantos*, being in this case the only way to let both Pound and me off the hook. 'I suppose', says Pound in the passage from Canto 95, 'I suppose St Hilary looked at an oak-leaf'. And Michael Alexander rejoins smartly: 'The suppositiousness... is pretty marked'. But surely 'I suppose' functions quite precisely in poetic discourse just as does in discourse of another kind, 'I propose' or 'I postulate'; stated or unstated (and here it is stated), it reiterates what Philip Sidney declared when he said that as for the poet 'he nothing affirmes, and therefore never lyeth'. This declares that the business of the poet is serious play – play between signifiers, letting the signified for the nonce go hang.

Accordingly, as the first earnest attempt to read *The Cantos* from a structuralist standpoint, John Steven Childs's 'Larvatus Prodeo: Semiotic Aspects of the Ideogram in Pound's *Cantos*' has considerable importance, though it is limited, as the title makes clear, from being focused on the special case of how the Chinese ideograms function. The structuralist authority that Childs most often cites is, not surprisingly, Roland Barthes. And some of the passages cited from Barthes are as usual vitiated by declaring or assuming an absolute discontinuity between the poetry that can be called 'modern' and that to be called 'classique'. One of them, however, has peculiar pertinence in that it links up with what Barthes could not have known about and Childs does not notice: the work that has been done on how *forma*, a concept that originated apparently with Allen Upward, figures alike in Pound's theory and his practice:

> Dans la Poétique moderne... les mots produisent une sorte de
> continu formel dont émane peu à peu une densité intellectuelle
> ou sentimentale impossible sans eux; la parole est alors le temps
> épais d'une gestation plus spirituelle, pendant laquelle la 'pen-
> sée' est preparée, installée, peu et peu par le hasard des mots
> (*Pai*, 92, 305).

What Barthes with characteristic incautiousness predicates of all
modern poetry is certainly true of one body of that poetry, the
Rock-Drill Cantos; in those cantos at any rate (in others less insis-
tently) the *res* to which Pound's *verba* point is ultimately not this or
that *thing*, still less this or that proposition. What is pointed to, and
earnestly invoked, is a disposition of mind and feeling, a disposition
which *precedes* the framing of propositions or the making of distinc-
tions, which precedes, and in the event of course may make unneces-
sary, the distinguishing between mediaeval Church history (St
Denys, St Hilaire) on the one hand, and on the other pagan and
perennial morality (*hilaritas*, the Dionysian); which refuses the
demand to know whether 'Druas' and 'Dione' and 'Erynnis' belong
in entomology or in classical mythology. (The names belong in both
realms; and it is just their dual belonging which, it may be argued,
makes them sanative and harmonizing.) This realm of thought and
feeling *before* the crystallizing out and the making of distinction is
precisely what Upward and Pound alike seem to have understood
by the realm of 'the *forma*'; and so that apparently so reasonable plea,
'But come, distinguish', is just what they are vowed not to satisfy.

Nevertheless, Michael Alexander must have some right on his
side. There must be some point at which we feel (and can vindicate
the feeling) that Pound's word-play ceases to be serious and becomes
frivolous. For me, and I think for some others, the point comes by
and large between the conclusion of *Rock-Drill* and the beginning
of *Thrones*. From this point of view nothing is so disappointing in
John Steven Childs's discussion as his assumption that *Rock-Drill*
and *Thrones* are much of a muchness. I will return to the beginning
of this article, and at the same time cite a case that I have used
elsewhere, by recalling that in the *Rock-Drill* Canto 94, and thereafter
in the *Thrones* cantos, we are required to extend the 'Helen' identifi-
cation to other Eleanors than Eleanor of Aquitaine; and that in the
Thrones Canto 107 one of these other Eleanors appears, Eleanor of
Provence, consort of Henry III of England:

> & this Helianor was of the daughters, heirs
> of Raymond Berengar
> and sister of Arch.   Cantaur
> (107/759)

We must note that the case of this Eleanor is not on a par with that of St Hilaire of Poitiers: the historical records tell us enough of this Eleanor, tell us in particular that she fiddled her kinsman into the see of Canterbury ('Arch. Cantaur'). What baffles and in the end exasperates us is not that we do not have this *res* to which to attach the *verba* about her, but that, the *res* thus established, we do not know what to do with it. Where does Eleanor's manoeuvring her relative into Canterbury fit into the still developing structure of Pound's poem? Are we to applaud her for the manoeuvre, or deplore it? In neither of these ways, nor in any other, does this *res* rhyme with, or hook on to, anything else in the poem. In other words, the identifying of this Eleanor with the older and greater Eleanor, and through her with Helen of Troy, offends us because it has no *structural* significance, not because it has no meaning in terms of the historical record. This suggests – I may dare to say, it *shows* – that, whereas few structuralists care to stoop to value-judgements, nevertheless their own procedures permit of such judgements being made. They would disarm the prejudices of some of us if they showed more interest in pursuing that possibility. There is *logopoeia* that is legitimate (St Denys identified with Dionysus), and other *logopoeia* that is not (Eleanor of Provence identified with Helen of Troy); and the test of legitimacy is not any appeal to authorities outside the poem, but on the contrary appeal to the poem's own structural requirements.

I shall assume (for I have argued the case elsewhere)[1] that what goes on in these lines about Eleanor of Provence is fairly typical of the *Thrones* sequence as a whole; that among the rather many things wrong with these cantos is word-play of this tired and pointless sort, *logopoeia* pursued at the expense of *phanopoeia* and *melopoeia*, and also of common sense. This is still a minority opinion, but one that I think is gaining ground – a great deal of *Thrones* is simply a bore. However, some *Thrones* cantos are better than others; and in the better ones one encounters *logopoeia* that is, to put it grudgingly, at least a borderline case. A rather crucial instance is Canto 106:

> Help me to neede
> By Circeo, the stone eyes looking seaward
> Nor could you enter her eyes by probing.
> The temple shook with Apollo
> As with leopards by mount's edge,
> light blazed behind her;
> trees open, their minds stand before them

1 See pp. 198-200 above.

As in Carrara is whiteness:
        Xoroi. At Sulmona are lion heads.
        Gold light, in veined phylotaxis.
By hundred blue-gray over their rock-pool,
    Or the king-wings in migration
        And in thy mind beauty, O Artemis
Over asphodel, over broom-plant,
     faun's ear a-level that blossom.
        Yao and Shun ruled by jade.
Whuder ich maei lidhan
           helpe me to neede
the flowers are blessed against thunder bolt
            help me to neede.
That great acorn of light bulging outward,
     Aquileia, caffaris, caltha palistris,
        ulex, that is gorse, herys arachnites;
Scrub oak climbs against cloud-wall –
     three years peace, they had to get rid of him,
     – violet, sea green, and no name.
Circe's were not, having fire behind them.
     Buck stands under ash grove,
        jasmine twines over capitols
        Selena Arsinoe
So late did queens rise into heaven.
     At Zephyrium, July that was, at Zephyrium
     The high admiral built there;
         Aedificavit
TO APHRODITE EUPLOIA
     "an Aeolian gave it, ex voto
     Arsinoe Kupris.
        At Miwo the moon's axe is renewed
        HREZEIN
Selena, foam on the wave-swirl
     Out of gold light flooding the peristyle
     Trees open in Paros,
        White feet as Carrara's whiteness
         (106/754–755)

This passage is a sort of tie-beam. Considered as a structural member, it carries much weight, resolves many stresses. On the one hand, it reaches far back into preceding cantos, picking up for instance ('violet, sea green, and no name') the three pairs of differently coloured eyes which figured so hauntingly and repeatedly in *The Pisan Cantos*, picking up also from *Rock-Drill* Canto 91 ('Help me to neede... Whuder ich maei lidhan') Brutus's prayer to Diana in Layamon's *Brut*, beseeching her to lead him to a new realm, the third Troy that Layamon identified with Albion. On the other hand, the passage also reaches forward, for instance to 'the great acorn of light' in Canto 116. Among the matters thus picked up from quite far back in the poem, and then conveyed forward, is the matter of butterflies. For 'the king-wings in migration' clearly 'rhymes' (structurally) with the 'farfalla' passage that we have looked at in Canto 92, and carries that forward to what may well be the last lines of the entire poem, among the 'Notes for Canto CXVII et seq.':

> Two mice and a moth my guides –
> To have heard the farfalla gasping
>   as toward a bridge over worlds.
> That the kings meet in their island,
>   where no food is after flight from the pole.
> Milkweed the sustenance
>   as to enter arcanum.
>
> To be men not destroyers.
>
> <div align="right">(<i>D&F</i>, 802)</div>

For the Monarch butterfly (*Danaus plexippus*), which does indeed live on the poisonous milkweed, in mid-September migrates southward, if not from the pole at least from arctic Canada, along skyways that have been mapped; and there are known locations where large flocks of them can be found resting, at staging posts on the migration. (The northward migration in spring is less marked, because apparently less marshalled.)

Thus, what in this way binds Canto 92 through Canto 106 with Canto 117 is a 'rhyme' of *res*, not of *verba*. The only word-play involved is the easy substitution of 'king' for 'monarch'. And so this transition can be (and should be, I think, for surely it is masterly) applauded as warmly by non-structuralists as by structuralists.[1] The 'borderline' cases come later in the passage when, if 'king-wings in migration' have alerted us to the presence of butterflies, we ponder the lines:

> Selena Arsinoe
> So late did queens rise into heaven.
>   At Zephyrium, July that was, at Zephyrium
>   The high admiral built there;
>
> (106/755)

---

1 To take the full force of it one needs to consult the elegant and learned examination by Sieburth in *Paideuma*, 4 : 2 & 3, 329-32.

For there is a butterfly called *Boloria selene* (the silver-bordered fritillary), and every one knows that there are butterflies called Admirals. One species of Admiral (the Viceroy) we have met already under the name *basilarch*; the other two species are named for or after a Greek goddess, whose name has resounded many times in the cantos and will resound even more loudly in the cantos that remain – they are *Limenitis arthemis* and *Limenitis arthemis astyanax*. So whoever the high admiral is in human terms (one thinks perhaps wrongly of Drake, for 'Zephyrium' means 'western promontory' and one promontory that might qualify is Circeo, with which Francis Drake was memorably connected in Canto 91), one cannot, and perhaps one should not, exclude the possibility that the admiral is as much insectile as human. If this is fanciful, a good deal less so is the nimbus or aura that hangs around 'So late did queens rise into heaven'. What this recalls first is a line from Canto 97, 'Bernice, late for a constellation, mythopoeia persisting'; and another from Canto 102, 'Berenice, a late constellation'. A look into Lemprière will identify the Queen Berenice in question, and sketch the myth which transforms her, or rather the hair of her head, into a constellation. But what are we then to make of the perhaps unwelcome information from the invaluable Alexander Klots, that there is a Queen butterfly (*Danaus gilippus*), which in many ways corresponds in the Southern states to the Monarch in more northerly latitudes; and that one sub-species of the Queen is called *Danaus gilippus berenice*? Are the queens, like the admirals, insectile as much as they are human, or mythologically divine?

What strengthens this alarmed or alarming supposition is that a few lines earlier has occurred ('caltha palistris... herys arachnites') what we may take to be an allusion to Linnaean botany – an important foreshadowing, if so, of the otherwise unheralded veneration to be given to Linnaeus in the *Drafts and Fragments*. For of course the classification of butterflies is itself Linnaean, and some of the taxonomic namings (notably that of the Monarch) are credited to Linnaeus himself. When in the last cantos Linnaeus is named for veneration along with Mozart and Ovid, is he in fact honoured as 'natural scientist'? Is he not rather, or equally, honoured as a genius of language, a masterly inventor of, and source for, interlingual punning (*logopoeia*) between Greek and Latin on the one hand, English and presumably Swedish on the other? According to Harry Meacham, in *The Caged Panther*, Pound's interest in Linnaeus dated from the St Elizabeths' years, and may have been prompted by the devotion to Linnaeus of the then Secretary-General of the United Nations, Dag Hammarskjold. It would be interesting to know precisely the grounds on which Hammarskjold venerated his great compatriot.

One of the rather few commentators who can help us in difficult speculations like these is Guy Davenport. His essay, 'Persephone's Ezra' is illuminating for instance on the relation between tree and marble pillar which accounts, in the passage we have been considering, for

> trees open, their minds stand before them
As in Carrara is whiteness:...
>
> (106/754)

and

> Trees open in Paros,
> White feet as Carrara's whiteness...
>
> (106/755)

And plainly, what we have more particularly been looking at is glossed when Davenport says in the same essay: 'Pound cancelled in his own mind the dissociations that had been isolating fact from fact for four centuries. To have closed the gap between mythology and botany' (or, we may add, lepidoptery) 'is but one movement of the process;...' However, when we return these sentences to their context we cannot help but wonder if the commonsense objections of a Michael Alexander are being given what is after all their due. For Davenport is quite uncompromising:

> To say that *The Cantos* is 'a voyage in time' is to be blind to the poem altogether. We miss immediately the achievement upon which the success of the poem depends, its rendering time transparent and negligible, its dismissing the supposed corridors and perspectives *down* which the historian invites us to look. Pound cancelled in his own mind the dissociations that had been isolating fact from fact for four centuries. To have closed the gap between mythology and botany is but one movement of the process; one way to read the cantos is to go through noting the restorations of relationships now thought to be discrete – the ideogrammatic method was invented for just this purpose. In Pound's spatial sense of time the past is here, now; its invisibility is our blindness, not its absence. The nineteenth century had put everything against the scale of time and discovered that all behaviour within time's monolinear progress was evolutionary. The past was a graveyard, a museum. It was Pound's determination to obliterate such a configuration of time and history, to treat what had become a world of ghosts as a world eternally present   (p.157).

This is wonderfully eloquent, and phrase after phrase in these sentences speaks justly to what we experience, and respond to, when we are reading *The Cantos* at their best. Yet is it not clear that in this passage Davenport, whether or not he intends it, is handing over the entire poem to the synchronic or synchronizing vision of the structuralist? He speaks of Pound as cancelling 'the dissociations that have been isolating fact from fact'; but of course, as any structuralist will point out with glee, it's not clear that *facts* figure in any poetic discourse whatever. We can't any longer suppose, naïvely, that a fact gets into a poem as soon as it is named there. For a fact, and the name of that fact, are different; and it is only the name, not the thing named, that is at home in the verbal universe that is a poem. As John Steven Childs remarks with obvious satisfaction, 'modern poetry' (in which clearly he includes *The Cantos*) 'is based on the exploitation of non-referential discourse'. If we do not share his satisfaction, if we want the discourse of *The Cantos* to be in some ways or in some degree referential, the *res* that we look for must be something different from what Guy Davenport means by 'facts'. It must be, I have suggested, what Upward meant by the *forma*; and I glossed this provisionally as a state of mind and feeling anterior to the making of distinctions. Thus where Davenport speaks of the cancelling of dissociations (which a Michael Alexander would surely, and with much reason, rephrase as the blurring of distinctions), we might do better to speak of the postponement, or the 'willing suspension', of distinctions. And I think this is more than nit-picking. For it permits of, and indeed requires, a *diachronic* vision, such as we might expect of a poet who told Grazia Livi in 1962: 'The modern world doesn't exist because nothing exists which does not understand its past or its future'. (Guy Davenport, who quotes this with approval, must be confident that it doesn't make against his reading of *The Cantos*, though to my mind it certainly does.)

These difficult matters are best dealt with in relation to some particular crux in our reading of the poem. Accordingly I will cite one more such crux, from Canto 110, the first of the *Drafts & Fragments*:

> The purifications
>> are snow, rain, artemisia,
>> also dew, oak and the juniper
>
> And in thy mind beauty, O Artemis,
>> as of mountain lakes in the dawn, . . .
>>
>>> (110/778)

The question is, very simply: Does it matter, for our reading of the poem aright, that we identify 'artemisia' as wormwood? If it does not matter, then the link from 'artemisia' to 'Artemis' is a mere adventitious jingle of sound, and so obvious that we might justly call it 'mechanical'. Even if we take note of John of Trevisa in 1398 ('Artemisia is callyd moder of herbes and was somtyme hallowed... to the goddess that hyght Arthemis'), we are still wholly in the realm of *verba* and moving from signifier to signifier by way of disputable etymology. If on the other hand we identify wormwood, and learn from *OED* that as early as 1535 wormwood was 'an emblem or type of what is bitter and grievous to the soul', we have moved from *verbum* to *res*; and the link to Artemis accordingly takes on substance and specificity. For we are compelled to infer that the Artemis who is so markedly the presiding deity of these cantos is every inch the Artemis of Canto 30, she by whom we 'maintain antisepsis', her special function the dispensing of what is, medicinally, 'bitter and grievous to the soul'. This means that the *forma* invoked and created in *Drafts & Fragments* is dark and tragically bitter in a way that, among the commentators, only Eva Hesse seems to have recognized. She must be right, I think, for if we move once more from *verbum* to *res*, we find the perception reinforced in those last lines where the Monarch butterflies 'meet in their island':

> Milkweed the sustenance
> as to enter arcanum
> (*D&F*, 802)

It is only by ingesting that which is to all others bitter and poisonous that the kings can enter, or think to enter, arcanum.

I conclude therefore that, much as structuralist criticism can illuminate for us what is going on in many pages of *The Cantos*, and however much non-structuralist criticism must refine its assumptions so as to allow for this, yet in the end Pound's claim to attend to *res* not *verba* can be, and must be, vindicated; and that a thoroughgoing or dogmatic structuralism milks this text, as presumably any other, of human pathos and human significance.

Adrian Stokes Revisited

Fifty years ago, when Pound in *The Criterion* applauded Adrian Stokes's *The Quattro Cento*, he exclaimed:

> It is almost incomprehensible that any man can have as great a concern for the shapes and meaning of stone beauty as Stokes has, without its forcing him to take the tools in his hands. In fact one can only suppose that he in some way regards himself as the fore-runner of some sort of sculptural amelioration, or at any rate is trying to clear up incomprehensions and to distinguish between pure and mixed sculptural values.

The comment is endearingly characteristic of Pound, who could never make a distinction, nor endorse one made by some one else, without at once *doing something about it*, taking the tool in his hands. But the reflection is a natural one, all the same: if Stokes wasn't himself going to sculpt (as he wasn't), and if he didn't want principally to clean up messy notions about sculpture and also architecture (as it soon appeared that he didn't), then what *was* his concern in *The Quattro Cento* (1932), *Stones of Rimini* (1934), and *Colour and Form* (1937)?

It was only incidentally the concern of a judicious historian, distinguishing in a given period the positive or healthful tendency from others that were dubious. And it was not the concern of the critic, if by 'critic' we understand (with a humility nowadays hardly met with) some one who discriminates among pleasures so as to sharpen them for himself and others. Although these splendid books did have that effect – and some of us are profoundly grateful for being thus educated by them – that seems not to have been Stokes' conscious motive for writing them. Before long we were to see that he approached his subject not as an artist, not as historian, not as critic, but as *clinician* – and in a strikingly narrow sense.

In the first years after Stokes learned from Melanie Klein to relate his art studies to infantile behaviour, construing his initial distinction between carving and moulding into allegedly analogous binary oppositions (rough and smooth, aggressive and reparative, inside and outside), his monographs continued for a while to interest those of us whose interest wasn't therapeutic. But it didn't last; and soon, for my part, I was throwing his books aside with a disappointed yawn. One reason for this was Stokes's prose-style, which had always been what Pound called it: 'floribund'. Once the prose could not be checked against particular art-works experienced, its 'waftiness' became tedious. Moreover, whereas one had begun by believing that Melanie Klein's kind of Freudianism did not have to be reductive, one came to see that it was as reductive as any other kind, when applied to art-works. Even at Stokes's hands artefacts were being explained by being explained away. Predictably, his discourse became interesting to aestheticians and philosophers in proportion as it became boring to artists and those artists' admirers. The finest connoisseur of his generation had turned into a theorist with a following.

If Melanie Klein's revisionist Freudianism is reductive, much more so is the sort currently on offer, the revised Freudianism of Jacques Lacan, as we encounter it in Alan Durant's *Ezra Pound, Identity in Crisis* (1981) and Paul Smith's *Pound Revised* (1983). Indeed, reduction could hardly go further than in an essay by Marcelin Pleynet from *Tel Quel*, a piece that both Durant and Smith cite admiringly, in which all that we need to know of the author of *The Cantos*, and all we need so as to estimate justly that and all his other works, is deduced from animated pondering of, and associating around, the three syllables of his name: 'EZ-RA-POUND'. This, we must all agree, is a wondrously labour-saving device; a trenchant simplification such as could have occurred only to a compatriot of René Descartes. And we may be grateful to Smith and Durant for tracking the piercing perception through one or two pages of Pound's verse and prose, so as to make it accessible to us slow and earth-bound Anglo-Saxons.

Paul Smith (p.43) explicitly adduces the Stokes/Pound relationship to support his and Durant's and Pleynet's contention that Pound's vision can be discounted because it is manifestly 'phallocentric'. (Not to worry too much, however; for so, it appears, is Homer's – Smith, p.53.) Giving me the credit some of which should go to Sister Bernetta Quinn, Paul Smith writes:

> Davie has noted the variable recurrence in the poem of images of stone, marble, glass and crystal, water and so on. These notions, derived from Adrian Stokes's emphasis on the kinship of marble and water, are corroborated by a certain connection of Jung's: there, the body 'is carbon... also it is well known that the diamond is a carbon crystal. Carbon is black – coal, graphite – but the diamond is purest water.'

The text from Carl-Gustav Jung (which is quoted only from an essay by 'E. Mottram') is not presented to us as part of any commentary on Canto 17 or on any other of the Cantos, nor on renaissance stonework. It comes to us therefore simply as one Swiss psychotherapist's meditation on certain elementary facts of physical chemistry. Accordingly it can constitute 'corroboration' only to those for whom a psychological theorist like Jung enjoys a specially privileged status, so as to be a last court of appeal in all forms of discourse whatever. If we refuse to give psychological theory this pre-eminence, we are back where we started from, not a whit the wiser. But behold what this specious 'corroboration' opens before us! –

> 'This formula's metonymic connections may be used' [Note that 'may be', and ask: 'By what code of scholarly decorum or relevance *may* it be?'] . . . 'This formula's metonymic connections may be used to underscore Pound's thematics: not only does it position the blackness of historical ignorance from which the crystal is supposed to arrive in Pound's poem, but in its connection about (*sic*) the body it produces the suggestive possibility of the body itself becoming the crystal, and so it presages the metamorphosis of the ball of crystal into 'That great acorn of light bulging outward' in almost comic suggestion of the glans of the penis . . .'

Not almost but entirely comic, we may think, is this train of speciously logical links by which the overt concern of Stokes's and Pound's ruminations – that is to say, the worked stone of Venice and the Rimini *tempio* – is unmasked as being really (and much virtue in that 'really') what always tediously awaits us at the end of every such chain in Freudian discourse: the penis. The penis; or else the anus. For Smith's case against Pound is that by him, as not by Joyce in *Finnegans Wake*, the penis is consistently (and how illiberally!) preferred before the anus. That is what is meant by calling Pound distressingly 'phallocentric'. And Smith is not so much shocked as resignedly unsurprised when I, pointing out the contribution to Canto 47 of Stokes's analogies between the male act in copulation, the carver's carving of the block, and the ploughman's grooving of the earth, fail to shake my head at the phallocentrism of, or behind, these analogies. Rather plainly I and also Stokes are phallocentric, even as Pound is. Since we already know that Homer stands convicted of the disability, I at any rate (since Stokes and Pound are dead) am not disturbed by this revelation about myself as Paul Smith thinks I ought to be. And meanwhile the multifarious juxtaposed or contending images and actions in *The Cantos* are reduced to one: penis (or if you like phallus) versus anus. It is such a reduction as

Adrian Stokes, even at his most benightedly Kleinian in later life, did not aspire to; nor would he (I like to think) have countenanced it.

Alan Durant's *Ezra Pound. Identity in Crisis* is an altogether weightier affair. Indeed Paul Smith's subsequent slim volume is much of the time only a grotesque parody-version of Durant's much more rigorous and powerful application of Lacanian theory to the body of Pound's work. It is certainly because of Durant's greater good sense that he nowhere engages with Stokes directly, as Smith tries to do. In his pages, as in Smith's, Lacan's Freudianism is reductive of Stokes's and Pound's insights. But with Durant this can be shown only by a teasing out of buried implications – a process which takes longer, but is that much more educational, since it involves us in pondering, as both Stokes and Pound did, the specific nature of sculpture among the other fine arts. On the other hand it's no good pretending that this process is anything but tedious: Lacan's terminology is deliberately – some would say, insolently – obfuscating in French; the anglicizing of it, whether by translators or by epigones like Smith and Durant, produces a discourse so thoroughly larded with gallicisms that only by a sort of legalistic fiction can we regard it as English at all. What it is, is *franglais*: an inherently free-floating lingo (not strictly a jargon, nor yet a dialect) in which virtually all fashionable criticism is now conducted, including criticism that is not at all under the aegis of M. Lacan. Accordingly most of the time, when we want to profit by literary criticism now in vogue, we are committed to translating *franglais* into English. And it may as well be said that in general the game isn't worth the candle; the profit to be gained cannot justify the effort.

In the present case the exercise will be worthwhile only if it provokes us to recall, to re-experience, just what it is like to see the stonework of Agostino di Duccio and Matteo de Pasti at Rimini, of the Lombardo brothers at Santa Maria dei Miracoli in Venice, or more generally of hand-worked and weather-worn stone anywhere at all. And already I have deliberately begged the question, or set a trap. For I have spoken of *seeing* these sculptures. But of course all theories of sculptural effect confirm what we have experienced for ourselves if we have ever seriously tried to take the impact of sculpture: that seeing it is only the beginning of the experience; that the encounter with it is kinetic or tactile at least as much as it is visual. This is why those who know the sculptures of the *tempio* only through photographs, however good, cannot be said to know those sculptures at all. Early in *The Cantos* Pound writes of this, of the sculptor's vision as comprehending the inside and the outside, the back and the front and the sideways all at once, even before the first stroke of the chisel upon the block. We all know this when we delay judging a free-standing sculpture until we have at least walked round it. Low-relief sculpture like that in the *tempio* cannot be walked around; but we are failing to experience this sculpture also, if we station ourselves at a fixed point and merely look at it as if it were a picture in stone. (That way for instance we precisely miss the miracle of several receding planes established in the depth of only a few millimetres skinned off the original stone-surface.) What, then, are we to make of Alan Durant's glossing a sentence from *The Chinese Written Character as a Medium for Poetry* by saying (p.82): 'Gaudier-Brzeska could, according to Pound, read Chinese quite well by bringing to bear his sculptor's visual sensibility'? Might we not say that merely by that unthinking conjunction – 'sculptor's/ visual' – this commentator has shown himself incapable of understanding just what it was about sculpture that most interested both Stokes and Pound?

This may be thought nit-picking, and unfair. And so it would be, if it were an isolated instance. On the other hand, this is a matter quite central to the Lacanian thesis, as both Smith and more particularly Durant expound it. What are involved are two Lacanian terms which Durant translates as 'specularity' and 'scopic field'. And here I start trying to translate Lacanian terms into plain English, knowing full well what elegant and necessary ambiguities they have, and are meant to have, in French. 'Specularity', then, appears to mean the giving to the eye undue pre-eminence over all the other organs of perception; and 'scopic field' appears to mean that vista which we can from a fixed point command. The notion of 'command' is vital to the Lacanian analysis, because the imperiousness implicit in the word enables the eye to stand in for the phallus; and thus from a Lacanian standpoint an art which is insistently visual is by just that token 'phallocentric', or likely to turn out so. (Those who know even a little of Freudian procedures, and the crucial role played in such procedures by the neat manoeuvre 'Heads I win, tails you lose', will not need to be told that the most phallocentric male writers are those whose possession of the phallus is least secure.) Thus, in so far as Pound is an artist determined to *see* and to make us see, this characteristic strengthens the case that he is a phallocentric artist, a man who, because his possession of the phallus is uncertain must repress his anxieties on that score by vehemently and insistently claiming otherwise. But what happens to this argument if Pound is *not* a visually oriented artist? Durant thinks he is, and arrays quotations, variously persuasive and less persuasive, to prove as much. But as we have seen, Pound's respect for the sculptor's vision, and his invocations of it, are taken as proof of this alleged predisposition, whereas in truth they prove rather the opposite. And there is other evidence: for instance an article by Pound in *The Criterion* for January 1923, in which he assails Ford the self-declared impressionist 'because he bases his criticism on the eye, and almost solely on the eye. Nearly everything he says applies to things *seen*. It is the exact rendering of the visible image, the cabbage field *seen*, France *seen* from the cliffs'.[1] And for that matter Durant himself quotes from Canto 94, inattentively (p.172):

> Was it Frate Egidio – per la mente'
>   looking down and reproving
> 'who shd/mistake the eye for the mind'...

– a warning against trusting the eye too implicitly, just the same warning in fact that Pound made in prose (citing the same Egidio, commentator on Cavalcanti), when he introduced reproductions of paintings by La Martinelli. Thus Pound has been at considerable pains *not* too give the eye pre-eminence over other organs of perception. But of course the Freudian fail-safe device – 'Heads I win, tails you lose' – is equal to this, as to all other emergencies: 'Why is he at such pains not to exalt the eye, if he were not tempted to do so?' There is no arguing with a logic thus self-sealed at both ends.

However, for those who have open minds, the entire Lacanian enterprise is endangered by such considerations as these. For as Durant usefully and carefully makes plain, Lacan's revision of Freudian doctrine (a radical revision, for the Viennese pioneer is declared to have been wrong about the unconscious from the start) rests on two importations from linguistics: first, Saussure's distinction between the signifier and the signified; and second, Jakobson's differentiation of metonymy from metaphor. And we cannot help but wonder, when such favoured status is claimed for verbal language and the linguistic arts, what status is left for what we are used to call the vocabularies of the other, the non-linguistic arts. Is this a slack usage that we must learn to abjure? Is there no acceptable sense in which we may speak of architecture or sculpture as possessing each its own artistic 'vocabulary'? Certainly on the face of it there seems no place for either metonymy or metaphor, whether in architecture or sculpture. And yet metonymy and metaphor are declared to represent the two determining impulses behind psychic life (roughly, metaphor encoding repression, metonymy encoding desire). If the non-verbal arts cannot incorporate either of these alternative and contending mechanisms, or even one of them, must we conclude that these arts are necessarily much more imperfect vehicles for the human condition than the arts of literature: Lacan, perhaps foreseeing this objection, has invaded at least one of the other arts, painting; and his admirers are ready to think that his privileged status in the theory of psycho-analysis enables him to beat the art-critics at their own game, as well as the literary critics. It is indeed Lacan's examination of a painting, Holbein's *The Ambassadors*, that introduces into Lacanian discourse both 'specularity' and 'the scopic field'. But as we have seen, though these concepts can with some difficulty be brought over from painting to apply to literature, it is not clear how they can be made applicable to either sculpture or architecture.

We may pass over Durant's Lacanian solemnity about inadvertent and in fact illusory puns, and also his dexterous use of the Freudian fail-safe device to as to explain how it is that this allegedly so 'specular' poem, *The Cantos*, sets up as specially authoritative witnesses the two *blind* persons, Tiresias and Homer. We may gratefully return from these sterilities to the young Stokes, whose inspired meditations about architecture and sculpture so excited Pound, after he and Stokes in the 1920s had met on the tennis-courts in Rapallo. I will dare to complain that, whereas my argument for a Stokesian presence in Cantos 17 and 47 has been generally accepted, no one to my knowledge has looked for that presence in other cantos where it seems to me much in evidence. This is particularly the case in *The Pisan Cantos* where, as I read the sequence, Pound *in extremis* was stayed and comforted time and again by just what the young Stokes had compellingly purveyed: a well-curb, a coign of worked marble, some emblem (figurative or not) out of renaissance Rimini or Venice or Urbino; in any case magnificently enhanced by what Stokes first perceived and named as stone-bloom or stone-blossom, lichens and weathering and the soft attrition of human hands. In Stokes's understanding, by this conjoined operation of human and non-human agencies the stone artifact became splendidly expressive without being self-expressive of any one person – all of it *outward*, all (Stokes's own word) 'manifest'. It is especially pitiful that when Stokes himself was *in extremis* – we now have eighteen poems of his written when he knew himself under death-sentence from cancer[1] – such emblems, which had comforted Pound, comforted Stokes not at all, nor did he turn to them so that they should. His Freudian indoctrination had been too thorough, over too many years, for him any longer to have access to the consolations that his own youth had uncovered for others.

What we see in Stokes's career as a whole is a determining crisis after which he turned back to specifically *human* nature away from that larger than human nature which Pound had reminded him of when, reviewing *Stones of Rimini*, Pound had remarked: 'Stokes's

1 Adrian Stokes, *With All the Views*, ed. Peter Robinson, (1981).

"water" concept is, whether he remember it or no, in harmony with the source of all the gods, Neptune, in Gemisto's theology'. For this crucial turn in Stokes there were compelling human reasons – Stokes had a schizophrenic daughter. All the same, we do not have to accept nor even understand the role of Gemistus Pletho in Pound's eclectic metaphysics, to take the point that Pound was offering Stokes a metaphysical significance that Stokes would not accept. What, in Stokes's conditioning or his temperament, turned him back from the elemental energies that his own attention had uncovered – predominantly water, and stone, and the one folded within the other – to drearily calculable variations on the infant's experience of breast-feeding? Why the turn back in, never thereafter outward? The discoveries that Stokes had made in the Rimini *tempio* – discoveries not in the first place scholarly, but unearthed simply by a finely tuned sensibility – could be glossed either psychologically, or metaphysically. Why did Stokes decide that the psychological gloss automatically had priority?

These questions may be regarded as rhetorical. For every one of us of the post-Poundian generations has been conditioned so as to think that, whenever there is a choice between metaphysical and psychological explanation, still intellectual integrity demands that the latter always be preferred. Thus Alan Durant (pp.86-88), after considering with sufficient care the verbal arrangement of twenty-five or so lines from Canto 17 (beginning, 'Flat water before me...'), declares with no real danger of being challenged: 'What this structure of difference sets up is not the intuition of the unseen, but the conditions of the unconscious, and of desire'. If we respond, 'Prove it!' this will be thought a breaking of the rules. And indeed it is so; for the tacit rule is that if a passage can be elucidated by appeal to a psychology – in this case, the very special psychology that depends on a Lacanian understanding of 'desire' – such an elucidation *necessarily* takes precedence of any elucidation resting on 'the intuition of the unseen'. Of course all movements of the psyche are 'unseen', and psychology of whatever school consists of nothing but intuitions of or about them, but Durant hasn't noticed this. The point is so obvious that I blush to spell it out. A passage in Durant (p.30) on Derrida and Saussure will do as well as any other to make the point that all the behaviourist sciences – including, quite notably, linguistics – are of their nature atheist; and from them a theist – as it happens polytheist – artist like Pound cannot in any circumstances earn anything but a 'thumbs down'.

We come back to the situation of the young Adrian Stokes or the young Pound or it may be ourselves, confronting the sculptures in the Rimini *tempio* and trying to find words in which to articulate the effect that this art-work has on us. Stokes, it will be remembered, articulated it by saying: 'the stone block is female, the plastic figures that emerge from it on Agostino's reliefs are her children, the proof of the carver's love for the stone'. To the gallant Paul Smith (p.46) this betrays a 'neglect of the feminine', by which 'a damage is done, a sexual *parti pris* firmly taken'. Does he accordingly, having confronted these sculptures himself, offer us an alternative fantasy, a different and better articulation? Of course not. For in the overwhelmingly verbal universe of the Left Bank word-spinners, as of those in the UK and the USA who wait upon their pronouncements, our encounters with sculpure and architecture have no status and no significance. It was not thus that either Stokes or Pound regarded the monuments, past and present, of these classic arts.

PN Review 35, vol 10: no.3 (1983).

Pound's Friends

Peter Makin, *Pound's Cantos*. Allen and Unwin, 1985.

Christine Froula, *To Write Paradise: Style and Error in Pound's Cantos*. Yale University Press, 1985.

Peter Nicholls, *Ezra Pound: Politics, Economics and Writing*. Macmillan, 1984.

Number ten in the Unwin Critical Library, Peter Makin's book is very good. No one can say with any confidence that it will attract new readers to Pound's immense poem; and in fact one of its great virtues is that it doesn't try to minimise how difficult *The Cantos* is, and always will be. The difficulties are of three kinds: first, those inseparable from the nature of the enterprise (i.e. epic); second, those inseparable from Pound's temperament; lastly, those involved with the political and other vicissitudes endured by Pound through his more than fifty years labour on the poem. Devoted work by commentators through now several decades has in one sense 'cleared up' difficulties in each of these areas: for, though *The Cantos* have attracted a quota of pedants and loonies, that quota is surprisingly small, and most Poundians have worked harder and more responsibly than, for instance, the Hardyans have. But their clearings-up necessarily partake of the refractory and multifarious and arcane nature of the text that they work with, and of the sources of that text; and so mastering the elucidations is not much easier than mastering the poem. *The Cantos* is or are, and through any foreseeable future will remain, 'caviare to the general': and yet there they sprawl, a labyrinthine ruin (to put the case at its worst) plumb in the middle of whatever we understand by Anglo-American Modernism in poetry. Anyone may be excused for deciding that life is too short for coming to terms with *The Cantos*: but if we make that decision we thereby disqualify ourselves from having any opinion worth listening to, about the poetry in English of this century.

What incessantly threatens to disable and demoralise commentators on Pound is precisely this clear-sighted recognition that the poet to whom they devote themselves can never have in any ordinary sense 'a public'. It's against the permanent drag of this dispiriting awareness that we should measure, and applaud, the élan that Peter Makin finds, nine times over, to impel him on to seven or nine or ten or twenty cantos at a time, from Canto One to Canto 117 – this after six chapters of preliminary and necessary throat-clearing. True to his briefing from Claude Rawson as general editor, Makin doesn't restrict himself to summarizing what previous commentators have uncovered (though he's good at that, scrupulous and thorough – for instance, noting German and Italian writing as well as English), but he has pursued his own researches and presses his own line – nowhere to better purpose that on Canto 36, the translation of Cavalcanti's 'Donna mi prega', where his elucidation of the psychology and metaphysics of Albertus Magnus is so far as I know unprecedented, and awesomely illuminating. Moreover, having to decide with each batch of cantos those that he will concentrate on, he honourably steers clear of those that are most winning, most 'lyrical' – scanting in his Chapter Eight Canto 17 for the more rebarbative Cantos 21 and 25; or in Chapter Ten passing over Canto 47, which can be, and has been, applauded by some to whom the thrust of *The Cantos* as a whole is unappealing.

Over quite long stretches it doesn't appeal to Makin either. Written at speed in the last months before war broke out, Cantos 52 to 71, known to initiates as the Chinese History Cantos followed by the John Adams Cantos, seem to him as to many of us wrongly conceived as well as sloppily executed. His dislike of them takes a special turn, however, when for the failure of the Adams sequence he blames John Adams, not Pound: 'What flatness, undifferentiation, the section none the less has seems to come from Adams. Both Adams's morality and his aesthetic seem negative, stoic, Horatian...' I'd quarrel with this. The writings by Adams that Pound takes his scissors to can be shown to be repeatedly livelier and more humane as Adams wrote them than after Pound has performed his slapdash surgery. But in any case notice how Makin would bully us into accepting that in morality and aesthetics 'stoic' and 'Horatian' are self-evidently words of ill omen. A helluva lot of people through the centuries have thought them very honourable words indeed, as Peter Makin certainly knows. There is a brazenness about the manoeuvre which in an odd way I find engaging, as it is in the young Hugh Kenner from whom I would guess Makin learned it. But someone who so dashingly cuts his corners – he does so at one point about the iambic pentameter, and elsewhere (really rather deplorably) about the British Great War poets – has to be watched, all the more because he is trenchant, rapid, brilliant – that's to say, persuasive.

The put-down of John Adams isn't a side-issue. It's almost true to say that Makin sees Adams as Pound's evil genius, sidetracking him time and again from what was his true gift and the glory of his poem: a recovery for our time of the perceptions that the Romance languages in the 12th and 13th centuries were carrying forward from the Roman bequest of Ovid (*not* Horace, and not Virgil either). Makin's previous book was *Pound and Provence*, and it's clear where his heart lies. He is sure that Pound was right to discern that the perceptions in question carried with them, implicitly *were*, a morality – and a morality that can be formulated and talked about, not just sealed in the amber of Walter Pater's cadences. His own talk about it, particularly when he shows it in splendid action in Ovid's *Metamorphoses*, is as good as Pound's talk, and comes, as Pound's does, from taking seriously what is being talked about by Guinicelli and Cavalcanti as well as Dante. But how was any of this to be brought to bear on the condition of being an American in the 1930s? That was Pound's problem, and it was no good telling him that there couldn't be a connection, for the connection was *there*, in him: he was both a devotee of the Mediaeval Romance literatures embodied, and an American patriot. Panicked, like everyone else of alertness, by the drift (not to say, torrent) from Depression towards War, Pound had not the time to work out what could only be a circuitous and tenuous connection anyway. The connections he made in his politico-economic tracts have convinced hardly anybody, ever (certainly not the Italian Fascists). The connection he made inside the ongoing poem has convinced more people, but still not many. The problem there was how to get from the nature and essence of light as explored by poets and philosophers of the *duecento* to the light implied in the intellectual historian's term, 'the Enlightenment' – especially, for Pound the patriot, in the American Enlightenment of which Jefferson and Adams were luminaries. And Pound himself later came to acknowledge that the connection he was looking for, if it existed, was much less direct than in the 1930s he rashly and urgently supposed. None of this, however, gets us any nearer accepting Makin's implication that Pound's interest in Adams, and incidentally in Jefferson, was a simple aberration or (worse still) an avoidable wrong move in poetic strategy. Not far under the surface of Makin's writing on these matters is a series of polarities which look downright silly when brought into the open: Ovid good, John Adams bad; Mediterranean good, North Atlantic bad; Romanism and Paganism good, Protestantism bad; Middle Ages good, Enlightenment bad; and finally (inside Pound), translator of Cavalcanti good, Philadelphia Prebyterian bad.

And yet... not only has Makin solidly done his fair-minded

homework on figures like Adams whom he finds unsympathetic,
but time and again his feeling for verse and for the ghostly half-
remembered presence of earlier verse in later, triumphs over the
skeletal armature of history-of-ideas prejudice which orders his dis-
course for him, but need not for us. Thus the Philadelphia Presby-
terian who survives into the polytheistic poet from his laxly con-
ditioned boyhood has never been discerned more brilliantly than
when a strenuous passage from the Pisan Canto 83, overtly Greek
and Chinese in colouring (over the indispensable base of acute sen-
suous perception), is set beside 'the hymnology of Pound's youth':

> It breaths in the air,
> It shines in the light,
> It streams from the hills,
> It descends to the plain,
> And sweetly distils
> In the dew and the rain.

Unfair that we neither know nor care that the author of 'O Worship
the King' was Robert Grant (1785-1838). Grant's visual anonymity
is the clearest proof that he has entered into the folk-memory, his
verses remembered or half-remembered by those who neither know
nor care – nor need they – what it is they remember. And who can
doubt, once Makin has suggested it, that the polyglot author of *The
Cantos* participated in this folk-memory, and profited by it, along
with (one may still hope) the rest of us?

I have a further and specialized though quite important quarrel
with Makin about his lumping together, as much of a muchness, the
two late Canto-sequences, *Rock-Drill* and *Thrones*. *Rock-Drill* strikes
me as much the better, and I believe Makin's own citations and his
commentary bear me out. But this bone may be picked elsewhere.
For now I'll quote one more sentence, about lines from Canto 49,
the so-called 'Seven Lakes' canto, which stands apart from all the
others: 'Such verse seems to demonstrate that emotion works by a
negative law: mere absence of aggression, distortion, haste allows
us to read into things (qualified only as to texture, shade and other
exact physicality) powers that favour human well-being'. Extremely
distinguished itself, in diction and (yes) cadence, this sentence is on
the one hand an exceptionally exact registering of the effect that
certain verse-lines have on us and, at the same time, precisely by
virtue of that exactitude, it opens up vast vistas, not just on what
poetry is and does, but on how we do – or might, or should – traffic
with 'things', whether verbally or non-verbally. There are other
sentences like this, in a book that ideally should reach people with
no special interest in Pound or Pound's poem.

There is a certain naïveté, which I'd be the last to reprehend, about supposing that poetry traffics with 'things' at all, or with any things other than the verbal things called words. This is what deconstructionists say, and they are not easy to rebut even though experience continually belies them. Deconstructionism says also that the poet can't lose, because he can't win; he's not to blame for what goes wrong in his poems, because he gets no credit for what goes right in them. Christine Froula, who follows up her fresh and idiosyncratic commentary on *Selected Cantos* with what is the first thoroughgoing deconstructionist reading of Pound's poem, adheres at all points to this latter precept. The received text of *The Cantos* (not that there is one, but let that pass) is riddled with errors; and, to leave aside the mistakes made by printers and proof-readers and officiously well-meaning editors, many of the errors not only originate with Pound but were perpetuated by him. Often, having the errors pointed out to him, he refused to sanction changes. This is a black mark against him? Not at all, says Ms Froula: the very fact that he refused revisions when these were offered shows that he repudiated for and in his poem any conception of human history as possessing a factual truth beyond the variously unreliable witnesses through whom (culminating in the poet himself) the historical record is transmitted to us. His and their orthographical and other errors are themselves part of the historical record, a most important and salutary part since they disabuse us of the delusion that what we call history comes down to us except as, innocently or not, corrupted by each and every chronicler and historiographer in the chain by which the past, or a version of it, is communicated to the present. Thus every howler that Pound commits, whether intended or inadvertent (and mostly we can't tell the difference) counts unto him for virtue.

This argument is much harder to retort to than hearty common sense will suppose. Many of Froula's pages are closely argued, and some are eloquent. Moreover, as the first scholar to work directly from the work-sheets which, astonishingly voluminous and complete, are now available in the Beinecke Library at Yale, she has written a book that has to be called indispensable, even as one shudders to think how many less intelligent books that Beinecke archive is sure to spawn. Her focus is on Canto Four, a choice by no means arbitrary nor ill-considered; and her publishers deserve much credit for reproducing, in hardback at this price, drafts and variants and diagrammatic *stemma* – the full bibliographical apparatus.

When a book has so many virtues, it seems unfair to launch an attack on it at its weakest. But the points at issue are important enough to require this. So here goes – with a justly famous poem, 'On First Looking Into Chapman's Homer':

> Much have I travell'd in the realms of gold,
> And many goodly states and kingdoms seen;
> Round many western Islands have I been
> Which bards in fealty to Apollo hold.
> Oft of one wide expanse had I been told
> That deep-brow'd Homer ruled as his demesne;
> Yet did I never breathe its pure serene
> Till I heard Chapman speak out loud and bold:
> Then felt I like some watcher of the skies
> When a new planet swims into his ken;
> Or like stout Cortez when with eagle eyes
> He star'd at the Pacific – and all his men
> Look'd at each other with a wild surmise –
> Silent, upon a peak in Darien.

Keats made a mistake: it wasn't Cortez but Balboa who first saw the Pacific. The editors of *The Norton Anthology of English Poetry* say that this error 'matters to history but not to poetry'; and Christine Froula, rashly I think, agrees with them. But, she goes on to say, this excuse for Keats won't hold for Pound, because *The Cantos* is 'an epic, not a lyric; a self-proclaimed poem including history, not a fantasy of poetic power or a literary rhapsody'. Whereupon, having dismissed this simple-minded excuse for Pound's errors, she proceeds to her own more sophisticated excuse for them. But meanwhile what has happened to Keats? Are we to take his poem as 'a fantasy of poetic power' or 'a literary rhapsody'? That's not clear; what is clear is that neither description does it justice. Keats's sonnet includes history, just as *The Cantos* claim to do, and the history it includes is a sort of history *The Cantos* are much concerned with – the transmission of cultural values (from Homer via George Chapman to John Keats). The error about Cortez doesn't matter, not for the reason the Norton editors give or imply, but because it is an error in the history of European discovery and colonizing of the New World – and that is not, except incidentally, the history that Keats's poem is concerned with. Should we not say in fact that, if there can be such a thing as an epic sonnet, Keats has written it? We cannot say anything else so long as we accept Froula's definition of the epic, following Pound, as 'a poem including history'. The definition will not serve; more than this must be asked of a poem before it can qualify as an epic, just because Keats's sonnet meets the one declared condition as clearly as *The Cantos* do. But if this is granted, most of Christine Froula's intricate argument falls to the ground.

It is a very 'concerned' argument. She is anxious to see the end of 'the Western *epos*, grounded since the *Iliad* in a tradition of conquest by violence'; and so, at the opposite pole from those who cannot forget nor forgive that Pound was a Fascist, she wants to think that with *The Cantos* 'the history of epic takes a radically different turn' – towards an inclusive humanity, recognizing without prejudice, for instance, the Chinese along with the European cultural and ethical traditions. But the plain fact is that *The Cantos* hymn the martial virtues among others; that Sigismundo Malatesta might as well have been a conquistador, and that if he isn't exactly lauded for this, he isn't in *The Cantos* censured for it either. Though we need not deny that Pound launched himself on his long poem out of revulsion and indignation at the loss of life in World War One, all the same his poem cannot be squared with *bien-pensant* liberal sentiments as smoothly as Christine Froula believes, and would persuade us.

It is rather disgraceful that 'epic' and 'lyric', terms bequeathed to us by a poetics we no longer believe in, should still figure so largely (never properly nor strictly defined) in our own discourse. Taking advantage of this laxity, we can say that, much as Christine Froula harps on the epic nature of *The Cantos* (inadequately defined, as we have seen), in fact she responds most fervently to the dimension of the poem that can reasonably be described as 'lyric'. This is a not uncommon response, and isn't to be sneered at, since it measures up to at least one dimension of the poem. It most often shows up in readers for whom the Pisan Cantos constitute so obviously the most moving sequence that they lament the rest of the poem was not written in the same mode; and though Ms Froula's scheme allows her only a few pages for the Pisan Cantos, it's notable that she writes there with uncommon ardour. What's more, even as she argues for the poetics of Canto Four as thoroughly Modernist (with genuflections to Kandinsky and Brancusi and others), she speaks of 'a poetics based not on words as signs but on their powers of suggestion', and of how Pound 'was more attracted to what the words of his sources did not say than to what was there on the page'. This is as much as to say that as late as the 1920s Pound was still working in terms of a Ninetyish aesthetic that sought 'moods' and 'the ineffable' – a suspicion borne out on inspecting the drafts, which show a poet doggedly (not to say, sickeningly) diligent indeed, self-critical and self-demanding, but in the service of an aesthetic which still valued the fugitive and evanescent over the overtly stated: a lyrist in fact, though, as Froula compassionately and rightly persuades us, desperately in earnest about gearing up his Imagist-lyric talent to epic requirements. One has noticed before how easily what looks like austere Modernism – in Kandinsky, for instance – can be rendered back into the vocabulary of the Nineties. The crucial point surely is whether the sensibility on display is that of the agonizing poet (in which case we are still in the world of lyric), how far it is that of some one else, of 'the hero' (at which point we have moved into epic). Christine Froula makes just and witty play out of how the epic hero is always errant, prone to error, wandering both in geography and morally. But in *The Faerie Queene* it is the Redcrosse Knight whom we see making errors, not Edmund Spenser, whereas in *The Cantos* it is not Malatesta nor John Adams nor any other hero whom we see erring, but their chronicler, the poét.

For me the case breaks wide open when Froula quotes with approval Otto Rank saying that the modern artist 'does not practise his calling, but *is* it, himself, represents it ideologically'. A very dangerous sentiment, and very German! It is plainly what underwrote the careers of the late Robert Lowell, the late John Berryman. And Froula, by endorsing it as a judgement on Pound's career, in effect debases *The Cantos* to the level of Lowell's *History*, with the agonizing poet at centre stage. Is that what Froula really thinks? I suspect it is, though she might be ready to credit Pound with more finesse, for instance in the inventing of cadence. But Pound's attempt to move out of lyric into epic, though in the event it may not have succeeded, was surely more sustained and more arduous than anything Robert Lowell conceived of. And when Pound refused to clear up spelling errors that were pointed out to him (some he cleared up, but not all), his refusal can be vindicated short of sharing Froula's and Hayden White's sour scepticism about historiography generally. The elderly Pound, as Froula uneasily concedes, was not thus sceptical – which commits her to the familiar deconstructionist assumption that the critic (herself) knows what the poet is up to, better than the poet does. I'm afraid that about this admirably painstaking but seldom commonsensical book the hard thing to say is what needs saying: with friends like this, what poet needs enemies?

Peter Nicholls's dry and difficult but necessary book makes Peter Makin look very old-fashioned. Nicholls is up to the minute. His index lists Althusser, Barthes, Benjamin, Derrida, Eagleton (Terry), Foucault, Gramsci, Lukacs (and yes, in case you wondered, Davie); but it has no entries for Ford (F.M.), Gaudier-Brzeska, Hulme (T.E.), Ovid, Adrian Stokes, Yeats. Some of this is not easily excusable: it is timely to point out where the young Pound was in debt to Pater, but not without considering Yeats as possible intermediary; and it is outrageous to connect Pound's interest in metamorphosis with Emerson rather than Ovid. (For an American of Pound's generation not to be bothered with Emerson is remarkable and significant; but others before Nicholls have shown themselves determined to read Emerson between the lines from which he is conspicuously excluded.) Suppressing the names of Gaudier and Hulme, both killed in the Great War and many times indignantly recalled by Pound for just that reason, allows Nicholls to write that it was Pound's reading of Major Douglas's *Economic Democracy* in 1919 which 'suddenly alerted him to tensions in society'. A man who, having lived 1914 to 1919 in London, needed a *book* thus to alert him would have to be a cerebral monster. Pound was a very bookish poet, but not so bookish as that.

Books are what Nicholls is good at, and at home with. Because he is content to imagine Italian Fascism wholly in terms of its books (Gentile's, Odon Por's, others), he can depict Pound's embrace of that cause temperately, without any of the vindictive self-righteousness that has disfigured other accounts. This is much to the good. Yet it comes through as singularly bloodless, in more senses than one; what was wrong with Mussolini's Italy can hardly be located, plausibly, in a wrong or disputable reading of a passage from Aristotle's Politics, or of 18th-century physiocrats. Still, it's just here that Nicholls is at his strongest. Stripping away the heated bogeyman aura from Pound's Fascism, he is able to show that this was no avoidable aberration on the poet's part, rather an almost inevitable consequence of the aesthetics and the psychology that he started out with; and equally that after 1945 there was not, as in honesty there could not be, the recantation of Fascism that Pound's well-intentioned apologists have foisted on him – the Pisan Cantos are defiant, not (except in the private and domestic sphere) contrite. Others have been sure this must be so, but Nicholls, so cool about it and also doggedly omnivorous, is the first to carry conviction – to those, that is, who will trudge with him through some of the most arid stretches of the poem.

Nicholls is not just an 'ideas' man. He can make discriminations about style, showing, for instance, how line after line of the winning Canto 17 duplicates rhythmically lines from poems by Swinburne that no one reads, showing, too – conclusively to my mind – how Pound's style in the Adams cantos had to travesty Adams – had to technically, but ideologically also. And yet, though he can explain why Pound wrote, for instance, the Chinese History cantos in the way he did, he doesn't thereby make them any more readable. And indeed that's no part of his intention. His coolness is clinical. Impossible to say what pleasure he took in writing this book, or in reading *The Cantos* so as to write it. Impossible equally to say, when we get to the end, how he feels about Pound or Pound's poem. He's neither friend nor enemy. The sickness, whether of poet or poem, turns out to be deep-seated, complicated, and of long continuance: accordingly, diagnosis is intricate, and has to proceed by stages. The only pleasure offered (and it is considerable) is that of seeing the diagnostician practising his remorseless, learned and scrupulous skills. Those skills are Marxist? Structuralist? Freudian? Peter Nicholls is impassively eclectic. It is all rather unnerving to woozy and ardent characters like me or, if I may co-opt him, Peter Makin.

Poundians Now

If I am called a Poundian, that does not offend me, I am quite pleased. But in this I surprise myself. For in private and sometimes in public I am impatient with other traders in the market place who trade too openly under the self-styles: Chaucerian, Shakespearean, Miltonist. Do not the expressions, 'Poundian', and 'Pound Studies', testify equally to the breaking up and sharing out of literature – even in English, not to speak of other languages – into jealously defended and happily exclusive principalities, so many cosy specialisms? In some circumstances, and in some people's mouths, I fear 'Poundian' may carry that implication. But not on the whole; or not yet. For in the first place 'Poundian' – so I tell myself – describes a person who, just because of the author to whom he has devoted himself, is vowed and compelled to breaking through fences: between authors, between periods and languages, between disciplines. Supposing one starts as a student of English or American literature, there is no way to read *The Cantos* except by chancing one's arm as a classicist today, an historian tomorrow, a Sinologist, even (though here some of us lose our nerve) an economist. The Poundian, like his poet, lives by taking risks; and from time to time – such is the nature of the game – he must come a cropper. This is not at all the way of the specialist. And accordingly the specialists – Chaucerians, classicists, economists, whatever – have characteristically (there are shining exceptions as we know) opposed Pound studies, and oppose them still. For this is the second thing about being a Poundian: it is an embattled condition, and always has been ever since Hugh Kenner in 1952 broke the ground so as to make Pound studies possible. In thirty years the occupation has become less dangerous, but it is still true that the avowed Poundian takes not just intellectual risks but professional risks too. To avow a consuming or even a principal scholarly interest in Ezra Pound is not the best way to commend oneself to an interviewing committee – not in the academic world nor, I suspect, in other worlds either.

Accordingly people who want an easy life, who dread insecurity professionally and in other ways, do not become students of Pound's poetry. And this means, so I have found, that the community of

Poundians is bound together as only embattled communities are – 'If we weren't stupid, we wouldn't be here', as someone says in the D.T.C. at Pisa. But equally this community does not exist for mutual support and assurance; it is not cosy. When Poundians communicate, their communications do not take the form that they have in communities of the insecure – that is to say, in my experience, blandishments on the surface and backbiting underneath. No one for instance thinks it odd or requiring an apology that, precisely because Hugh Kenner did the pioneering work for us, hardly a book on Pound now appears in which the author does not at some point take issue with Hugh Kenner. This is as it should be, this is how knowledge advances. Poundians, I am saying, are used to giving and taking hard knocks – as their poet was. It's in the light of that, and of the value I put on it, that I proceed to some critical reflections on certain directions that I see Pound studies taking, now and in recent years.

One current that runs strongly in recent Pound scholarship can be exemplified by an essay in *Paideuma* 13 : 3 (Winter 1984). It is by Angela Elliott, who exclaims admiringly at one point (p.336): 'A subtle and lovely syncretism'. One is grateful for such explicitness: Ms Elliott is one of many enthusiastic readers of *The Cantos* for whom the main thrust of that poem, or perhaps among its several thrusts the one that they are happiest with, is *syncretic*. That there is such a dimension to *The Cantos* cannot be denied; the crucial collection that Ms Elliott cites in her title – 'Pound's "Isis Kuanon"' – undoubtedly signals a syncretic intention on the poet's part, and invites the sort of interpretation that she duly or dutifully proceeds to, by which the vast circumstantial differences between ancient Egypt ('Isis') and ancient China ('Kuanon') are painstakingly ironed out so as to persuade us that they can be ignored.

The really ambitious syncretist is not content to reconcile only two systems of thought and belief; he is happiest when he has four or five balls in the air. And in fact what elicits Angela Elliott's admiring exclamation is a snatch of lines from *The Cantos* which, though they occur in a context impregnated with egyptology, deal explicitly with neither Egypt nor China, but with Graeco-Roman antiquity on the one hand, and on the other hand Provence of the troubadours. They are the last lines of Canto 93:

> You have stirred my mind out of dust.
> Flora Castalia, your petals drift thru the air,
> the wind is ½ lighted with pollen
> > diafana,
> e Monna Vanna... tu mi fai rimembrar.

Ms Elliott comments: 'With his philological and punning interests, Pound was probably thinking of the reassembling of the dismembered Osiris, engaging the concept of remembering as Platonic and Egyptian restitution – a subtle and lovely syncretism'. The betraying word is 'probably'; for what is probable to one cast of mind is improbable to another. Angela Elliott – and this is to her credit – nearly always builds into her arguments an escape-hatch of this kind: 'may be', 'it is possible', 'may well be...'. This is scholarly procedure; but it cannot help raising a doubt whether or to what extent a way of proceeding that requires such constant shadings and hesitations, which proffers us probabilities at best, can ever satisfy. And indeed this is the unavoidable character of syncretism, a word of which the *Shorter OED* austerely warns that it is 'usually derogatory'.

In the preceding issue of *Paideuma* (13 : 2) there was an intricate and learned essay by Colin McDowell which proceeded in a similar way and was open to the same objections. Because at one point McDowell referred to my essay '*Res* and *Verba* in *Rock-Drill* and After' (see above pp.327-39), I was able to lodge a protest, and I repeat that protest now because what is at issue strikes me as important. McDowell, remarking (pp.195-6) on 'the butterfly, traditional symbol of the soul', then devoted to me a querulous footnote: 'Donald Davie almost seems to go out of his way not to mention this very traditional equivalence, perhaps because it answers his rhetorical questions too quickly'. He is right: the 'traditional equivalence' does indeed answer my questions all too quickly, too quickly for my liking because too quickly to do justice to Pound's writing as a verbal fabric, rather than a message in code. If, reading as breakers of a code, we obey Colin McDowell's instruction as decoder-in-chief, 'For butterfly read soul throughout', the butterflies, in all their insisted-on variety, no sooner flit into the text than they immediately flicker out again: the seeming *res*, 'butterfly', is only *verbum*, the true *res*, 'soul', is elsewhere. And this is typical of the sort of reading that McDowell would incite us to, when he assures us that in Pound's writing is to be found the system of symbolism called the Perennial Philosophy, and asks us to find in that writing much that might appeal to 'someone like Kathleen Raine, who writes of the "tradition" in Yeats and Blake' (p.195). McDowell's own exegesis certainly proceeds along lines that we are familiar with if we have read much of Kathleen Raine: faced with the fact that in *The Cantos* Persephone's role in the spirit-world is associated now with a gate, now with a bridge, now with a cave, now with a bower, McDowell's procedure is to rummage through lexicons, Islamic, Zoroastrian, Coptic, Egyptian, Hindu – the attraction to the Near and Middle East is typically Rainean – so as to persuade us that gate = bridge

= cave = bower. So also with insects: faced with 'spider' in one place and 'butterfly' in another, McDowell follows the same learned and eclectic procedure so as to persuade us that spiders are essentially the same as butterflies. Yet this is surely just what Fenollosa castigated in 'The Chinese Written Character as a Medium for Poetry'; the habit (supposed by Fenollosa to be peculiarly 'Western') of erecting logical pyramids, of which the apex is for instance 'redness' whereas the particular examples of redness – flamingos, iron-rust, cherries – survive only, as it were stunned by the weight above them, at the pyramid's base. Pound when he edited and annotated Fenollosa's treatise certainly endorsed Fenollosa's warning that this was no way to arrive at any valuable or nutritious truths; and for McDowell's case to stick he surely needs to prove, as he doesn't attempt to do, that Pound later changed his mind.

To be sure, Pound's long association with Yeats had made him open to, and intrigued by, studies in Comparative Religion like G.R.S. Mead's; Pound himself seems not to have realized that Fenollosa's way of thinking, and Mead's, could hardly be reconciled. And if McDowell had limited himself to showing how those old interests surfaced – particularly in *Thrones* – so as to fabricate connections and transitions far more of *verbum* than of *res*, he would have done valuable service. But his more presumptuous claim runs smack up against the surely indisputable fact that the experience of reading *The Cantos* isn't remotely like the experience of reading Kathleen Raine's poems, or Blake's; and isn't much like the experience of reading Yeats. The same objection can be levelled at Angela Elliott.

The great and salutary merit of deconstructionist readings of *The Cantos*, of which we have few so far, is that they start at the opposite extreme from the syncretists, and indeed deny the implicit postulate that the syncretists proceed from. That is to say, the deconstructionists, in theory at any rate, refuse to let us move off or behind the verbal surface of the poem – and this for the good reason that that surface is stretched over a void or else, in a milder version, that we cannot prove that it isn't. 'Gate', and 'bower' and 'cave' and 'bridge', 'Isis' and 'Kuanon', exist on the verbal surface, as part of a verbal fabric. There is no space or depth behind the text into which we may delve, as Elliott and McDowell want us to, so as to reconcile or conflate gate with bower, or Isis with Kuanon. If Elliott and McDowell want to 'go behind' in this way, no one can stop them, but they should not suppose that the products of such readings have any more authority, as interpretations, than the products of free, of the free-est, association and reverie. To this the syncretist's first line of defence consists in invoking the author's professed intention or, failing that, the author's temperament, his cast of mind. This is what

Angela Elliott provides for when she reminds us of Pound's 'philo-
logical and punning interests'. But however it may be with other
authors, with Pound this defence must fall to the ground, because
Pound was a chameleon, capable of pursuing at different times or
even at the same time intentions that were logically incompatible.
A disciple of Fenollosa could not logically have been also an admirer
of G.R.S. Mead; and Michael André Bernstein no less than Massimo
Bacigalupo has been forced to concede that at least by the time of
Thrones Pound was proceeding in ways for which his resounding
declaration, '*res* not *verba*', gave no warrant at all. Nothing has given
more offence in the deconstructionists' theory than their contention
that once an author has set words and cadences in play, he loses the
power of controlling and directing them, or the reader's response
to them.[1] But we do not have to accept that this is true of all respect-
able authors, to concede that it is rather often true of the author of
The Cantos. And thus, having no wish to declare myself a decon-
structionist, I none the less believe that deconstructionist readings
of *The Cantos* could be – and have been already, in the work of
Bacigalupo for instance – very illuminating. One effect of them
would be, if not to stall exegesis, at any rate to make our exegetes
ask themselves just what they are doing; and that would be no bad
thing, as I have suggested in the case of the syncretists.

But alas, all this is so much whistling in the dark, since we are
unlikely to get any further deconstructionist readings of *The Cantos*
beyond those that we have already from Massimo Bacigalupo and
from Christine Froula in her *To Write Paradise: Style and Error in
Pound's Cantos*. For the deconstructionist critic is very hard to find,
despite the numerous 'View Halloo's urgently sounded to warn us
of his presence and his depredations. Deconstructionists are charac-
teristically not readers of poetry, but philosophers of language; and
their publications typically bluster about how they would turn criti-
cism upside down, could they ever find the time, and the patience,
to practice it:

> I will do such things, –
> What they are yet I know not; but they shall be
> The terrors of the earth.

Accordingly, deconstructionists mostly spend their time not criticiz-
ing but arguing about what it would be like to criticize, concluding

---

1 This is not true of bad authors of course; their language has so little
vitality of its own that the author remains all too plainly and lamentably
in total control of it.

for the most part that criticism is too dubious an activity for persons of their intellectual rigour to engage in. They spend their time squaring up for an encounter which in the end they retreat from. Hence such betraying titles as *Textual Strategies*, or *Tactics for Reading*. Tactics... strategies... How naïve we were, to think that reading was simply a matter of opening a book and scanning the first page, then the second! On the contrary, we are to think, the book is such an explosive article that, before we ever open it, we must arm ourselves in protective clothing and go through such an exhaustive series of fire-drills that we'd be well advised in the end not to open the book at all, so inflammable as it is. Thus, of the eight essayists assembled by Ian F.A. Bell[1] (one of the eight is Bell himself), two contrive not to quote a single verse-line, another quotes two lines, another three, and another eight. This means by my computation that in 196 pages supposedly devoted to a poet, only 13 lines of poetry are set before us. And so we see what the editor means when he attacks in his Preface 'the elusive, defensive claim that it is a sensitive appreciation of the poem on the page which matters, an appreciation sinuously articulated by the anaesthetizing discourse and narrow scholarship of the academies'. Obviously one way to get away from appreciating 'the poem on the page' is seldom to admit the poem, or any part of it, on to any page that one writes.

In fact, of these predominantly British essayists, only one, the American Joseph Riddel, writes as a deconstructionist. (He is the one who quotes eight lines – and those in his end-notes.) Nearly all the others seem to share the peculiarly sour and sullen Marxism which British teachers of literature avow ever more tenaciously as the voters of the United Kingdom ever more resolutely reject it. Peter Brooker seems to speak for most of them when at the end of his essay he proposes 'an active and unsullied opposition to the bouregois appropriation and ideological reproduction of art, language and the human subject in a class society'. Accordingly Pound's Fascism (that, far more than his anti-Semitism) is seldom out of their minds – another good reason why they read round and about *The Cantos*, rather than reading them; for who knows what defilement might come off on their fingers if they actually turned those so 'sullied' pages? No wonder if they are concerned to work out prophylactic tactics in advance of their ever doing so.

Deconstruction is my subject, more than Marxism – though to be sure the two are not for some people mutually exclusive. But before turning to Joseph Riddel, it is worth putting in front of those for whom *The Cantos* is first and foremost a Fascist poem, a snatch

1 *Ezra Pound: Tactics for Reading* (New York, 1982).

of discourse that I hope Ian Bell will not find 'anaesthetizing'. It is
Landor, writing in 1846:

> Before we pursue the details of a poem, it is customary to look
> at it as a whole, and to consider what is the scope and tendency,
> or what is usually called the moral. But surely it is a silly and
> stupid business to talk mainly about the moral of a poem,
> unless it professedly be a fable. A good epic, a good tragedy,
> a good comedy, will inculcate several. Homer does not repre-
> sent the anger of Achilles as being fatal or disastrous to that
> hero; which would be what critics call poetical justice. . . . In
> the *Odyssea* he shows that every obstacle yields to constancy
> and perseverance: yet he does not propose to show it: and there
> are other morals no less obvious. Why should the machinery
> of the longest poem be drawn out to establish an obvious truth,
> which a single verse would exhibit more plainly, and impress
> more memorably? Both in epic and dramatic poetry it is action,
> and not moral, that is first demanded.

But alas, I fear that to Peter Brooker and Ian Bell alike Walter Savage
Landor, aristocratic republican and apologist for tyrannicide, will
figure as irredeemably 'bourgeois'. (This Peter Brooker incidentally
both is and is not the same who did the admirable Faber *Guide* to
the *Selected Poems* of Pound; he was not always a tactician of reading
rather than a reader, nor did he always wear the ideological strait-
jacket that it seems he has now strapped himself into.)

Joseph Riddel's essay on 'Pound and "neo-Nietzschean clatter"'
– Pound's phrase in *Hugh Selwyn Mauberley* – supplies what we least
expect from a deconstructionist: a source for one of Pound's
strangest speculations about what it is that engenders and maintains
creative activity in the artist. This is the passage in his postscript to
the translation of Gourmont's *Physiologie de l'amour*, where Pound
wonders if creative energy is not just sexual but more narrowly and
specifically genital. Riddel sets beside this a passage from Nietzsche's
Will to Power which seems to say precisely the same thing, and this
is especially interesting because, whereas it is unthinkable that Pound
in his generation did not experience Nietzsche's influence, yet no
one to my knowledge has earlier found other than trivial traces of
Nietzsche in any Poundian text. The joke is that 'source' and 'influ-
ence' are precisely what the deconstructionist programme sets its
face against, as 'historicist'. Accordingly, so far from taking pride
in his discovery, Riddel huddles it away and passes on as fast as
possible, as if ashamed of it. To complicate matters further,
Nietzsche was enlisted by that deconstructionist authority, the late

Paul de Man, to enforce the deconstructionist contention that literary history's talk of before and after, of source and influence, is always fraudulent or at least obfuscating. Moreover the case is a strong one, especially when it is based, as it is by De Man, on a work so early in Nietzsche's career as *Birth of Tragedy*; for it is surely true there that, when Nietzsche casts his argument as a sort of narrative – the Dioynsian at some point supervening upon the Apollonian, or vice versa – we have to recognize this as a convenient and/or unavoidable myth. What Nietzsche really contends is that the two stresses which he calls 'Dionysian' and 'Apollonian' are just that, stresses simultaneously present at every point in time, whether we think of decades and centuries or of the very much shorter time-span in which the artist composes his artifact. It is not a matter of first this, then that; but of stress and counter-stress co-existing at every instant. Derrida himself saw Pound and Fenollosa, though also Mallarmé, as having arrived, independently of Nietzsche, at this perception. And when Riddel takes us through Pound's theoretical statements, particularly about 'Image' and about 'tradition', we are forced to see that simultaneity is indeed stressed time and again, and hence that when Pound wants to explain himself he is repeatedly driven towards the diagram, towards spatial rather than temporal analogies. This is particularly clear in how Pound conceives of tradition, a conception that we have been too ready to reconcile with the far more influential and less demanding formulations of Eliot. For Pound, as not for Eliot, tradition involves violent ruptures, eruptions or disruptions; creative energies over the centuries are repeatedly running down, and are as repeatedly wrenched violently into renewed life by the truly creative individuals. Moreover each renewal is indeed just that, a 'making new' of perceptual patterns or constellations, each of which is very old and has already appeared and re-appeared many times in the past. In this way tradition is for Pound something not just cyclical but, more challengingly, *repetitive*. And what is renewed is not just a lost accuracy, but rather a lost energy. This we may call 'natural', if only because it is, we perceive, a constant potentiality of the nature that we call 'human'. But since Nature as Fenollosa had said knows nothing of nouns and verbs, there is a disparity between Nature and any verbal formulation that we may address to it. This we readily acknowledge, saying that even the best poetry falls short of nature's copiousness. But it is equally possible to think of the disparity not as a falling short but an overshooting, not of Nature of course but of any natural occasion that poetry addresses. Riddel, if I read him aright, argues that this is how Pound sees the disparity. For I take it he is endorsing and paraphrasing Pound when he declares: 'Metaphor not only transports or carries over from one structure to another, but, like nature, branches and multiplies. It is a *law* of fecundity or super-abundance...' (pp.197-8). And certainly something like that seems true to the consistent dynamism in all Pound's formulations concerning metaphor or 'the Image'.

However it's not for nothing that I find myself writing 'I take it' and 'if I read him aright'. I have been trying to summarize the first half of Riddel's essay, and if I'm not sure that I've done so accurately, that of course may mean only that I am too obtuse to follow the speed and complexity of Riddel's thinking; but it may equally mean that Riddel has gone to rather great pains to make summarizing impossible. Certainly some French and British deconstructionists and post-structuralists have been thus perverse, and are quite ready to admit as much. As the Englishwoman Catherine Belsey contends, 'To challenge familiar assumptions and familiar values in a discourse which, in order to be easily readable, is compelled to reproduce these assumptions and values, is an impossibility'. (This very sentence is itself 'easily readable', however; which suggests a certain inconsistency.) The European deconstructionists are usually Leftist radicals of one sort or another; and so the 'familiar assumptions and values' are those of the 'bourgeois ideology' which they want to explode. Hence their wish not to be easily readable may be thought perverse, but has some reason behind it. American deconstructionists like Riddel, on the other hand, seldom seem to endorse Leftist or indeed any other analyses of society; and so it is hard to see why they take such pains to be unreadable. It seems to come about through a series of tics that they are unaware of, or else, more probably, so as to advertise their membership in an elect company that takes pride and pleasure in being exclusive, and manages to be so by using dense stylistic mannerisms which only the elect can with confidence decode. The staple of this distinctive style is a peculiarly insistent *franglais* made after the fashion of the deliberately deformed French employed by the original deconstructionist Derrida. In writing like Riddel's which deliberately affronts the lexical and syntactical norms of both English and French, it is impossible to decide which of the numerous solecisms are deliberate, which inadvertent. Add to that the possibility of typographer's and proof-reader's errors, which are likely to be many with a text so wayward, and we are faced with a discourse which is for most intents and purposes unreadable, since at hardly any point can we be certain that we are reading from the text what the writer thought he was putting there.

Another more serious and sinister reason for this style may be that, since poetry is almost by definition non-paraphrasable, to write prose which defies paraphrase is by implication to claim for it parity with poetry. And of course many modern writers about poetry do make that claim. Hence their impatience with the poetry that they write about, which by that very fact seems to enjoy logical priority over their own writing; and hence their reluctance to quote from such poetry. It is obvious that Riddel is far more interested in Pound's poetic theory than in his poetic practice; but perhaps a better way of putting it, in view of the title of this book, is that Riddel and most of the other essayists are less interested in Pound's writing of verse, than in his 'tactics for' such writing. It is the more surprising that from time to time in Riddel's pages we do encounter something that can be called criticism. This, for instance:

> To produce poetry, the poet introduces that which interferes or disturbs, but that which in itself does not totalize or order. For example, the Ovidian Dionysus in Canto 2.... Dionysus being that which inhabits any grammar or system (the ship on which he is transported) but cannot be reduced to it. Dionysus entangles and becalms the ideal of a completion of the voyage, and in his delay produces by resistance the most vigorous trans-formations of meaning while at the same time permitting an excess of metamorphic possibilities....

Though this is thrown out only in passing, as if grudgingly ('For example...'), and although it will be noticed that I have resorted to a lacuna in order that it should be readable, still what we have here surely is 'a sensitive appreciation' of Canto 1/2 'on the page', an appreciation moreover which attends to Landor's injunction: 'it is action, and not moral, that is first demanded'. We can see for our-selves how from this perceptive and original reading to draw conclu-sions about the significance of Ovid's *Metamorphoses* for *The Cantos* as a whole, and the significance of having a full-dress treatment of this Ovidian metamorphosis as early as Canto 2. This is criticism; but in Riddel's discourse it is an exception that proves the rule – the rule that criticism is seldom worth stooping to.

I have surveyed – rapidly and therefore in some degree unfairly – a dozen or so recent writers about Pound. Two of them I have called 'syncretists', several I have called 'Marxists', and one is a deconstructionist. All of them are scholars, but none (I have argued) is a critic. This is hardly a crying scandal. 'Critic' is not the most glorious of appellations, and so far as I am aware none of these writers has explicitly laid claim to it. Some of the contributors to Ian Bell's symposium, if we call them historians of ideas, can be respected: by exposing the scatty or cranky sides of people that Pound set much store by, such as Allen Upward and Ernest Fenol-losa, some of these scholars undoubtedly enrich our sense of the intellectual ambience that Pound moved in. What *is* a little scandalous is that by nearly all the writers I have considered (I except Herbert Schneidau) a body of poetry is harnessed to serve an ideology; for Colin McDowell's Perennial Philosophy is as much an ideology as the Marxist understanding of history, and rather more than Jacques Derrida's and Paul de Man's theory of language. What many or most of them will retort is that what I understand by 'criticism', what I look for and fail to find in their pages, is equally underpinned and legitimized by an ideology, the ideology that they call 'bourgeois'. But why should I deny this? I will grasp the nettle, admit the charge, and agree to call my frame of reference 'bourgeois'. Why not? 'Bourgeois', that bogey-word, describes – we can all agree – that culture which English-speakers and French-speakers (to go no further) inherit from the exertions, political and artistic, economic and intellectual, of our predecessors over the last three hundred years. Despite the long and unfinished catalogue of its crimes, this ideology has shown itself arguably more humane, and certainly more respectful of artistic and intellectual freedoms, than any alternative on offer in the past or today. Perhaps no other ideology permits of what I understand as criticism. Those who want something more exciting and inflammatory than criticism do well to look elsewhere.

More on the Muddle of *Thrones*

Considering the portrayal in *Thrones* (Cantos 96 to 109) of that last-come of all the *Cantos* heroes, Sir Edward Coke, Peter Makin has taken note of my own hardly temperate judgement that the historical perspective in which Pound places Coke is 'the notorious "whig interpretation" of English history in a sort of parody version for grade-school'.[1] Makin provides his own spirited gloss on 'the whig interpretation': 'that image of the glorious and special march of the English towards cultural (and economic) superiority, in which those Feet still walk on this sceptred Isle, under the aegis of middle-class individualism'. Moreover, in J.G.A. Pocock (*The Ancient Constitution and the Feudal Law*, New York, 1967) he has found an authority to vindicate my intemperance. According to Pocock:

> Coke and the Commons represented a rising landed gentry, solidly linked to a merchant class, using their economic power to bring to heel a king who in fact claimed no more absolute power than Elizabeth had. Their great propaganda weapon was the myth of the common law fused with the myth of Magna Carta. For Coke, Magna Carta and the common law circumscribed the powers of the king, and always had, 'time out of mind'. Coke's era arrived at this myth because it had no historical sense; could not well distinguish the habits of Elizabethans from the ways of Normans. Its assumptions put it at the mercy of a mass of legal apocrypha, and a habitual misreading of ancient documents. Thus Coke's contemporaries persuaded themselves that the common law had never changed; and in particular that it had always, even in the time of Magna Carta, circumscribed the King's prerogative through the institutions of Parliament and trial by jury, the antiquity of both being falsely deduced by Coke and his fellows from their documents.[2]

Thus my hunch is borne out; and I am duly gratified.

1 See above, 'Sicily in *The Cantos*', pp.247-53.
2 Makin, *Pound's Cantos* (London, 1985) pp.285-6.

Peter Makin however, unable (we might say) to leave well alone, went on burrowing or browsing and came up with another authority who, as it seemed to him, presents Pound's portrayal of Coke in a more favourable light. This is J.C. Holt, from whose *Magna Carta* (Cambridge, 1965) Makin learned that Coke's understanding of Magna Carta was not 'a myth created by the Stuarts [*sic*] and Elizabethans'; that on the contrary 'it was the fourteenth century which created, in almost finished form, that myth, and made it a functioning reality 250 years before Coke'; and that even in 1215, certainly by the time of Bracton (d. 1268), lawyers interpreted Magna Carta, or some provisions of it, as 'a fundamental law, which, by being a law, circumscribed the power of the King'. The question is, how much should this put me out of countenance? More is at stake than my *amour-propre*.

In the first place Pound (and Makin) cannot have it both ways: if what Coke asserted had already been widely accepted by say 1363, if 'Coke's extensions of this already ancient and functioning interpretation of Magna Carta were minor' (Makin p.286, summarizing Holt), then Coke may be applauded for his courage in standing up to the King, but hardly for his piercing intelligence. And yet it is the latter quality, the clarity of his mind, that is extolled in Canto 107:

> so that after one set of damned scoundrels (tonsured)
> another set of damned scoundrels
> > (untonsured)
> the foulest of all these Jimmy Stuart.
> > Coke: the clearest mind ever in England...

In fact it appears that neither Pocock's history nor Holt's credits Coke with a specially clear mind. Moreover, how can we trust as to clarity of mind a voice that relates history in the cops-and-robbers idiom of 'the foulest of all these Jimmy Stuart'? As soon as *Thrones* appeared, I objected to 'the pointless jocularity' (I should use harsher terms now) of what we have a little earlier in this Canto: 'Noll' for Oliver Cromwell, 'Charlie' for Charles the First. Now we have 'that slobbering bugger Jim First'. And neither Makin nor any one else has yet offered to deny that this is the language of the rabble-rouser.

In the second place a myth is no less a myth if with Holt we assign its fabrication to the fourteenth century than if with Pocock we date it in the late sixteenth. The fourteenth century is not, any more than the sixteenth century, that age of Henry II and Eleanor of Aquitaine in which Pound wants to implicate Sir Edward Coke:

> Coke, the clearest mind ever in England
> vitex, white eglantine
>   as tenthril thru grill-work
>   wave pattern at Excideuil
>   A spire level the well-curb

Makin explains: 'Henry II's reign is, for Coke, a legal Golden Age
– Glanville's age – and the Charter codified the good usages of it...
It is also the age of the troubadours, and of Henry's queen, Eleanor
of Aquitaine:... Now Pound brings in light from that period to
intesify Coke's, whose source was Magna Carta. Pound had seen
the gods' mark, the wave in the stone, at Excideuil, birthplace of
the troubadour Giraut de Borneil...' Thus both Coke and Pound
want to push their story further back than even 1215; and indeed
we should expect nothing else – 'time out of mind' was what Coke
demanded and asserted. So did the Whig apologists in the eighteenth
century:

> When Britain first, at Heaven's command,
>   Arose from out the azure main,
> This was the charter of the land,
>   And guardian angels sung this strain:
>   'Rule, Britannia, rule the waves;
>   Britons never will be slaves.'

> The nations, not so blest as thee
>   Must, in their turns, to tyrants fall;
> While thou shalt flourish great and free,
>   The dread and envy of them all...

Extraordinary! The one-time Anglophobe who had written *How
To Read*, and many stinging verses about the iniquities of the Bank
of England and Winston Churchill, now fervently endorses 'Rule
Britannia'! (James Thomson's 'nations, not so blest as thee' corres-
ponds to 'the french could not do it/they had not Magna Charta' –
in this same Canto.)[1] Might we not expect such a *volte-face* by Pound
at least to raise some eyebrows? Not really; for such bizarre reversals
are the rule in *Thrones*, as Peter Makin recognizes. The Eparch's
Book, extolled or at least approved in Canto 96, envisages 'an unim-
aginable and arbitrary bureaucracy', and this provokes Makin to two

---

1 Makin incidentally argues that Coke is a conservative whereas the Whig
interpreters weren't, but one can hardly get more conservative than 'When
Britain first' – from the undoubted Whig, Thomson.

brilliantly mordant sentences, at once entertaining and just: 'There seems to be no room for unauthorised young men like Pound's friend Gaudier-Brzeska, who set up shop under the railway arches and invade the territory of the professionals. Between Yeats's Byzantium of tin cockerels in glinting haze, and Pound's of harried shopkeepers, the choice is not attractive.' And similarly in Canto 98, that other new source, the Sacred Edict, shows the Confucian principle of filial deference ossified into an insistence on the unquestionable authority of the father-figure in all circumstances – thus, as Makin indignantly observes, making nonsense of Pound's earlier insistences on flexibility, the need to proceed by 'feel', in family relations as in all else. Thus the treatment of Coke is in line with what is going on in *Thrones* generally, where the trouble is not that Pound is changing his mind (and about matters of great import) but that he nowhere acknowledges this, and indeed seems unaware of doing it. On one issue after another he executes a 180-degree turn, and either never notices or else, and in any case, relies on us not to notice. The truth is that *Thrones* is largely rubbish, but no one likes to say so.

Peter Makin's way of not saying so is to pretend that whatever can be said of *Thrones* can be said of *Rock-Drill* also. But this is surely not true of *Rock-Drill* cantos like 90 and 91. Such cantos are open to objections, as Makin searchingly implies when he says that by the time of *Rock-Drill* 'Pound has become a Symbolist', and remarks that 'many will be satisfied to see Pound become a brilliant Symbolist, for to them that is what a Paradise is about: the transition to the purely spiritual, that which is of the mind only'. But the *Thrones* cantos are open to much broader and more damaging objections, of a quite different sort. Where the treatment of Coke is concerned, these objections turn on how far we can or should look for accuracy, consistency and plausibility in the historical narrative that the poem relates or insinuates. This is a vexed and hoary question, not to be answered in a hurry.

When Pound in a *Paris Review* interview defended what he had made of Sir Edward Coke, he reached back through time even further than to 'When Britain first': 'There *are* epic subjects. The struggle for individual rights is an epic subject, consecutive from jury trial in Athens to Anselm versus William Rufus, to the murder of Becket and to Coke and through Adams'. Now we have Whigs even in ancient Athens! But Peter Makin will accept this protestation: 'Whether or not the Cantos do justice to it, Coke's struggle is full and worthy epic material'. We ought to ponder this. What neither Pocock nor Holt denies is that everything about Coke's struggle, apart from his undoubted courage in Parliament, is a fiction. He was struggling to assert and get accepted a view of English history that is *mythical*. We may suppose that he sincerely believed it himself, but the fact remains that it is a myth, not in the sense of the stories in the *Metamorphoses* but in the sense of a propagandist fiction serving partisan political ends. Can we then agree that nevertheless it is 'full and worthy epic material'?

Perhaps we can. After all, some of those pretty stories in Ovid may have originated as, or served their turn as, propagandist fictions. Moreover some fictions are nourishing, in the sense that they incite men to live up to them, to transform (not just notionally but by positive action) the squalid fact until the nobler fiction supersedes it. And it would be easy to accept that the myth of citizens' inalienable rights has proved itself such an ennobling fiction many times over through the centuries. Makin says something like this on an earlier page where he discusses very valuably the USURA canto, 45. Of the image of a good communal life wistfully set before us in that canto, he points out that it would be 'difficult to locate in history or space':

> It is all cleaner than any real Middle Ages (where none but the richest merchants had stone houses at all); not as large-scale on the scientific, technical, industrial level as the European Renaissance, when men starved and held strikes. It is not as primitive as the Middle Ages sculpted by the Middle Ages; nor yet as palatial as the Renaissance painted by the Renaissance. The visual model is archaic myth-worlds, and idealized quasi-medieval pasts, painted (as by Fra Angelico) in the Renaissance.
>
> These are the methods of myth, and of course ahistorical and nostalgic. But one should not rule out the possibility that humankind may from time to time live up to myth – as the Ife bronzes, which to European eyes ought to be an imaginative invention of beauty, are found exemplified in living Nigerians.

It seems one might argue that if Canto 107 were as well written as Canto 45, then its portrayal of Coke could be justified in this way. Its myth would be as ennobling as the myth of each man having 'a house of good stone / each block cut smooth and well fitting'. And in that way the Coke material would be 'full and worthy'. But even so, would it be epic, or 'epical'? Pound, we all remember, defined epic as 'a poem including history'; whereas we seem to have found that both Canto 45 and Canto 107 *exclude* history. Their method is, says Makin, 'of course ahistorical'. How then can they figure in a poem that aspires to be epic, except as divagations, interludes if not indulgences? Makin shows us one way: since 'humankind may from time to time live up to myth', the history of humankind may or must include the myths, the beguiling or ennobling fictions that humankind has from time to time been seduced by. Yes, but in that case the fictions must be presented *as* fictions. And however it may be with Canto 45 (where it could well be argued that archaic diction and scriptural cadence do frame it as fiction), in Canto 107 the Magna Carta/Coke material is presented to us on the contrary as verifiable fragments of suppressed or forgotten or distorted but authentic historical records. Offering in this way to be history, it cannot but be discredited when we find it is no more than a fable.[1]

Let us not sophisticate further. When a poem offers us as excitingly rediscovered fact what we discover from other sources to be propagandist fiction, we cannot help thinking the worse of the poem, whether or not it declares itself an epic. The subject-matter either will or will not carry the weight that the poet wants to put on it. This is what Pound assumes when he asserts, 'There *are* epic subjects', and Peter Makin also when he endorses Pound: 'full and worthy epic material'. But this is precisely what currently influential theory is concerned to deny; deconstructionists and others will not have it that 'subject', or 'subject-matter', has any such autonomous existence – for them, since poetry is a verbal fabric and nothing else, it cannot be the case that certain verbal fabrications or formulations, for instance Magna Carta, are any more or less auspicious for poetic manipulation than any others. In this way, facing up to the unacceptability of *Thrones* is part of the struggle to maintain the traditional poetics that Pound subscribed to, against the post-structuralist and deconstructionist poetics currently on offer.

The astonishing recovery in *Drafts and Fragments* puts the calamity of *Thrones* in a new light. The recovery is artistic, not ideological; no ideological crux is resolved, and *Drafts and Fragments* offers us, as suffering persons, no comfort. But the poem that ends with 'Notes for 117 et seq.' – not with the spurious 'Canto 120' – does indeed as we experience it end with epic poetry. When we read in Canto 115, 'The scientists are in terror / and the European mind stops / Wyndham Lewis chose blindness / rather than have his mind stop', we are persuaded that the preceding cantos have provided enough spectacles of the European mind in action – for instance, the minds of Cavalcanti and Albertus Magnus in Canto 36 – for this judgement on its finally running out to be well-earned, and to carry sombre conviction. It is not the European mind of Pound's lifetime, of

---

1 It so happens that Pound's definition of epic is patently defective, since it would have us accept as epic Keats's sonnet on Chapman's Homer; but that is beside the point being made here.

Wyndham Lewis's, which grinds to a halt; but a mind which they inherited, and sought to perpetuate. What has erred, and now through Pound acknowledges its error, is not Ezra Pound's mind nor Wyndham Lewis's, but the European mind: Winston Churchill's and Jacques Maritain's, Lenin's and Mussolini's, as well as Cavalcanti's and Grosseteste's and even (American though he was) John Adams's. It is 'the end of an auld sang'; and what saves the record from elegy for epic is the strenuousness with which each doomed hero applied himself to the foredoomed enterprise. That the history which each mind sought to interpret can be seen as myth or fable, is perhaps beside the point; for myth or fable may be the only way in which the human mind can comprehend history.

And yet the fable of Edward Coke cannot take its place along with Cavalcanti's, nor even with Churchill's and Maritain's. Part of the reason is that it was brought into the reckoning too late in the poem, under the wrong auspices and in the wrong company. But this is still a structuralist objection: it is the structure of the poem that on this showing is thrown askew by *Thrones*. And does this fully account for our indignant exasperation with these cantos? I think not. What dismays us about the *Thrones* sequence, especially when we look back at it from the regained altitude of *Drafts and Fragments*, is its *levity*: the high-handedness with which Pound at that stage exploited several mutually inconsistent myths of history as if all were equally nourishing and proper. The *Thrones* sequence as written (though not apparently as the author conceived of it) cannot be saved from the structuralists and post-structuralists; and just that is what is wrong with it.

Index of names

Index of Pound's works